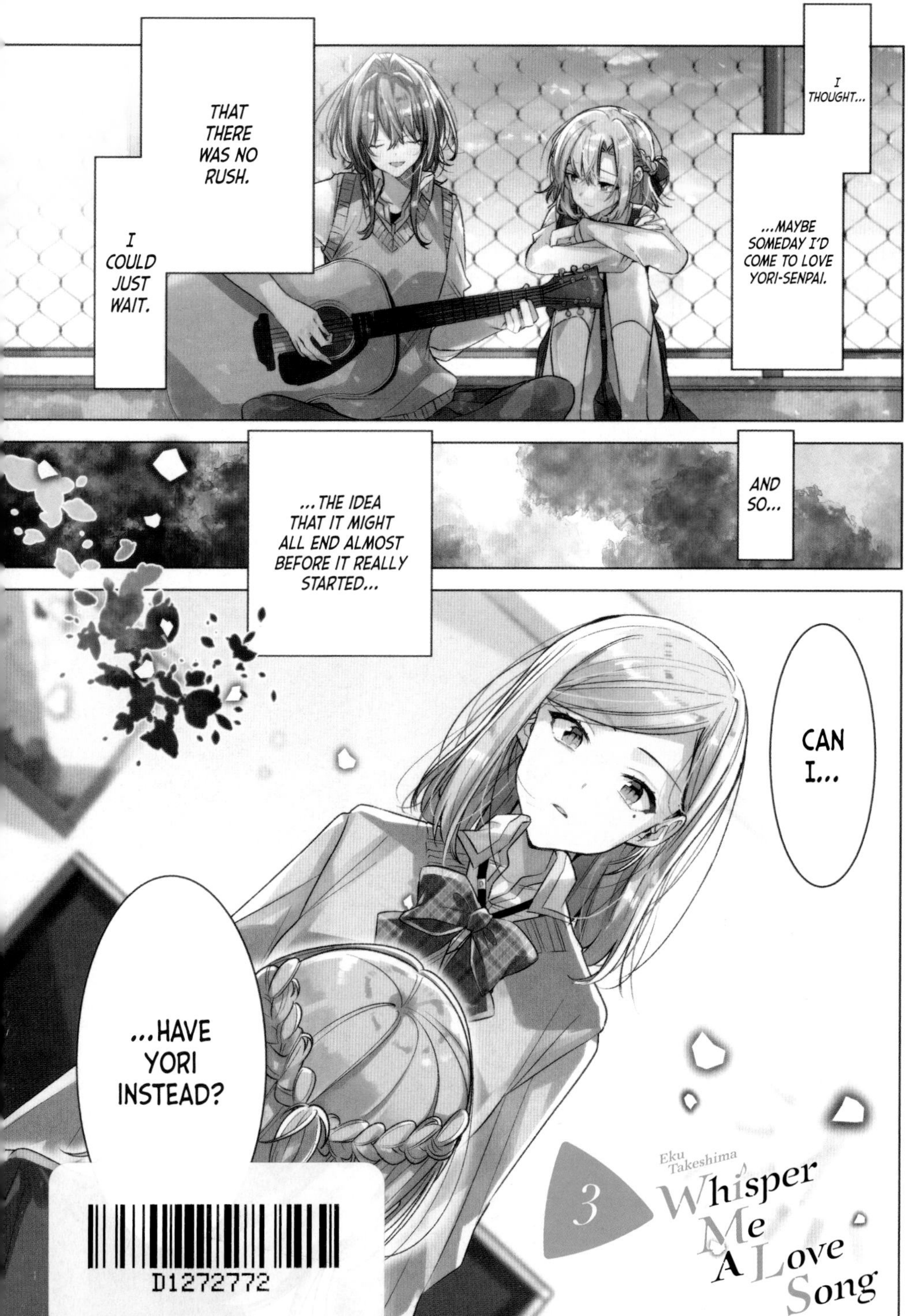
I THOUGHT...
...MAYBE SOMEDAY I'D COME TO LOVE YORI-SENPAI.
THAT THERE WAS NO RUSH.
I COULD JUST WAIT.
AND SO...
...THE IDEA THAT IT MIGHT ALL END ALMOST BEFORE IT REALLY STARTED...
CAN I...
...HAVE YORI INSTEAD?
Eku Takeshima
3
Whisper Me A Love Song

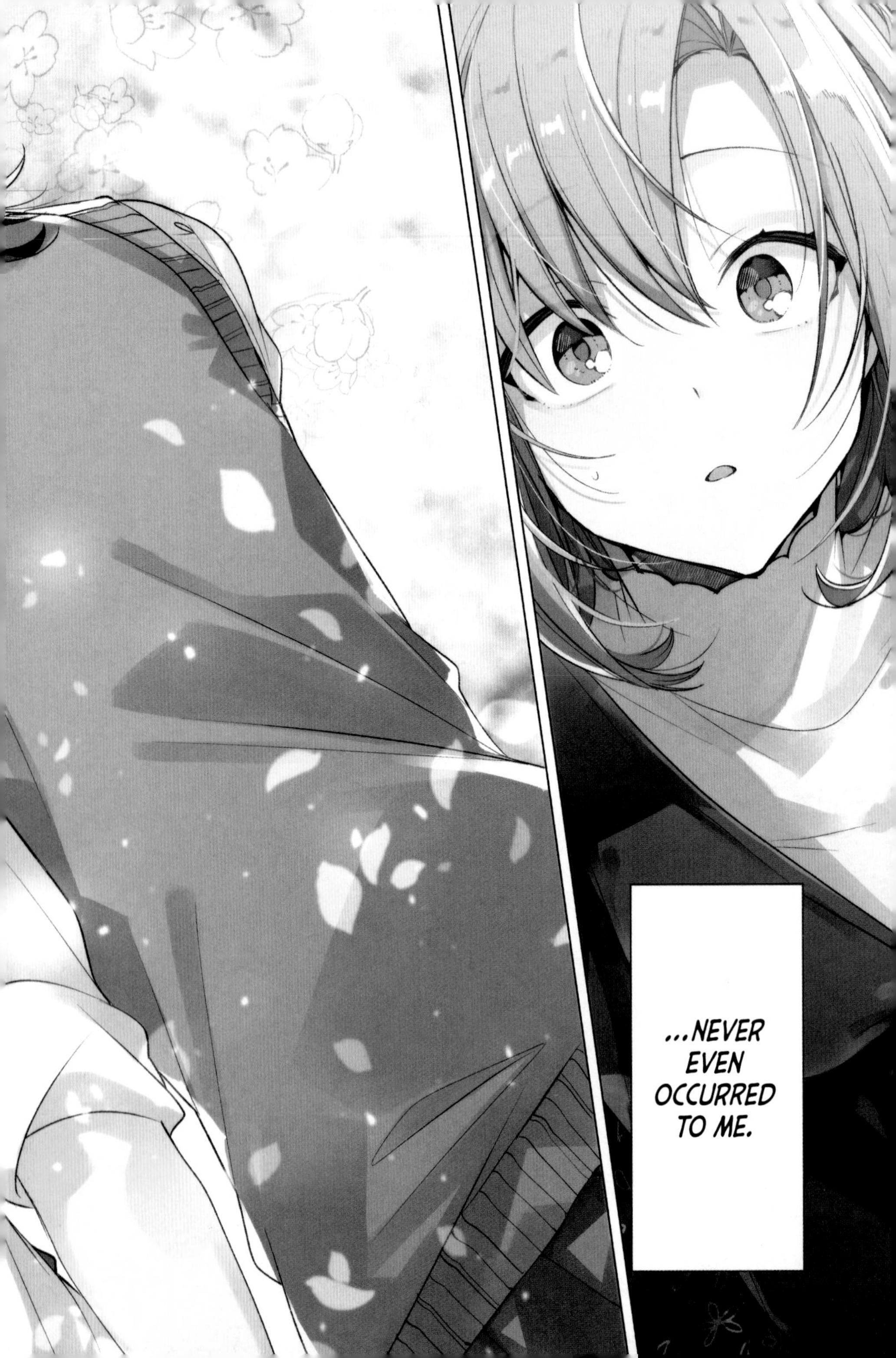
...NEVER EVEN OCCURRED TO ME.

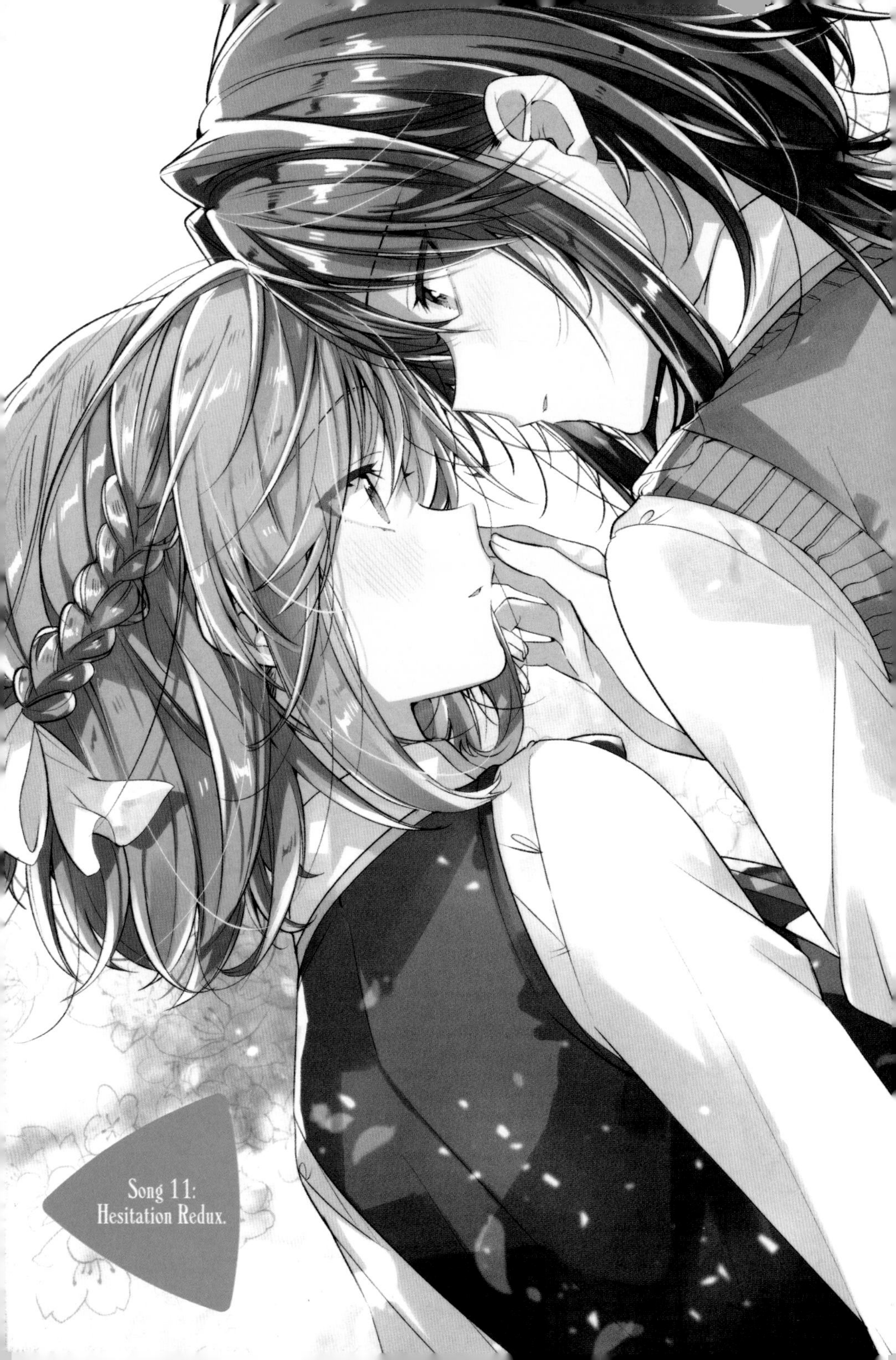
Song 11:
Hesitation Redux.

contents

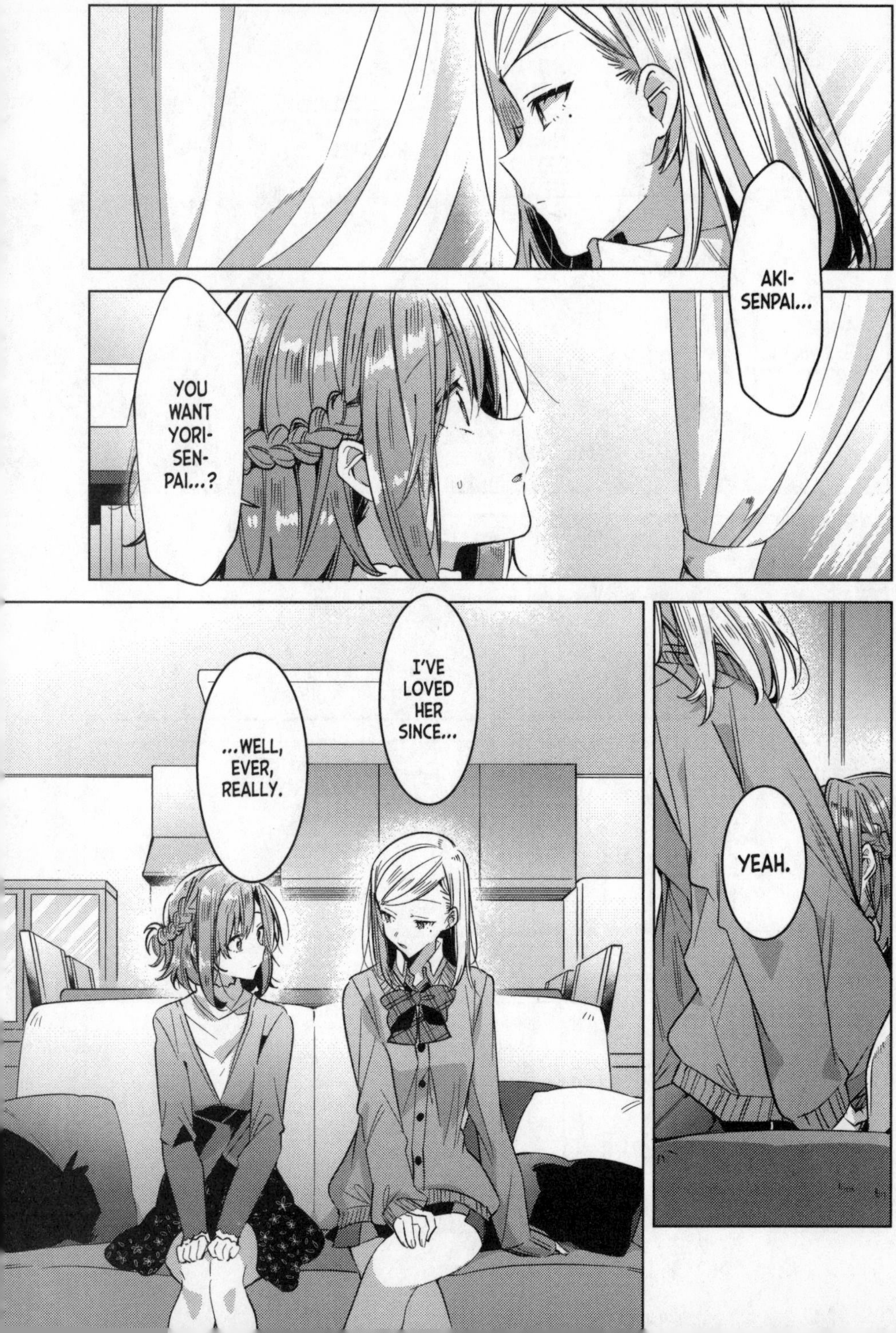
AKI-SENPAI...
YOU WANT YORI-SENPAI...?
YEAH.
I'VE LOVED HER SINCE...
...WELL, EVER, REALLY.

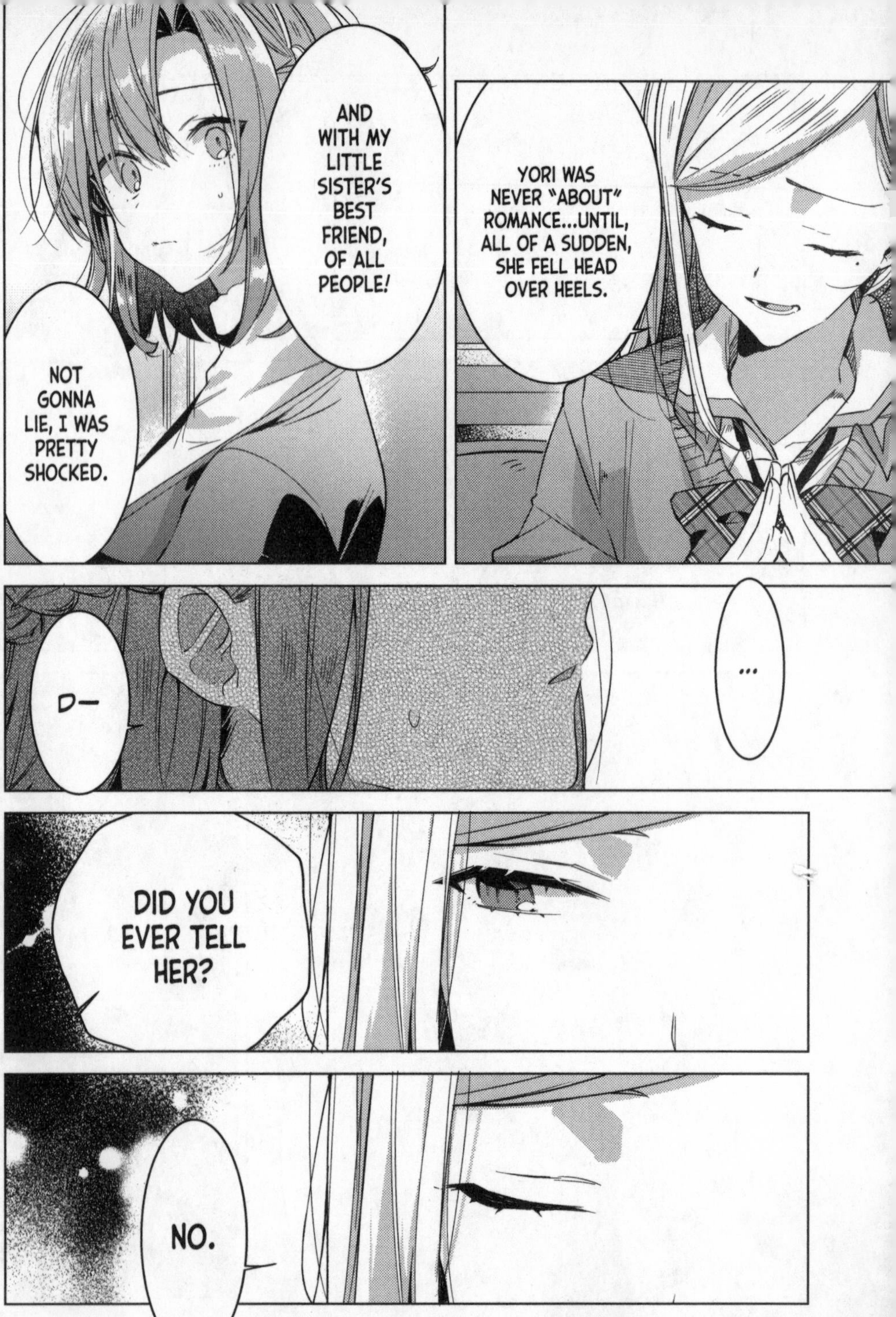
YORI WAS NEVER "ABOUT" ROMANCE...UNTIL, ALL OF A SUDDEN, SHE FELL HEAD OVER HEELS.
AND WITH MY LITTLE SISTER'S BEST FRIEND, OF ALL PEOPLE!
NOT GONNA LIE, I WAS PRETTY SHOCKED.
...
D—
DID YOU EVER TELL HER?
NO.

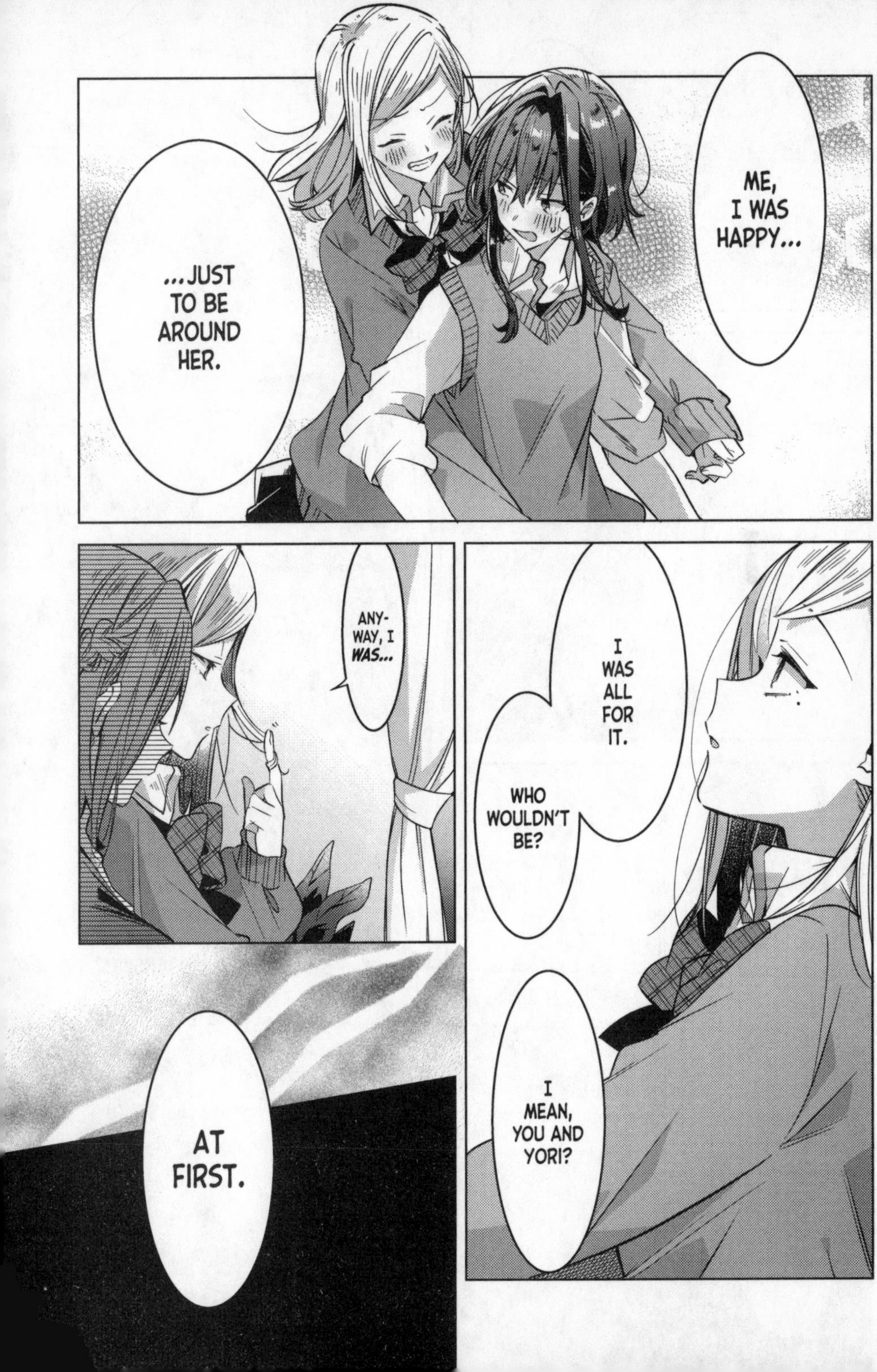
ME, I WAS HAPPY...
...JUST TO BE AROUND HER.
I WAS ALL FOR IT.
WHO WOULDN'T BE?
I MEAN, YOU AND YORI?
ANY-WAY, I *WAS*...
AT FIRST.

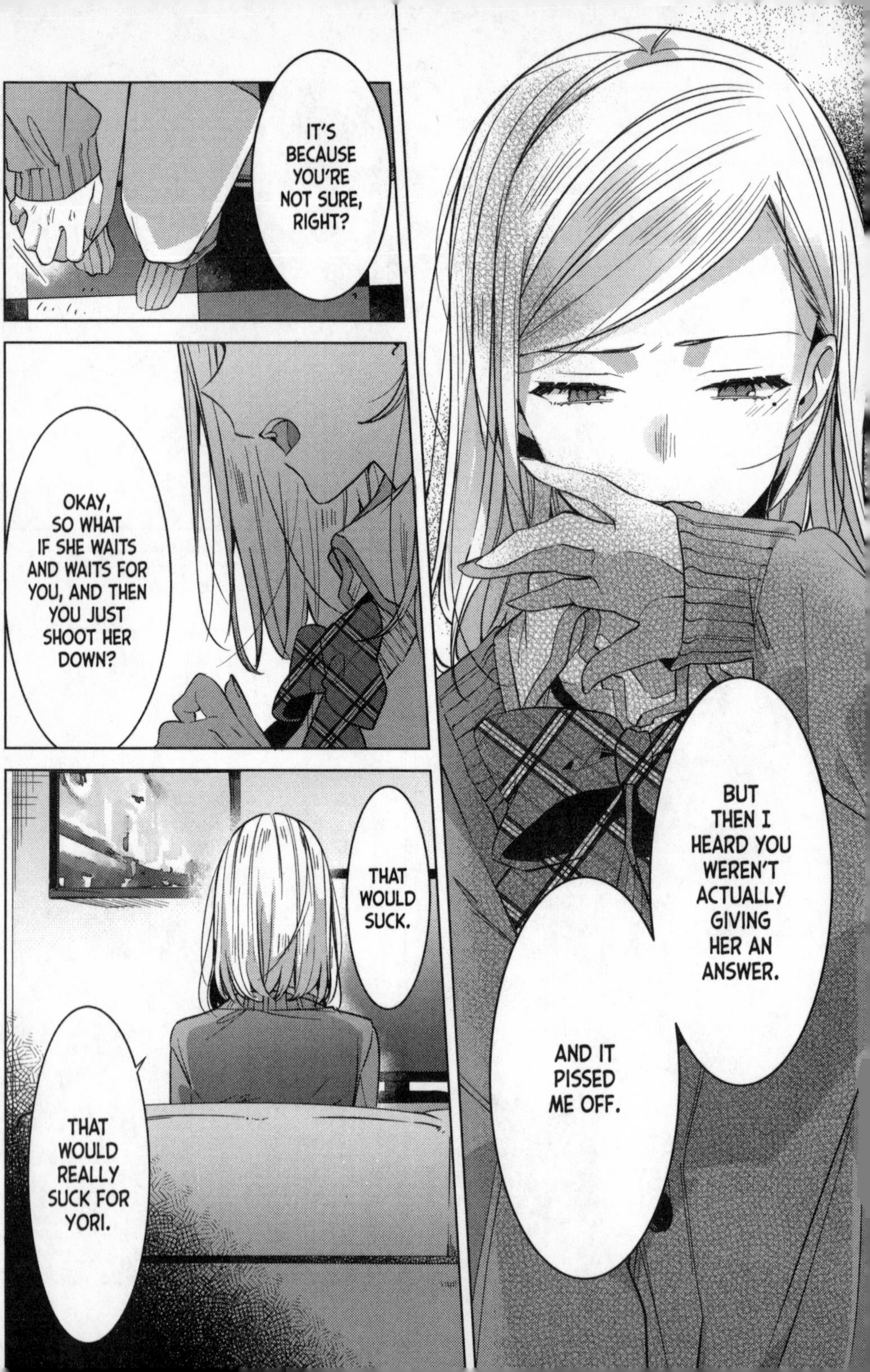
BUT THEN I HEARD YOU WEREN'T ACTUALLY GIVING HER AN ANSWER.
AND IT PISSED ME OFF.
IT'S BECAUSE YOU'RE NOT SURE, RIGHT?
OKAY, SO WHAT IF SHE WAITS AND WAITS FOR YOU, AND THEN YOU JUST SHOOT HER DOWN?
THAT WOULD SUCK.
THAT WOULD REALLY SUCK FOR YORI.

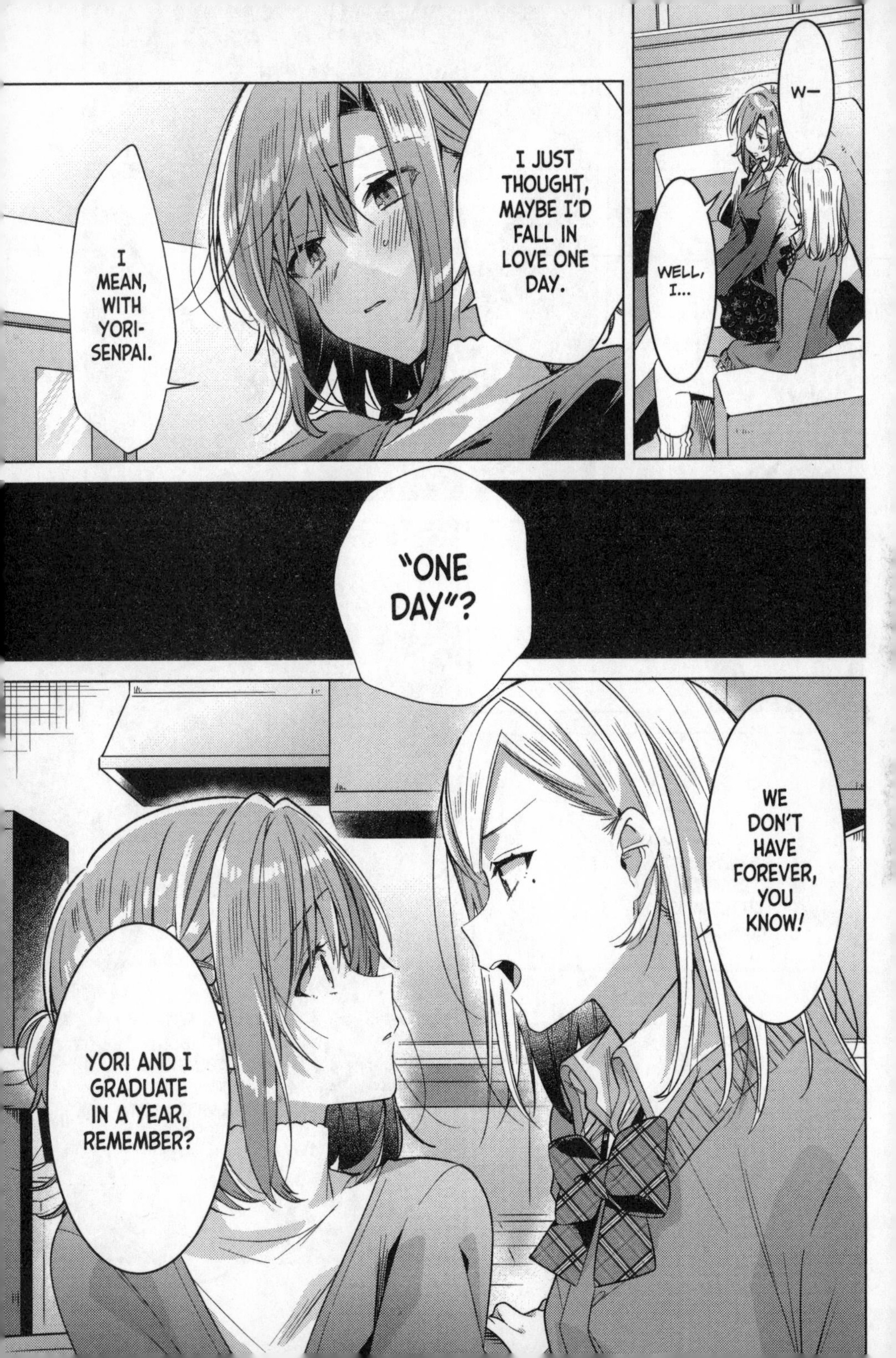
W—
WELL, I...
I JUST THOUGHT, MAYBE I'D FALL IN LOVE ONE DAY.
I MEAN, WITH YORI-SENPAI.
"ONE DAY"?
WE DON'T HAVE FOREVER, YOU KNOW!
YORI AND I GRADUATE IN A YEAR, REMEMBER?

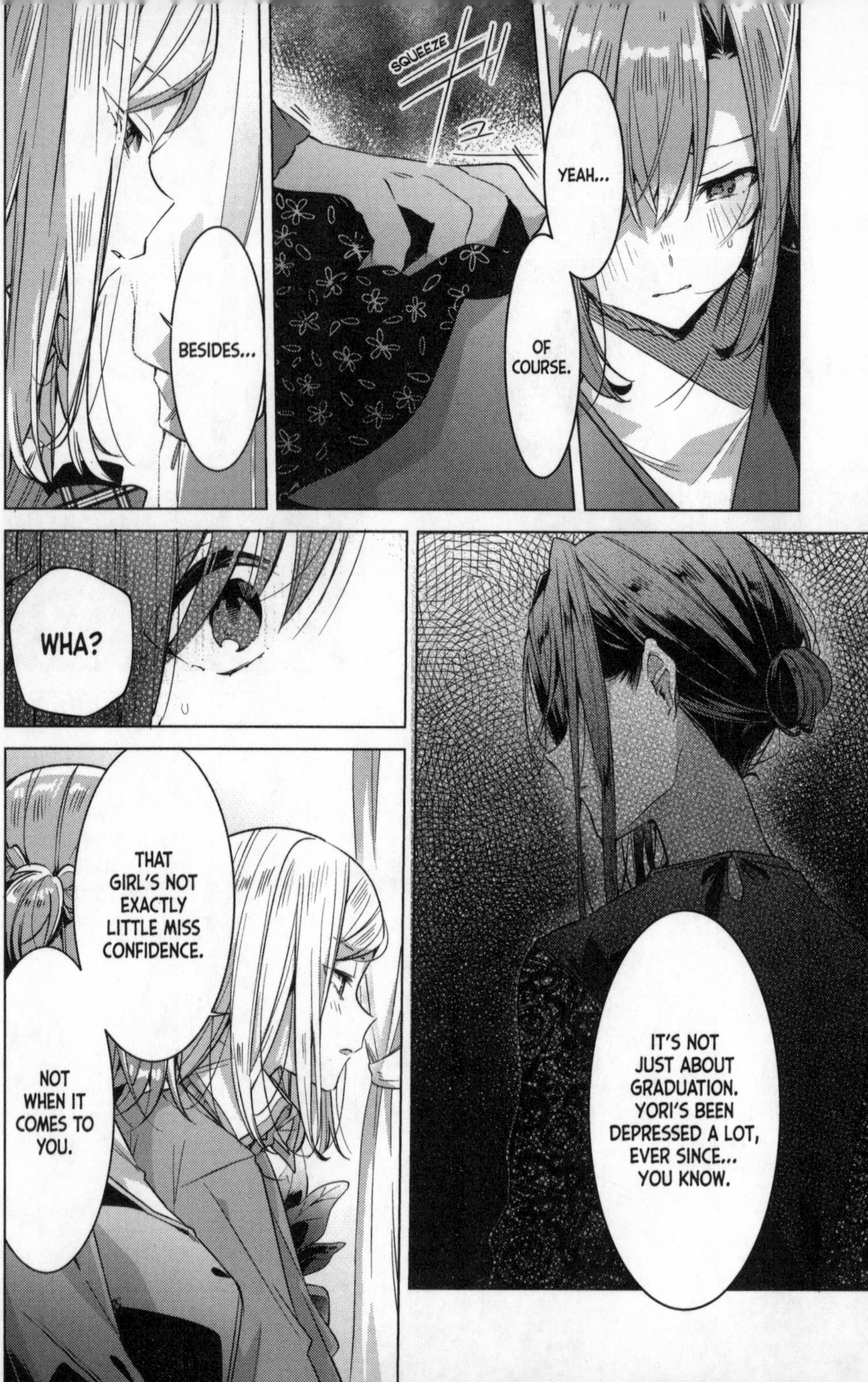
YEAH...
OF COURSE.
SQUEEZE
BESIDES...
IT'S NOT JUST ABOUT GRADUATION. YORI'S BEEN DEPRESSED A LOT, EVER SINCE... YOU KNOW.
WHA?
THAT GIRL'S NOT EXACTLY LITTLE MISS CONFIDENCE.
NOT WHEN IT COMES TO YOU.

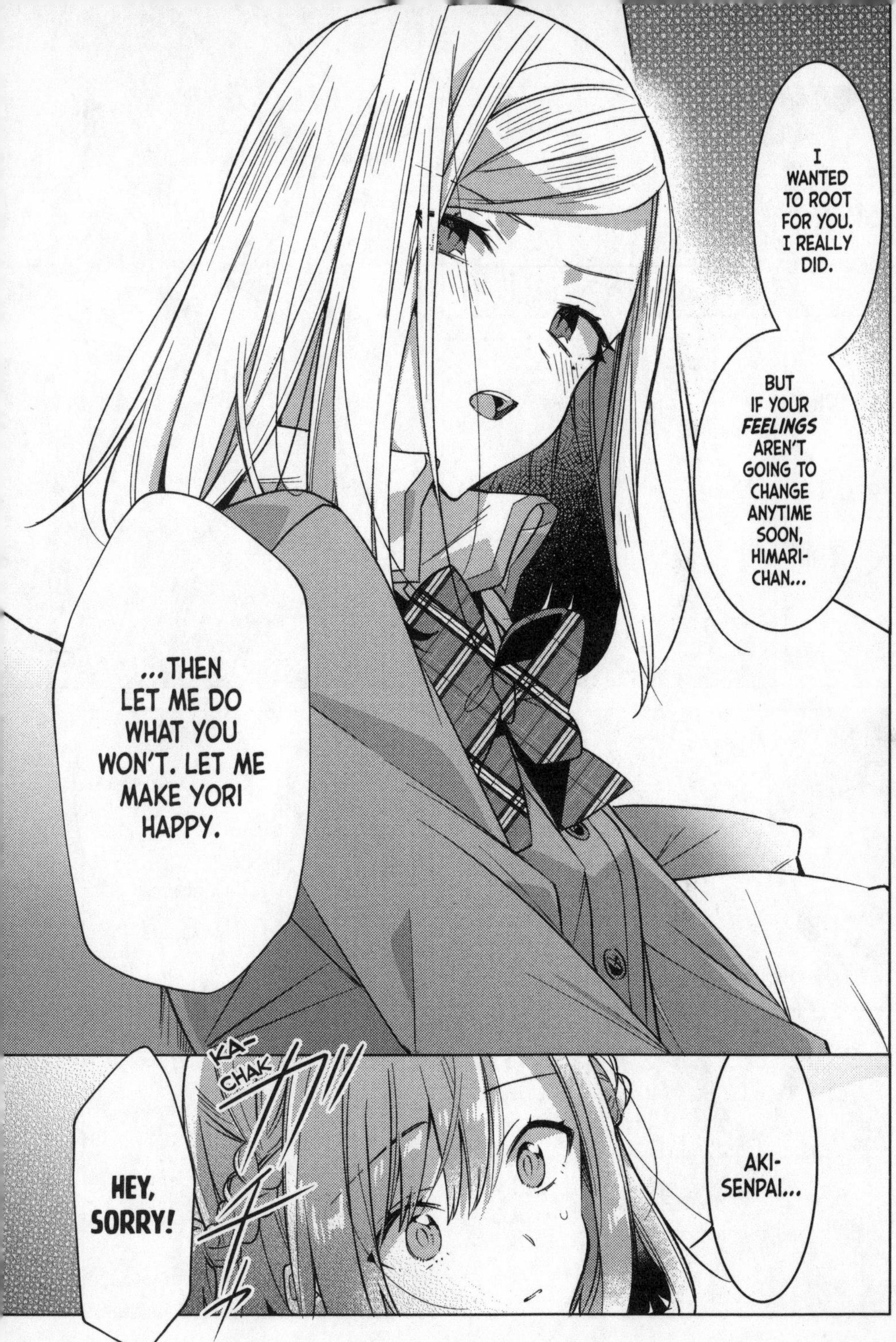
I WANTED TO ROOT FOR YOU. I REALLY DID.
BUT IF YOUR *FEELINGS* AREN'T GOING TO CHANGE ANYTIME SOON, HIMARI-CHAN...
...THEN LET ME DO WHAT YOU WON'T. LET ME MAKE YORI HAPPY.
AKI-SENPAI...
KA-CHAK
HEY, SORRY!

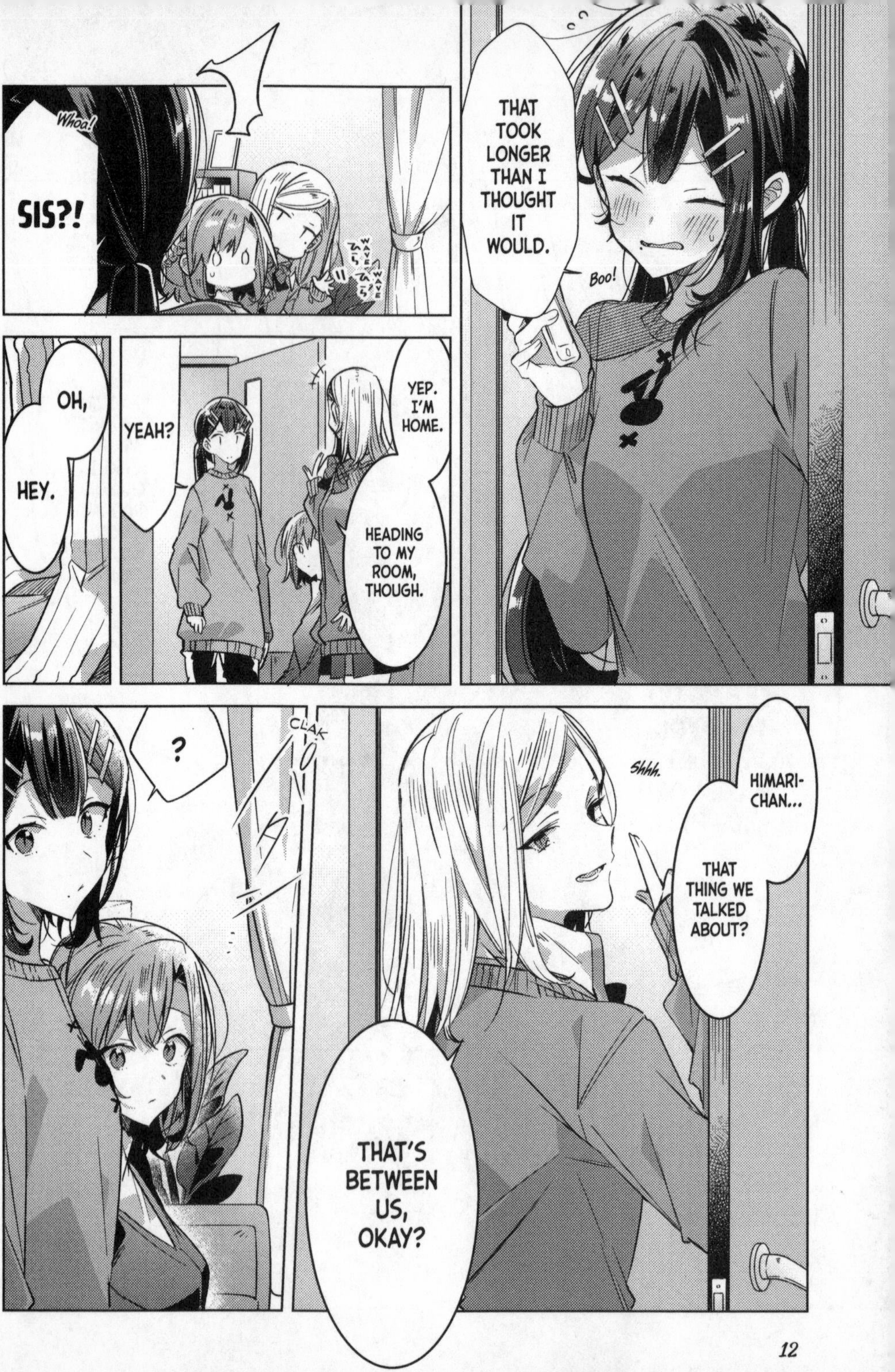
THAT TOOK LONGER THAN I THOUGHT IT WOULD.
Boo!
Whoa!
SIS?!
WAVE
WAVE
YEP. I'M HOME.
YEAH?
HEADING TO MY ROOM, THOUGH.
OH,
HEY.
Shhh.
HIMARI-CHAN...
THAT THING WE TALKED ABOUT?
THAT'S BETWEEN US, OKAY?
CLAK
?

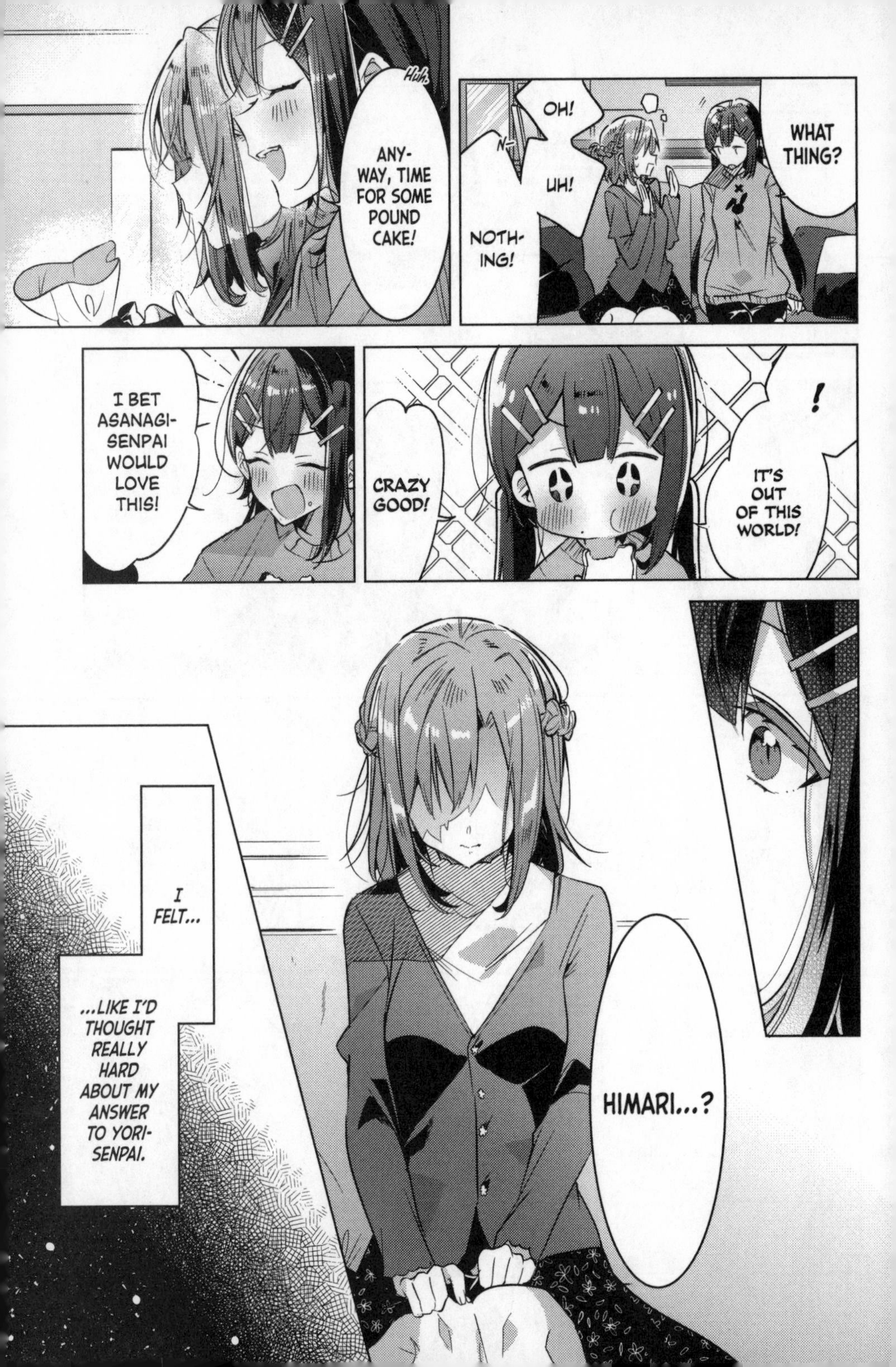
WHAT THING?
OH!
N-
UH!
NOTHING!
Huh
ANYWAY, TIME FOR SOME POUND CAKE!
!
IT'S OUT OF THIS WORLD!
CRAZY GOOD!
I BET ASANAGI-SENPAI WOULD LOVE THIS!
HIMARI...?
I FELT...
...LIKE I'D THOUGHT REALLY HARD ABOUT MY ANSWER TO YORI-SENPAI.

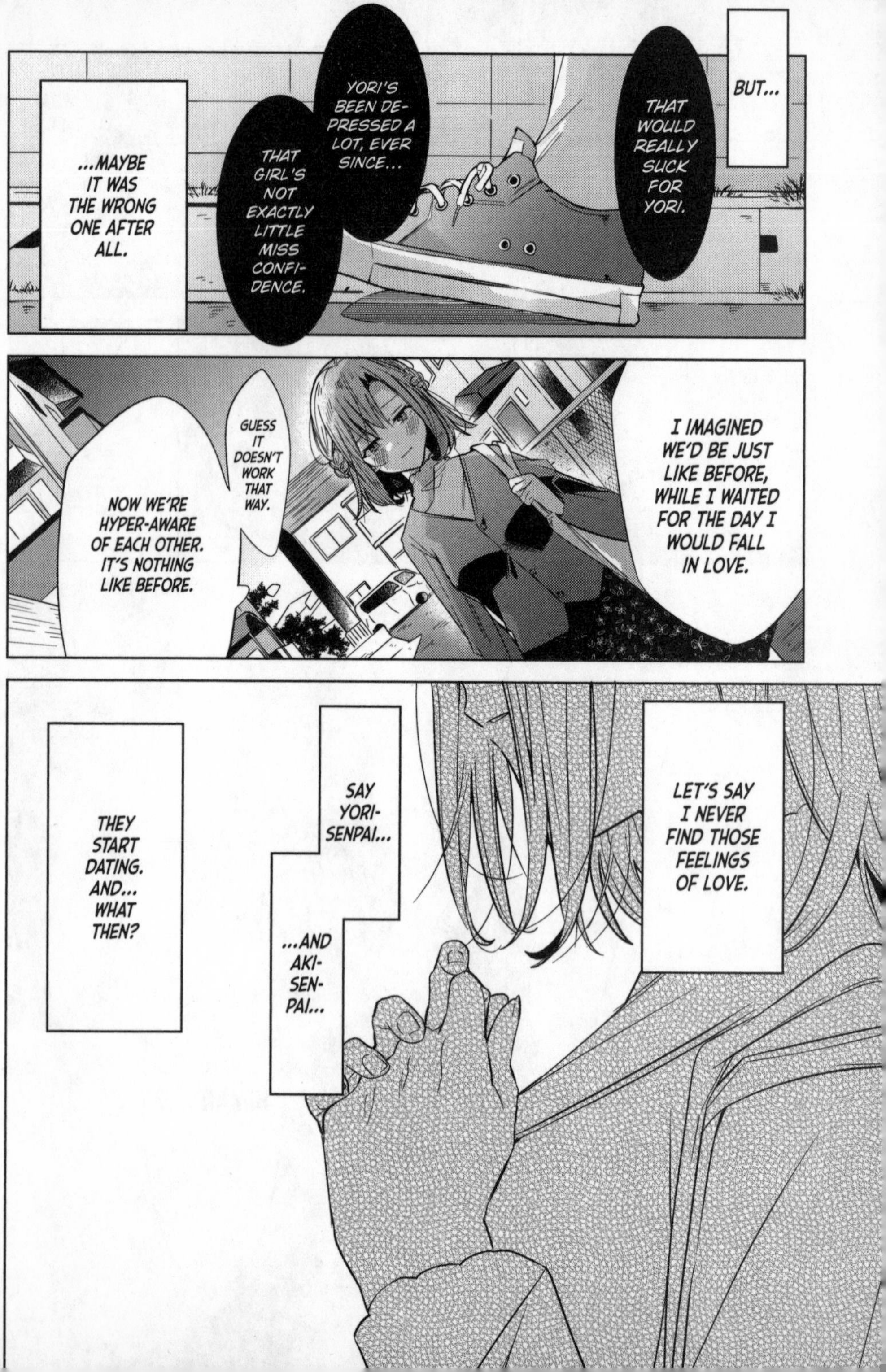
BUT...
THAT WOULD REALLY SUCK FOR YORI.
YORI'S BEEN DE-PRESSED A LOT, EVER SINCE...
THAT GIRL'S NOT EXACTLY LITTLE MISS CONFI-DENCE.
...MAYBE IT WAS THE WRONG ONE AFTER ALL.
I IMAGINED WE'D BE JUST LIKE BEFORE, WHILE I WAITED FOR THE DAY I WOULD FALL IN LOVE.
GUESS IT DOESN'T WORK THAT WAY.
NOW WE'RE HYPER-AWARE OF EACH OTHER. IT'S NOTHING LIKE BEFORE.
LET'S SAY I NEVER FIND THOSE FEELINGS OF LOVE.
SAY YORI-SENPAI...
...AND AKI-SEN-PAI...
THEY START DATING. AND... WHAT THEN?

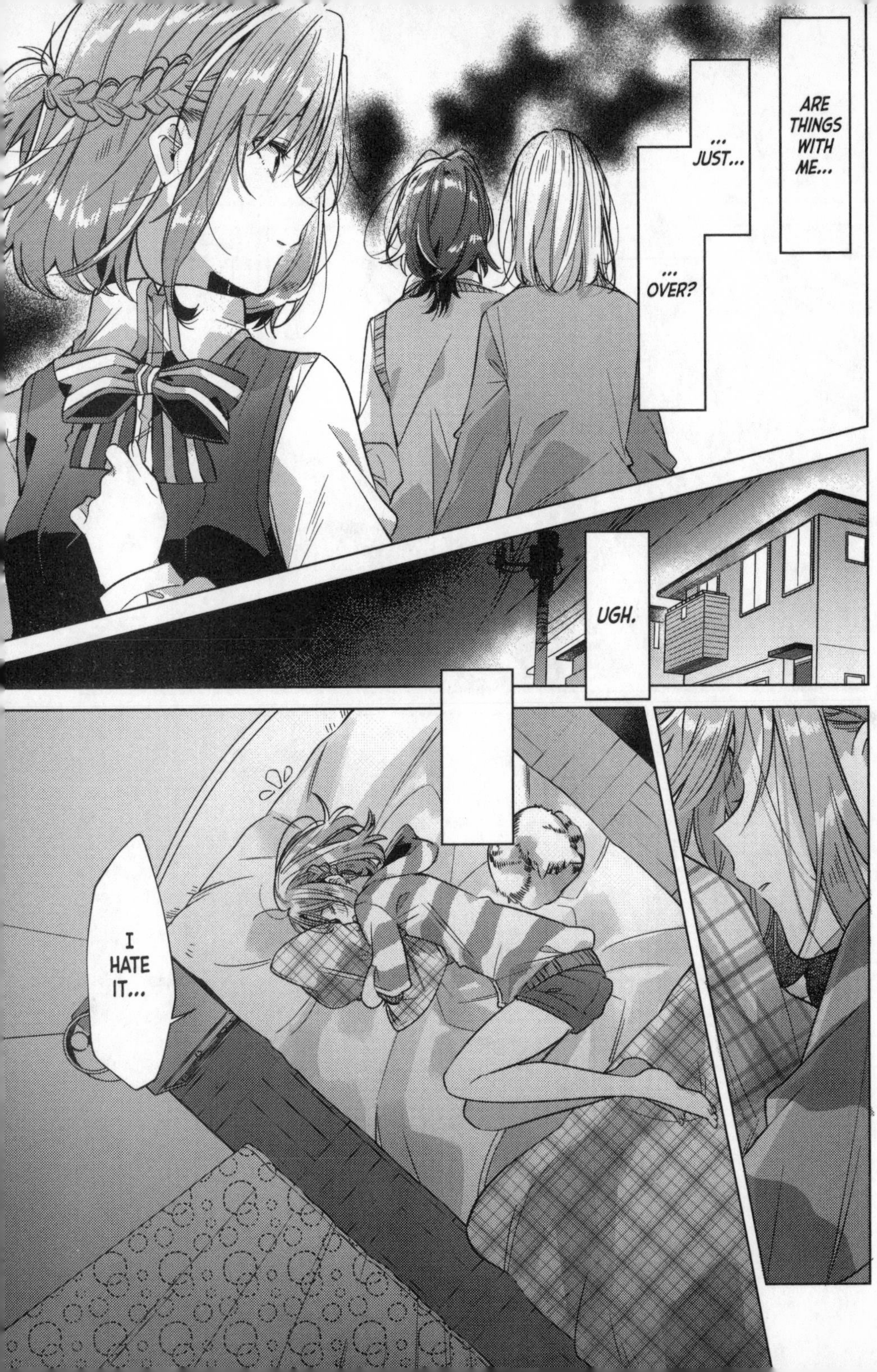
ARE THINGS WITH ME...
... JUST...
... OVER?
UGH.
I HATE IT...

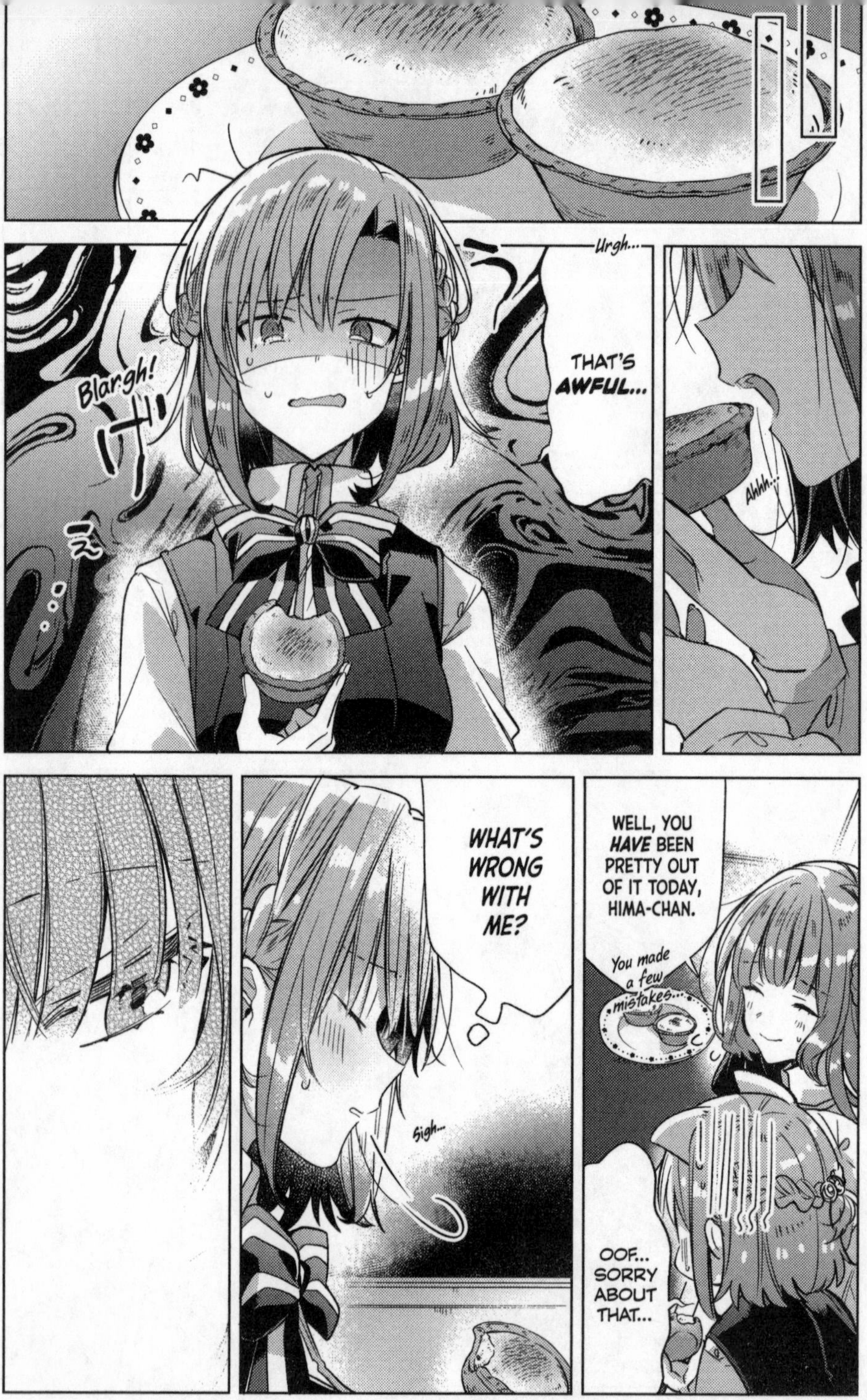
Ahhh...
Urgh...
THAT'S **AWFUL...**
Blargh!
げ
WELL, YOU **HAVE** BEEN PRETTY OUT OF IT TODAY, HIMA-CHAN.
You made a few mistakes...
OOF... SORRY ABOUT THAT...
WHAT'S WRONG WITH ME?
Sigh...

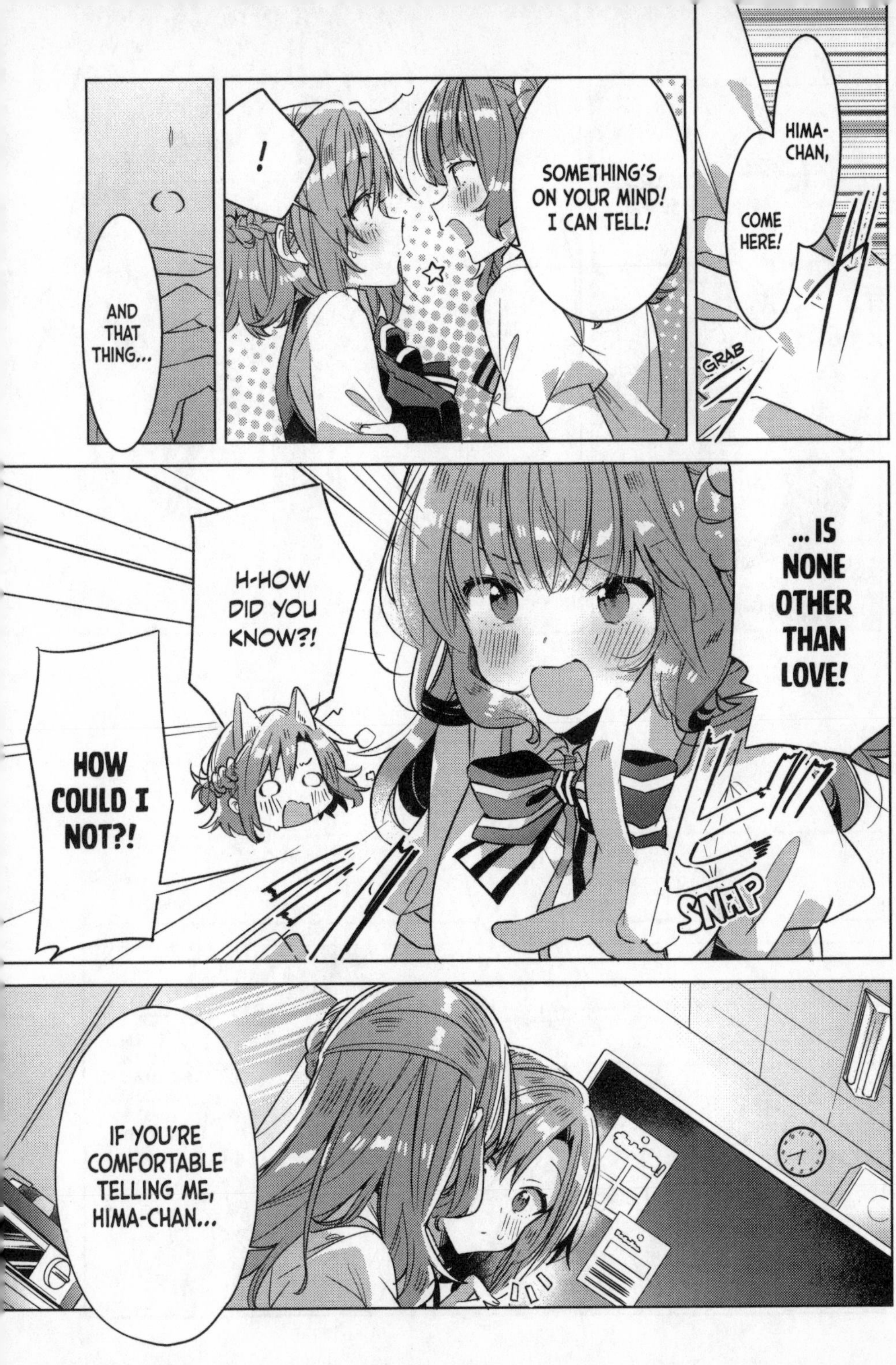
HIMA-CHAN,
COME HERE!
GRAB
SOMETHING'S ON YOUR MIND! I CAN TELL!
!
AND THAT THING...
...IS NONE OTHER THAN LOVE!
SNAP
H-HOW DID YOU KNOW?!
HOW COULD I NOT?!
IF YOU'RE COMFORTABLE TELLING ME, HIMA-CHAN...

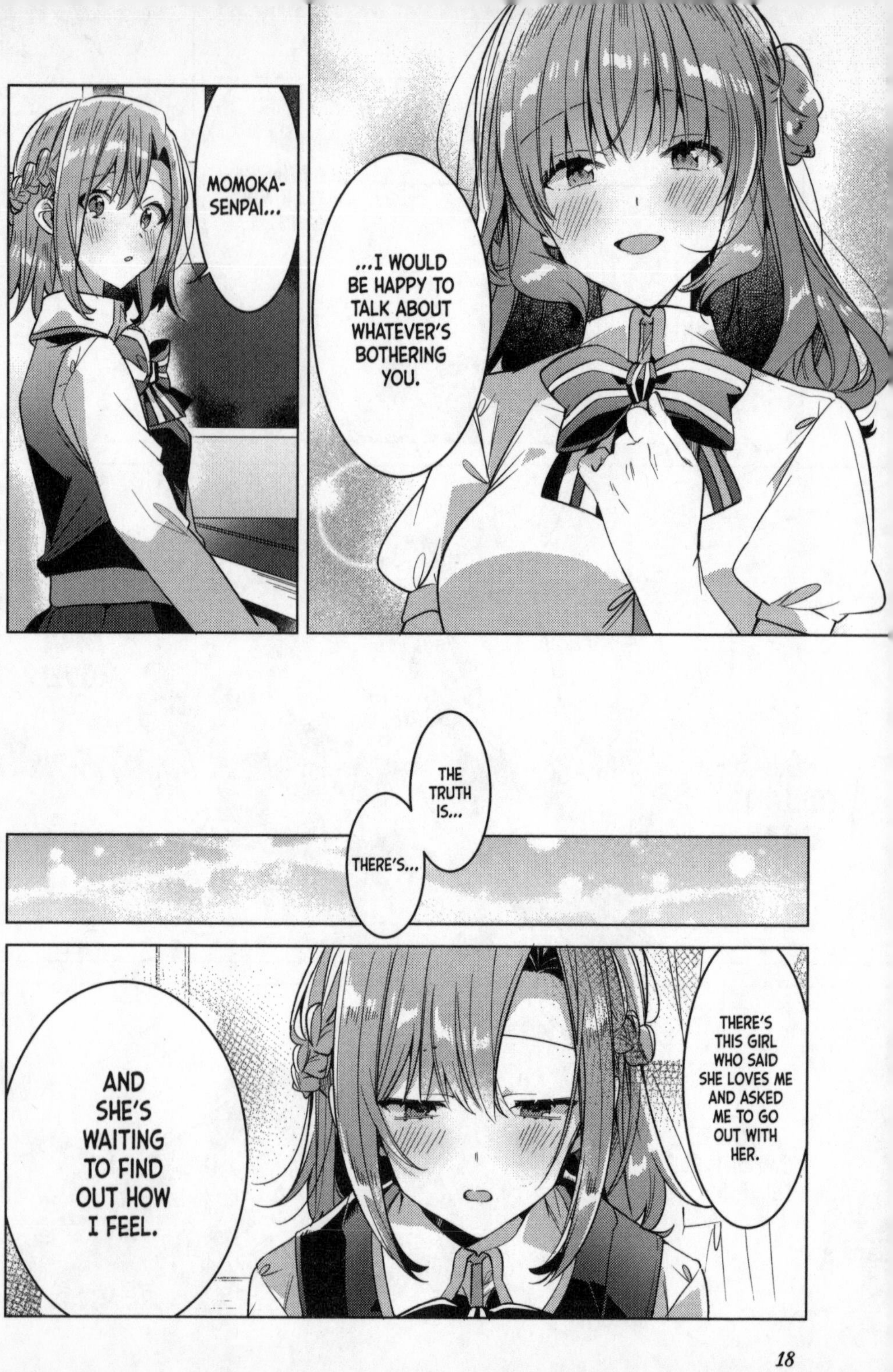
...I WOULD BE HAPPY TO TALK ABOUT WHATEVER'S BOTHERING YOU.
MOMOKA-SENPAI...
THE TRUTH IS...
THERE'S...
THERE'S THIS GIRL WHO SAID SHE LOVES ME AND ASKED ME TO GO OUT WITH HER.
AND SHE'S WAITING TO FIND OUT HOW I FEEL.

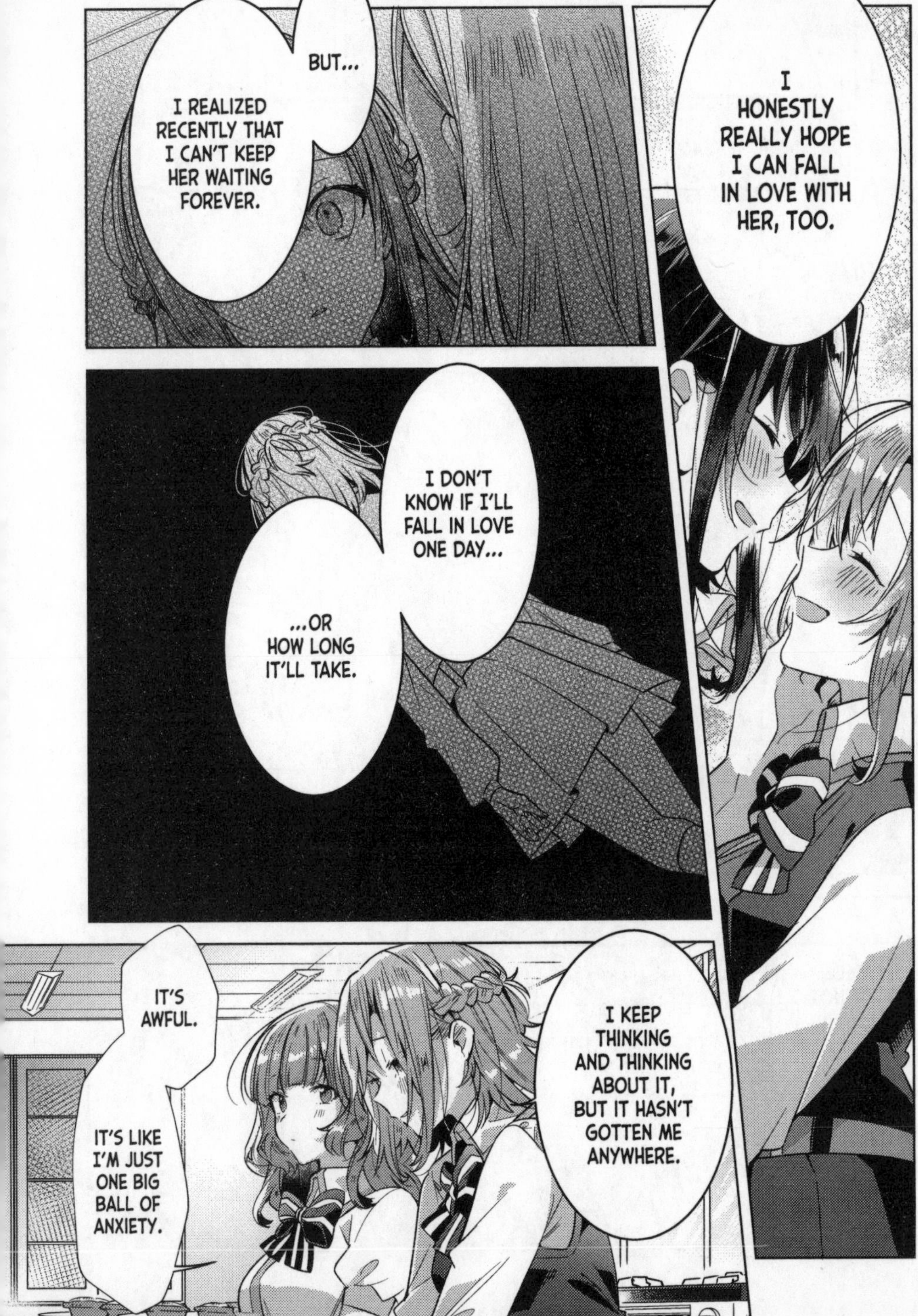
I HONESTLY REALLY HOPE I CAN FALL IN LOVE WITH HER, TOO.
BUT...
I REALIZED RECENTLY THAT I CAN'T KEEP HER WAITING FOREVER.
I DON'T KNOW IF I'LL FALL IN LOVE ONE DAY...
...OR HOW LONG IT'LL TAKE.
I KEEP THINKING AND THINKING ABOUT IT, BUT IT HASN'T GOTTEN ME ANYWHERE.
IT'S AWFUL.
IT'S LIKE I'M JUST ONE BIG BALL OF ANXIETY.

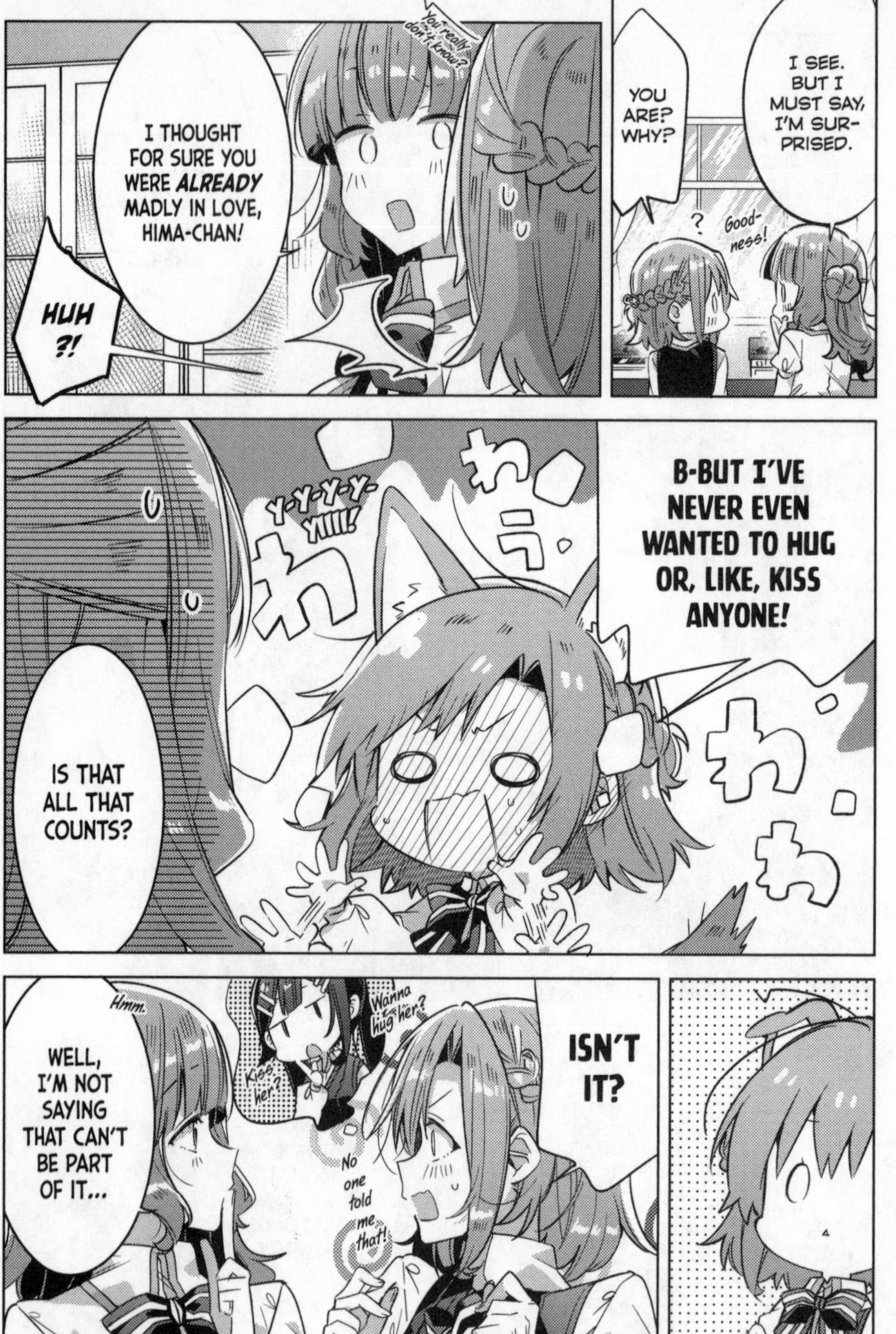
I SEE. BUT I MUST SAY, I'M SURPRISED.
Goodness!
YOU ARE? WHY?
?
You really don't know?
I THOUGHT FOR SURE YOU WERE *ALREADY* MADLY IN LOVE, HIMA-CHAN!
HUH ?!
B-BUT I'VE NEVER EVEN WANTED TO HUG OR, LIKE, KISS ANYONE!
Y-Y-Y-Y-YIIII!
IS THAT ALL THAT COUNTS?
ISN'T IT?
Wanna hug her?
Kiss her?
Hmm.
WELL, I'M NOT SAYING THAT CAN'T BE PART OF IT...
No one told me that!

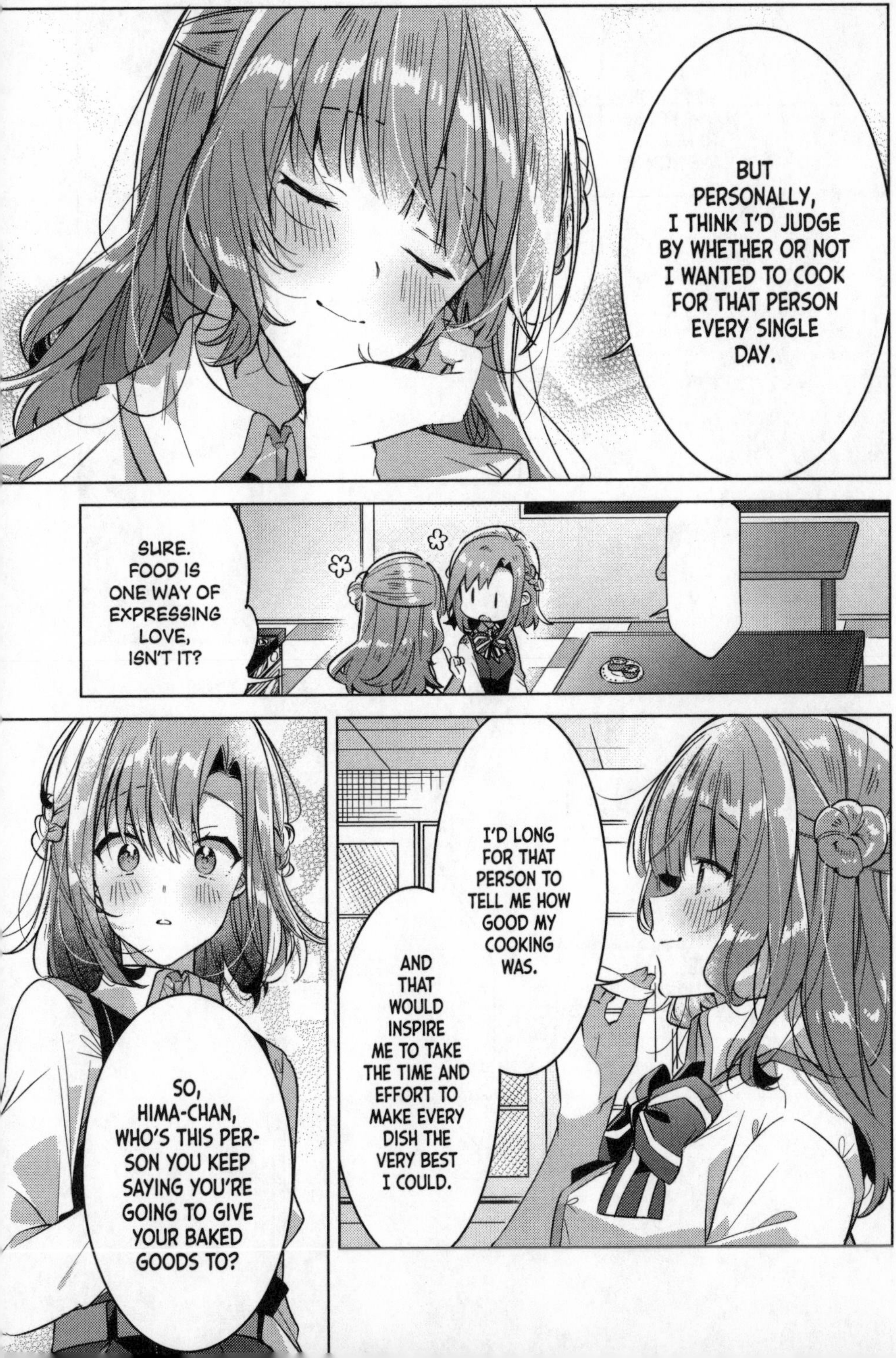
BUT PERSONALLY, I THINK I'D JUDGE BY WHETHER OR NOT I WANTED TO COOK FOR THAT PERSON EVERY SINGLE DAY.
SURE. FOOD IS ONE WAY OF EXPRESSING LOVE, ISN'T IT?
I'D LONG FOR THAT PERSON TO TELL ME HOW GOOD MY COOKING WAS.
AND THAT WOULD INSPIRE ME TO TAKE THE TIME AND EFFORT TO MAKE EVERY DISH THE VERY BEST I COULD.
SO, HIMA-CHAN, WHO'S THIS PER-SON YOU KEEP SAYING YOU'RE GOING TO GIVE YOUR BAKED GOODS TO?

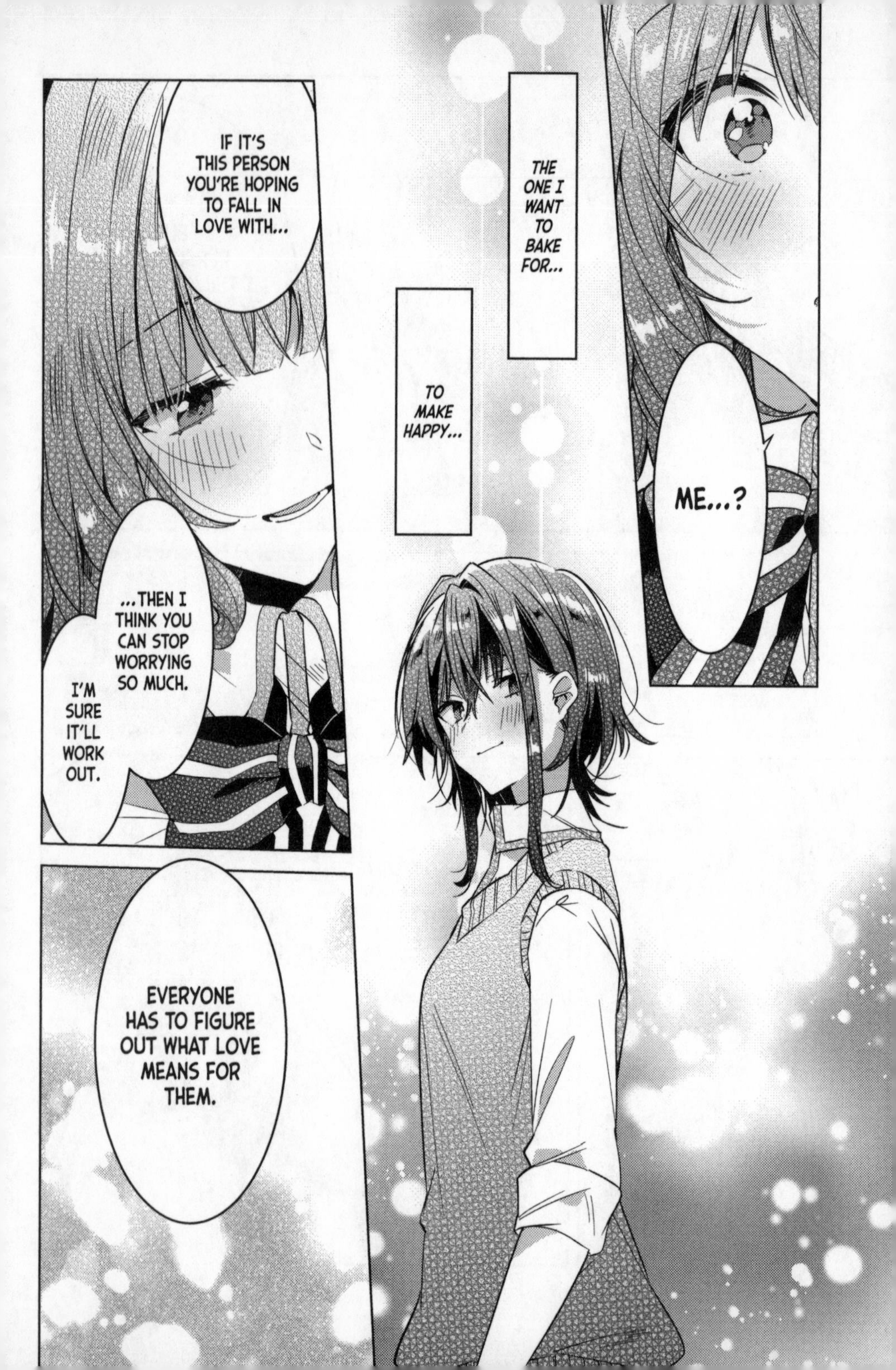
THE ONE I WANT TO BAKE FOR...
TO MAKE HAPPY...
ME...?
IF IT'S THIS PERSON YOU'RE HOPING TO FALL IN LOVE WITH...
...THEN I THINK YOU CAN STOP WORRYING SO MUCH.
I'M SURE IT'LL WORK OUT.
EVERYONE HAS TO FIGURE OUT WHAT LOVE MEANS FOR THEM.

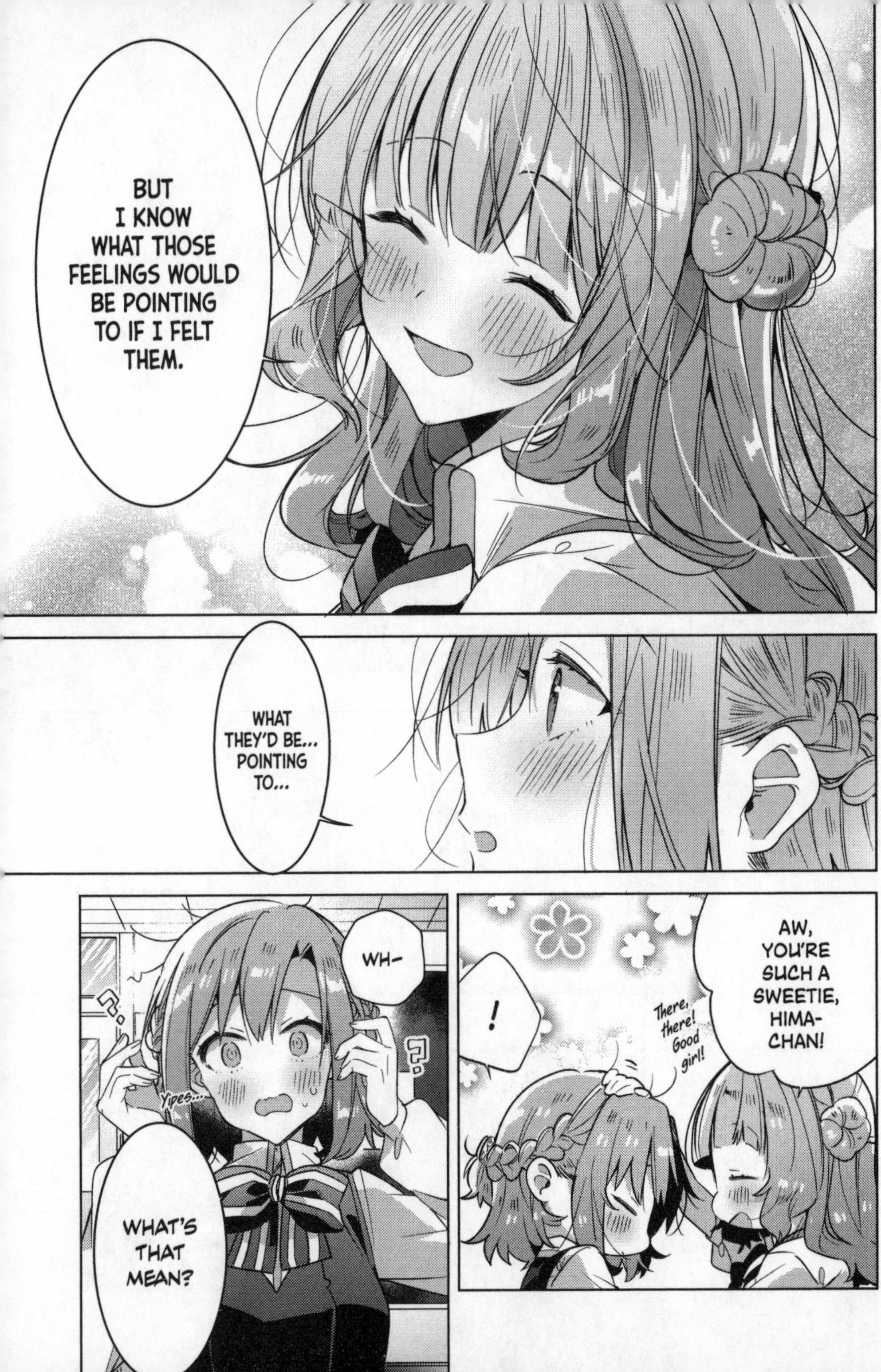
BUT I KNOW WHAT THOSE FEELINGS WOULD BE POINTING TO IF I FELT THEM.
WHAT THEY'D BE... POINTING TO...
AW, YOU'RE SUCH A SWEETIE, HIMA-CHAN!
There, there! Good girl!
!
WH-
Yipes...
WHAT'S THAT MEAN?

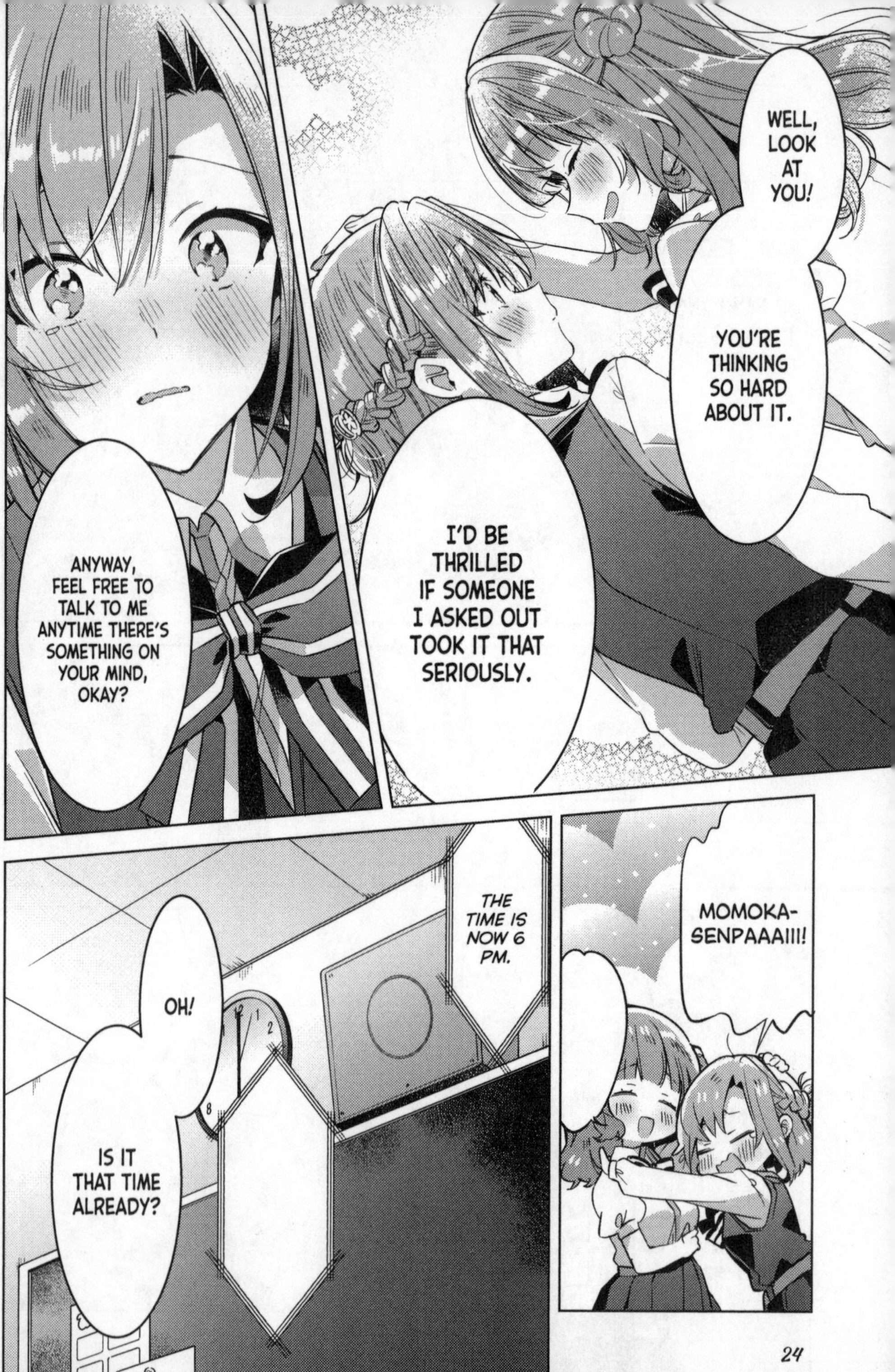
WELL, LOOK AT YOU!
YOU'RE THINKING SO HARD ABOUT IT.
I'D BE THRILLED IF SOMEONE I ASKED OUT TOOK IT THAT SERIOUSLY.
ANYWAY, FEEL FREE TO TALK TO ME ANYTIME THERE'S SOMETHING ON YOUR MIND, OKAY?
MOMOKA-SENPAAAIIII!
THE TIME IS NOW 6 PM.
OH!
IS IT THAT TIME ALREADY?

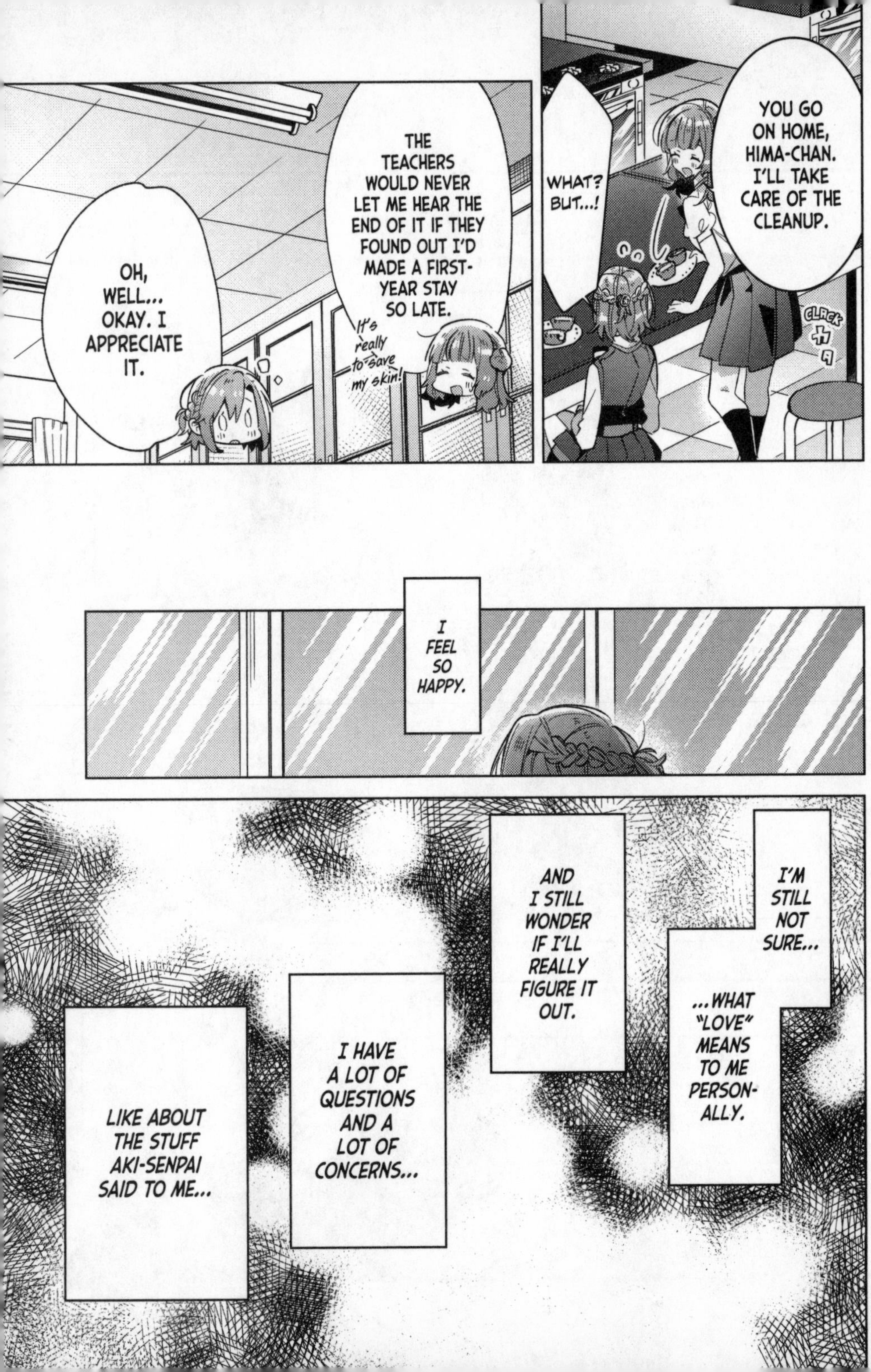
YOU GO ON HOME, HIMA-CHAN. I'LL TAKE CARE OF THE CLEANUP.
WHAT? BUT...!
CLACK カタ
THE TEACHERS WOULD NEVER LET ME HEAR THE END OF IT IF THEY FOUND OUT I'D MADE A FIRST-YEAR STAY SO LATE.
It's really to save my skin!
OH, WELL... OKAY. I APPRECIATE IT.
I FEEL SO HAPPY.
I'M STILL NOT SURE...
...WHAT "LOVE" MEANS TO ME PERSON-ALLY.
AND I STILL WONDER IF I'LL REALLY FIGURE IT OUT.
I HAVE A LOT OF QUESTIONS AND A LOT OF CONCERNS...
LIKE ABOUT THE STUFF AKI-SENPAI SAID TO ME...

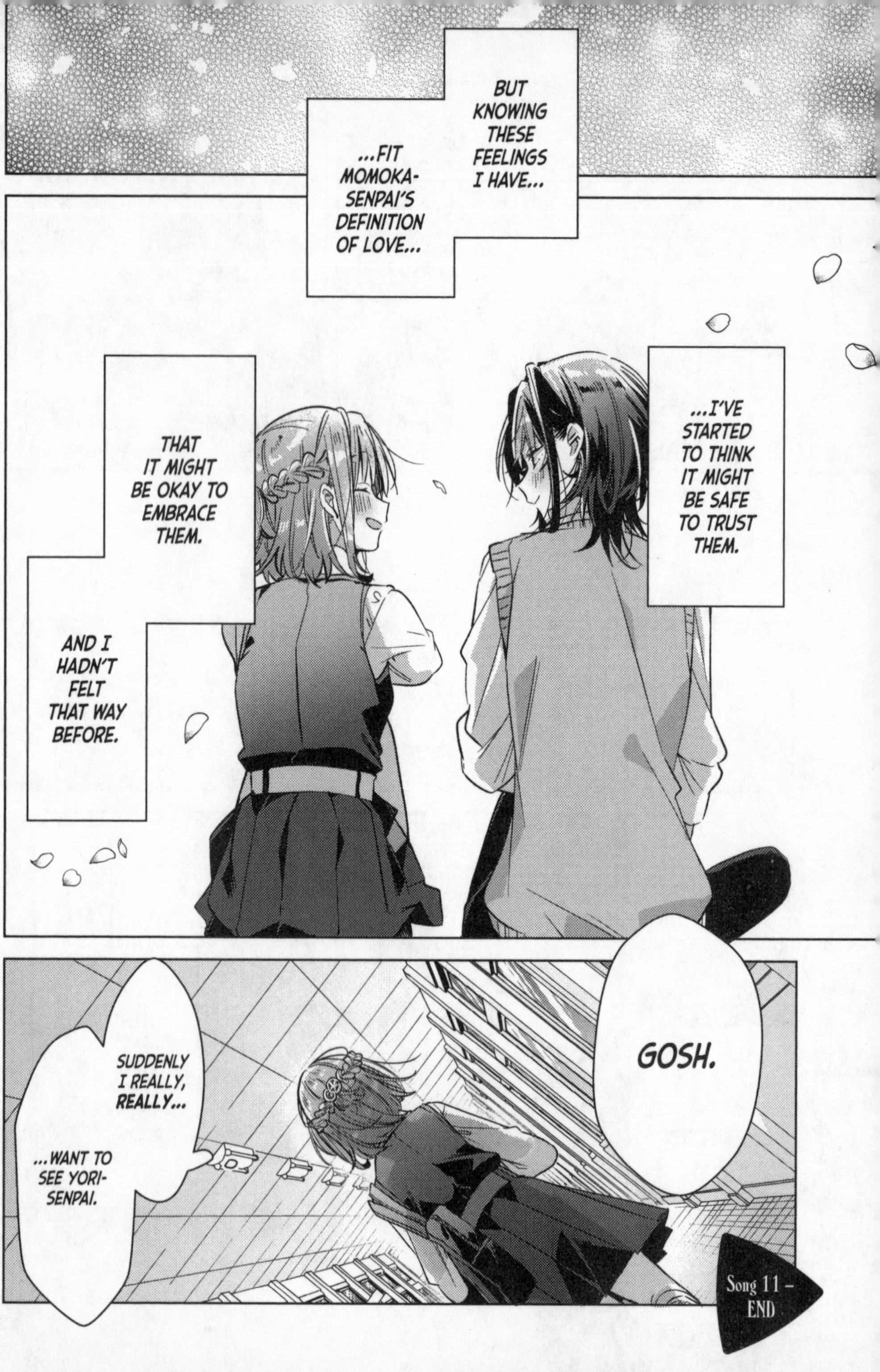
BUT KNOWING THESE FEELINGS I HAVE...
...FIT MOMOKA-SENPAI'S DEFINITION OF LOVE...
...I'VE STARTED TO THINK IT MIGHT BE SAFE TO TRUST THEM.
THAT IT MIGHT BE OKAY TO EMBRACE THEM.
AND I HADN'T FELT THAT WAY BEFORE.
GOSH.
SUDDENLY I REALLY, REALLY...
...WANT TO SEE YORI-SENPAI.
Song 11 – END

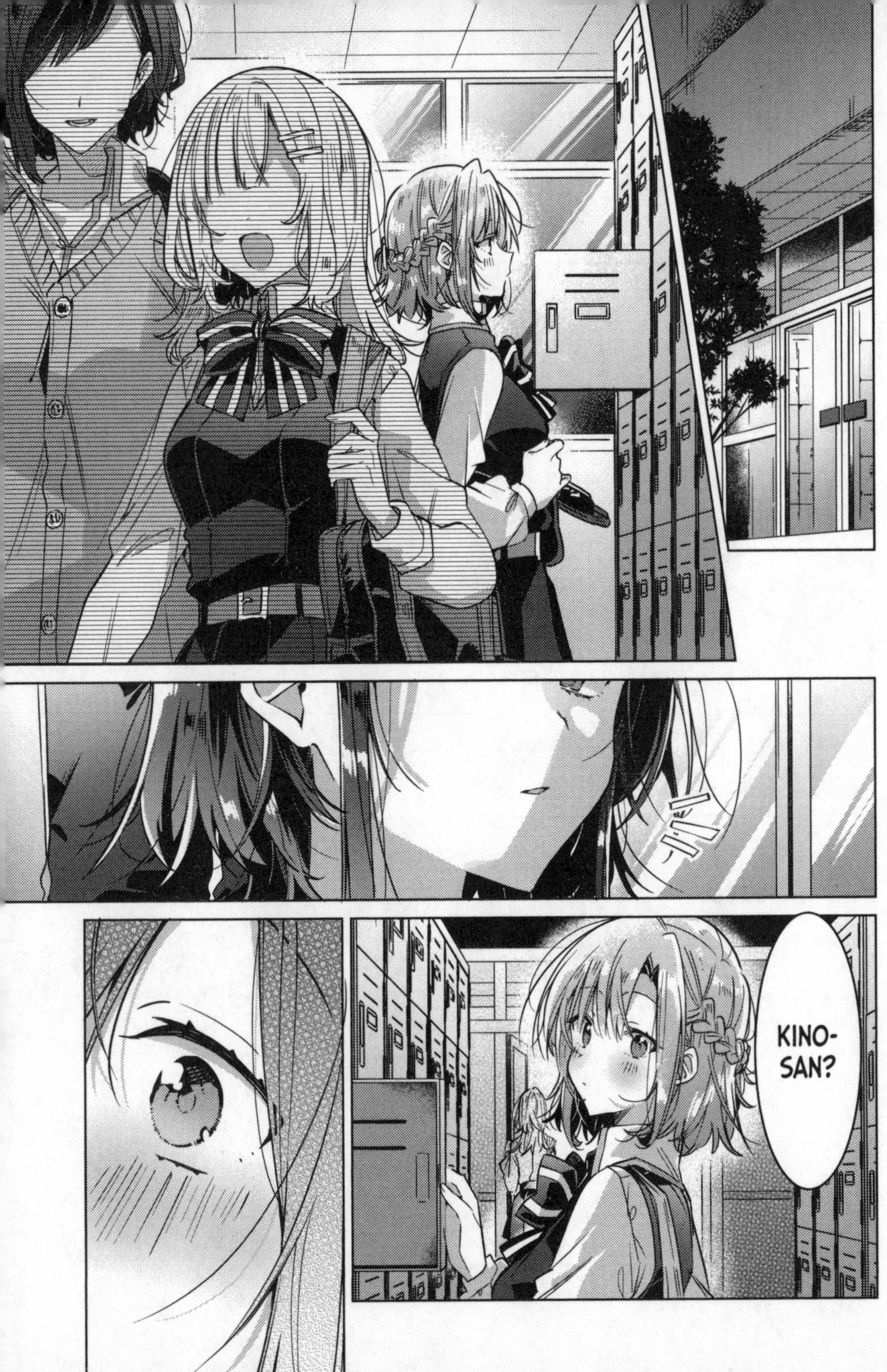
KINO-SAN?

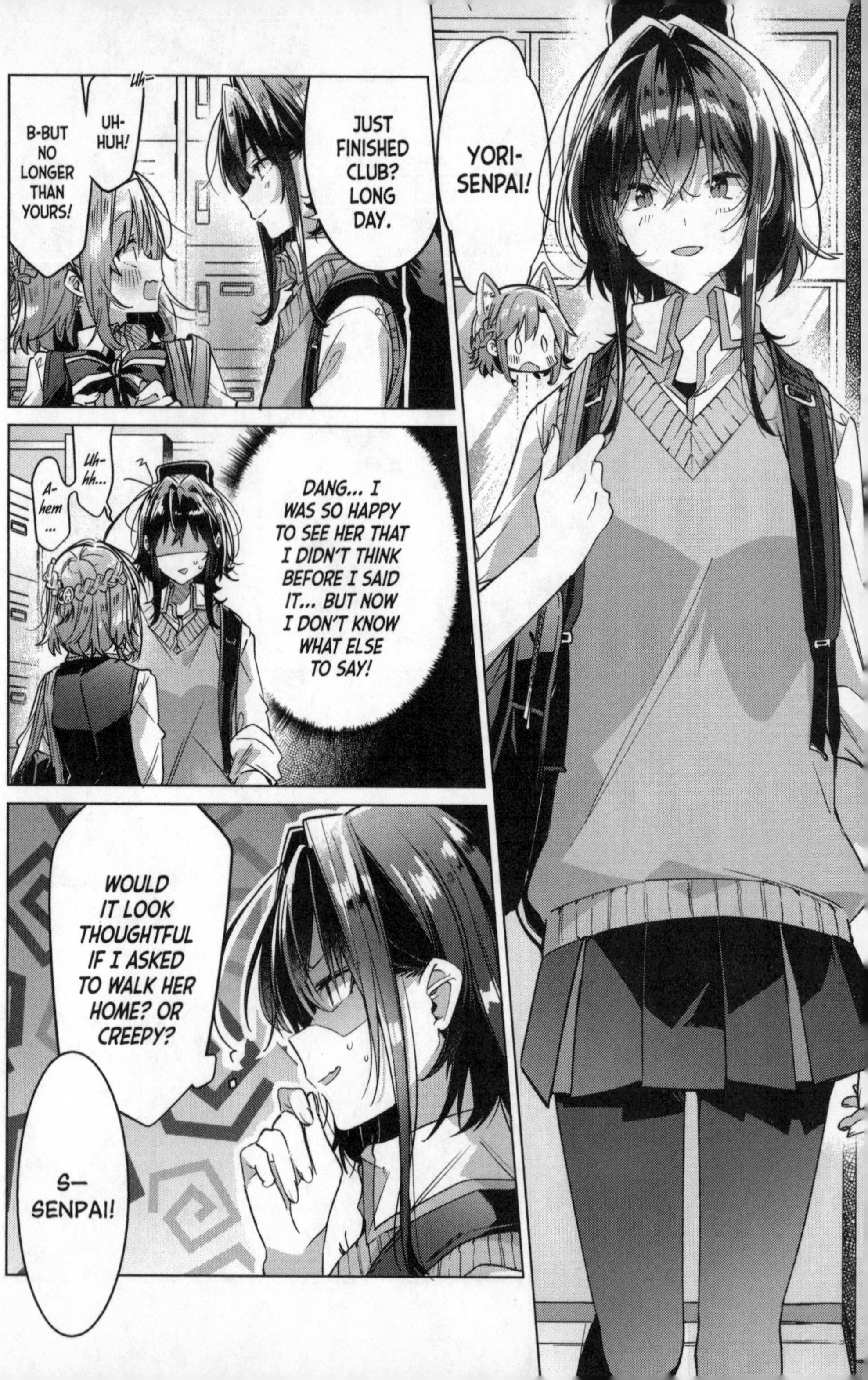
YORI-SENPAI!
JUST FINISHED CLUB? LONG DAY.
Uh—
UH-HUH!
B-BUT NO LONGER THAN YOURS!
DANG... I WAS SO HAPPY TO SEE HER THAT I DIDN'T THINK BEFORE I SAID IT... BUT NOW I DON'T KNOW WHAT ELSE TO SAY!
Uh-hh...
A-hem...
WOULD IT LOOK THOUGHTFUL IF I ASKED TO WALK HER HOME? OR CREEPY?
S—SENPAI!

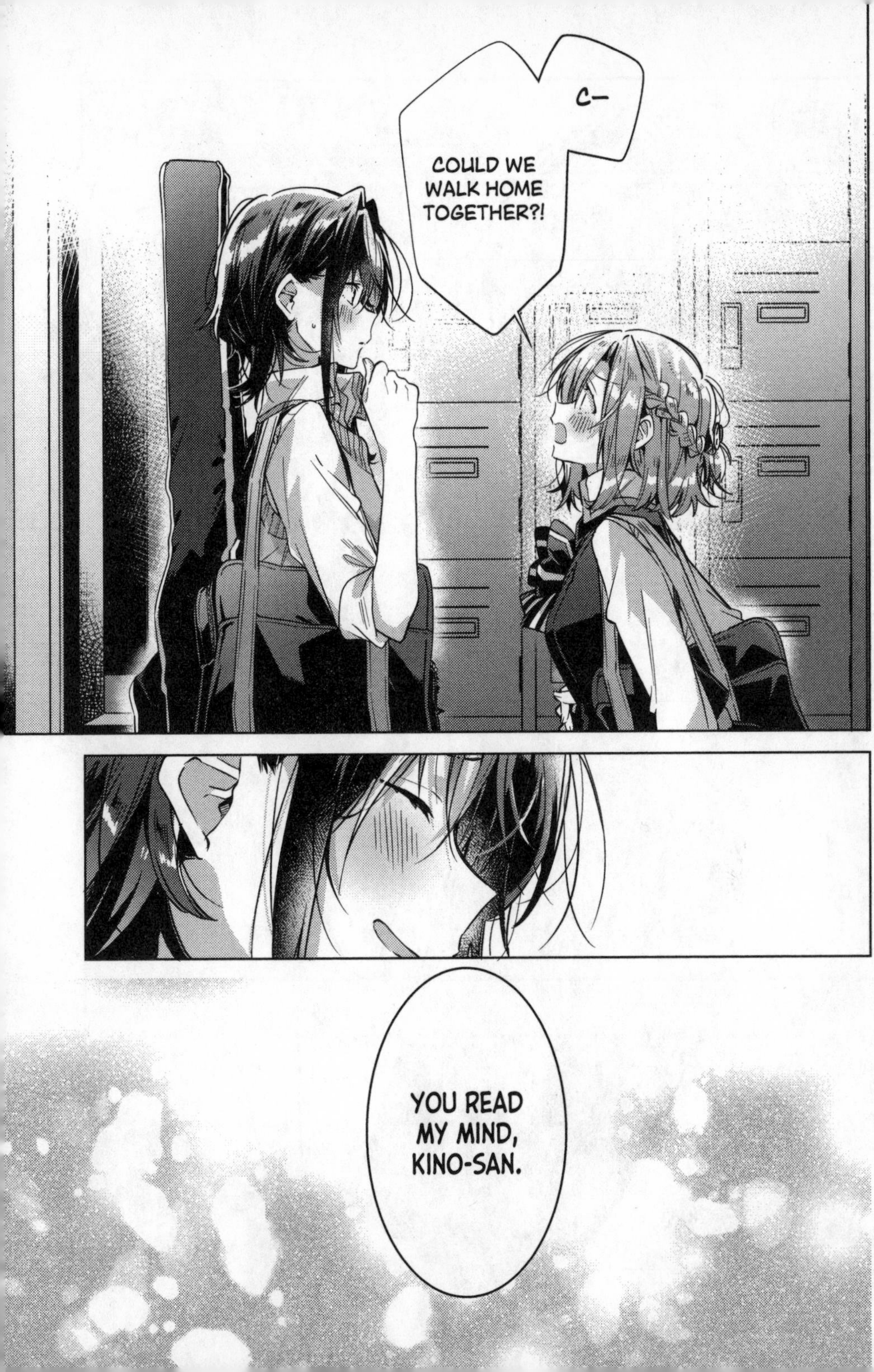
C—
COULD WE WALK HOME TOGETHER?!
YOU READ MY MIND, KINO-SAN.

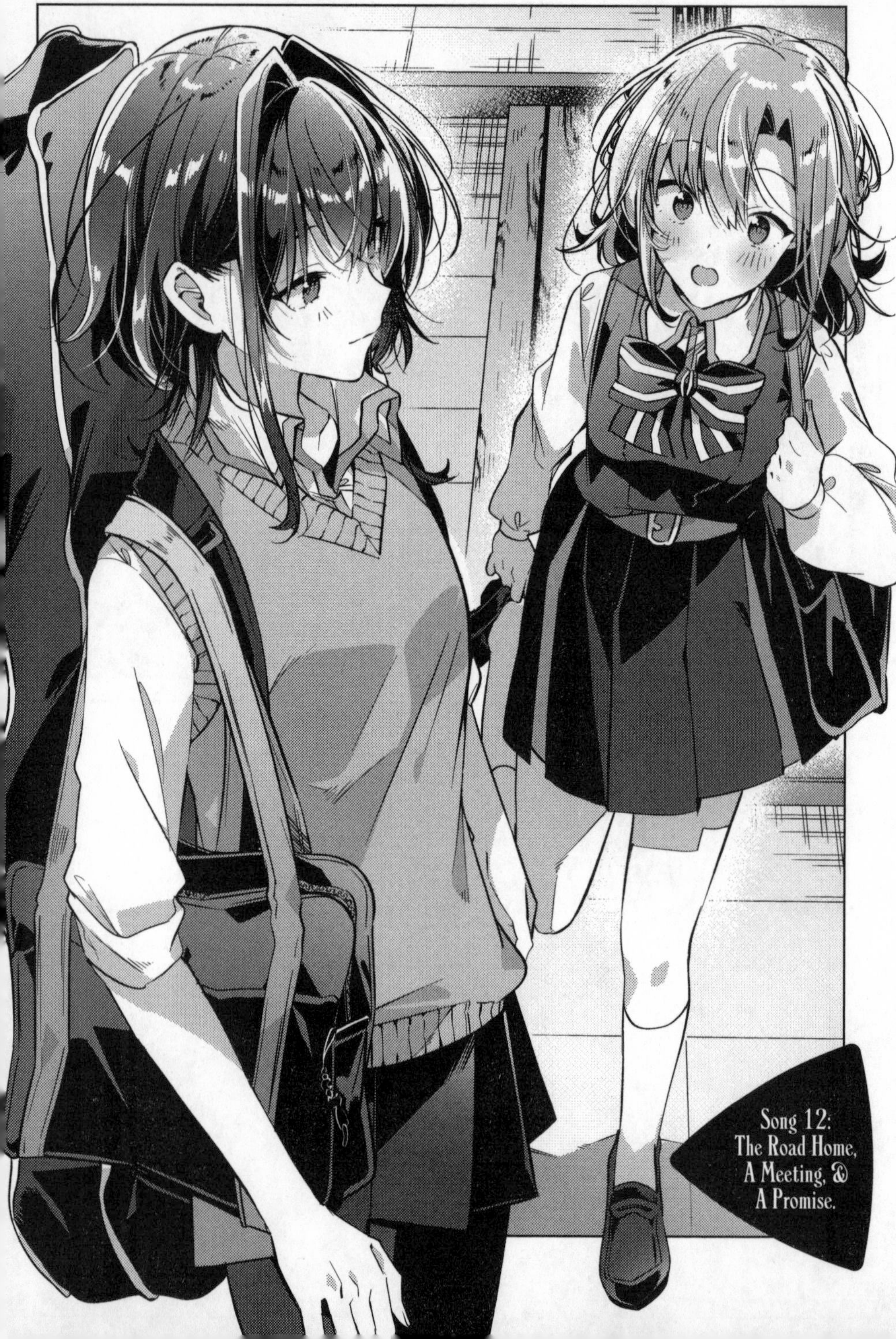
Song 12:
The Road Home,
A Meeting, &
A Promise.

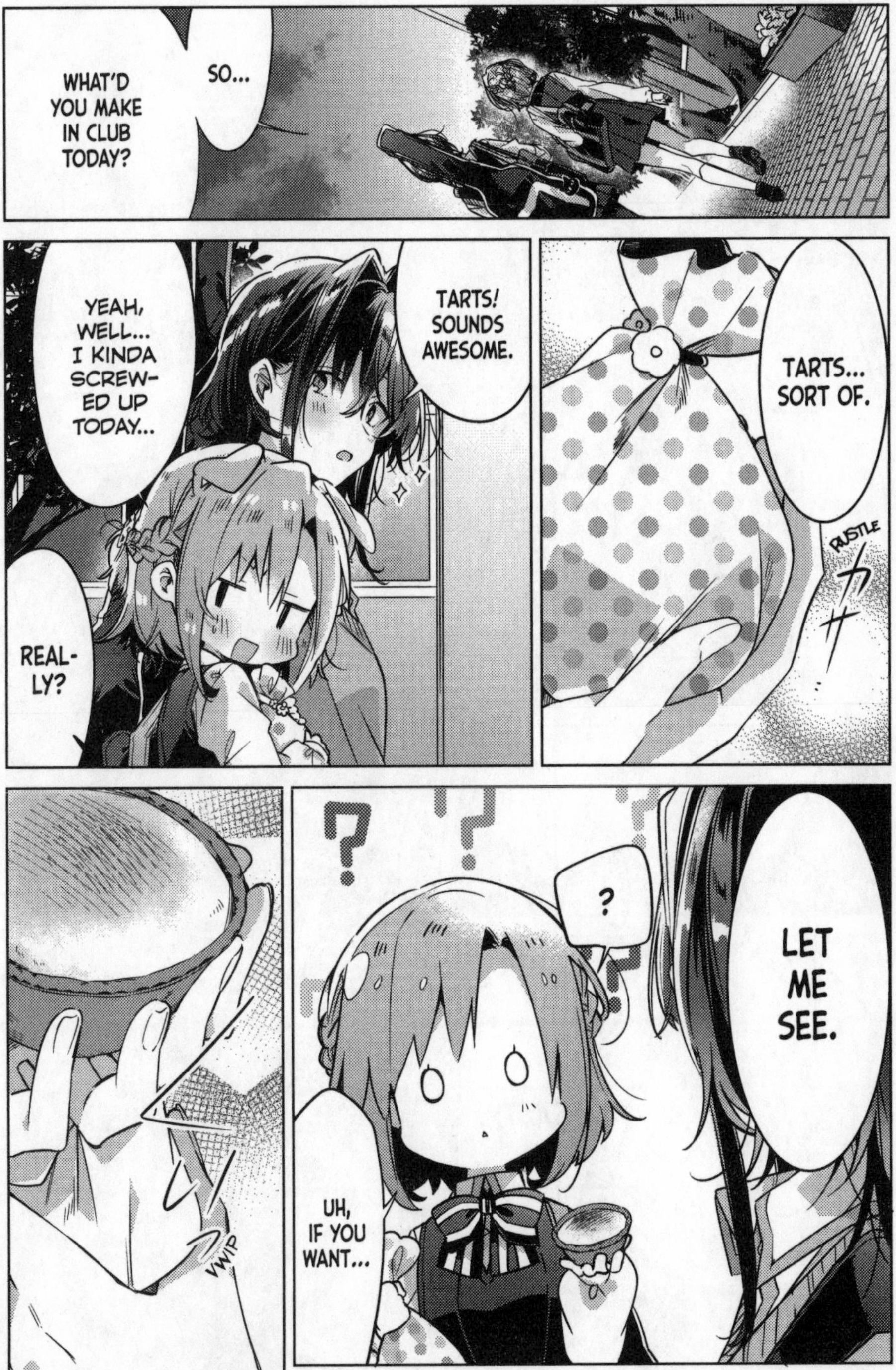
SO...
WHAT'D YOU MAKE IN CLUB TODAY?
TARTS... SORT OF.
RUSTLE
TARTS! SOUNDS AWESOME.
YEAH, WELL... I KINDA SCREW-ED UP TODAY...
REAL-LY?
LET ME SEE.
?
UH, IF YOU WANT...
VWIP

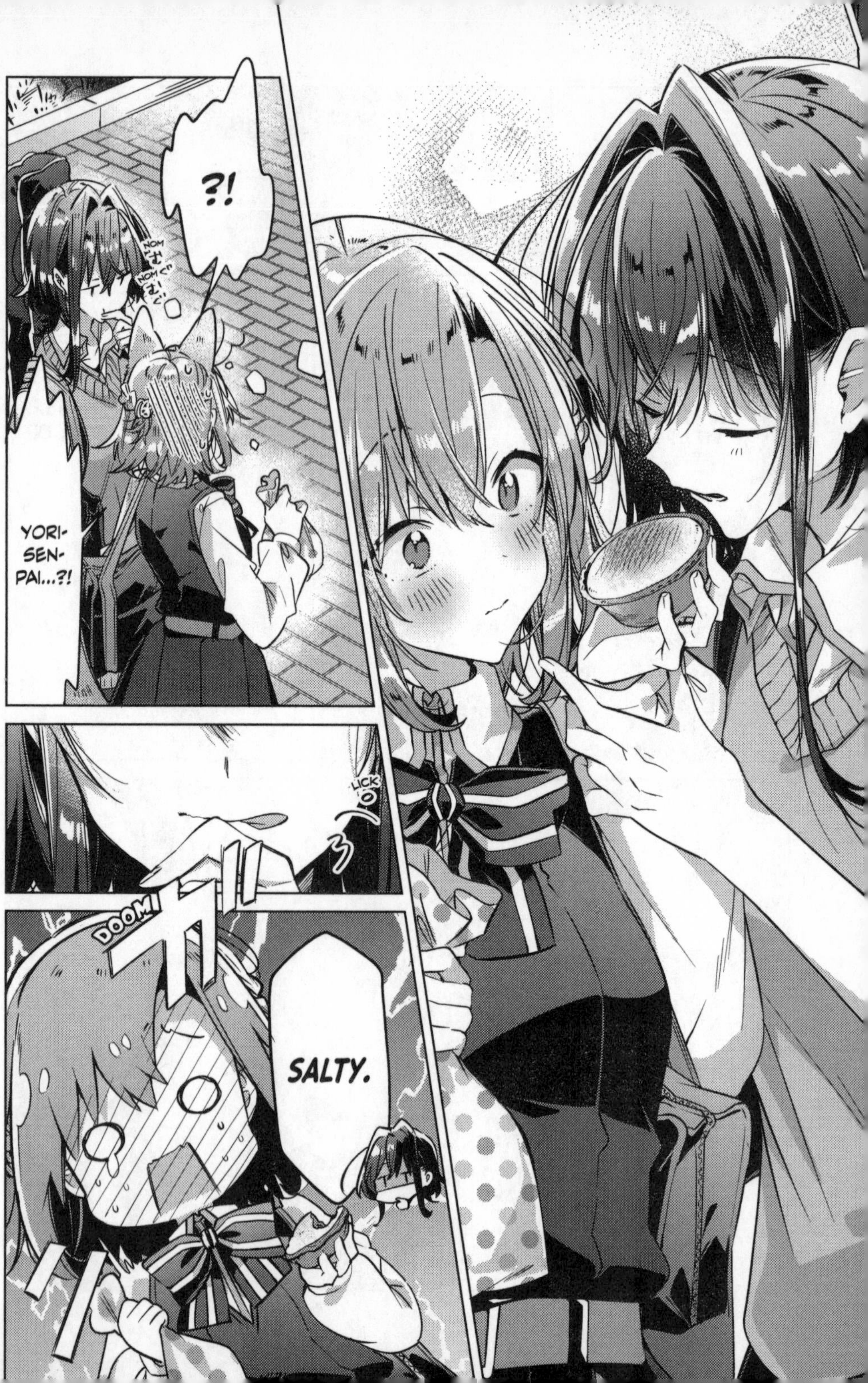

?!
NOM NOM
YORI-SEN-PAI...?!
LICK
DOOM!
SALTY.

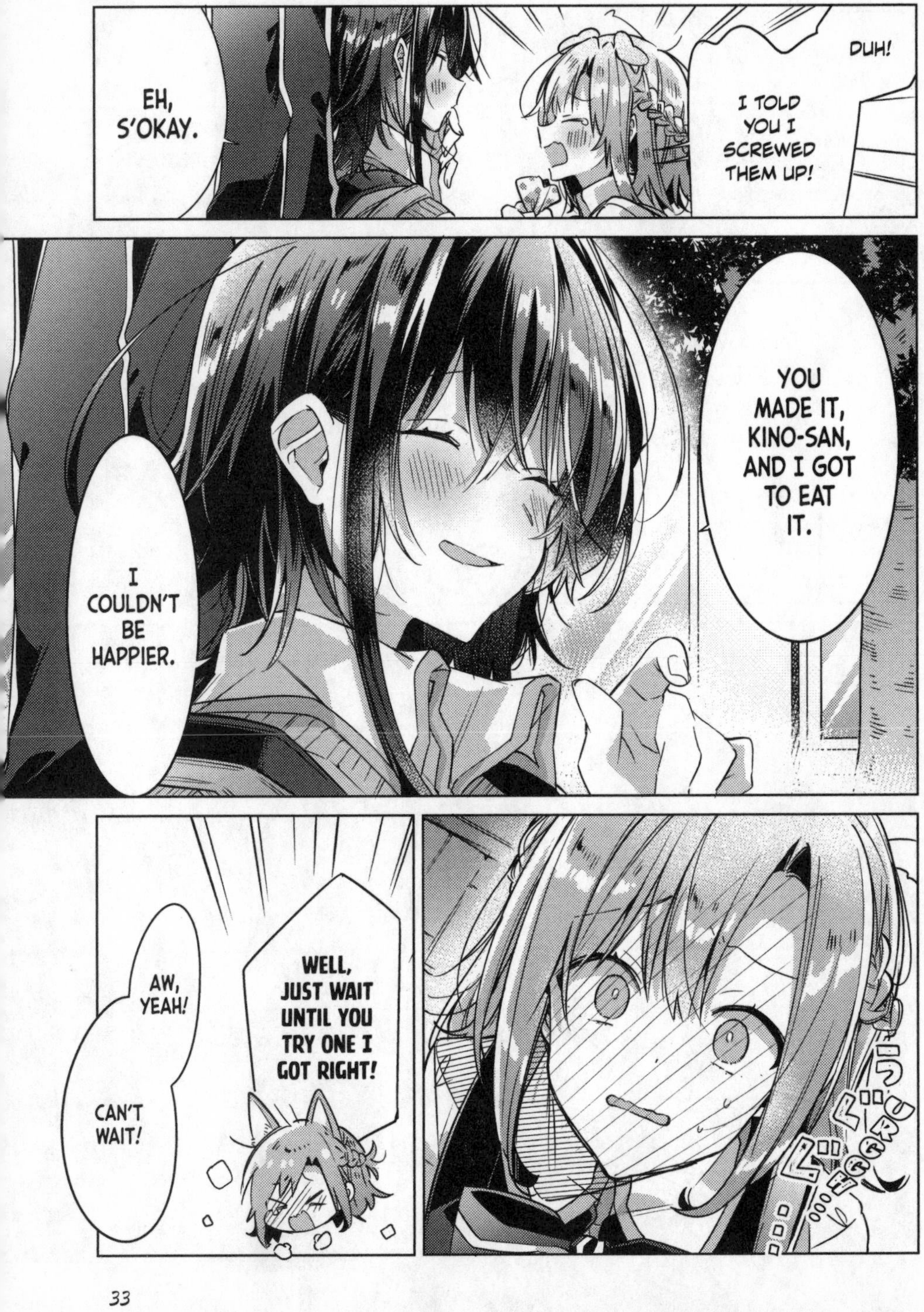
DUH!
I TOLD YOU I SCREWED THEM UP!
EH, S'OKAY.
YOU MADE IT, KINO-SAN, AND I GOT TO EAT IT.
I COULDN'T BE HAPPIER.
うぐぐ…
URGGH...
WELL, JUST WAIT UNTIL YOU TRY ONE I GOT RIGHT!
AW, YEAH!
CAN'T WAIT!

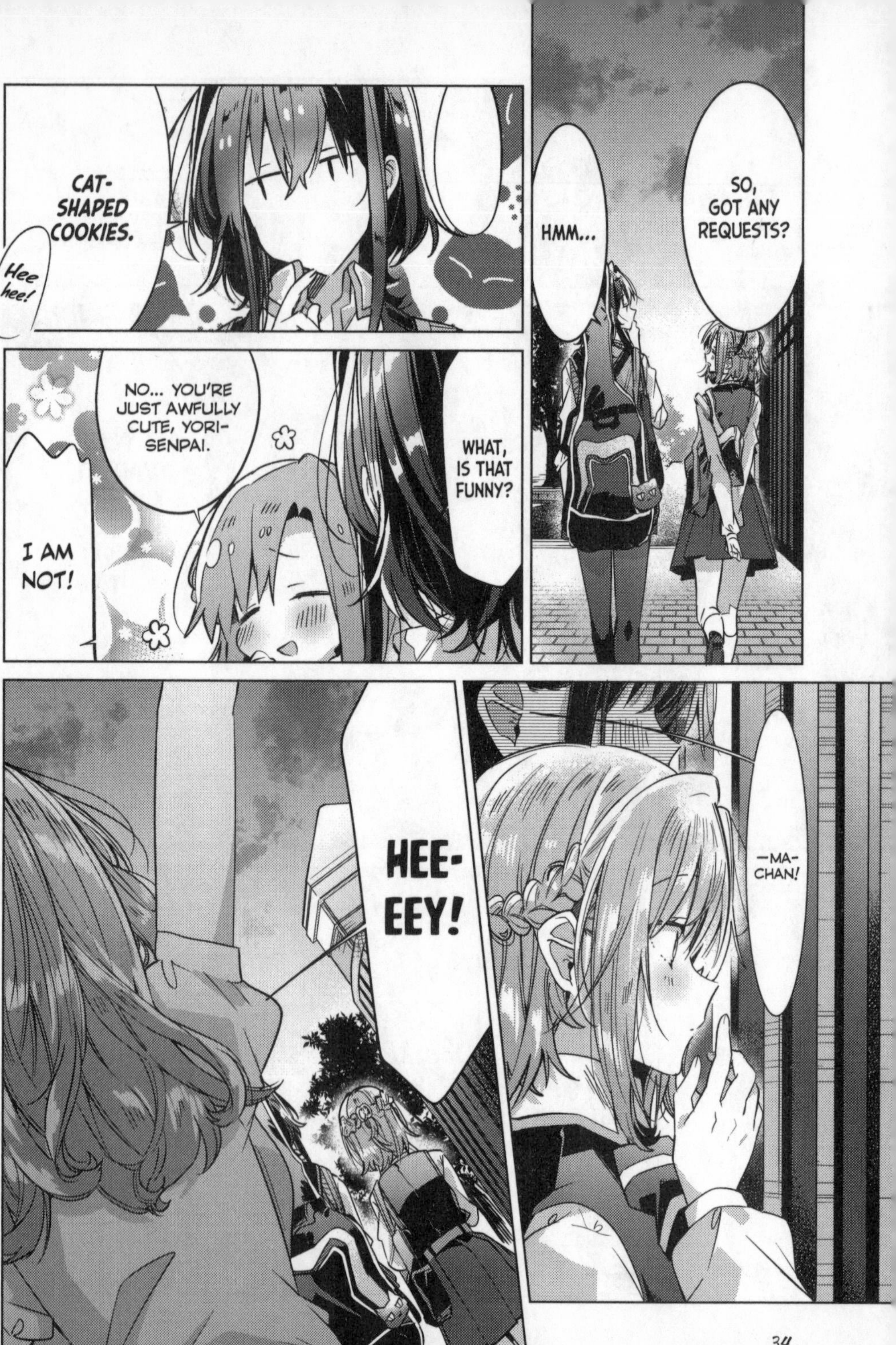
SO, GOT ANY REQUESTS?
HMM...
CAT-SHAPED COOKIES.
Hee hee!
WHAT, IS THAT FUNNY?
NO... YOU'RE JUST AWFULLY CUTE, YORI-SENPAI.
I AM NOT!
—MA-CHAN!
HEE-EEY!

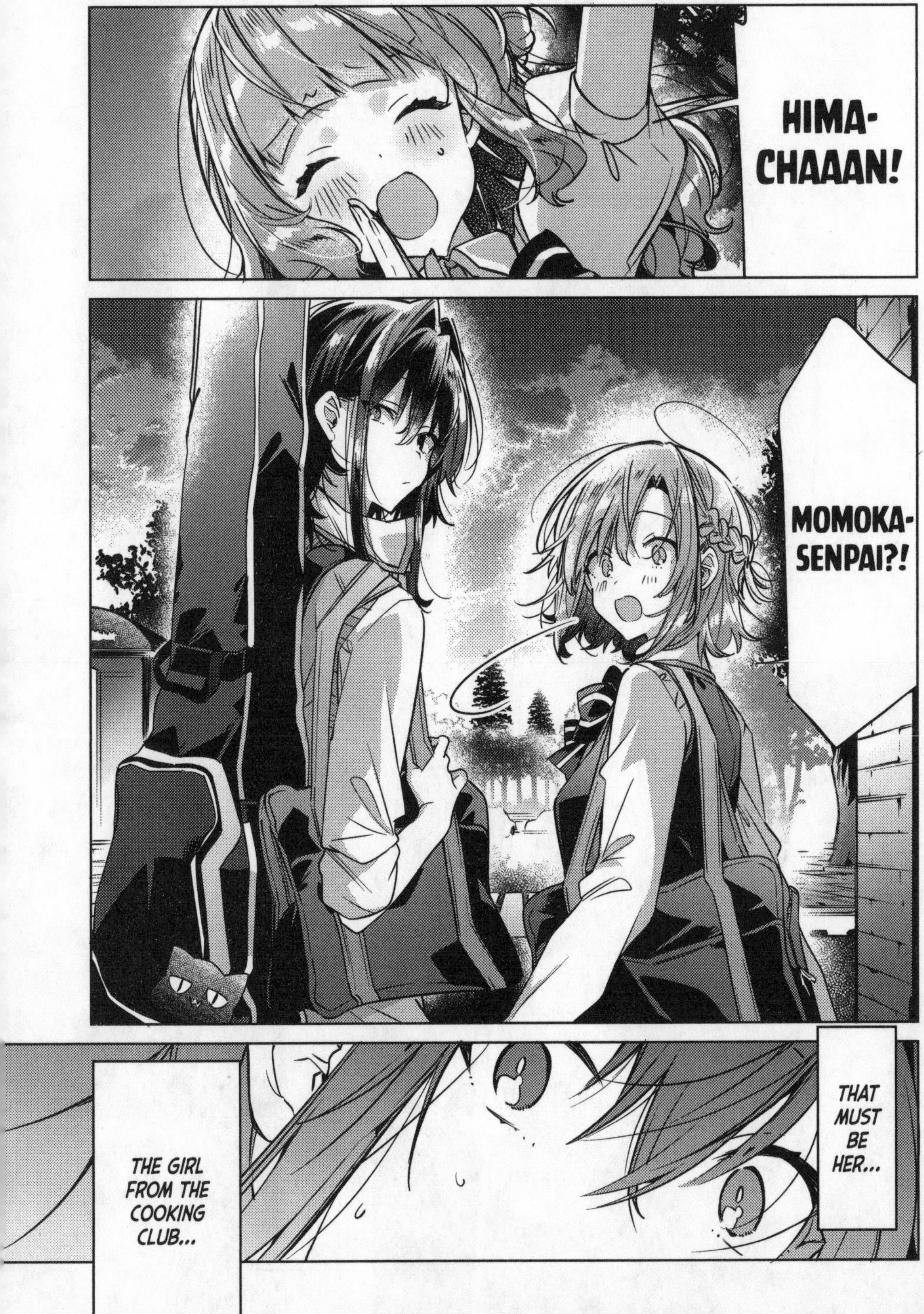
HIMA-CHAAAN!
MOMOKA-SENPAI?!
THAT MUST BE HER...
THE GIRL FROM THE COOKING CLUB...

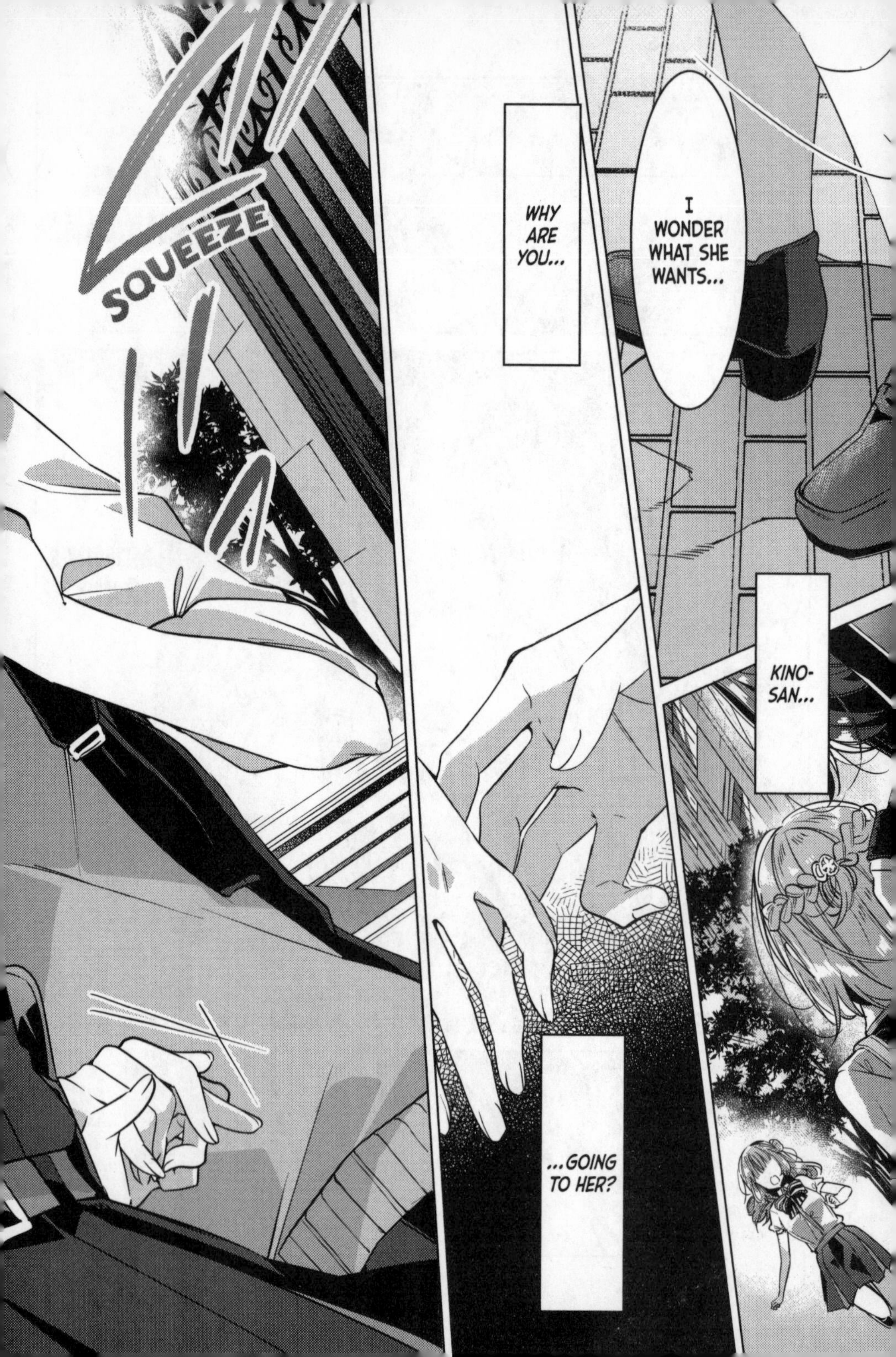
I WONDER WHAT SHE WANTS...
KINO-SAN...
WHY ARE YOU...
...GOING TO HER?
SQUEEZE

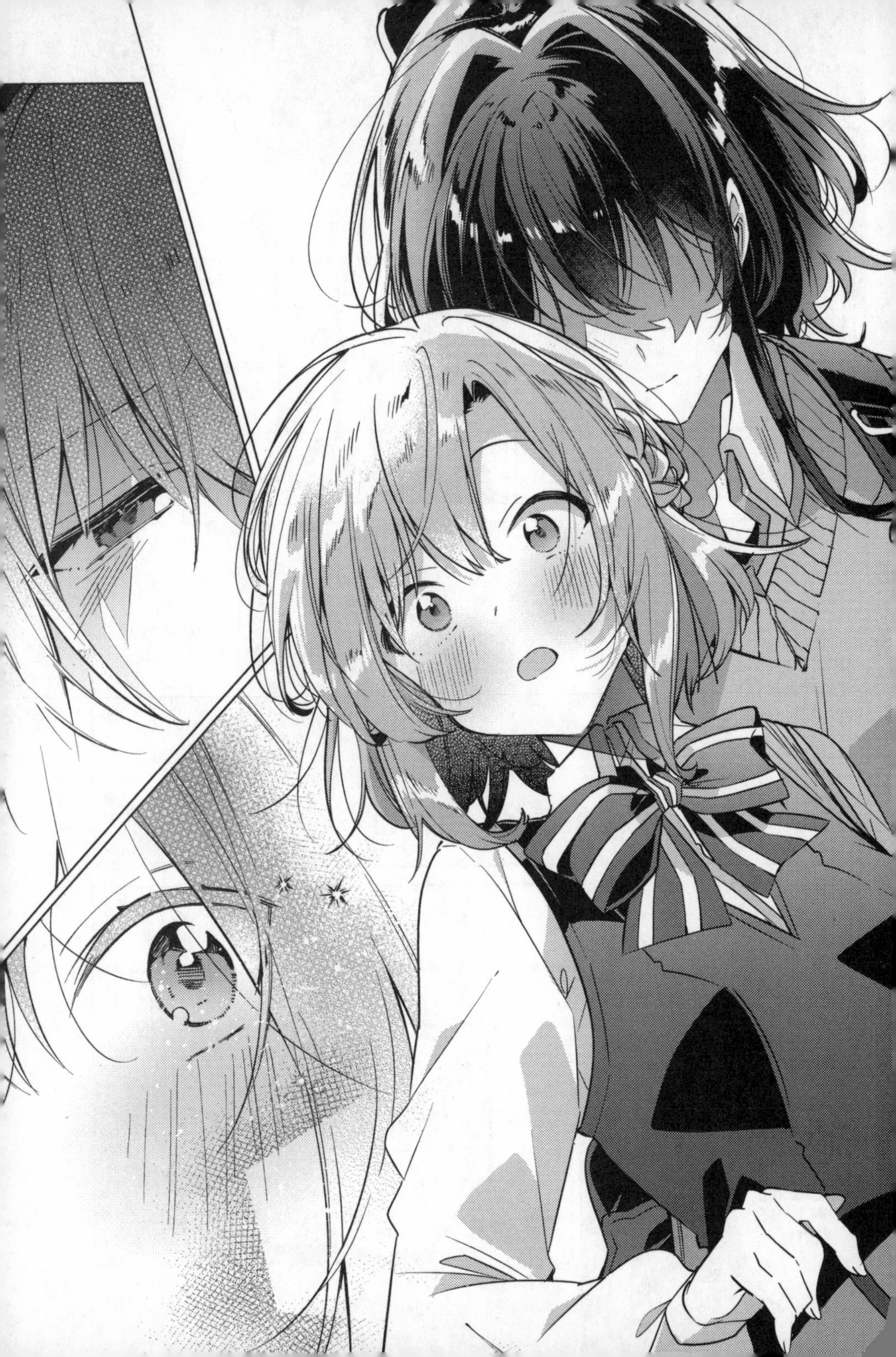

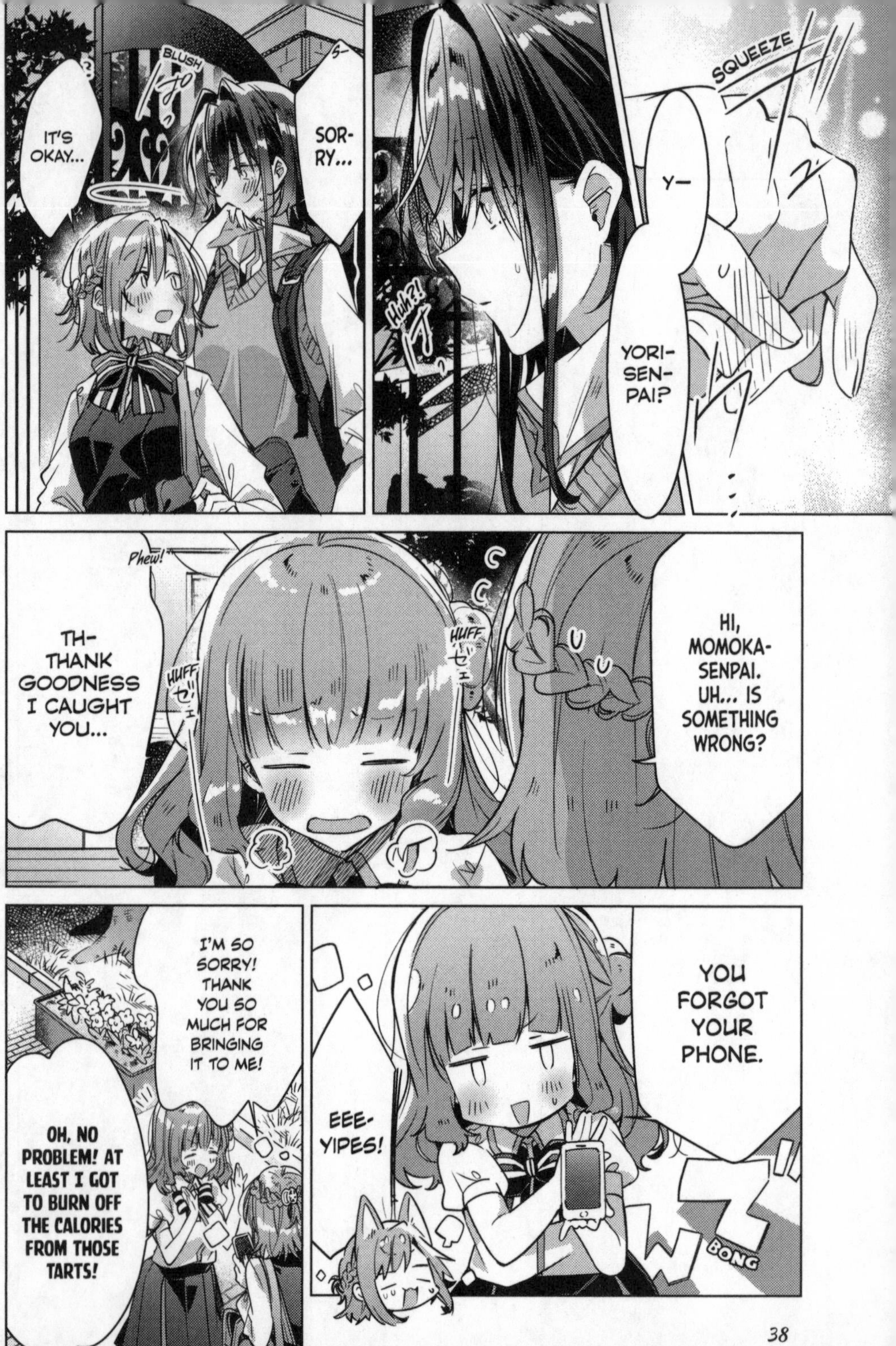
SQUEEZE
Y—
YORI-SENPAI?
Huh?!
S—
SORRY...
BLUSH
IT'S OKAY...
HI, MOMOKA-SENPAI. UH... IS SOMETHING WRONG?
HUFF
HUFF
Phew!
TH-THANK GOODNESS I CAUGHT YOU...
YOU FORGOT YOUR PHONE.
BONG
EEE-YIPES!
I'M SO SORRY! THANK YOU SO MUCH FOR BRINGING IT TO ME!
OH, NO PROBLEM! AT LEAST I GOT TO BURN OFF THE CALORIES FROM THOSE TARTS!

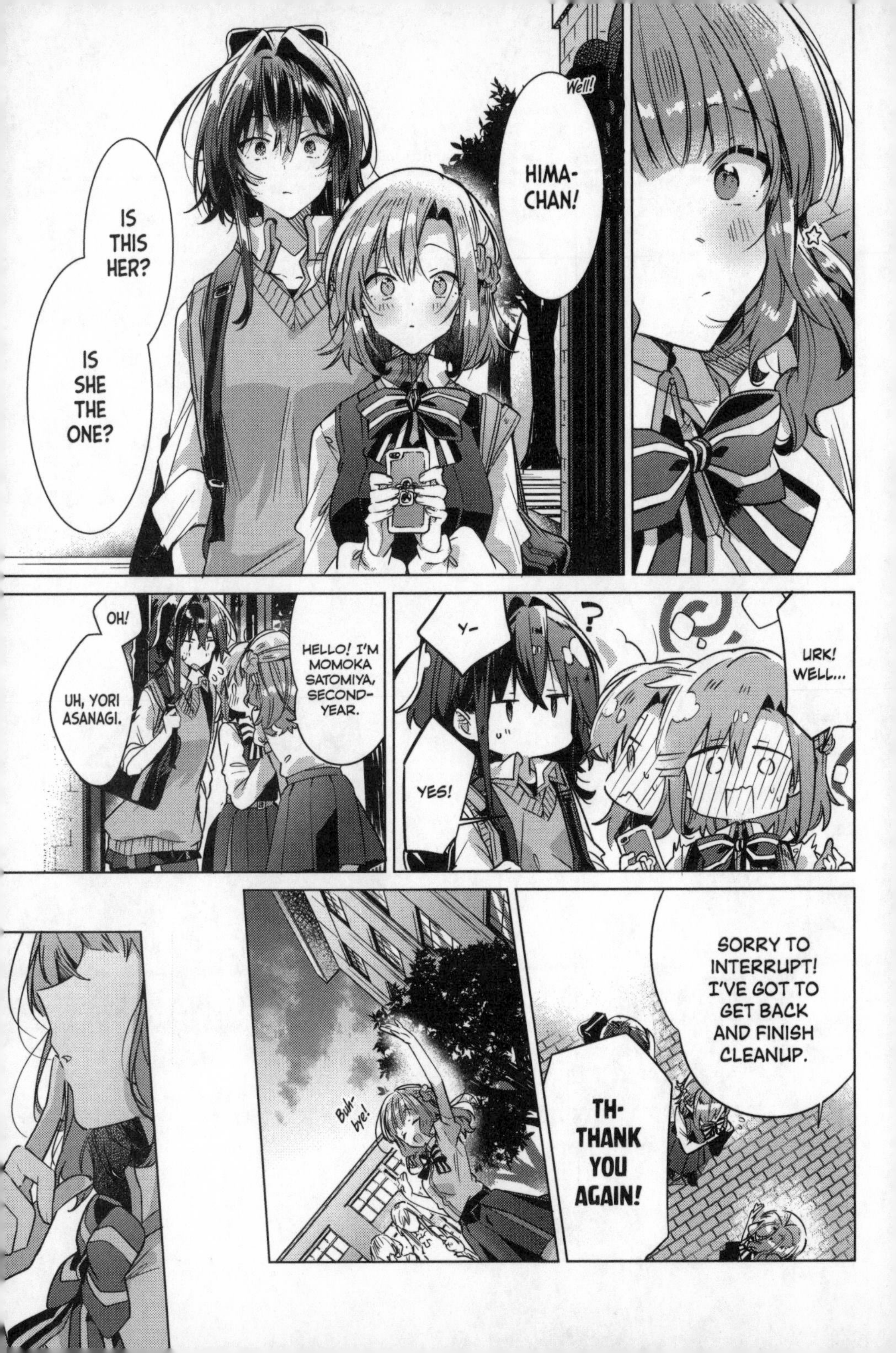
Well!
HIMA-CHAN!
IS THIS HER?
IS SHE THE ONE?
Y-
URK! WELL...
YES!
HELLO! I'M MOMOKA SATOMIYA, SECOND-YEAR.
OH!
UH, YORI ASANAGI.
SORRY TO INTERRUPT! I'VE GOT TO GET BACK AND FINISH CLEANUP.
TH-THANK YOU AGAIN!
Buh-bye!

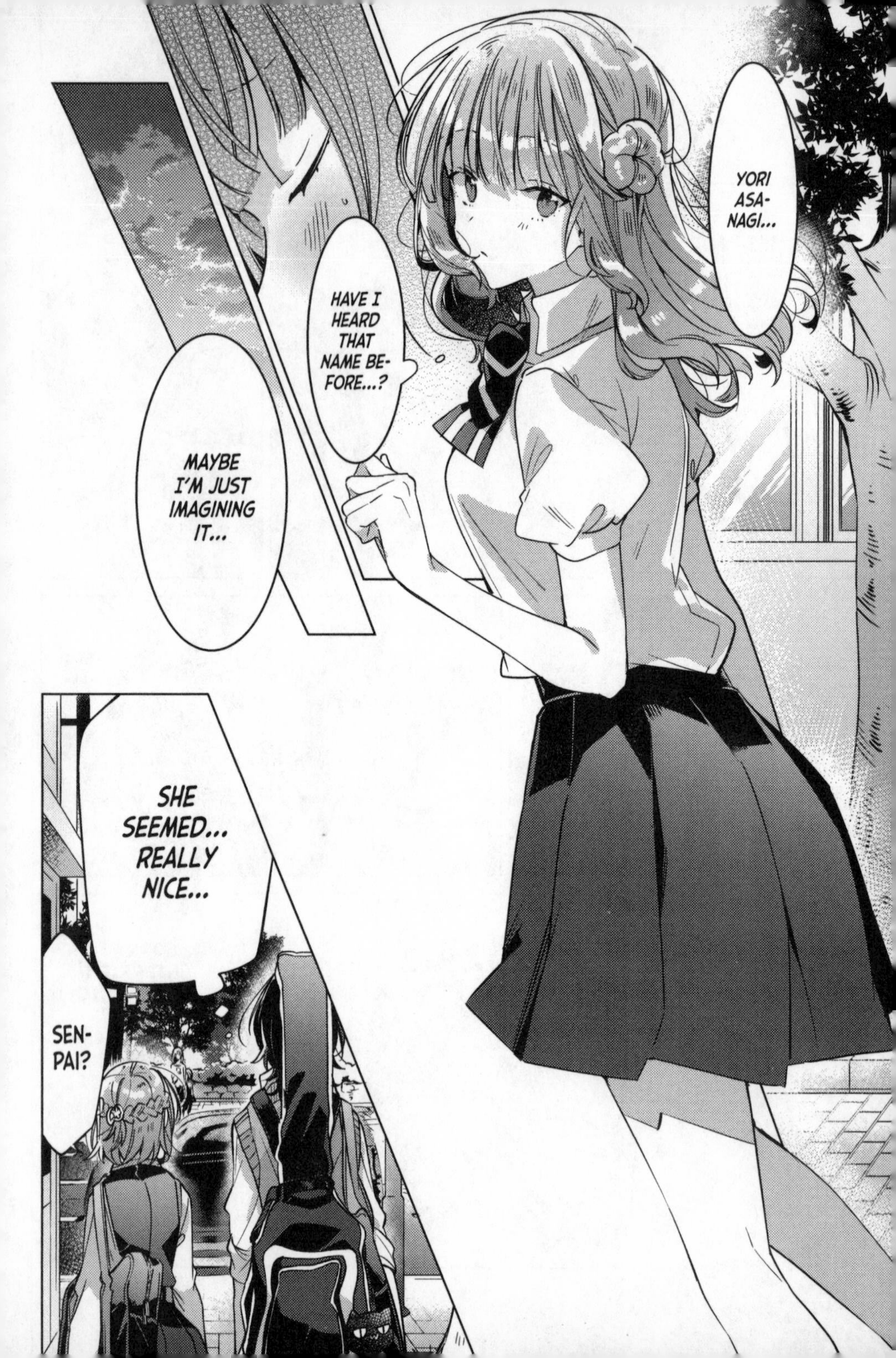
YORI ASA-NAGI...
HAVE I HEARD THAT NAME BE-FORE...?
MAYBE I'M JUST IMAGINING IT...
SHE SEEMED... REALLY NICE...
SEN-PAI?

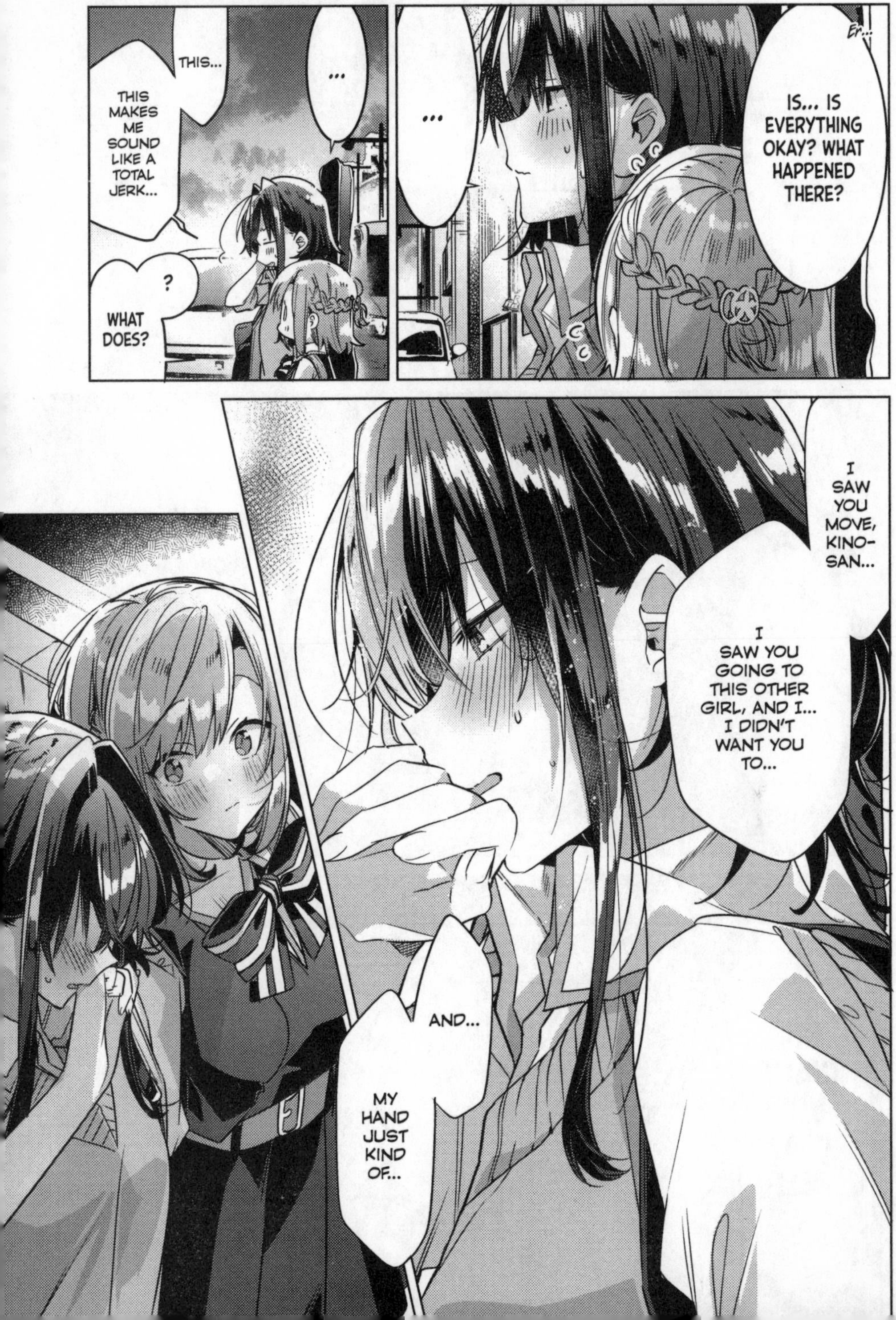
Er...
IS... IS EVERYTHING OKAY? WHAT HAPPENED THERE?
...
...
THIS...
THIS MAKES ME SOUND LIKE A TOTAL JERK...
?
WHAT DOES?
I SAW YOU MOVE, KINO-SAN...
I SAW YOU GOING TO THIS OTHER GIRL, AND I... I DIDN'T WANT YOU TO...
AND...
MY HAND JUST KIND OF...

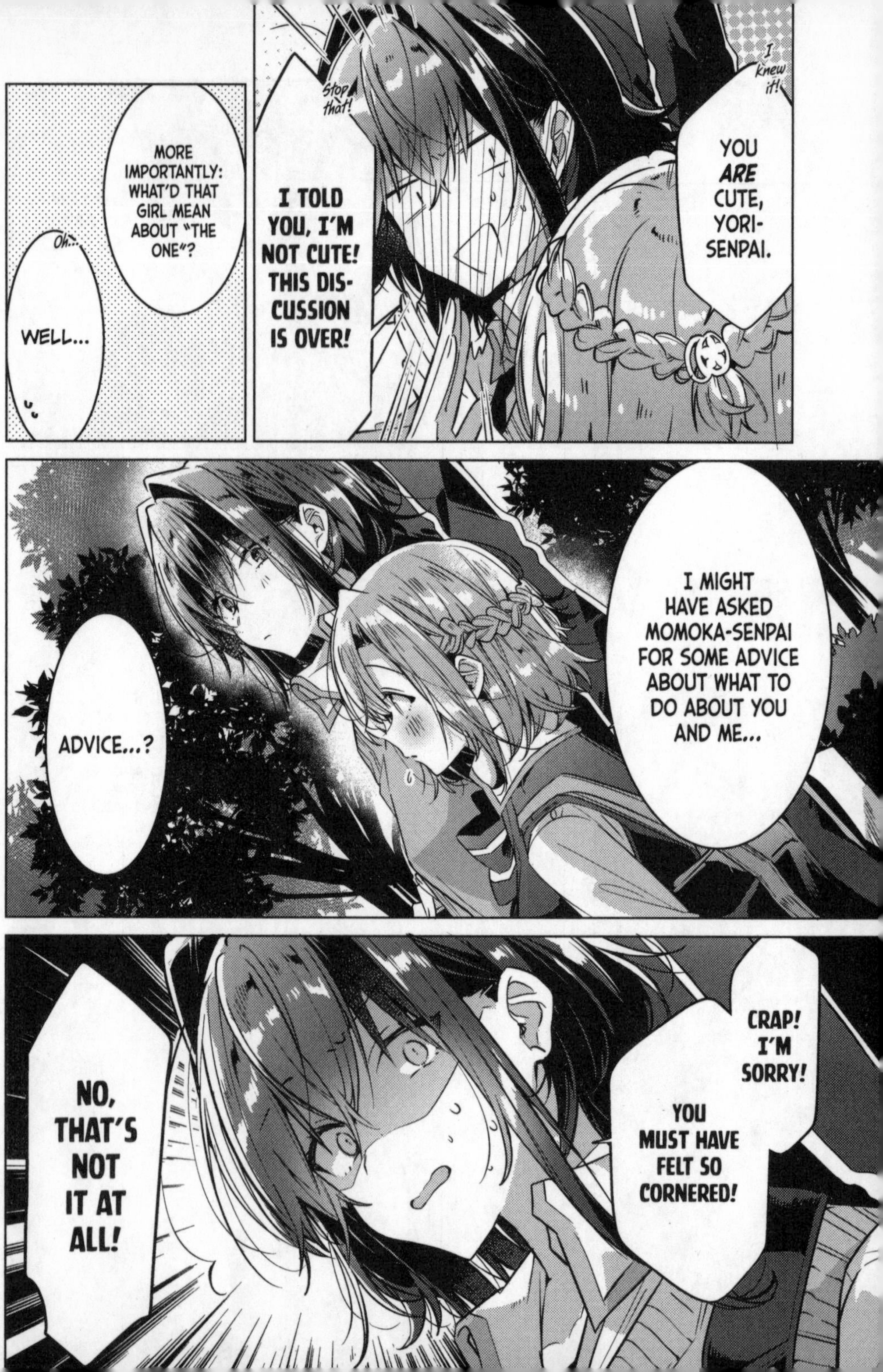
I knew it!
YOU ARE CUTE, YORI-SENPAI.
Stop that!
I TOLD YOU, I'M NOT CUTE! THIS DIS-CUSSION IS OVER!
MORE IMPORTANTLY: WHAT'D THAT GIRL MEAN ABOUT "THE ONE"?
Oh...
WELL...
I MIGHT HAVE ASKED MOMOKA-SENPAI FOR SOME ADVICE ABOUT WHAT TO DO ABOUT YOU AND ME...
ADVICE...?
CRAP! I'M SORRY!
YOU MUST HAVE FELT SO CORNERED!
NO, THAT'S NOT IT AT ALL!

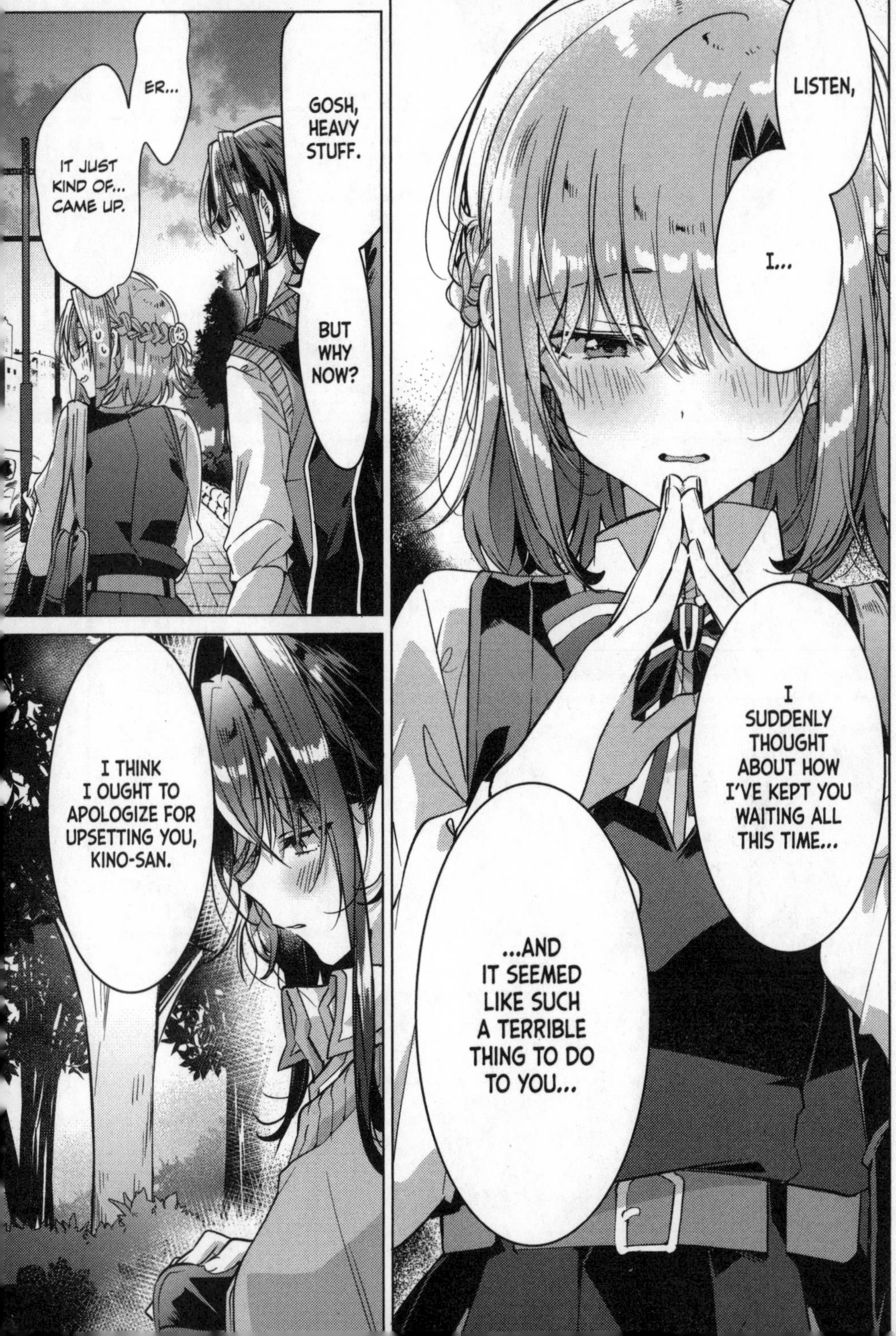
LISTEN,
I...
I SUDDENLY THOUGHT ABOUT HOW I'VE KEPT YOU WAITING ALL THIS TIME...
...AND IT SEEMED LIKE SUCH A TERRIBLE THING TO DO TO YOU...
GOSH, HEAVY STUFF.
BUT WHY NOW?
ER...
IT JUST KIND OF... CAME UP.
I THINK I OUGHT TO APOLOGIZE FOR UPSETTING YOU, KINO-SAN.

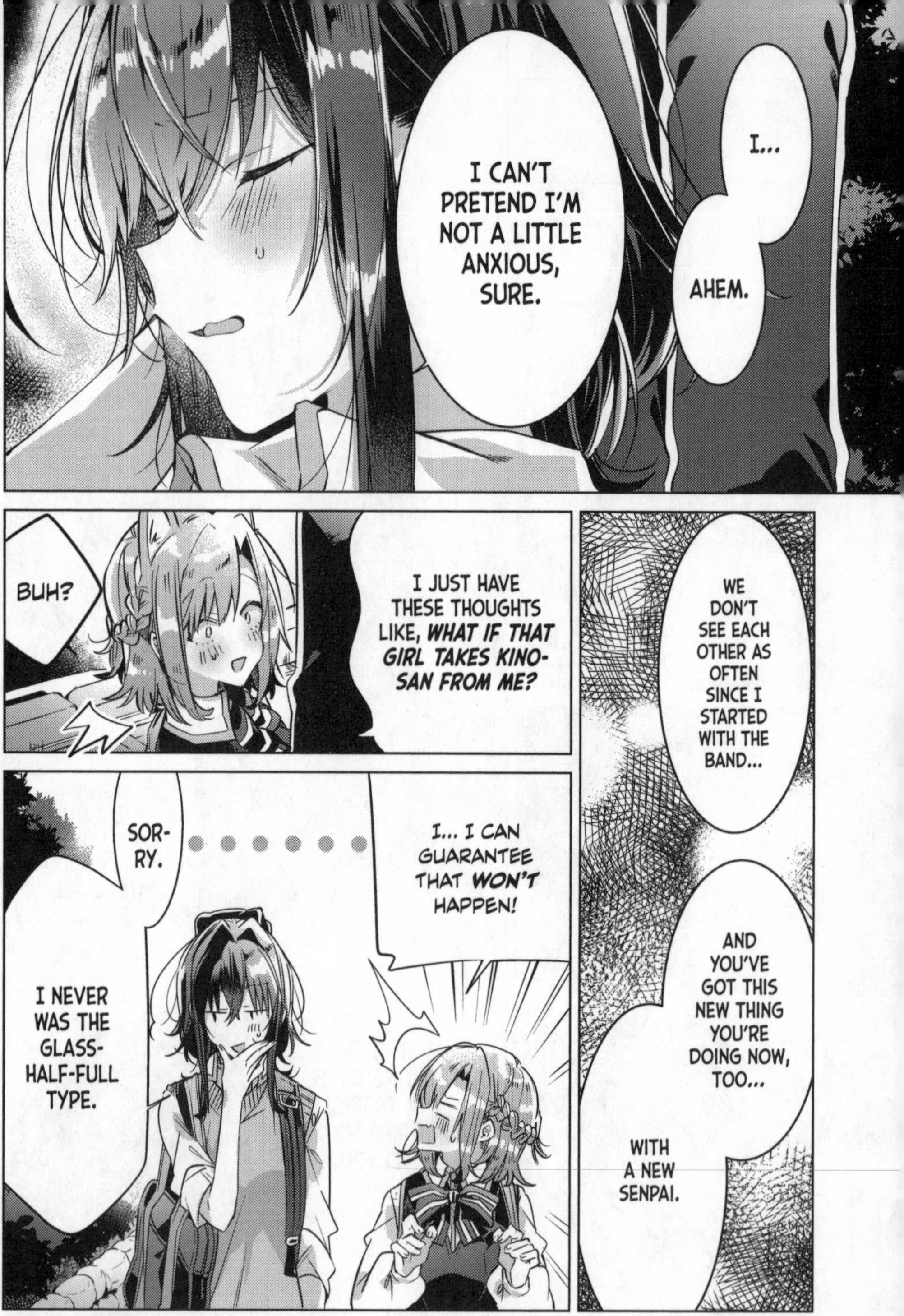
I...
AHEM.
I CAN'T PRETEND I'M NOT A LITTLE ANXIOUS, SURE.
WE DON'T SEE EACH OTHER AS OFTEN SINCE I STARTED WITH THE BAND...
AND YOU'VE GOT THIS NEW THING YOU'RE DOING NOW, TOO...
WITH A NEW SENPAI.
I JUST HAVE THESE THOUGHTS LIKE, *WHAT IF THAT GIRL TAKES KINO-SAN FROM ME?*
BUH?
I... I CAN GUARANTEE THAT *WON'T* HAPPEN!
SOR-RY.
I NEVER WAS THE GLASS-HALF-FULL TYPE.

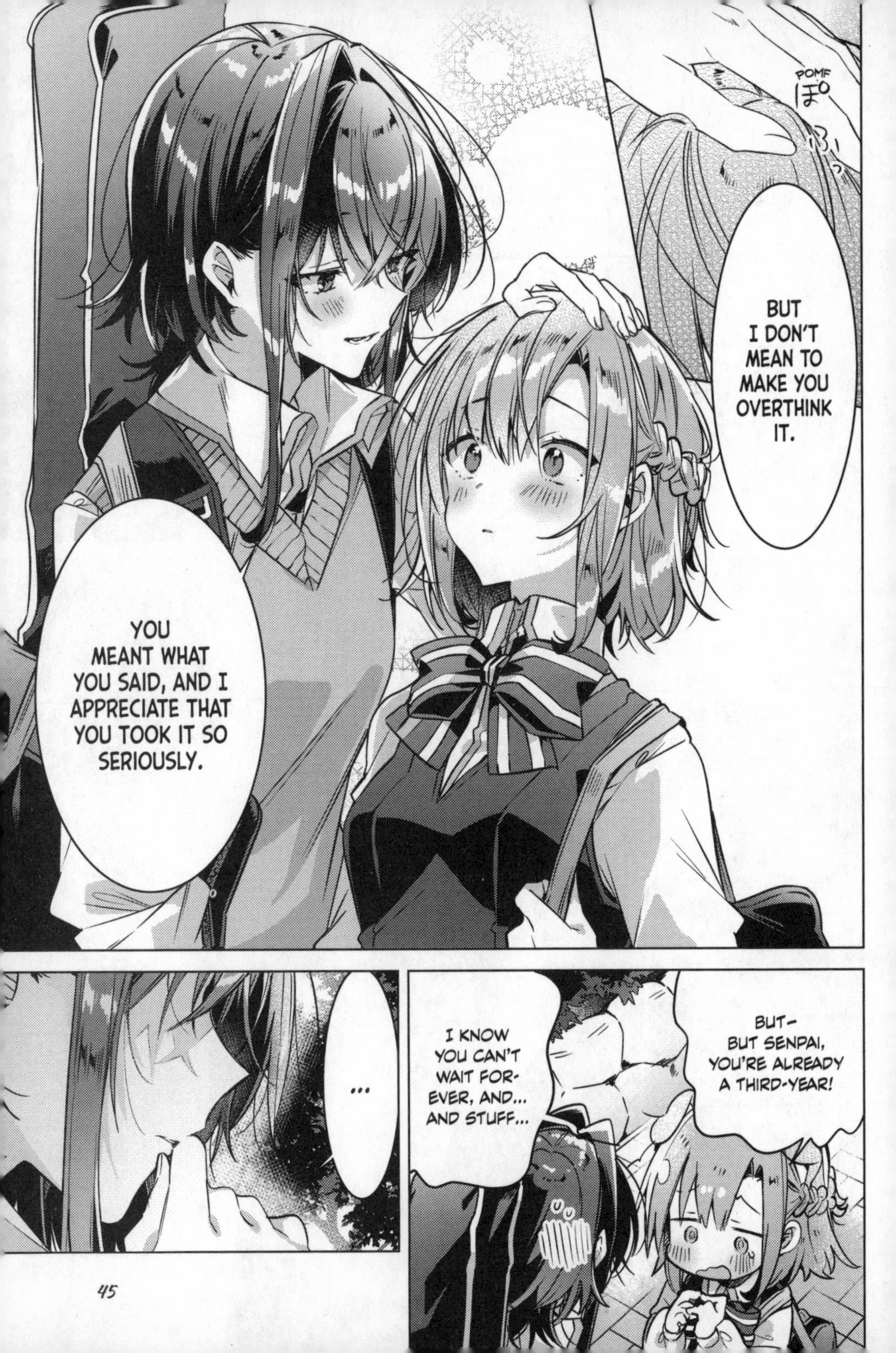
POMF
ぽふっ
BUT I DON'T MEAN TO MAKE YOU OVERTHINK IT.
YOU MEANT WHAT YOU SAID, AND I APPRECIATE THAT YOU TOOK IT SO SERIOUSLY.
BUT- BUT SENPAI, YOU'RE ALREADY A THIRD-YEAR!
I KNOW YOU CAN'T WAIT FOR-EVER, AND... AND STUFF...
...

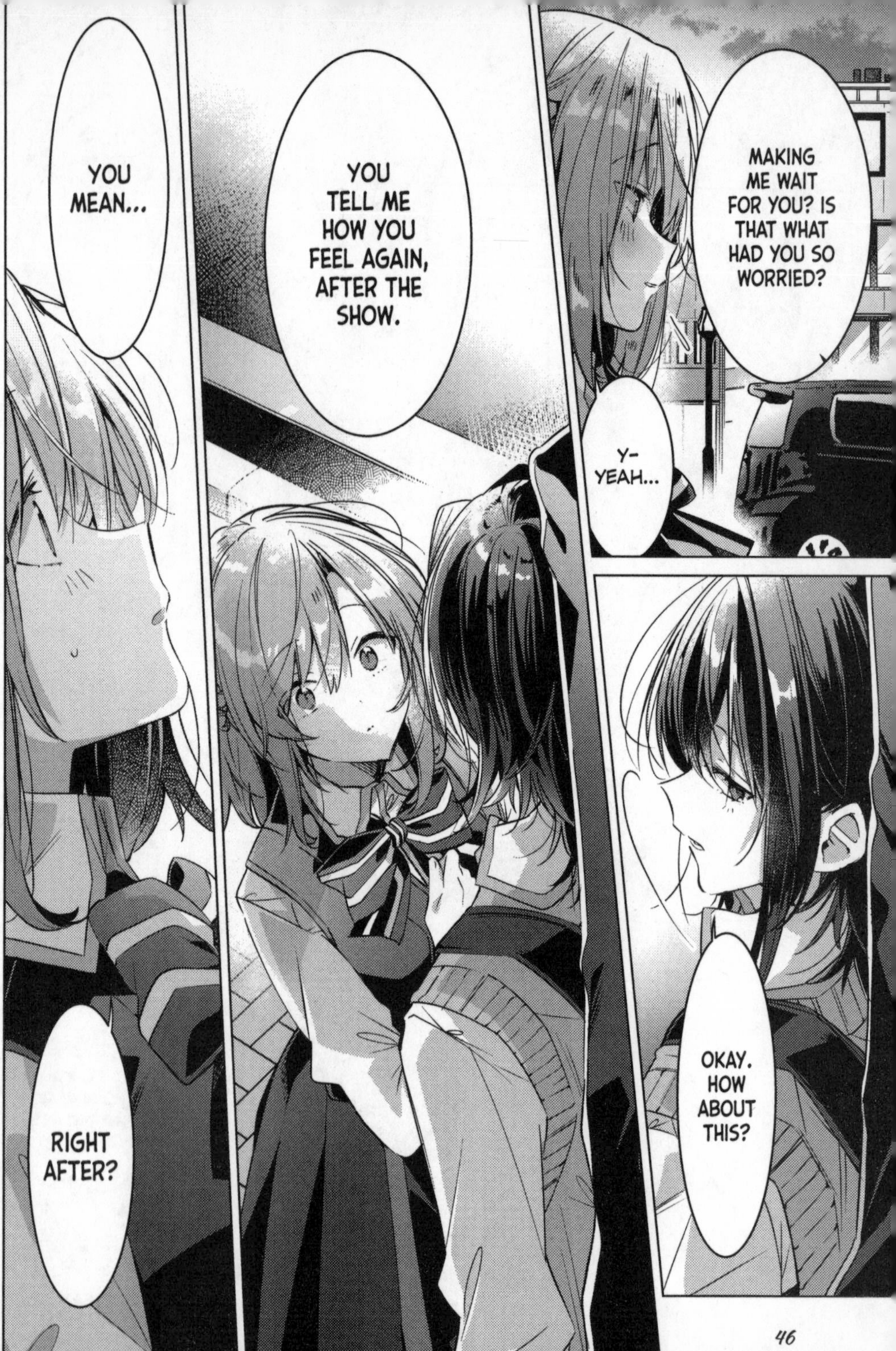
MAKING ME WAIT FOR YOU? IS THAT WHAT HAD YOU SO WORRIED?
Y-YEAH...
OKAY. HOW ABOUT THIS?
YOU TELL ME HOW YOU FEEL AGAIN, AFTER THE SHOW.
YOU MEAN...
RIGHT AFTER?

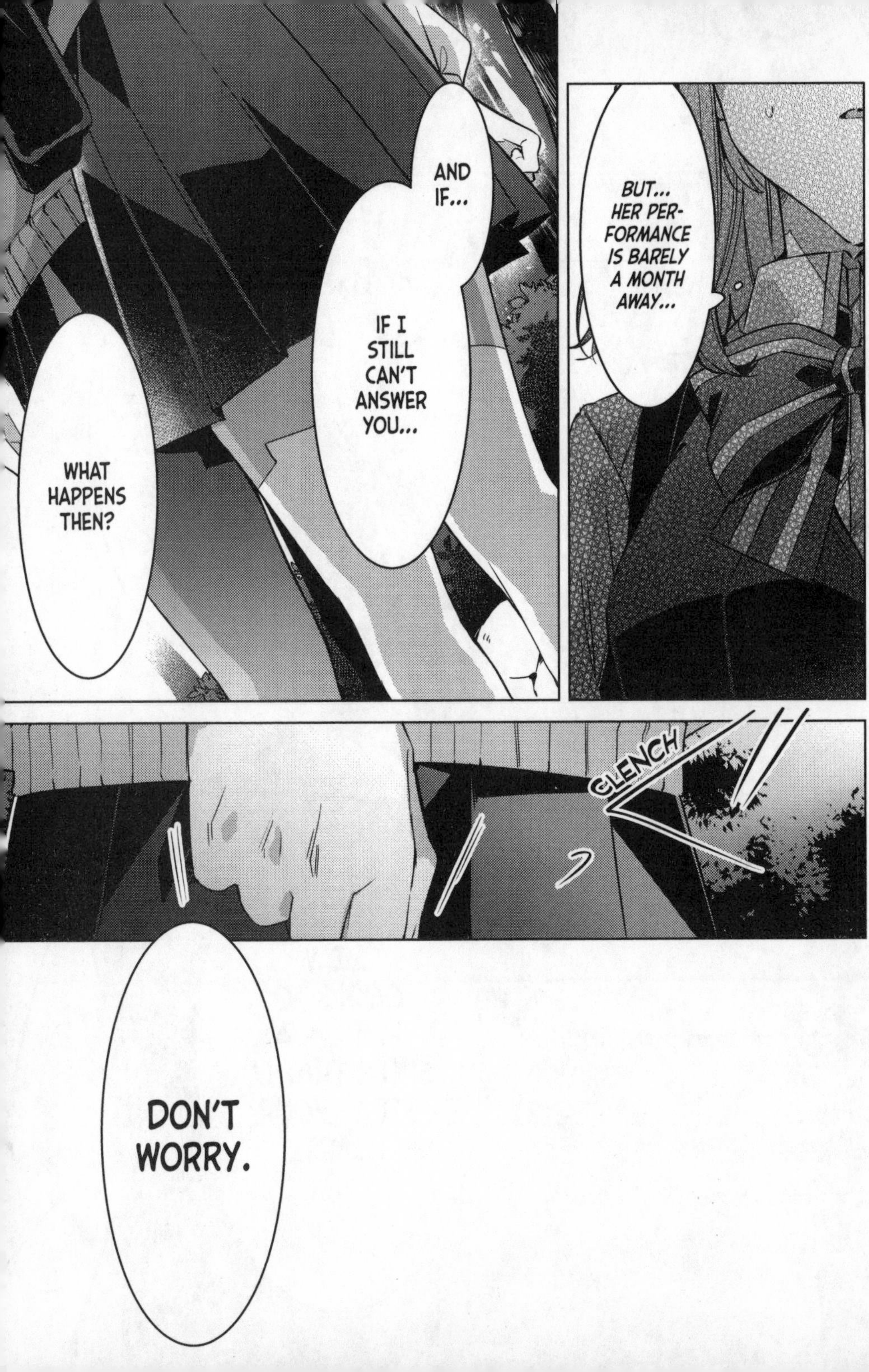
BUT... HER PER-FORMANCE IS BARELY A MONTH AWAY...
AND IF...
IF I STILL CAN'T ANSWER YOU...
WHAT HAPPENS THEN?
CLENCH
DON'T WORRY.

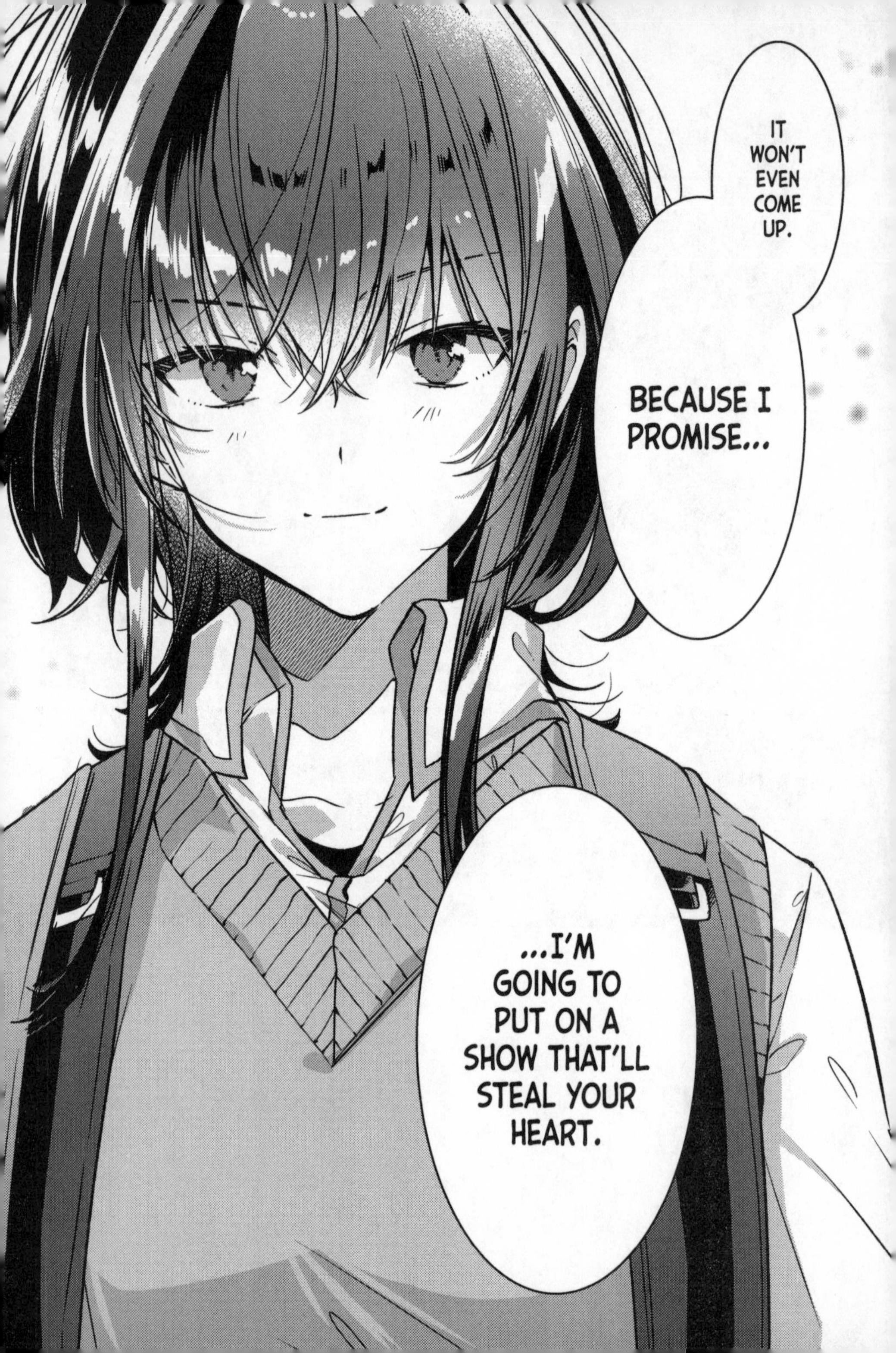
IT WON'T EVEN COME UP.
BECAUSE I PROMISE...
...I'M GOING TO PUT ON A SHOW THAT'LL STEAL YOUR HEART.

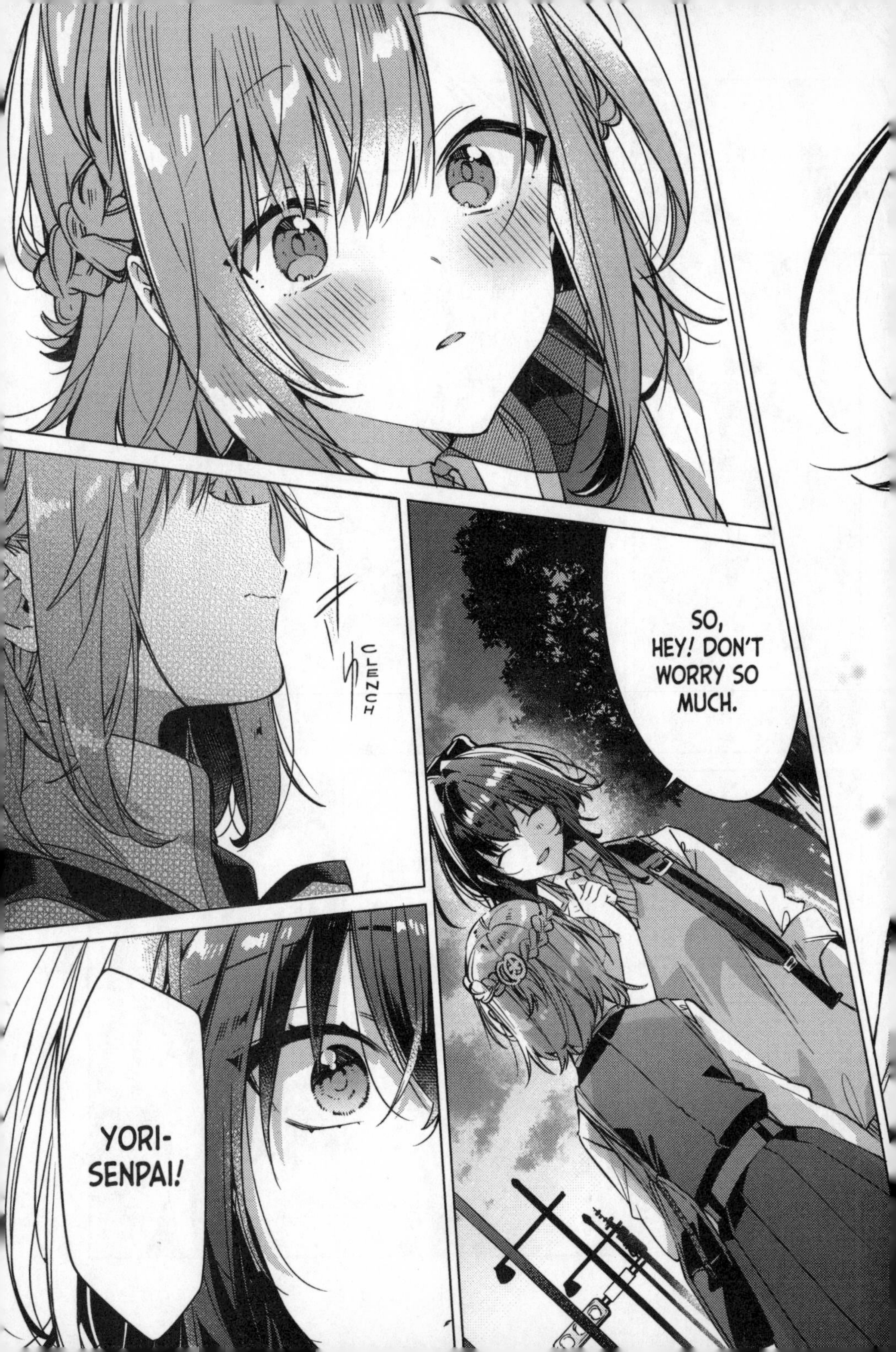
SO, HEY! DON'T WORRY SO MUCH.
CLENCH
YORI-SENPAI!

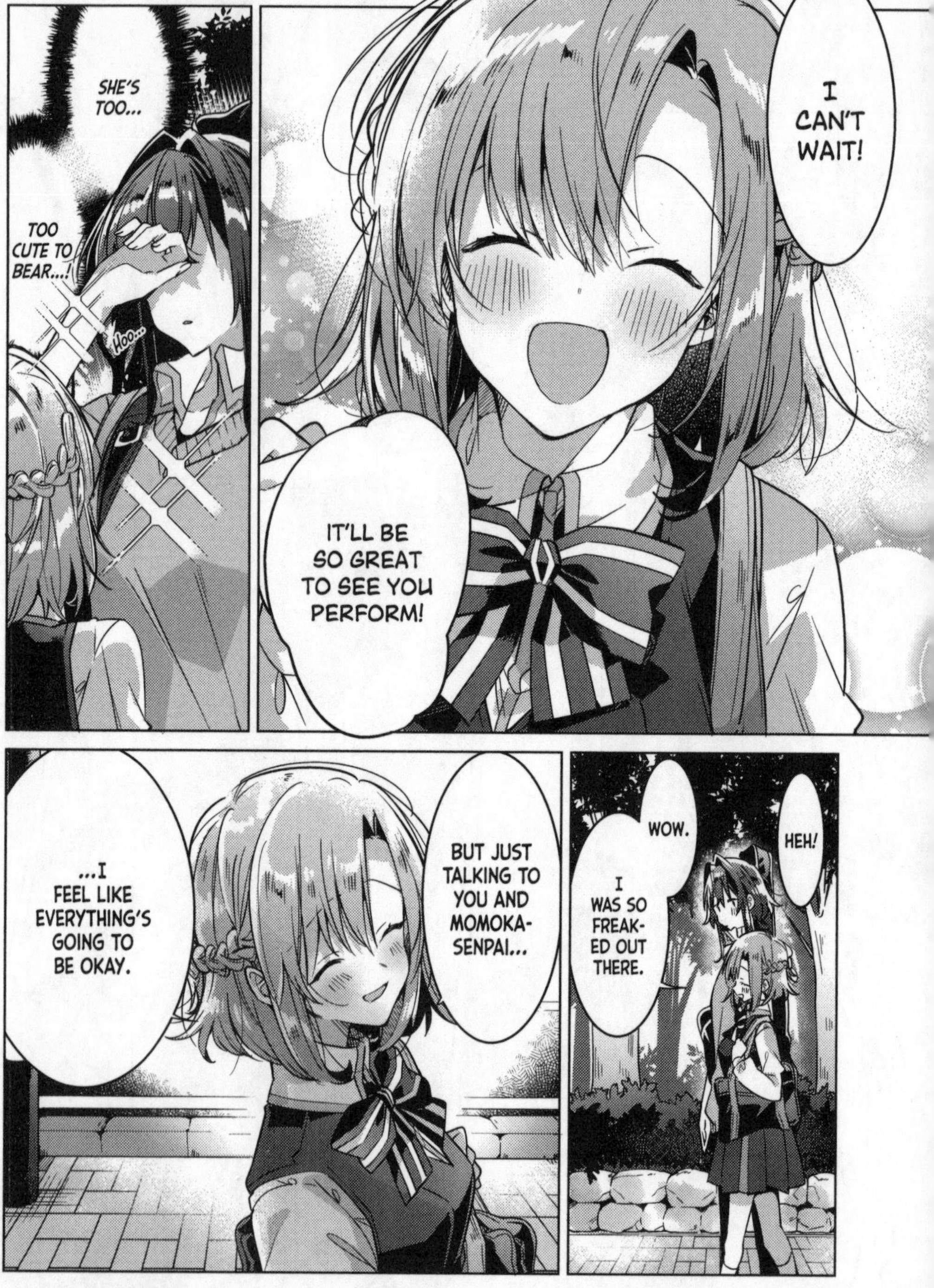
I CAN'T WAIT!
IT'LL BE SO GREAT TO SEE YOU PERFORM!
SHE'S TOO...
TOO CUTE TO BEAR...!
Hoo...
HEH!
WOW.
I WAS SO FREAK-ED OUT THERE.
BUT JUST TALKING TO YOU AND MOMOKA-SENPAI...
...I FEEL LIKE EVERYTHING'S GOING TO BE OKAY.

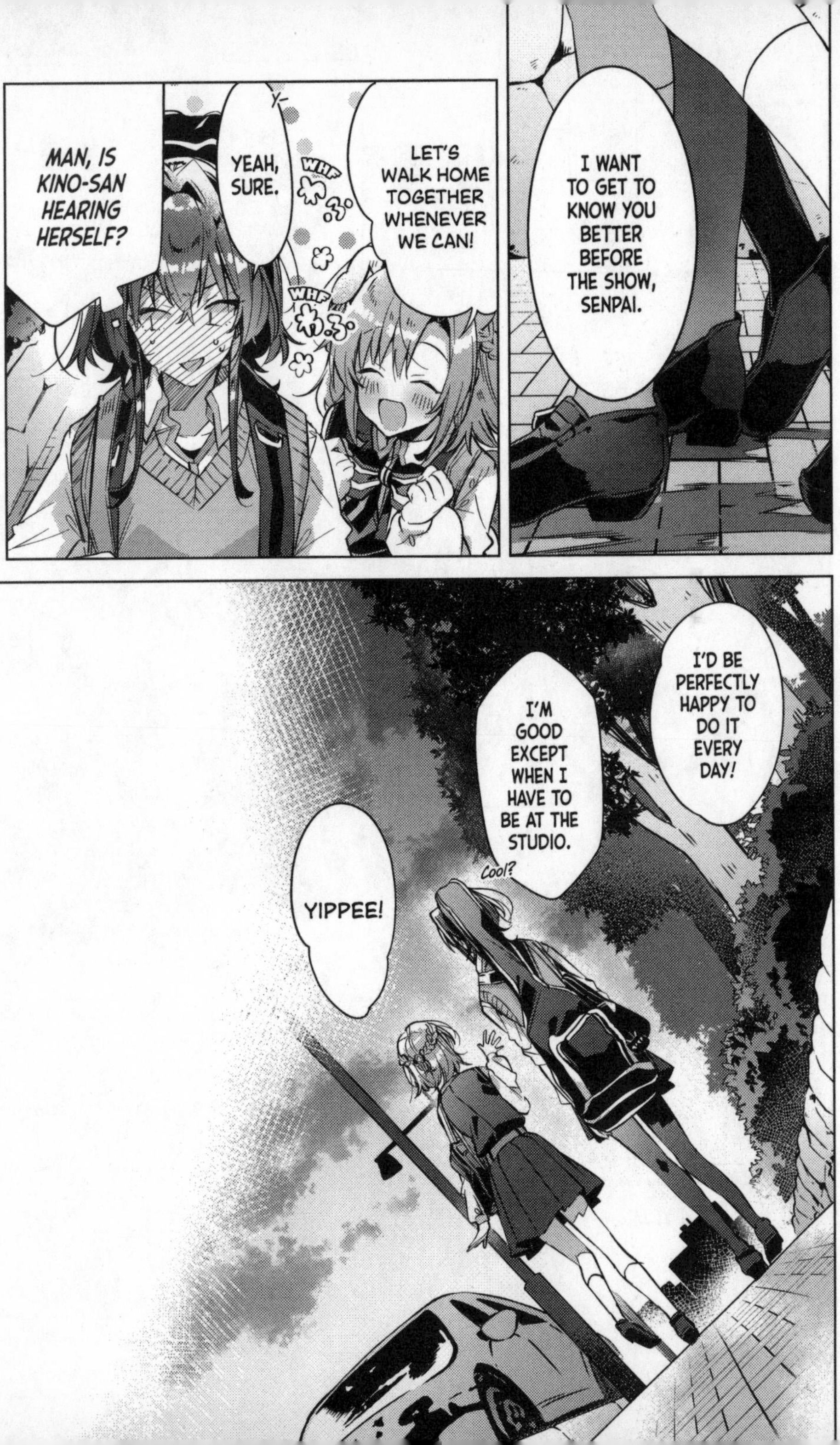
I WANT TO GET TO KNOW YOU BETTER BEFORE THE SHOW, SENPAI.
LET'S WALK HOME TOGETHER WHENEVER WE CAN!
WHF
WHF
YEAH, SURE.
MAN, IS KINO-SAN HEARING HERSELF?
I'D BE PERFECTLY HAPPY TO DO IT EVERY DAY!
I'M GOOD EXCEPT WHEN I HAVE TO BE AT THE STUDIO.
Cool?
YIPPEE!

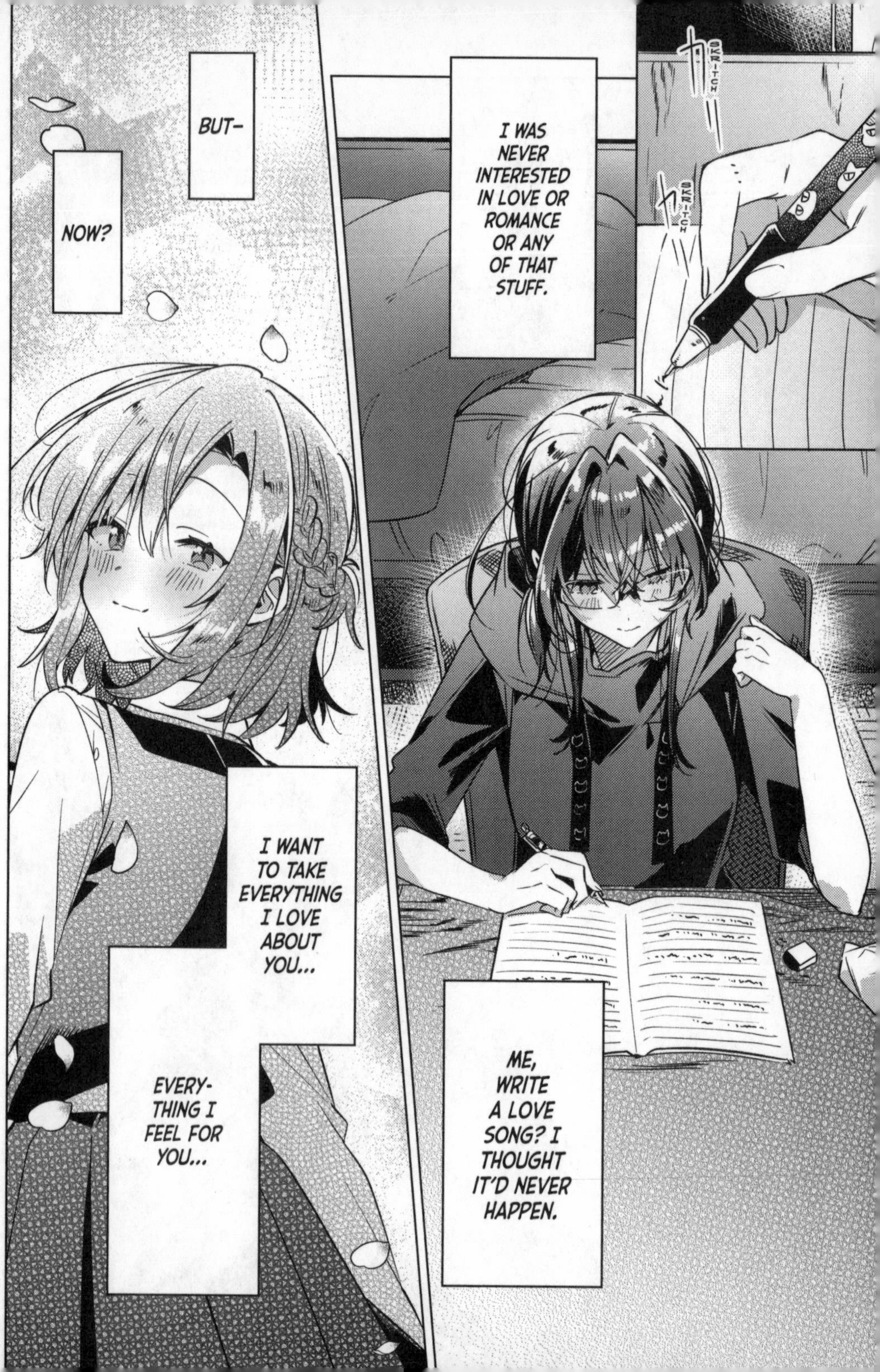

SKRITCH
SKRITCH
I WAS NEVER INTERESTED IN LOVE OR ROMANCE OR ANY OF THAT STUFF.
ME, WRITE A LOVE SONG? I THOUGHT IT'D NEVER HAPPEN.
BUT-
NOW?
I WANT TO TAKE EVERYTHING I LOVE ABOUT YOU...
EVERY-THING I FEEL FOR YOU...

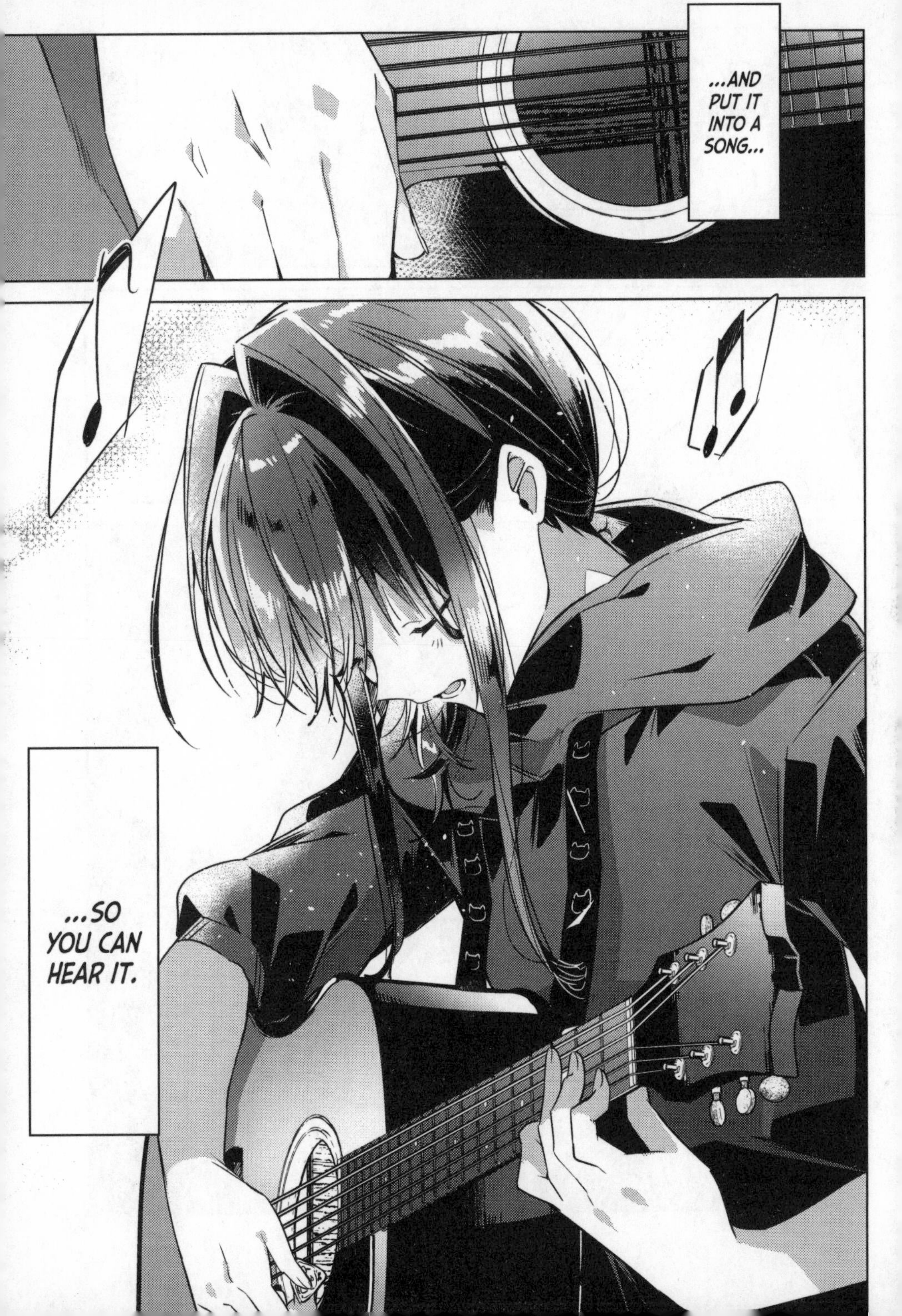
...AND PUT IT INTO A SONG...
...SO YOU CAN HEAR IT.

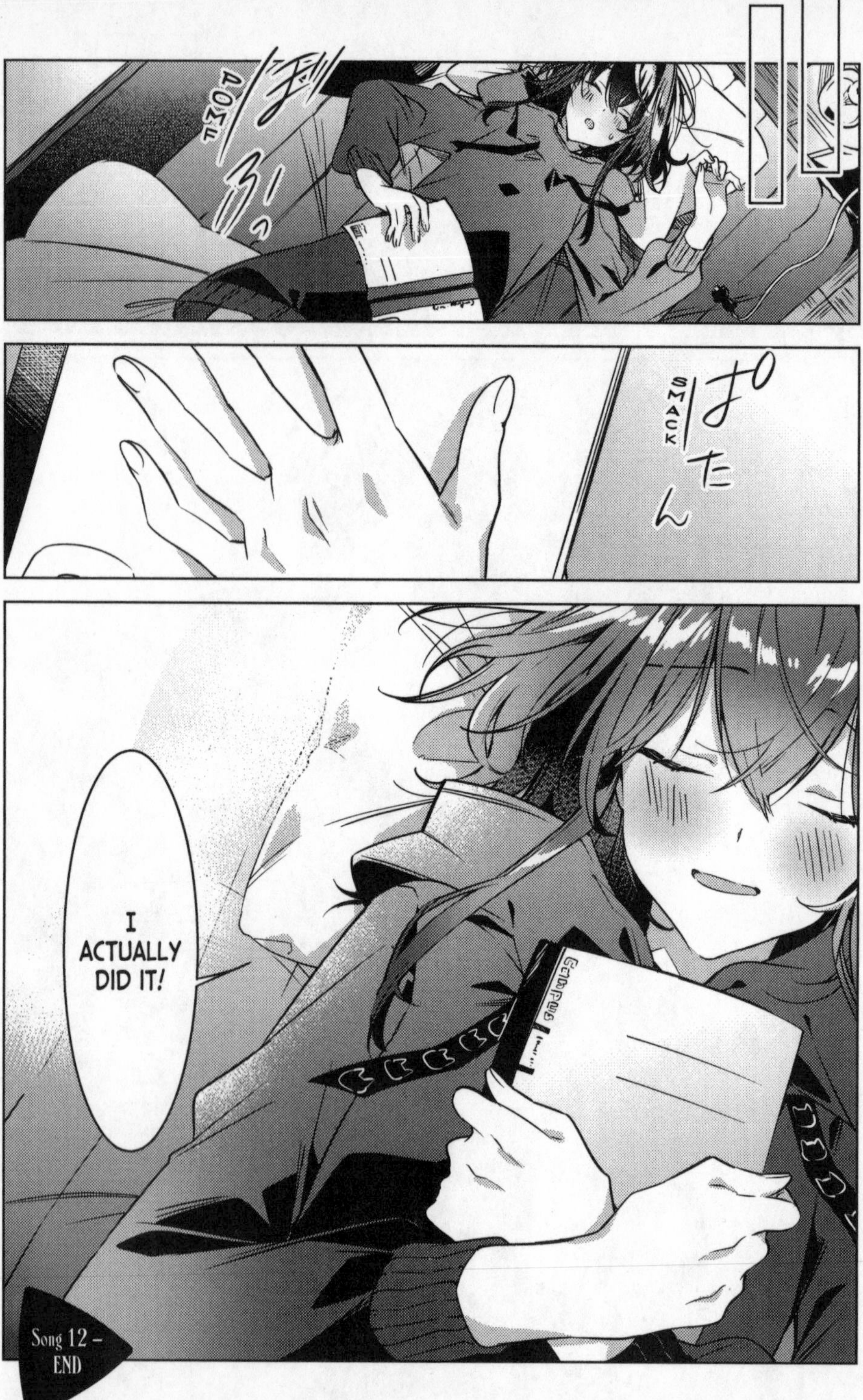
ぽふっ
POMF
ぱたん
SMACK
I ACTUALLY DID IT!
Song 12 - END

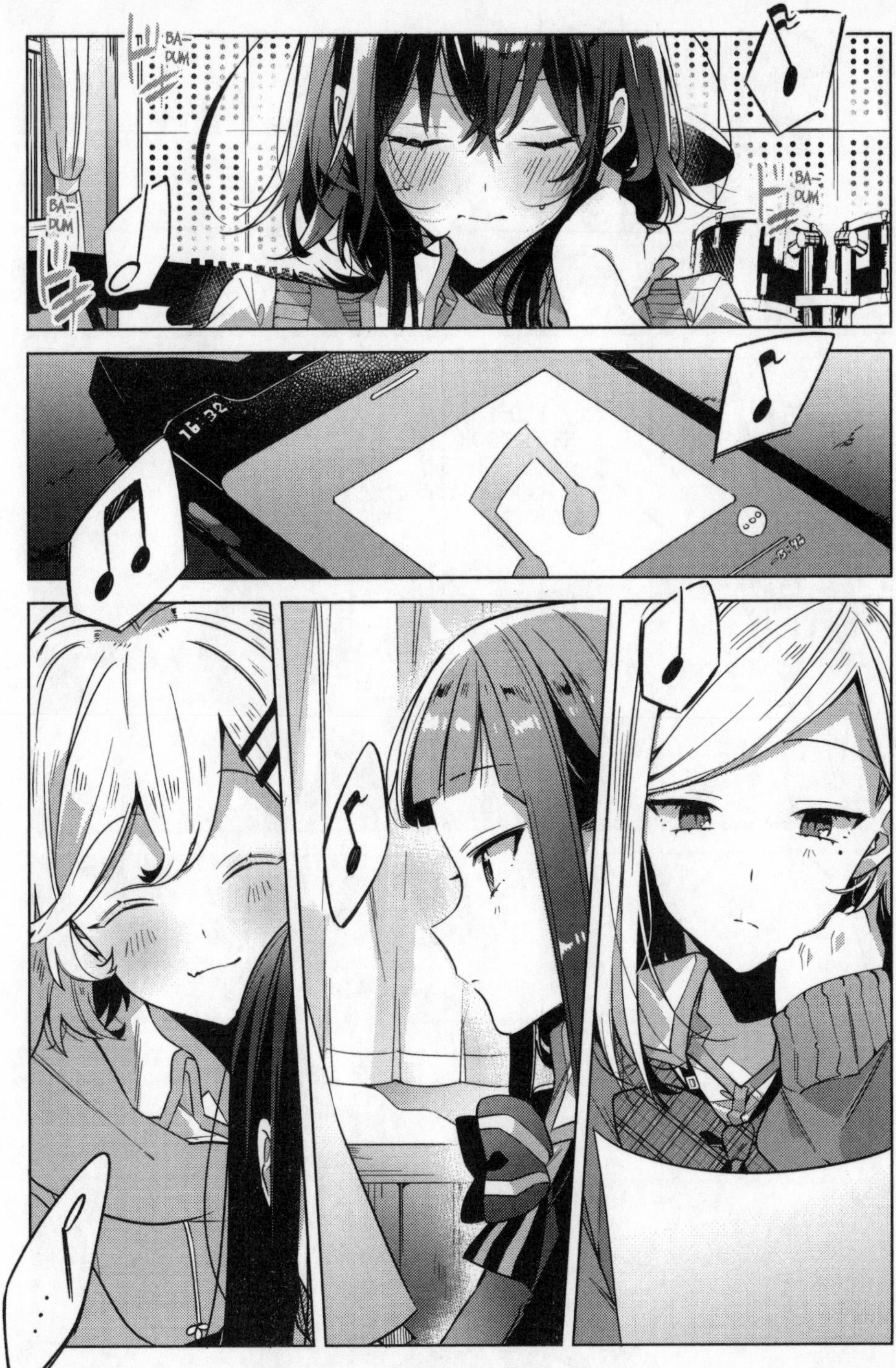
BA-DUM
BA-DUM
BA-DUM
16:32
. . .

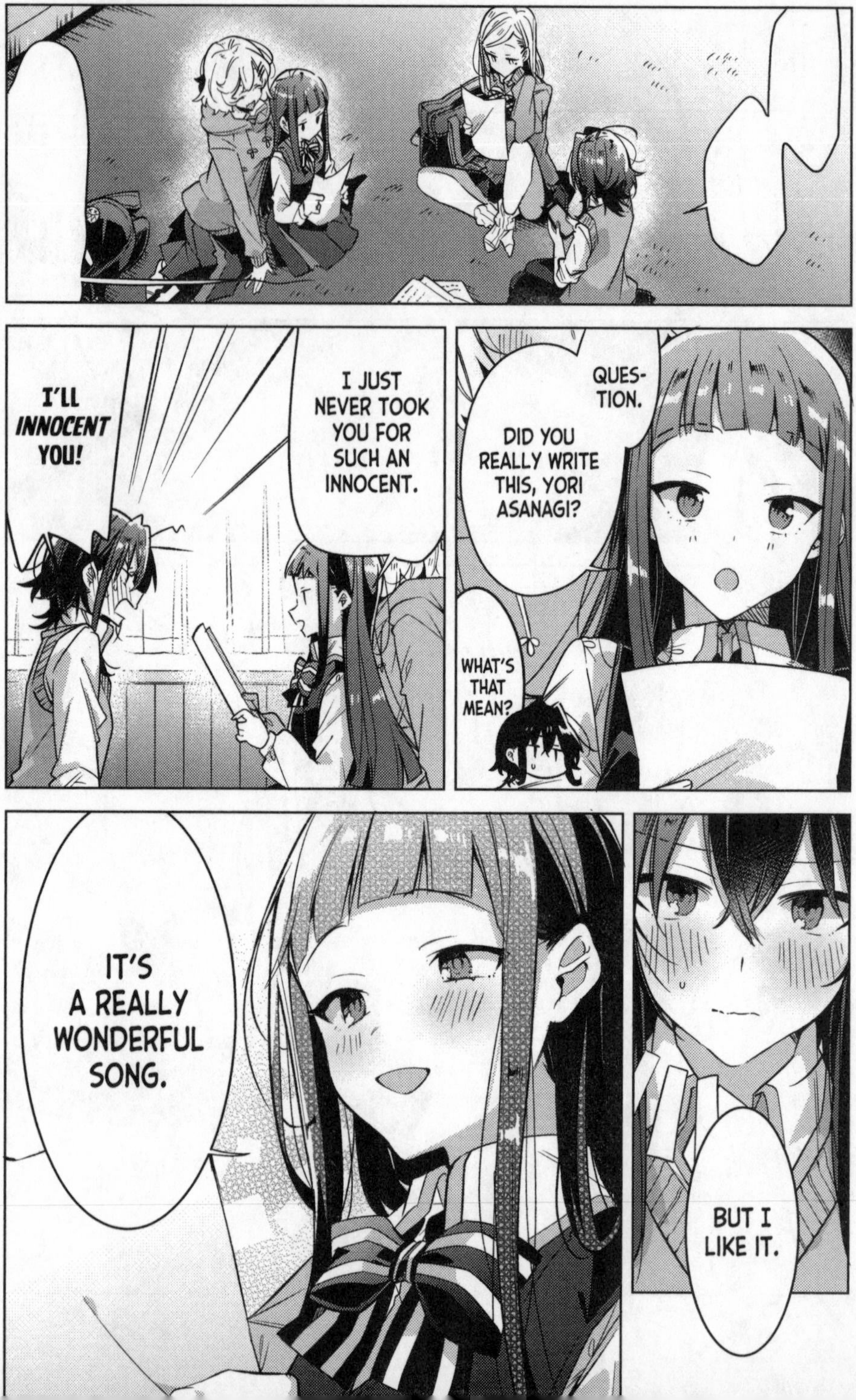
QUES-TION.
DID YOU REALLY WRITE THIS, YORI ASANAGI?
WHAT'S THAT MEAN?
I JUST NEVER TOOK YOU FOR SUCH AN INNOCENT.
I'LL *INNOCENT* YOU!
BUT I LIKE IT.
IT'S A REALLY WONDERFUL SONG.

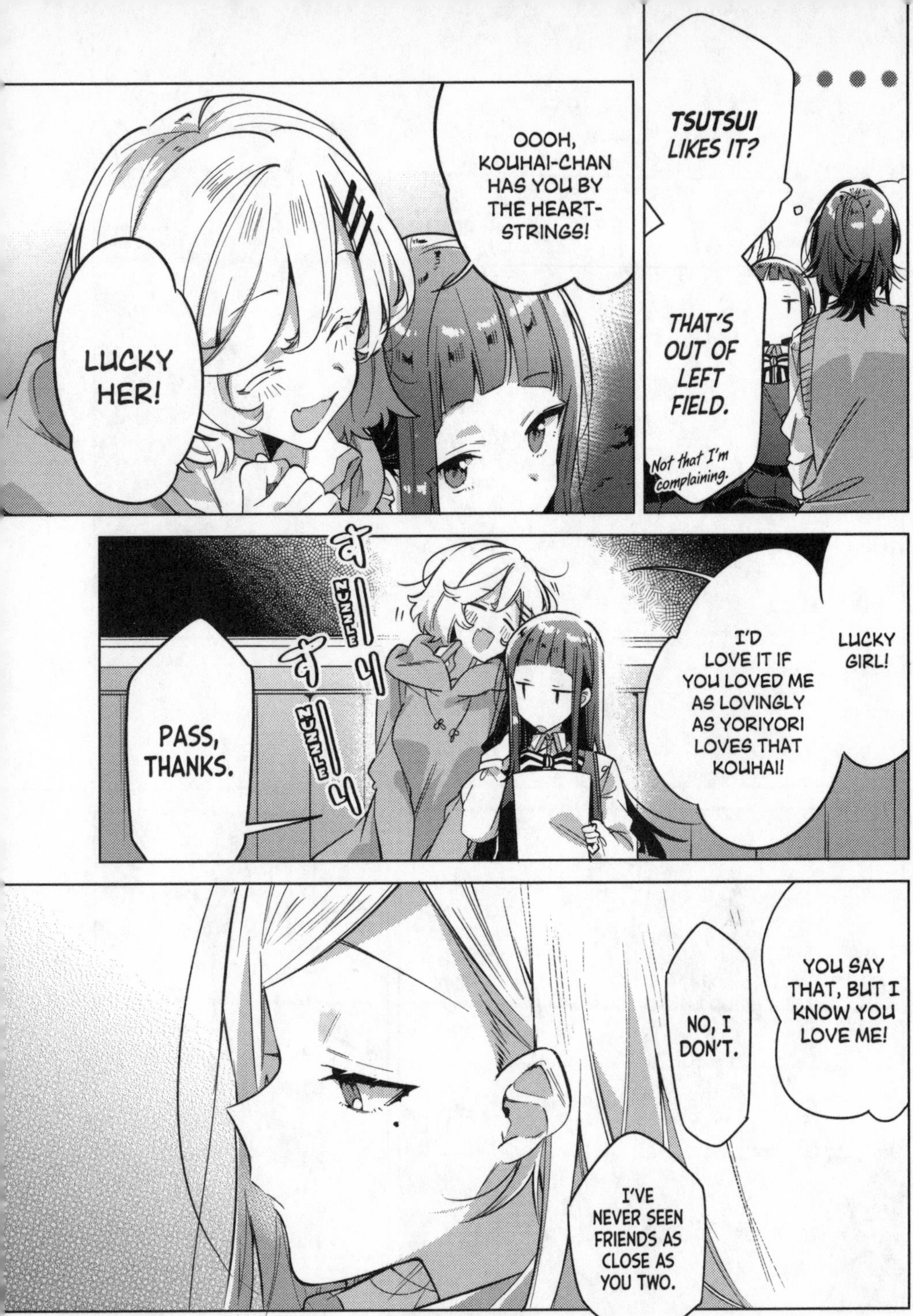

TSUTSUI LIKES IT?
THAT'S OUT OF LEFT FIELD.
Not that I'm complaining.
OOOH, KOUHAI-CHAN HAS YOU BY THE HEART-STRINGS!
LUCKY HER!
LUCKY GIRL!
I'D LOVE IT IF YOU LOVED ME AS LOVINGLY AS YORIYORI LOVES THAT KOUHAI!
NUZZLE
NUZZLE
PASS, THANKS.
YOU SAY THAT, BUT I KNOW YOU LOVE ME!
NO, I DON'T.
I'VE NEVER SEEN FRIENDS AS CLOSE AS YOU TWO.

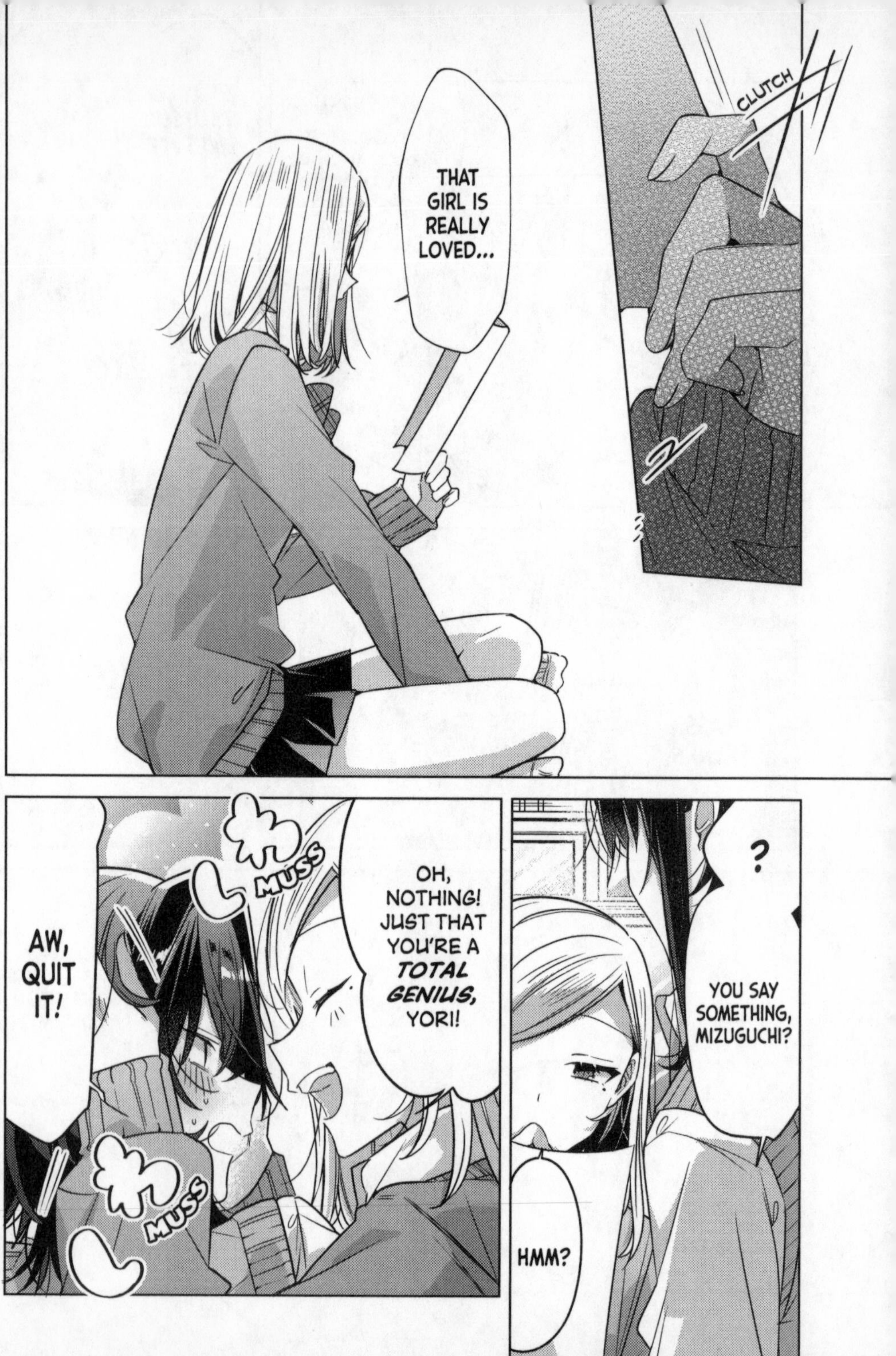
CLUTCH
THAT GIRL IS REALLY LOVED...
?
YOU SAY SOMETHING, MIZUGUCHI?
HMM?
OH, NOTHING! JUST THAT YOU'RE A *TOTAL GENIUS,* YORI!
MUSS
MUSS
AW, QUIT IT!

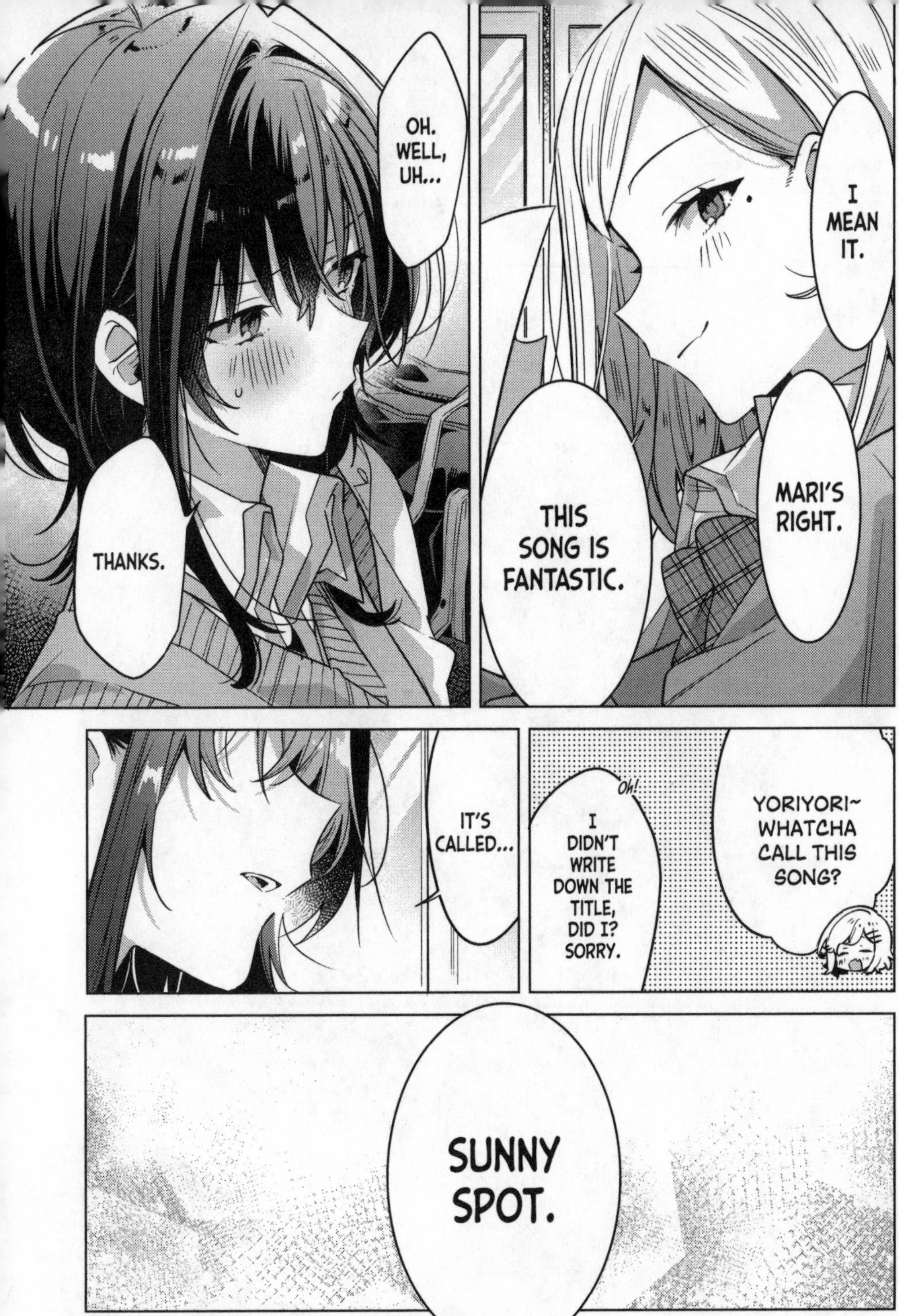
MARI'S RIGHT.
THIS SONG IS FANTASTIC.
I MEAN IT.
OH. WELL, UH...
THANKS.
YORIYORI~ WHATCHA CALL THIS SONG?
Oh!
I DIDN'T WRITE DOWN THE TITLE, DID I? SORRY.
IT'S CALLED...
SUNNY SPOT.

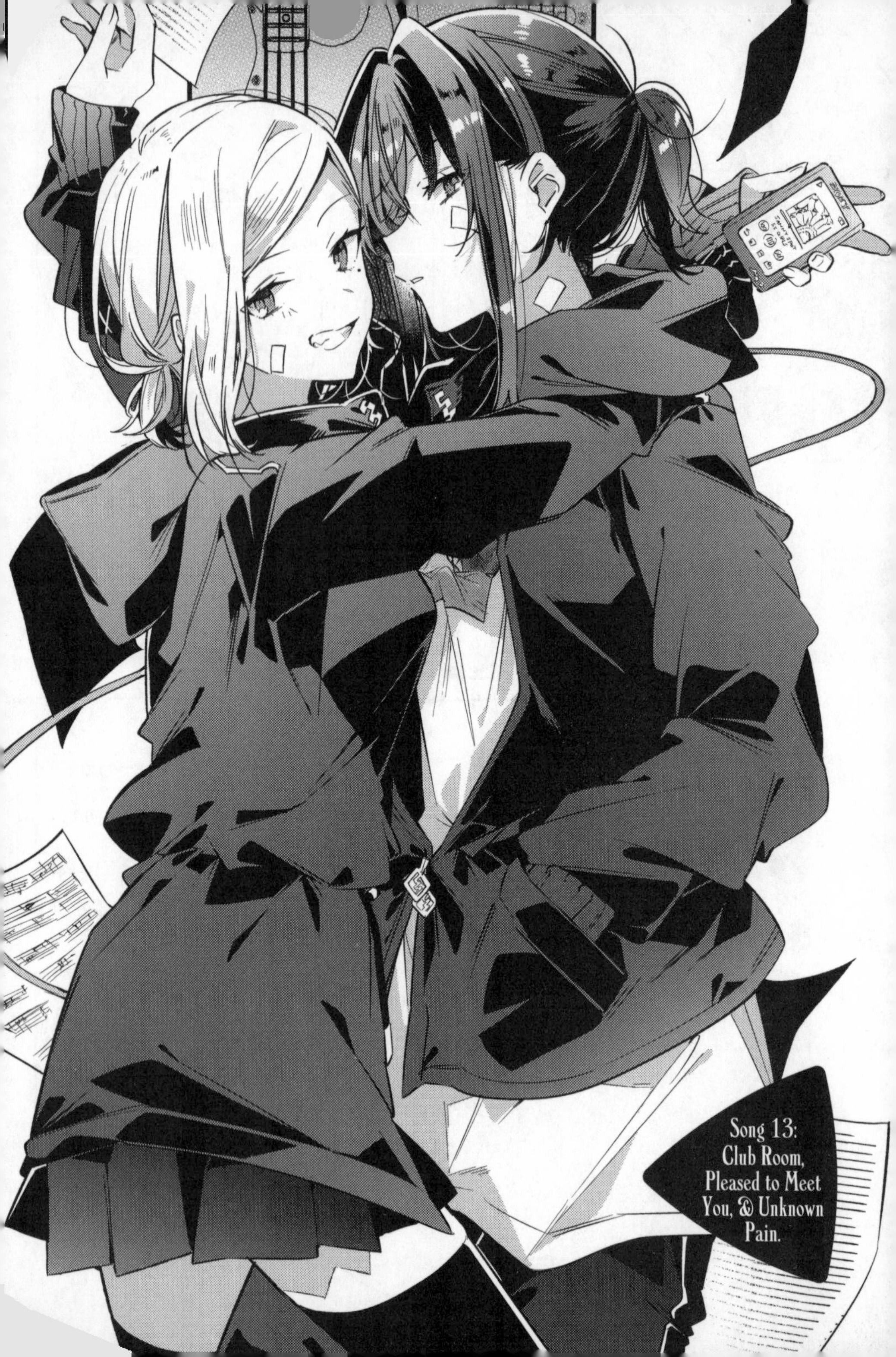
Song 13:
Club Room, Pleased to Meet You, & Unknown Pain.

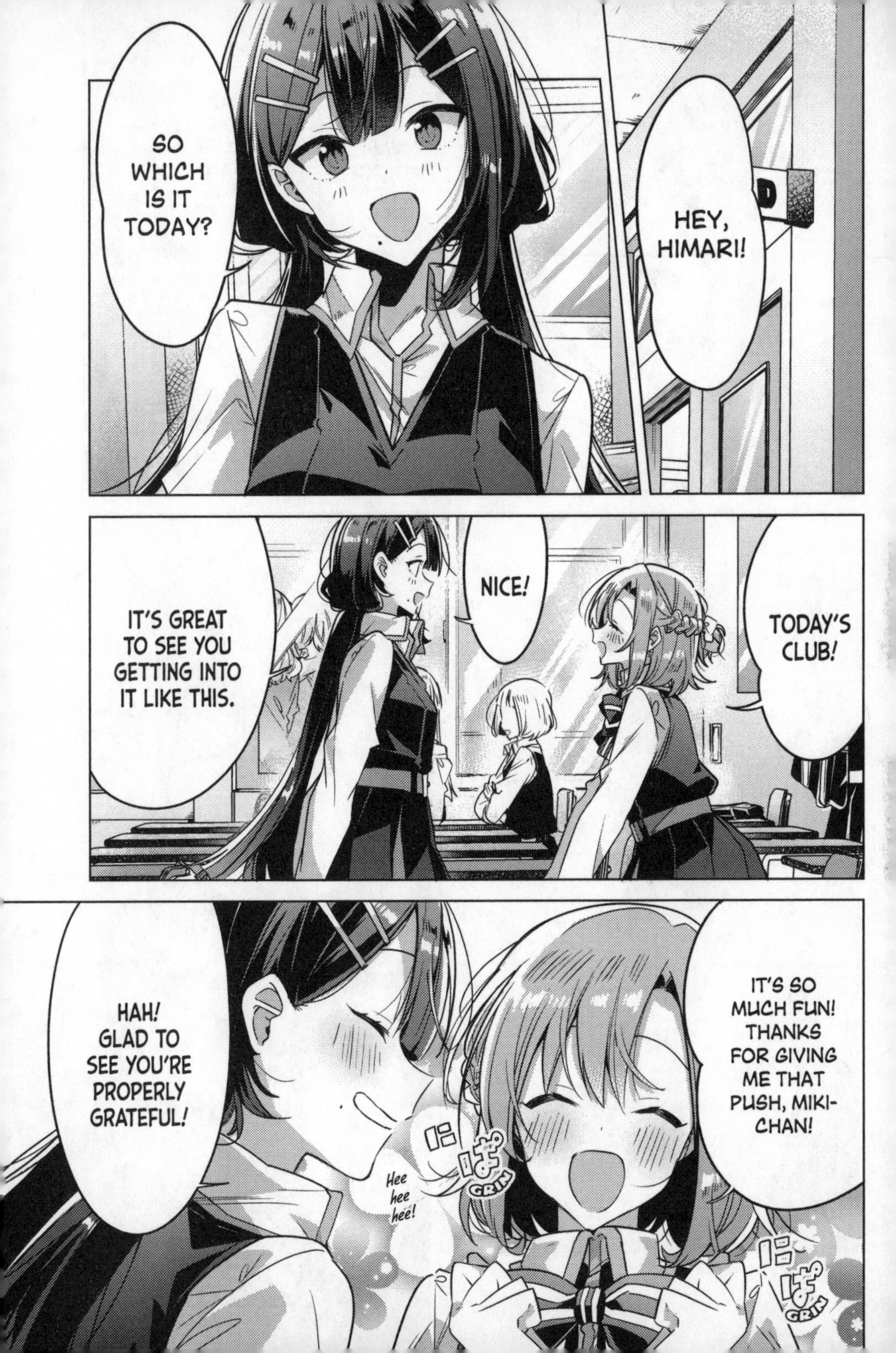
HEY, HIMARI!
SO WHICH IS IT TODAY?
TODAY'S CLUB!
NICE!
IT'S GREAT TO SEE YOU GETTING INTO IT LIKE THIS.
IT'S SO MUCH FUN! THANKS FOR GIVING ME THAT PUSH, MIKI-CHAN!
にぱ GRIN
にぱ GRIN
Hee hee hee!
HAH! GLAD TO SEE YOU'RE PROPERLY GRATEFUL!

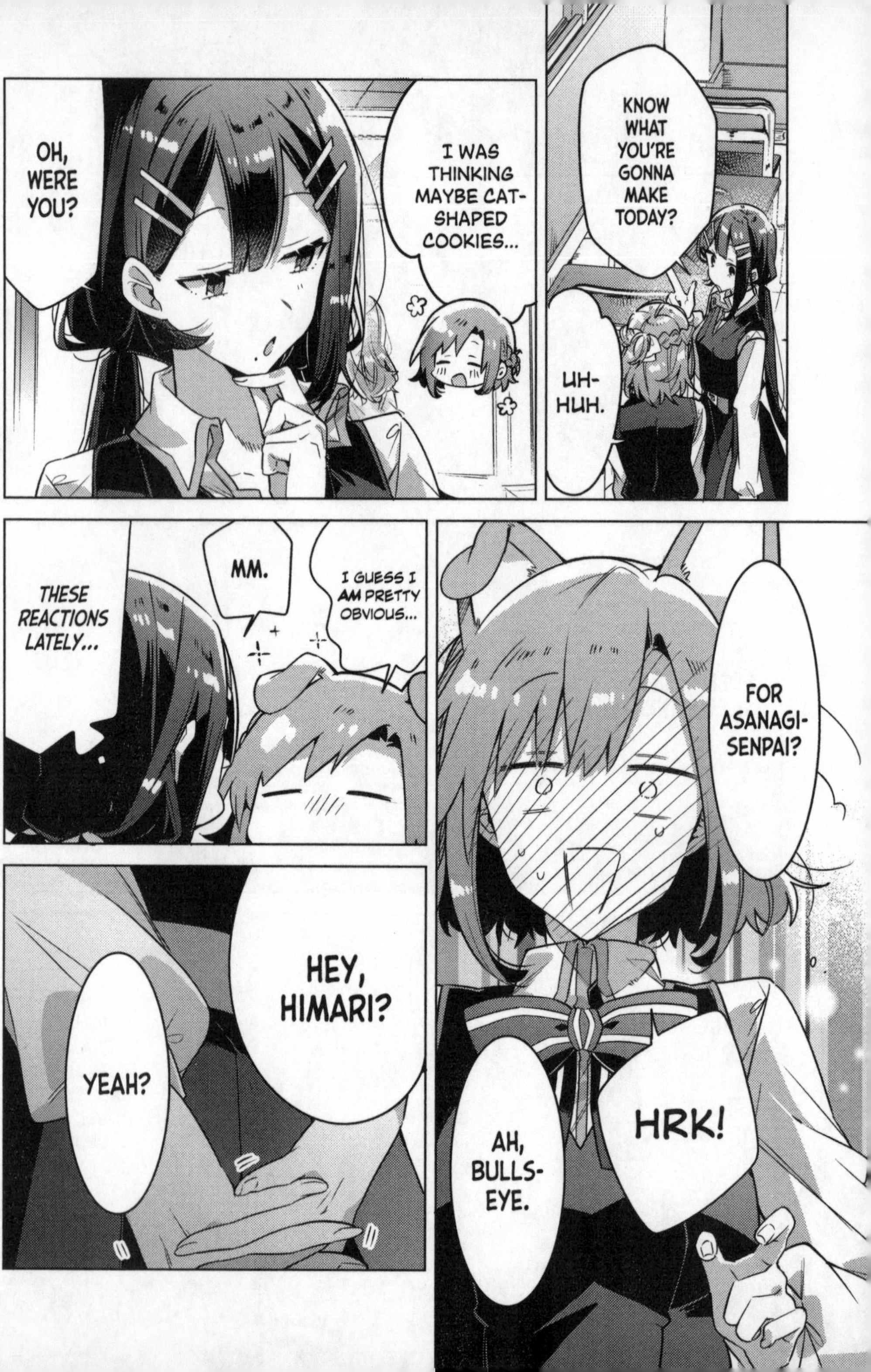
KNOW WHAT YOU'RE GONNA MAKE TODAY?
UH-HUH.
I WAS THINKING MAYBE CAT-SHAPED COOKIES...
OH, WERE YOU?
FOR ASANAGI-SENPAI?
HRK!
AH, BULLS-EYE.
I GUESS I AM PRETTY OBVIOUS...
MM.
THESE REACTIONS LATELY...
HEY, HIMARI?
YEAH?

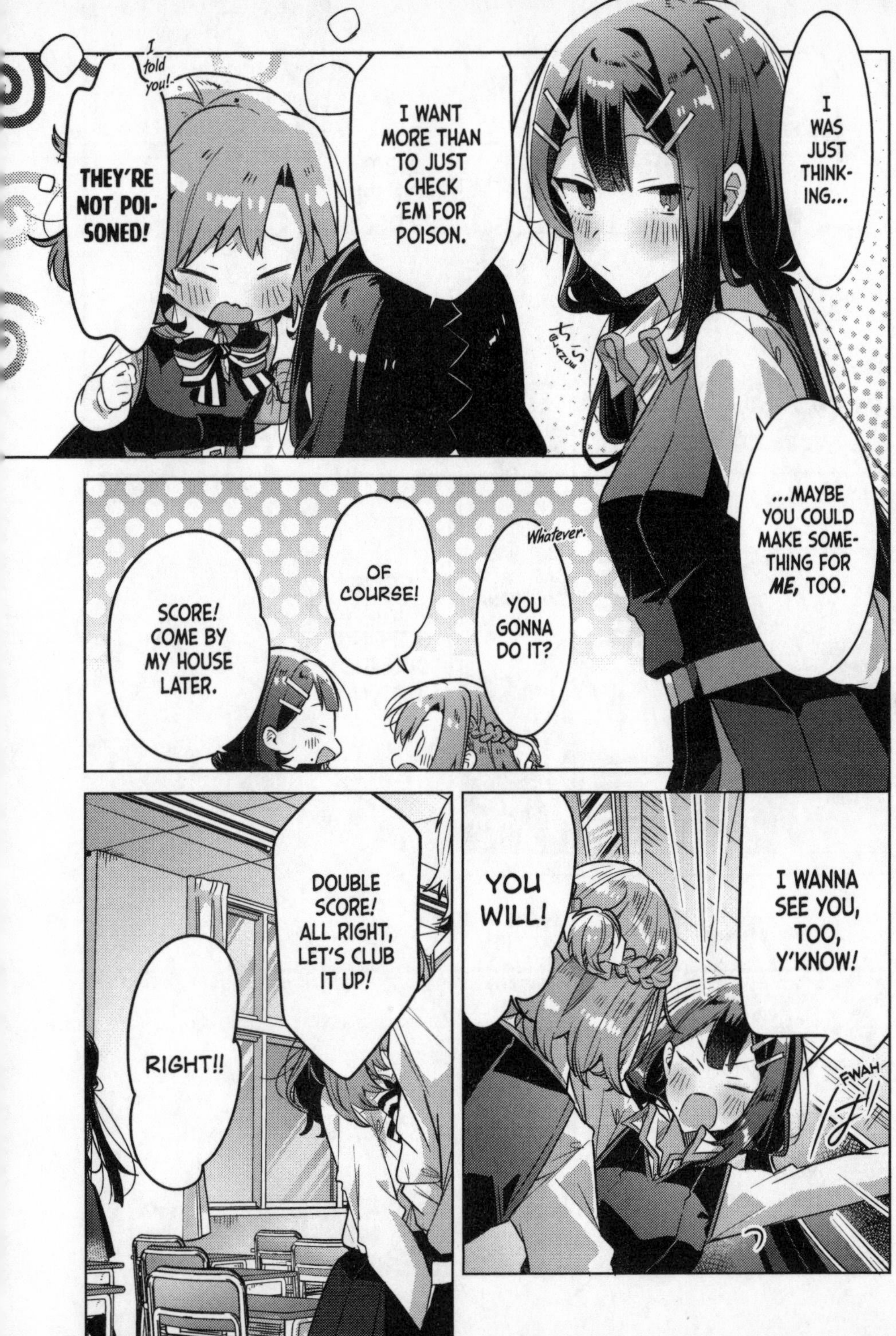
I WANT MORE THAN TO JUST CHECK 'EM FOR POISON.
THEY'RE NOT POISONED!
I told you!
I WAS JUST THINKING...
...MAYBE YOU COULD MAKE SOMETHING FOR *ME*, TOO.
Whatever.
YOU GONNA DO IT?
OF COURSE!
SCORE! COME BY MY HOUSE LATER.
I WANNA SEE YOU, TOO, Y'KNOW!
FWAH
YOU WILL!
DOUBLE SCORE! ALL RIGHT, LET'S CLUB IT UP!
RIGHT!!

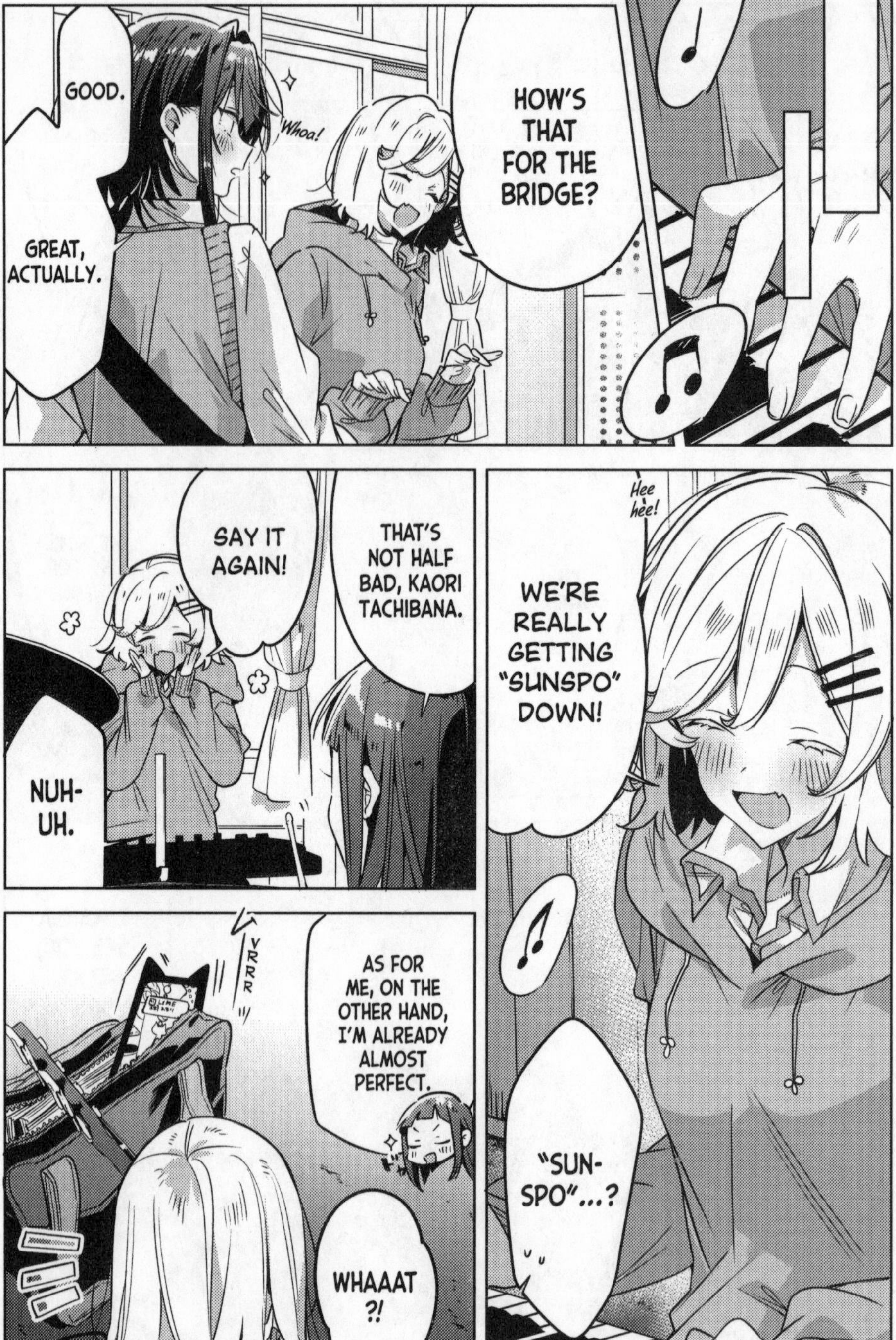
HOW'S THAT FOR THE BRIDGE?
Whoa!
GOOD.
GREAT, ACTUALLY.
Hee hee!
WE'RE REALLY GETTING "SUNSPO" DOWN!
"SUN-SPO"...?
THAT'S NOT HALF BAD, KAORI TACHIBANA.
SAY IT AGAIN!
NUH-UH.
AS FOR ME, ON THE OTHER HAND, I'M ALREADY ALMOST PERFECT.
VRRR
WHAAAT?!

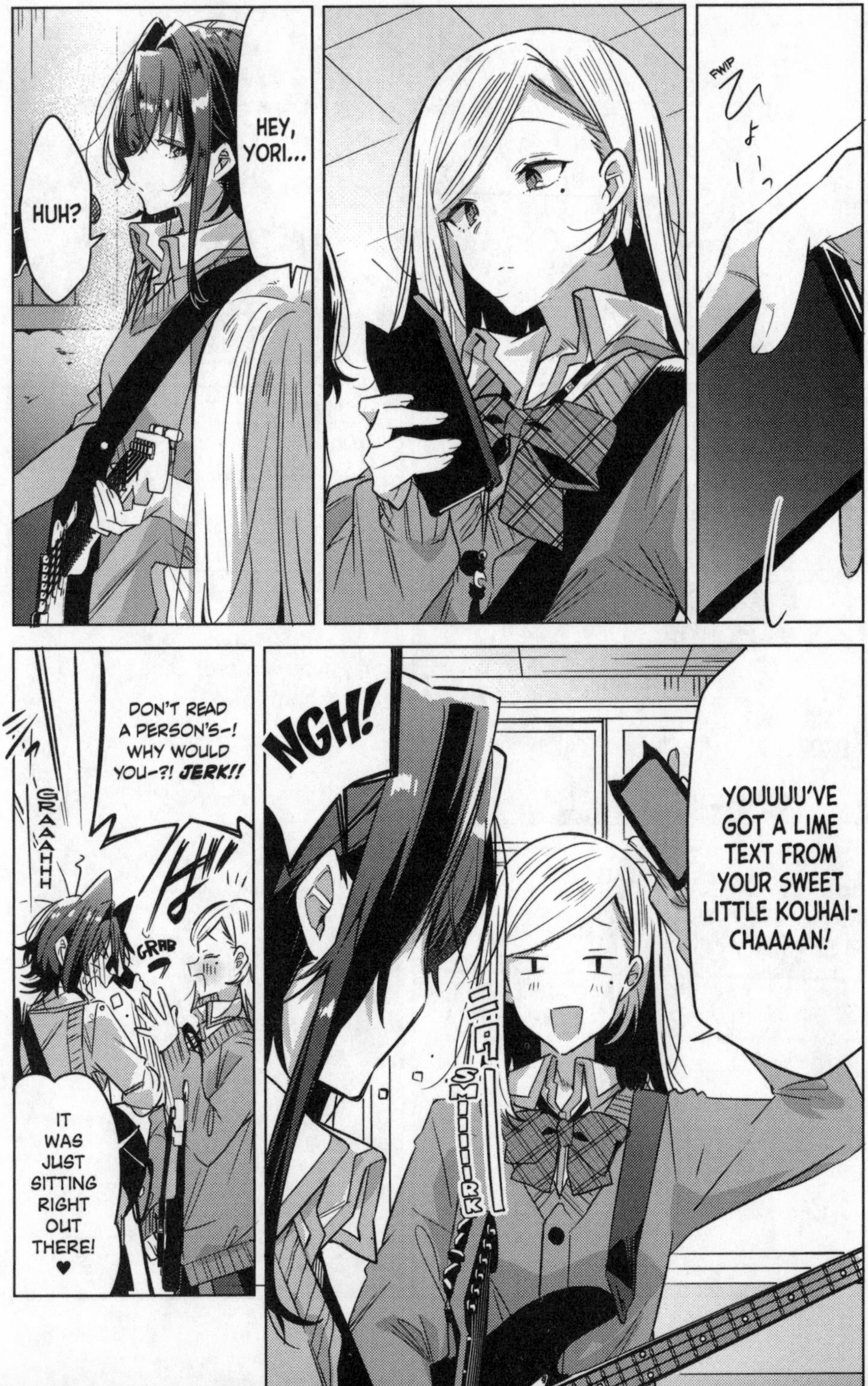
FWIP
ひょいっ
HEY, YORI...
HUH?
NGH!
YOUUUU'VE GOT A LIME TEXT FROM YOUR SWEET LITTLE KOUHAI-CHAAAAN!
SMIIIIIIRK
DON'T READ A PERSON'S-! WHY WOULD YOU-?! JERK!!
GRAAAHHH
GRAB
IT WAS JUST SITTING RIGHT OUT THERE! ♥

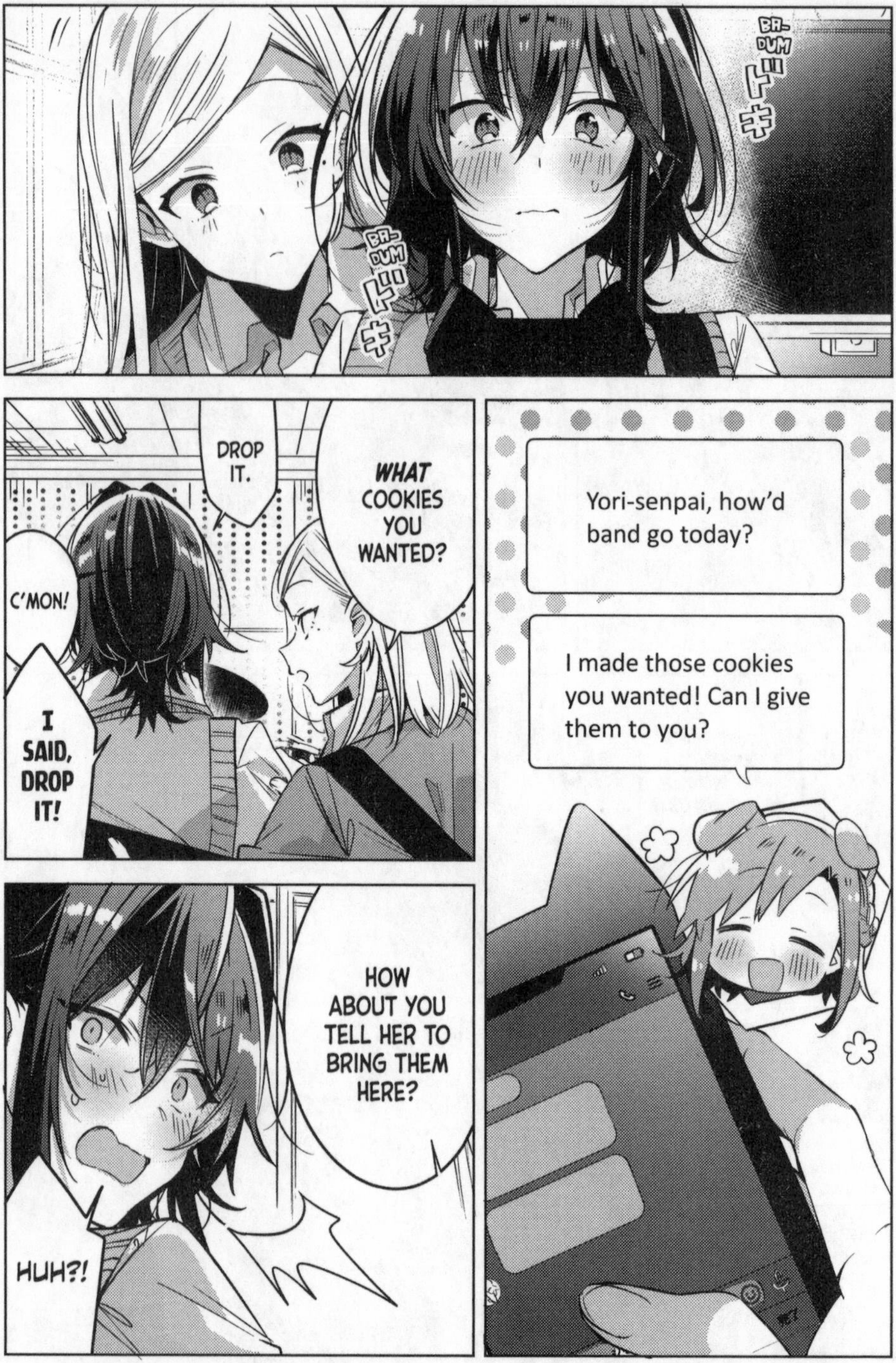
BA-DUM
ドキ
BA-DUM
ドキ
Yori-senpai, how'd band go today?
I made those cookies you wanted! Can I give them to you?
WHAT COOKIES YOU WANTED?
DROP IT.
C'MON!
I SAID, DROP IT!
HOW ABOUT YOU TELL HER TO BRING THEM HERE?
HUH?!

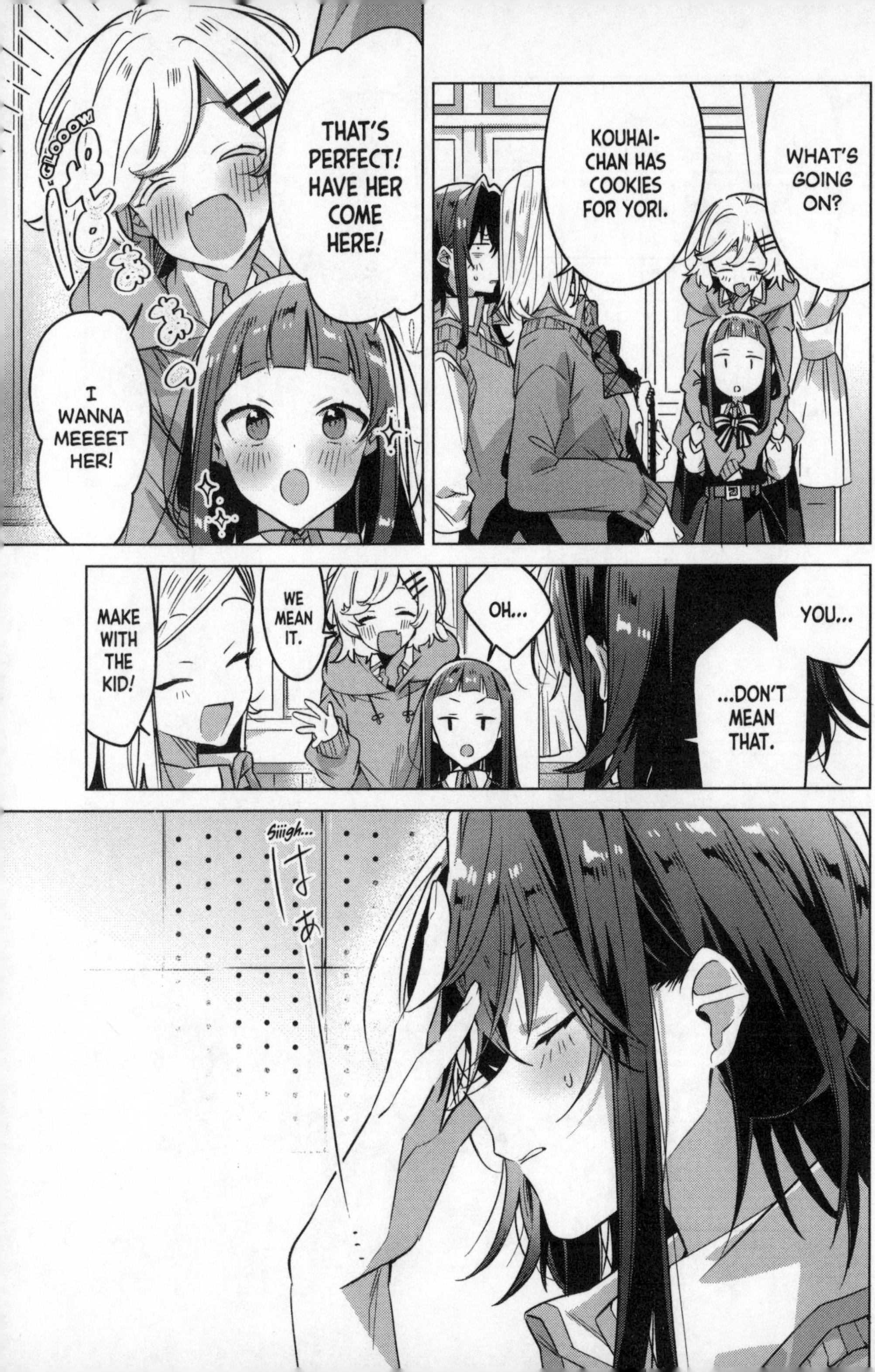
WHAT'S GOING ON?
KOUHAI-CHAN HAS COOKIES FOR YORI.
GLOOOW
THAT'S PERFECT! HAVE HER COME HERE!
I WANNA MEEEET HER!
YOU...
...DON'T MEAN THAT.
OH...
WE MEAN IT.
MAKE WITH THE KID!
Siiigh...

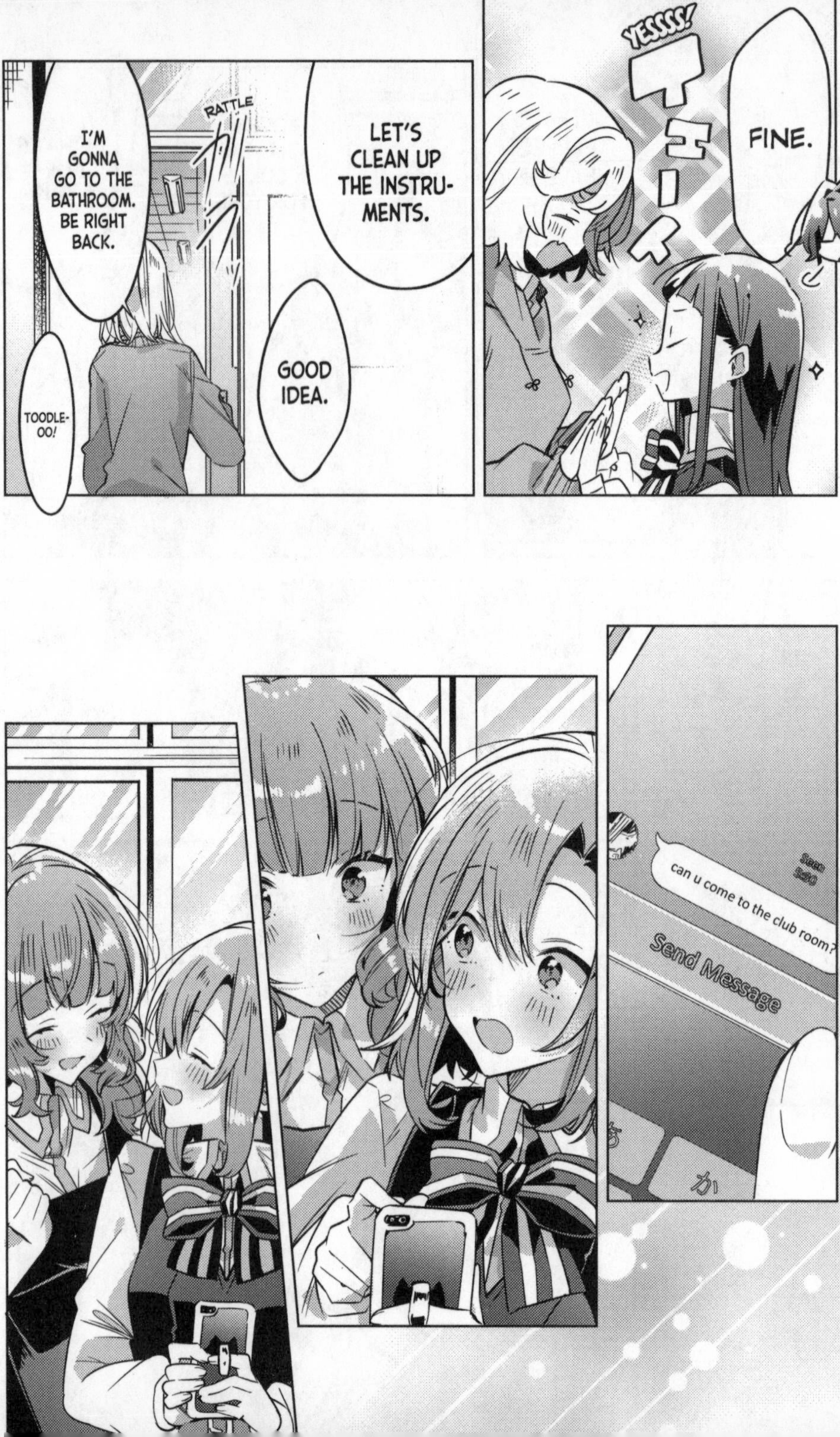
YESSSS!
FINE.
LET'S CLEAN UP THE INSTRU-MENTS.
GOOD IDEA.
RATTLE
I'M GONNA GO TO THE BATHROOM. BE RIGHT BACK.
TOODLE-OO!
Seen
can u come to the club room?
Send Message

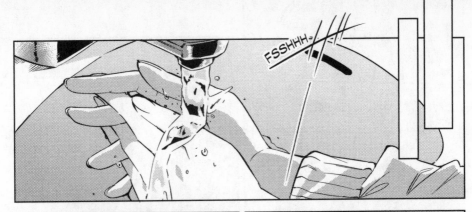

FSSHHH~

AKI-
SENPAI!

OH—

SQUEAK

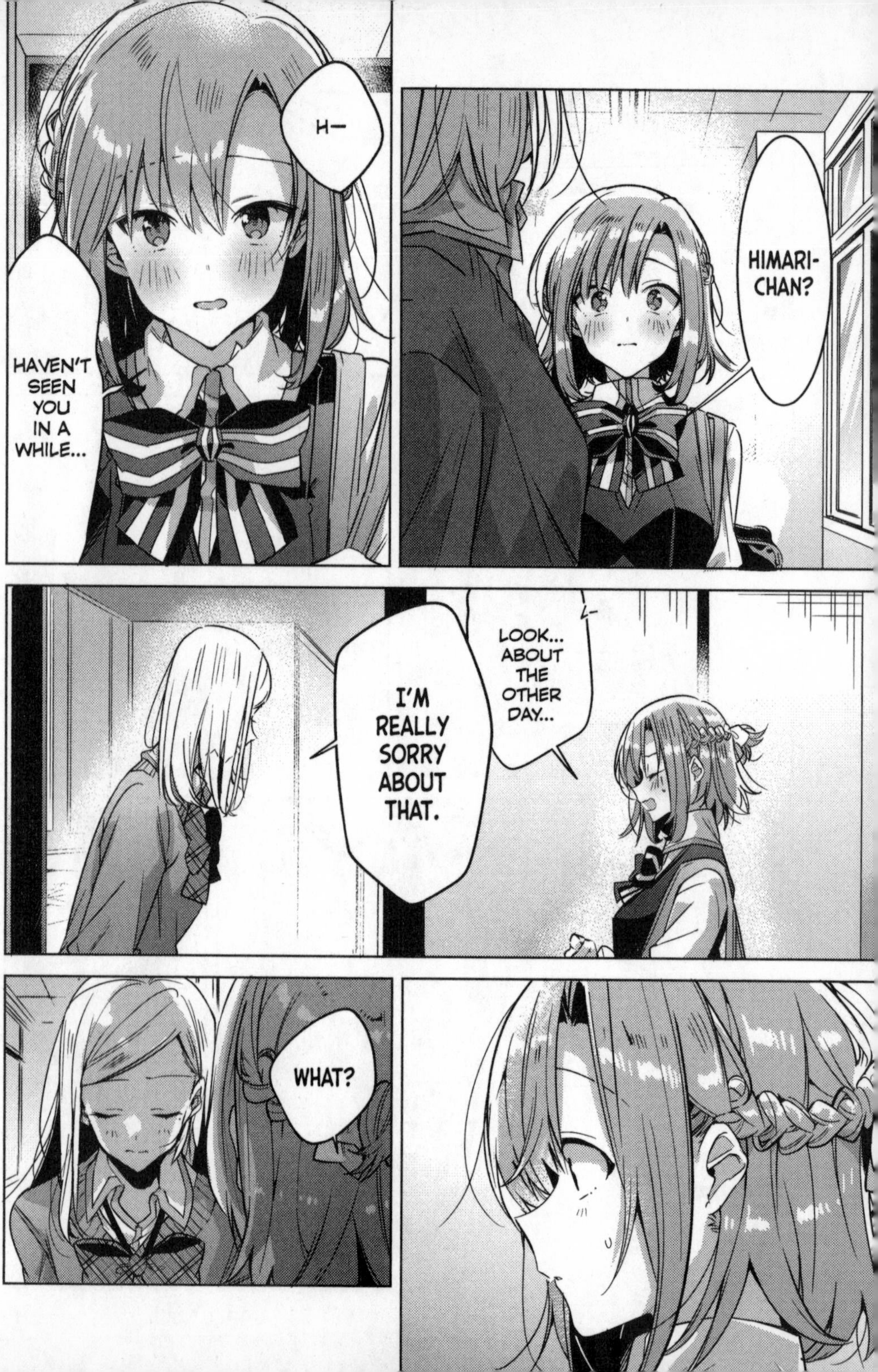
HIMARI-CHAN?
H—
HAVEN'T SEEN YOU IN A WHILE...
LOOK... ABOUT THE OTHER DAY...
I'M REALLY SORRY ABOUT THAT.
WHAT?

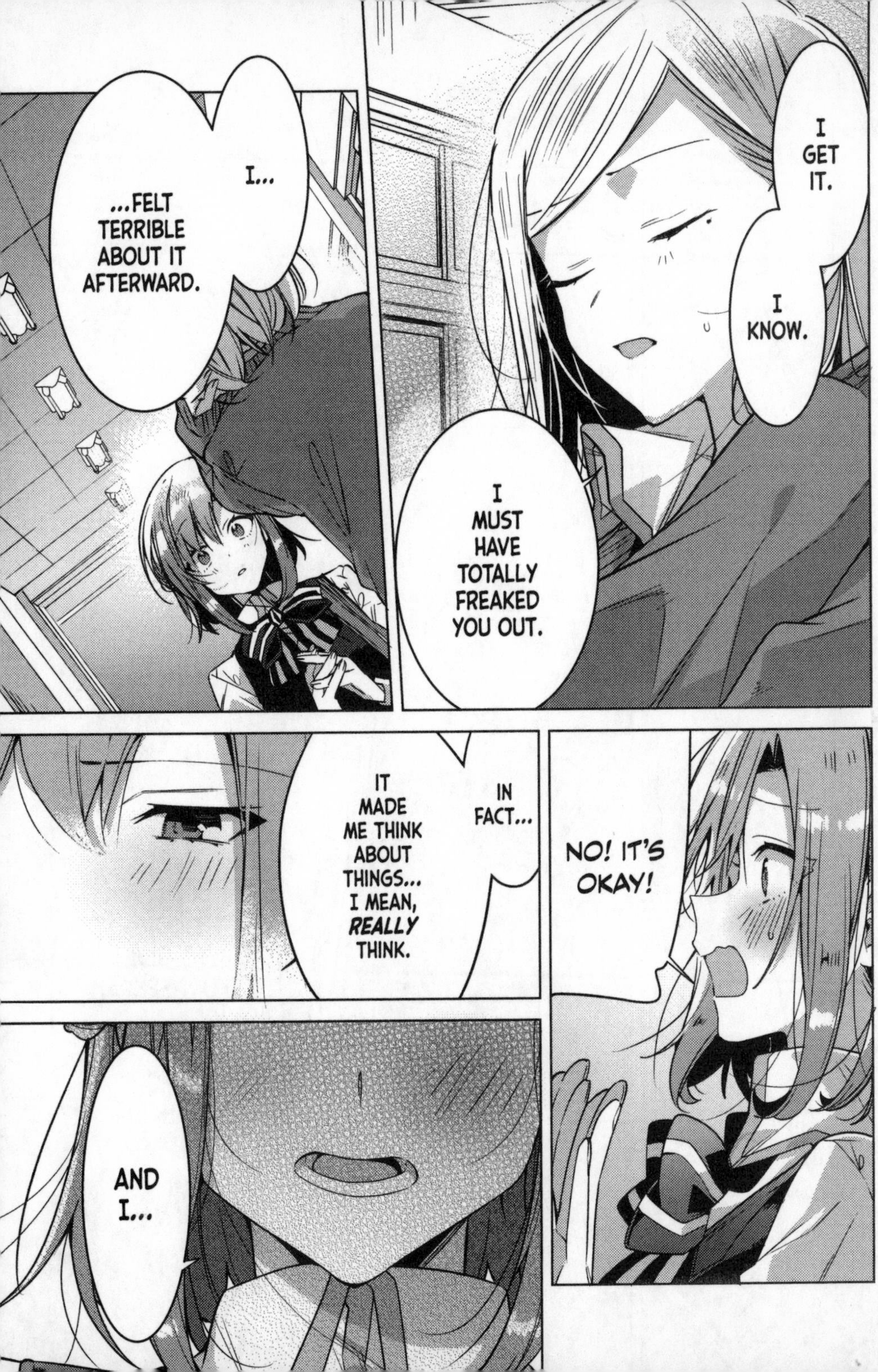
I GET IT.
I KNOW.
I MUST HAVE TOTALLY FREAKED YOU OUT.
I...
...FELT TERRIBLE ABOUT IT AFTERWARD.
NO! IT'S OKAY!
IN FACT...
IT MADE ME THINK ABOUT THINGS... I MEAN, *REALLY* THINK.
AND I...

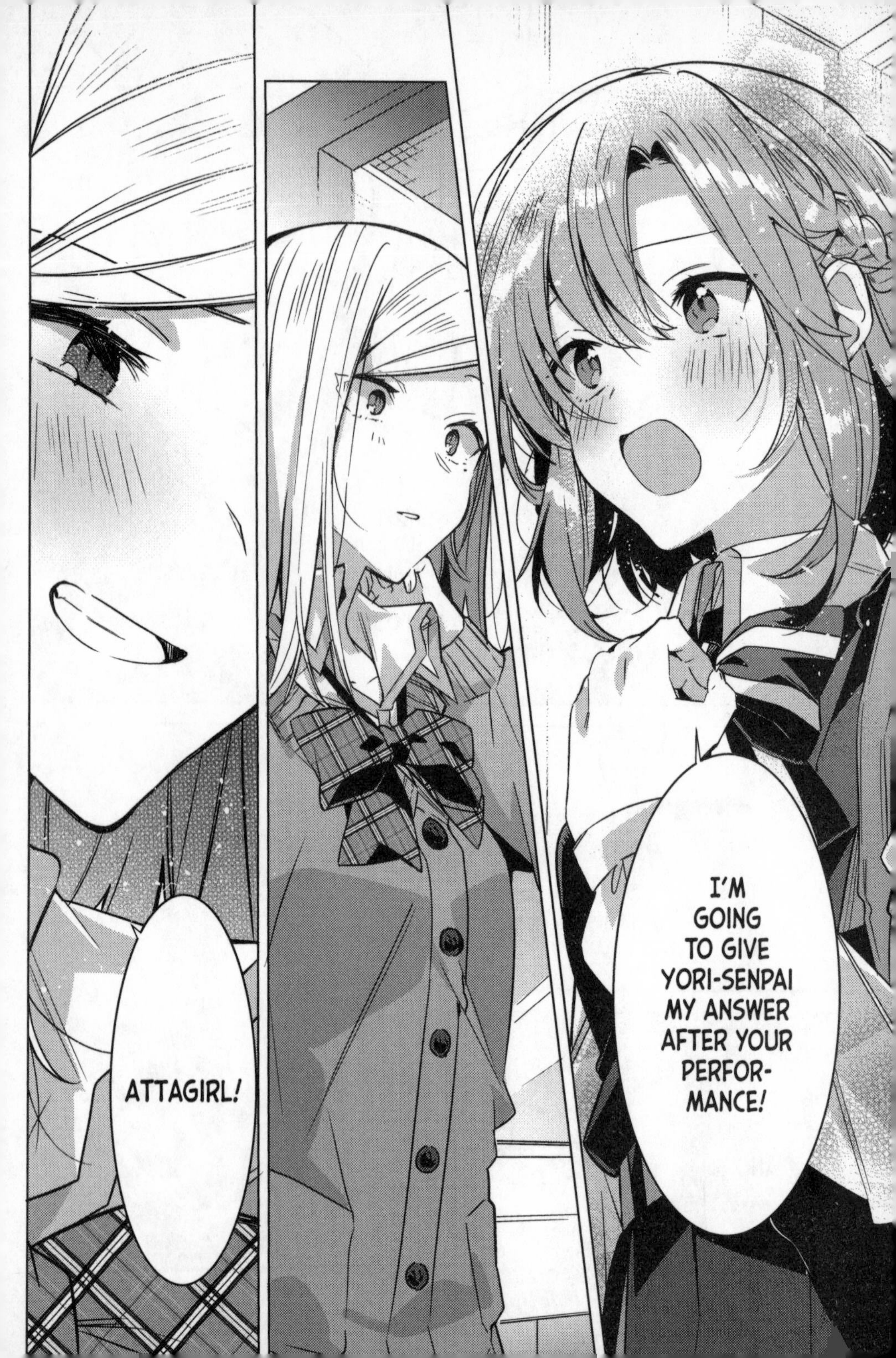
I'M GOING TO GIVE YORI-SENPAI MY ANSWER AFTER YOUR PERFOR-MANCE!
ATTAGIRL!

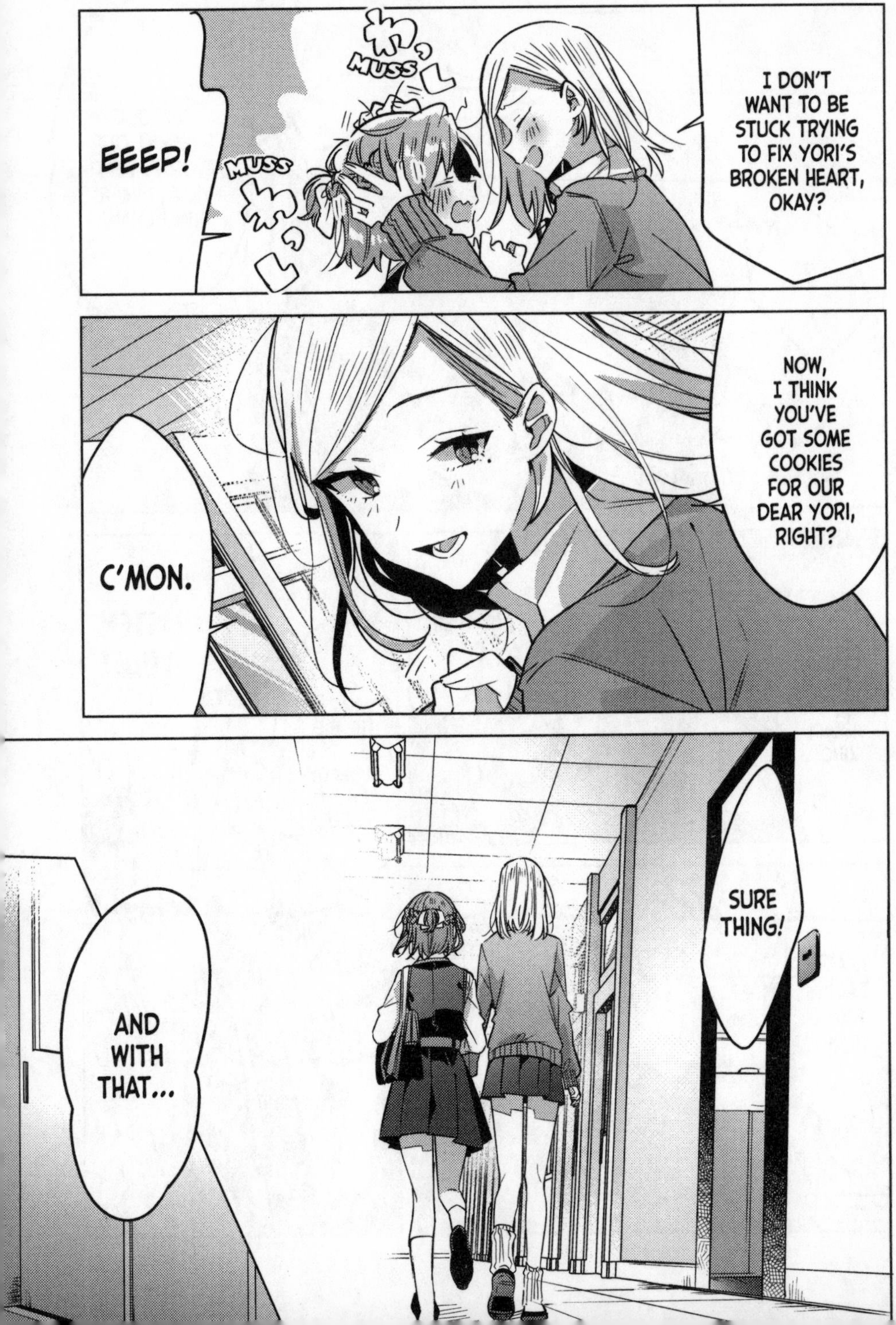
I DON'T WANT TO BE STUCK TRYING TO FIX YORI'S BROKEN HEART, OKAY?
MUSS
MUSS
EEEP!
NOW, I THINK YOU'VE GOT SOME COOKIES FOR OUR DEAR YORI, RIGHT?
C'MON.
SURE THING!
AND WITH THAT...

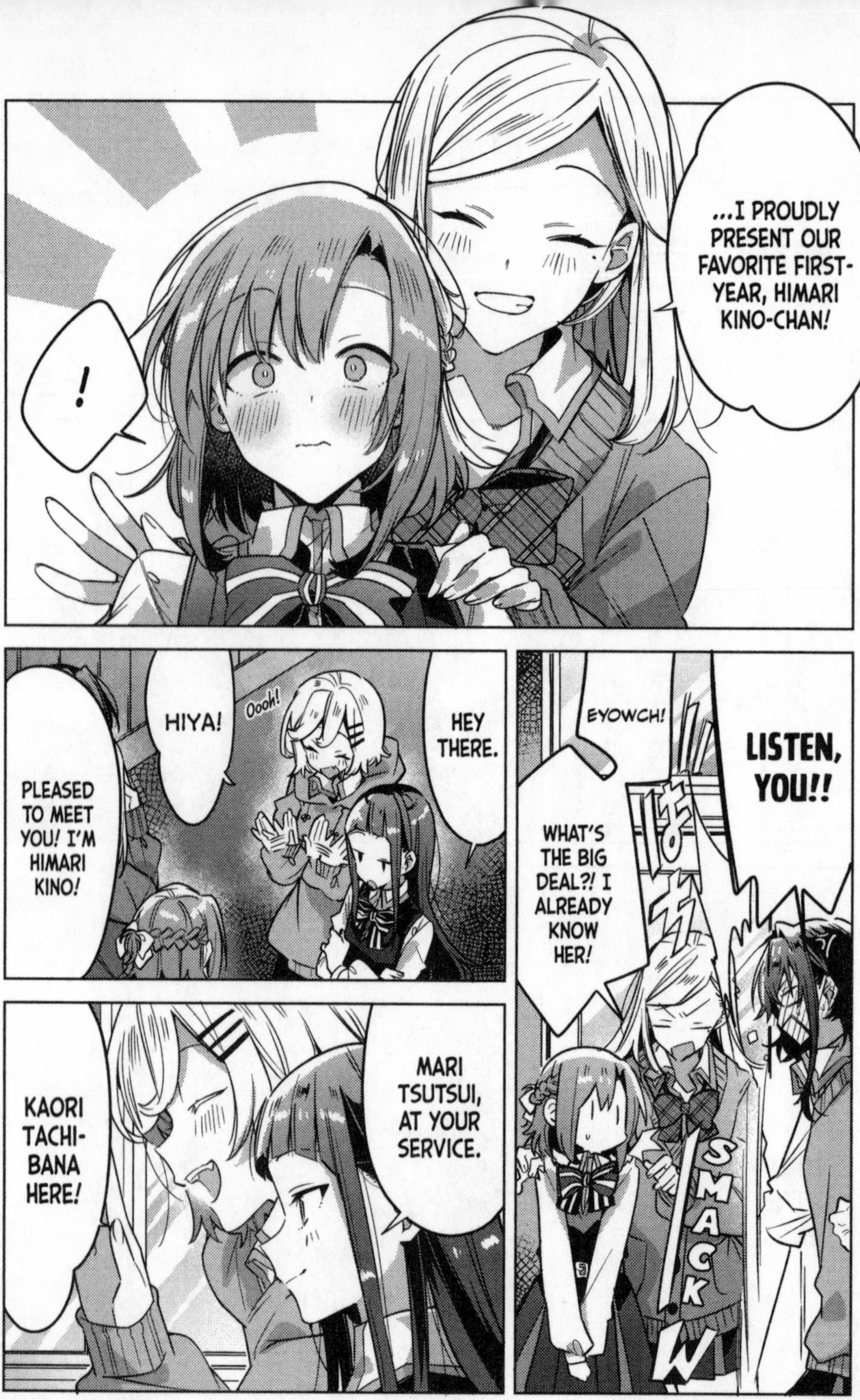
...I PROUDLY PRESENT OUR FAVORITE FIRST-YEAR, HIMARI KINO-CHAN!
!
LISTEN, YOU!!
EYOWCH!
WHAT'S THE BIG DEAL?! I ALREADY KNOW HER!
SMACK
HEY THERE.
Oooh!
HIYA!
PLEASED TO MEET YOU! I'M HIMARI KINO!
MARI TSUTSUI, AT YOUR SERVICE.
KAORI TACHI-BANA HERE!

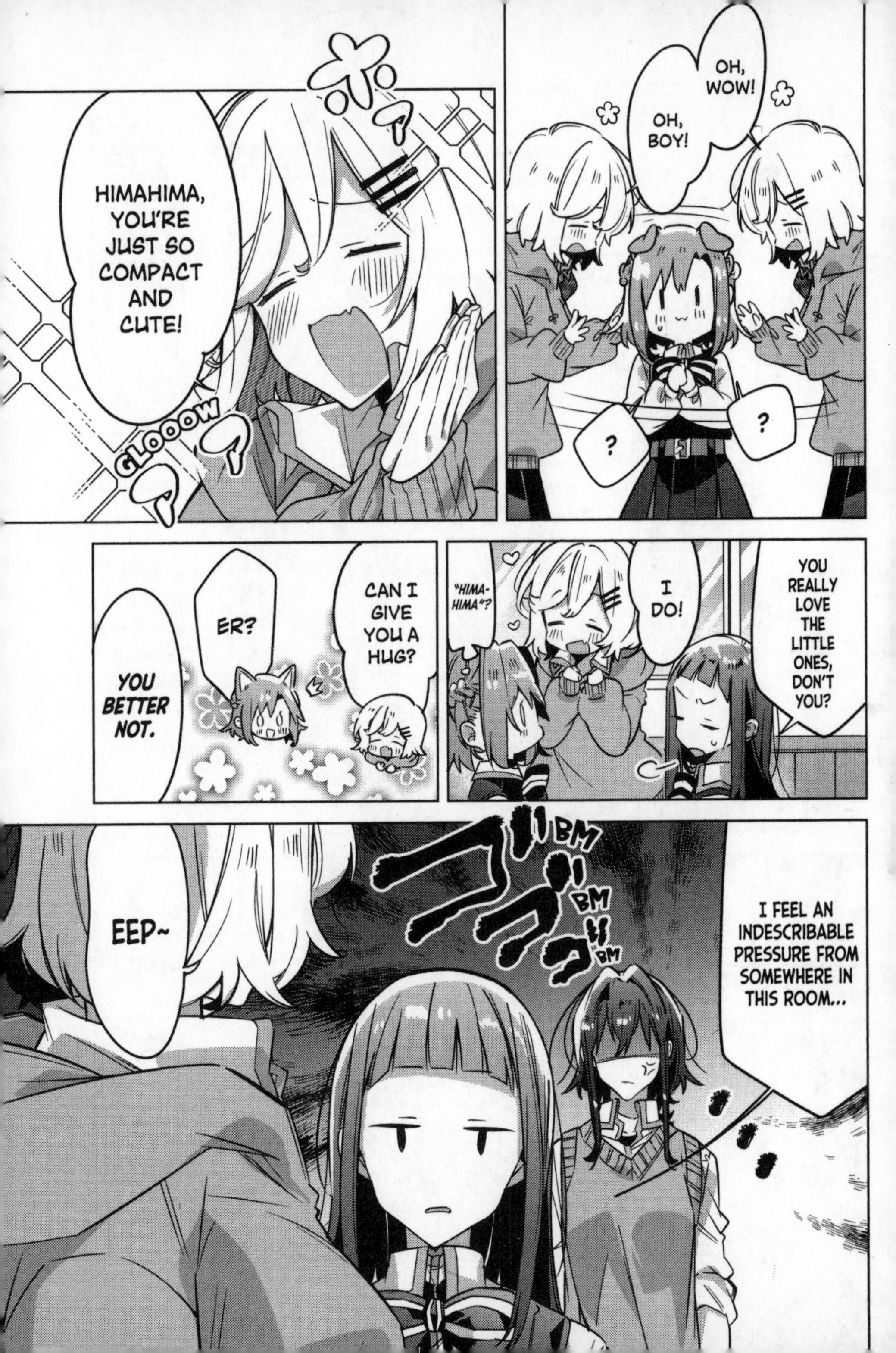
OH, WOW!
OH, BOY!
?
?
HIMAHIMA, YOU'RE JUST SO COMPACT AND CUTE!
GLOOOW
YOU REALLY LOVE THE LITTLE ONES, DON'T YOU?
I DO!
"HIMA-HIMA"?
CAN I GIVE YOU A HUG?
ER?
YOU BETTER NOT.
I FEEL AN INDESCRIBABLE PRESSURE FROM SOMEWHERE IN THIS ROOM...
BM
BM
BM
EEP~

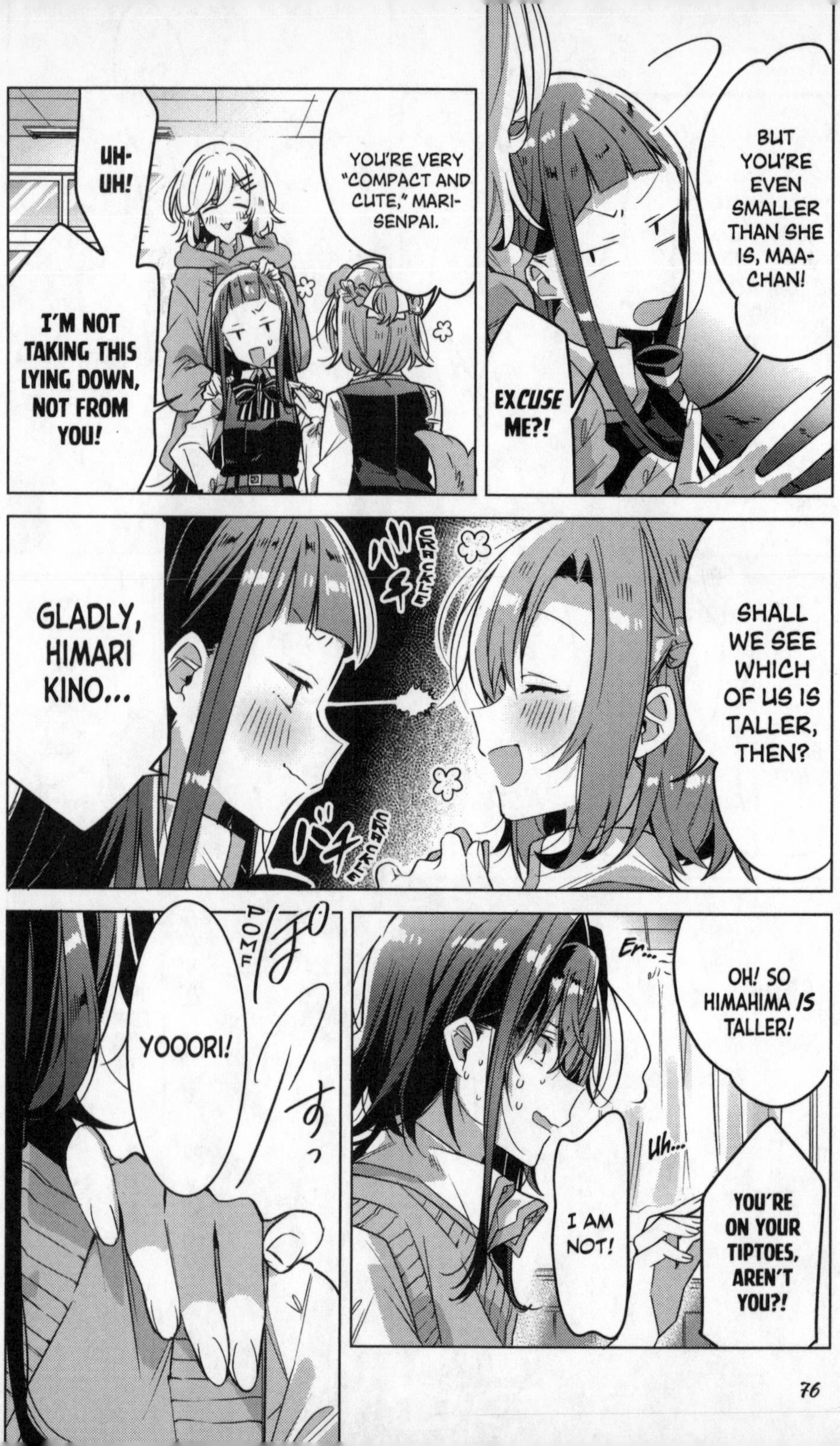
BUT YOU'RE EVEN SMALLER THAN SHE IS, MAA-CHAN!
EXCUSE ME?!
YOU'RE VERY "COMPACT AND CUTE," MARI-SENPAI.
UH-UH!
I'M NOT TAKING THIS LYING DOWN, NOT FROM YOU!
SHALL WE SEE WHICH OF US IS TALLER, THEN?
CRACKLE
GLADLY, HIMARI KINO...
CRACKLE
Er...
OH! SO HIMAHIMA IS TALLER!
Uh...
YOU'RE ON YOUR TIPTOES, AREN'T YOU?!
I AM NOT!
POMF
YOOORI!

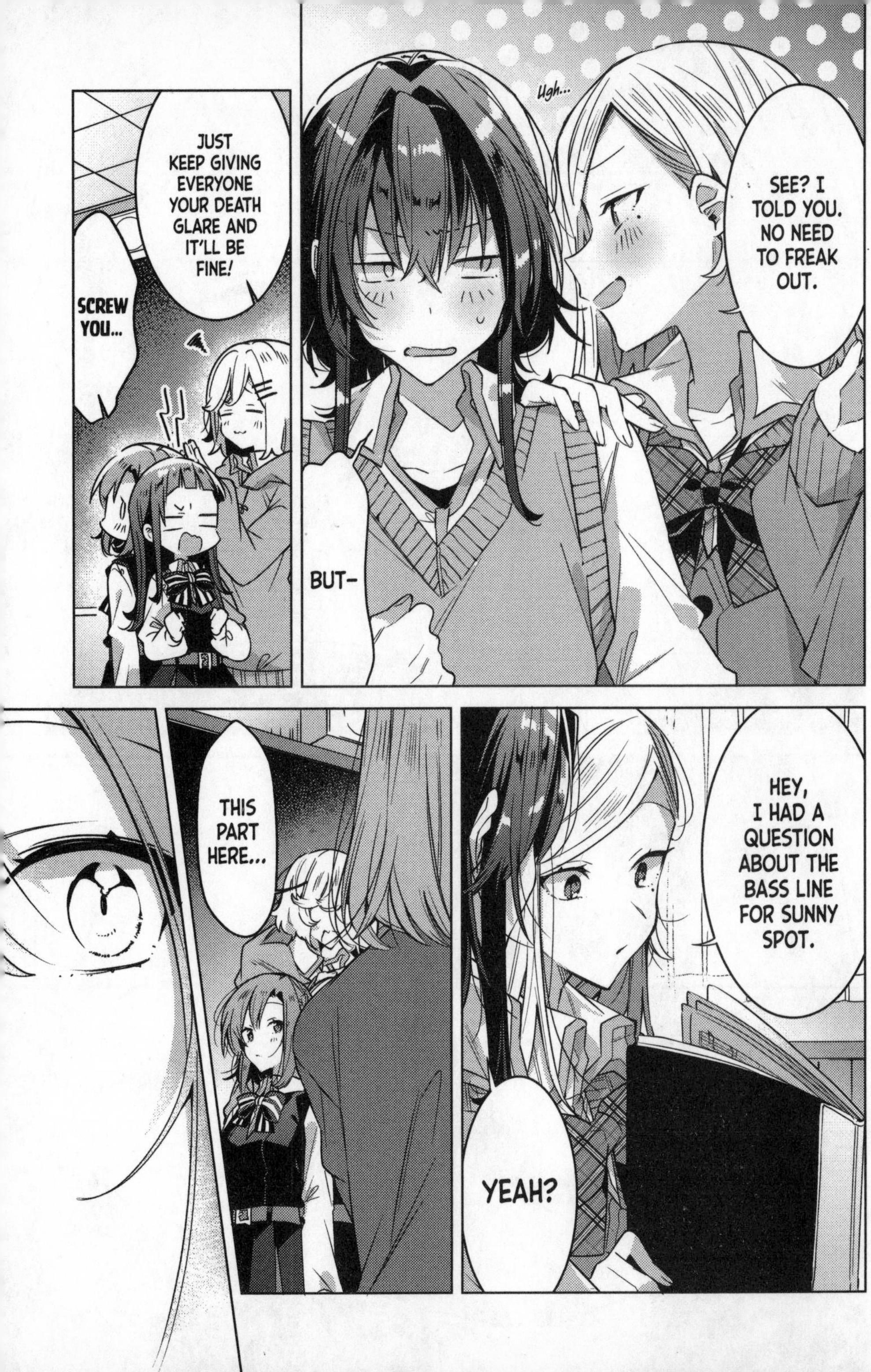
SEE? I TOLD YOU. NO NEED TO FREAK OUT.
Ugh...
BUT–
JUST KEEP GIVING EVERYONE YOUR DEATH GLARE AND IT'LL BE FINE!
SCREW YOU...
HEY, I HAD A QUESTION ABOUT THE BASS LINE FOR SUNNY SPOT.
YEAH?
THIS PART HERE...

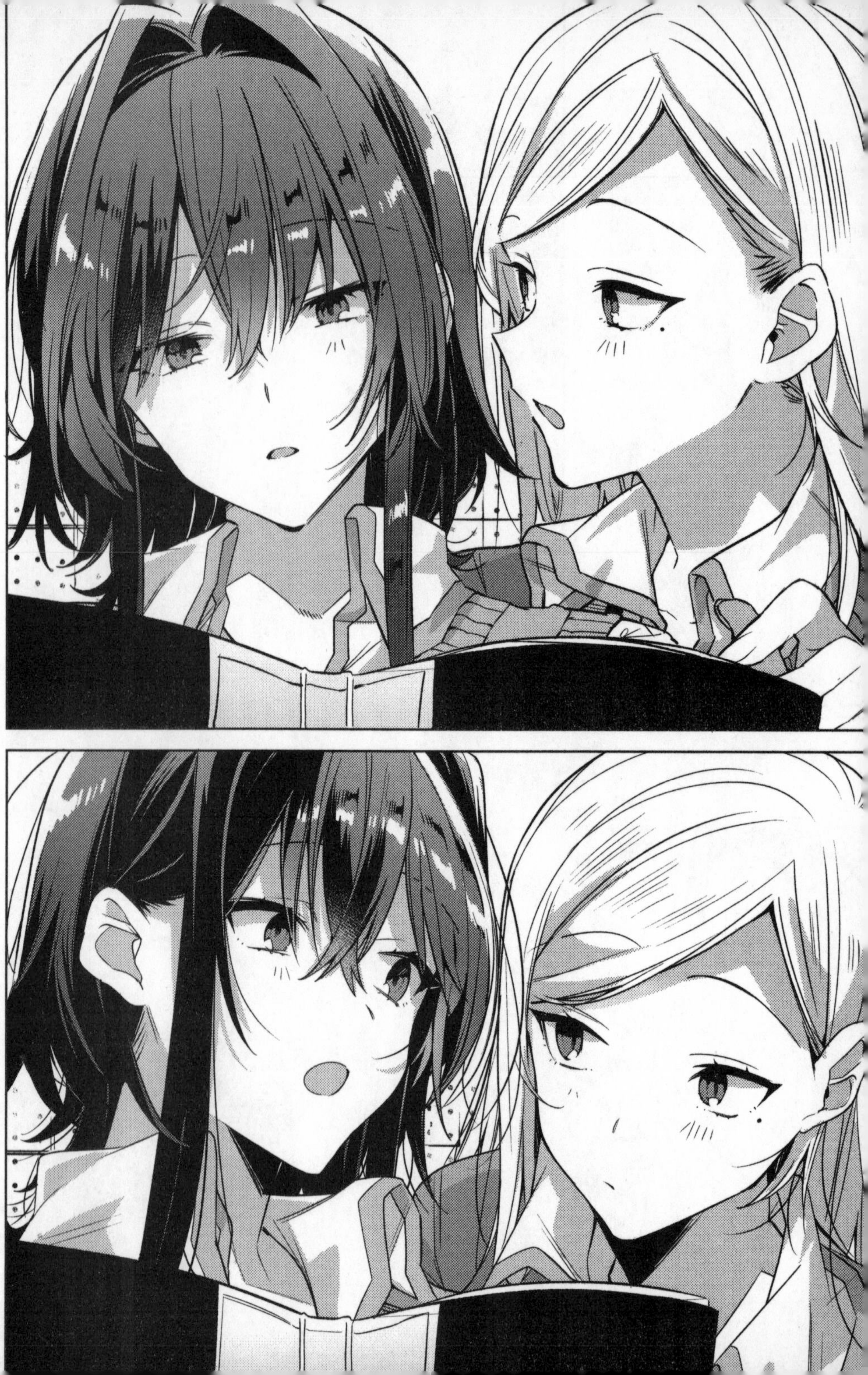

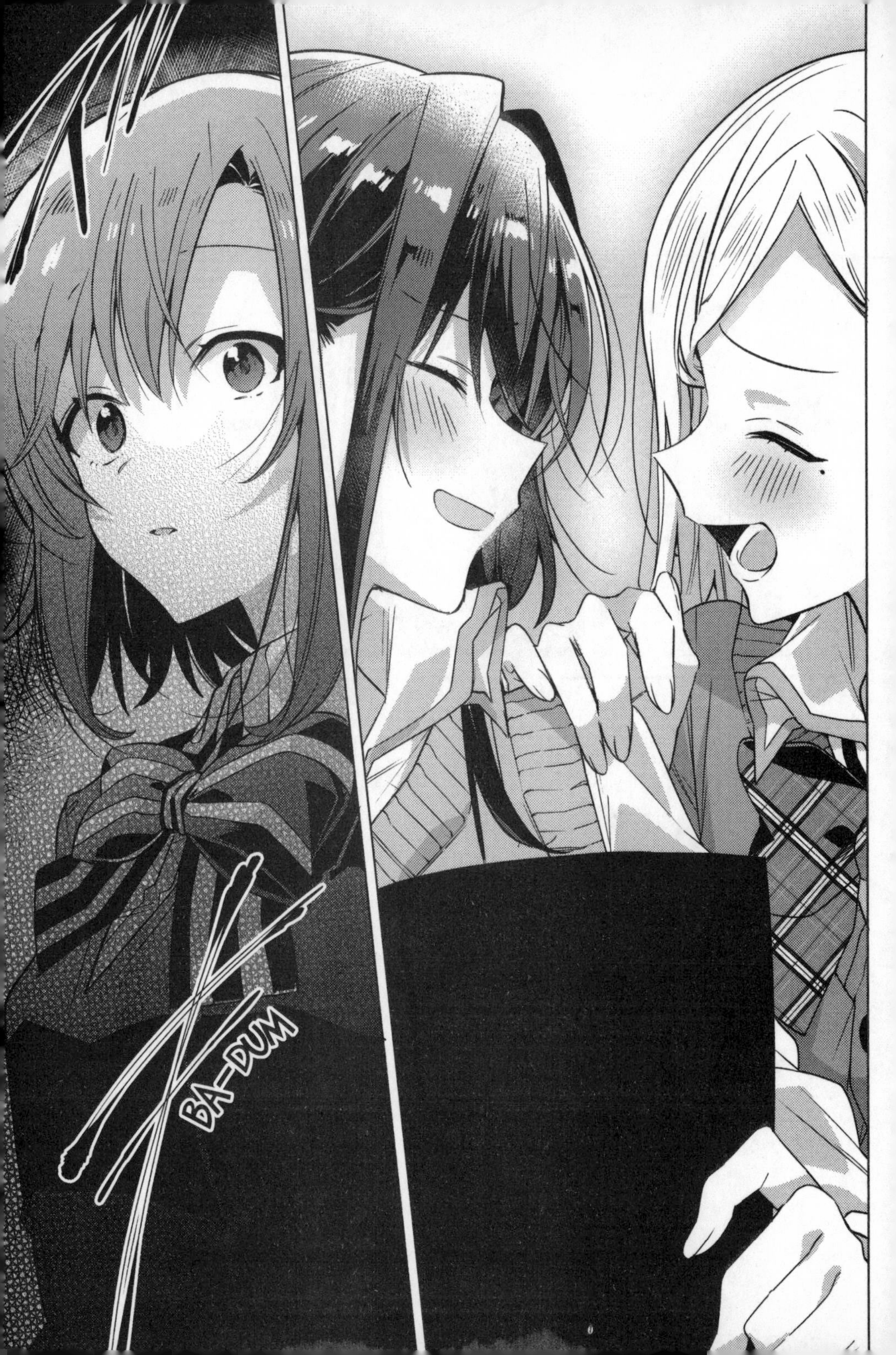
BA-DUM

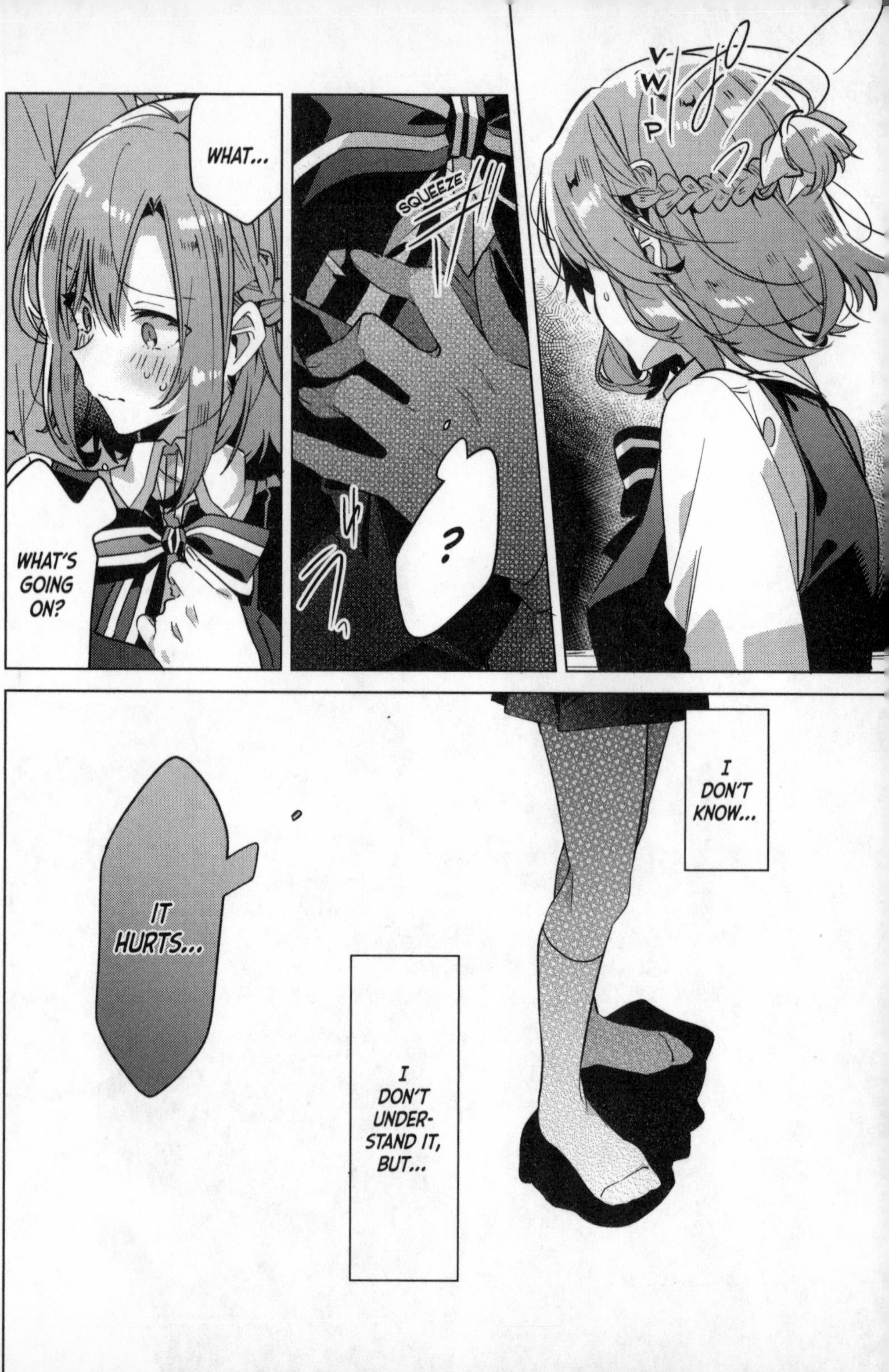
VWIP
SQUEEZE
?
WHAT...
WHAT'S GOING ON?
I DON'T KNOW...
I DON'T UNDER-STAND IT, BUT...
IT HURTS...

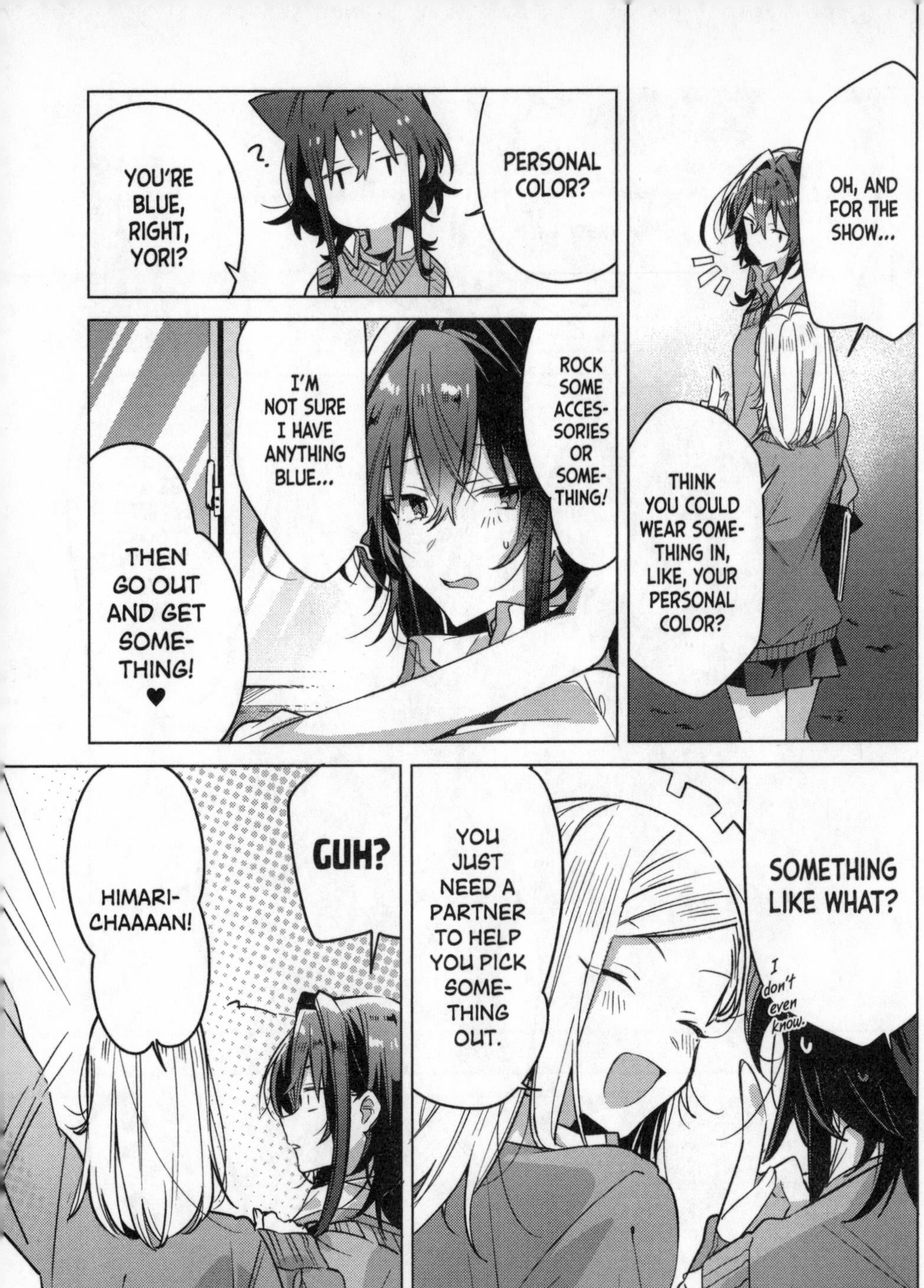
OH, AND FOR THE SHOW...
THINK YOU COULD WEAR SOME-THING IN, LIKE, YOUR PERSONAL COLOR?
PERSONAL COLOR?
YOU'RE BLUE, RIGHT, YORI?
ROCK SOME ACCES-SORIES OR SOME-THING!
I'M NOT SURE I HAVE ANYTHING BLUE...
THEN GO OUT AND GET SOME-THING! ♥
SOMETHING LIKE WHAT?
I don't even know.
YOU JUST NEED A PARTNER TO HELP YOU PICK SOME-THING OUT.
GUH?
HIMARI-CHAAAAN!

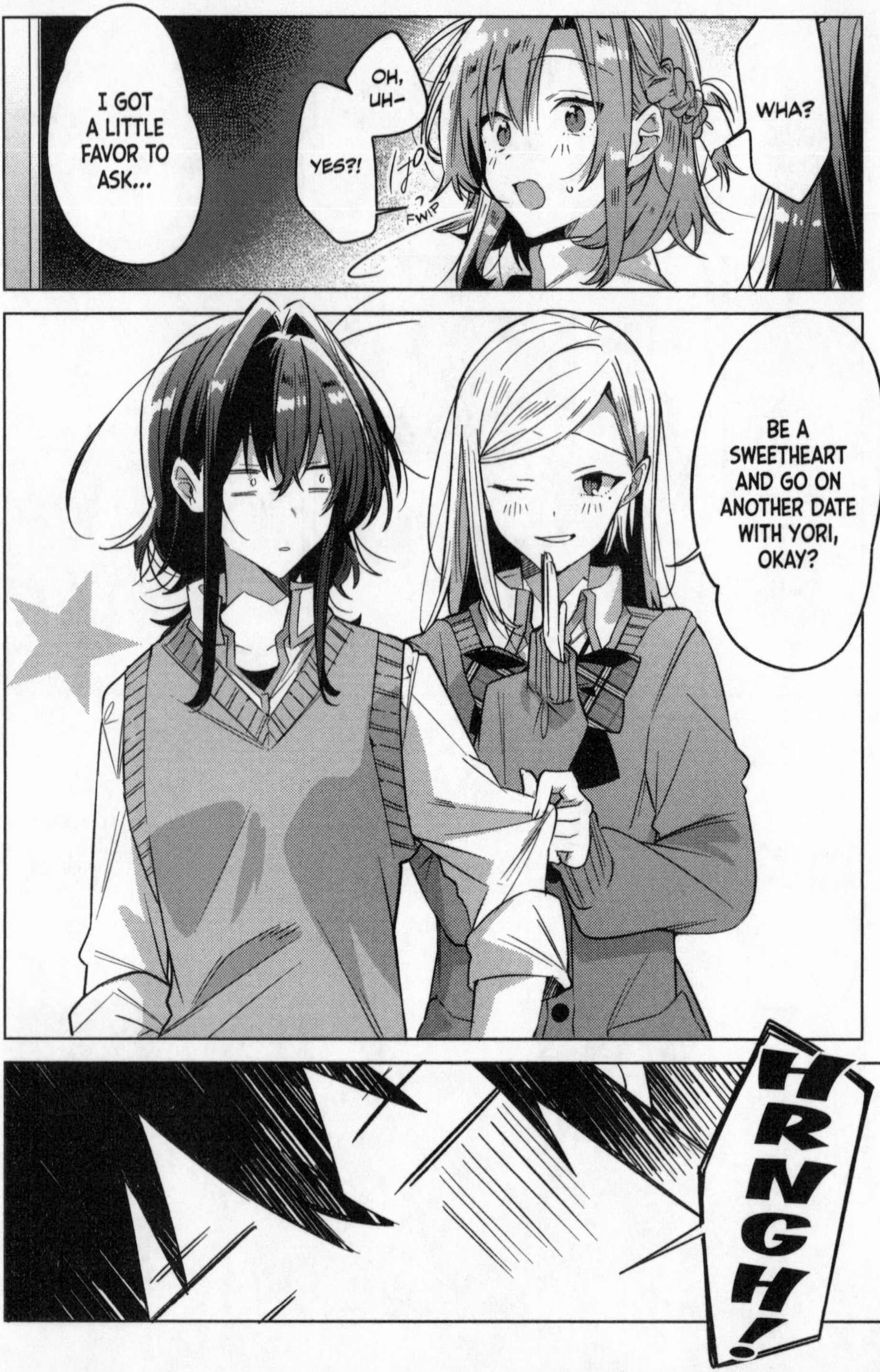
WHA?
OH, UH-
YES?!
FWIP
I GOT A LITTLE FAVOR TO ASK...
BE A SWEETHEART AND GO ON ANOTHER DATE WITH YORI, OKAY?
HRNGH!

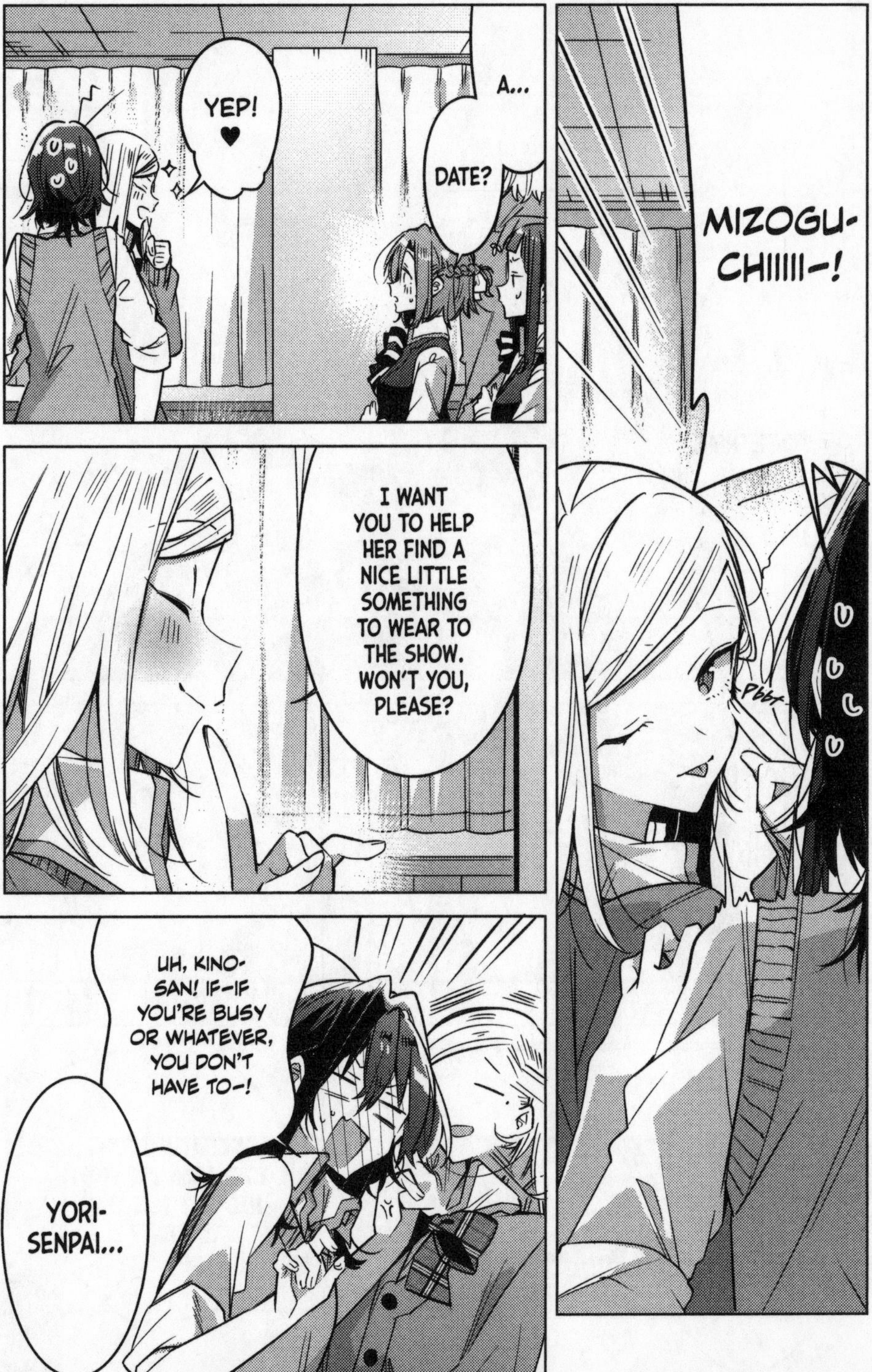
MIZOGU-CHIIIIII—!
Pbbt
A... DATE?
YEP! ♥
I WANT YOU TO HELP HER FIND A NICE LITTLE SOMETHING TO WEAR TO THE SHOW. WON'T YOU, PLEASE?
UH, KINO-SAN! IF—IF YOU'RE BUSY OR WHATEVER, YOU DON'T HAVE TO—!
YORI-SENPAI...

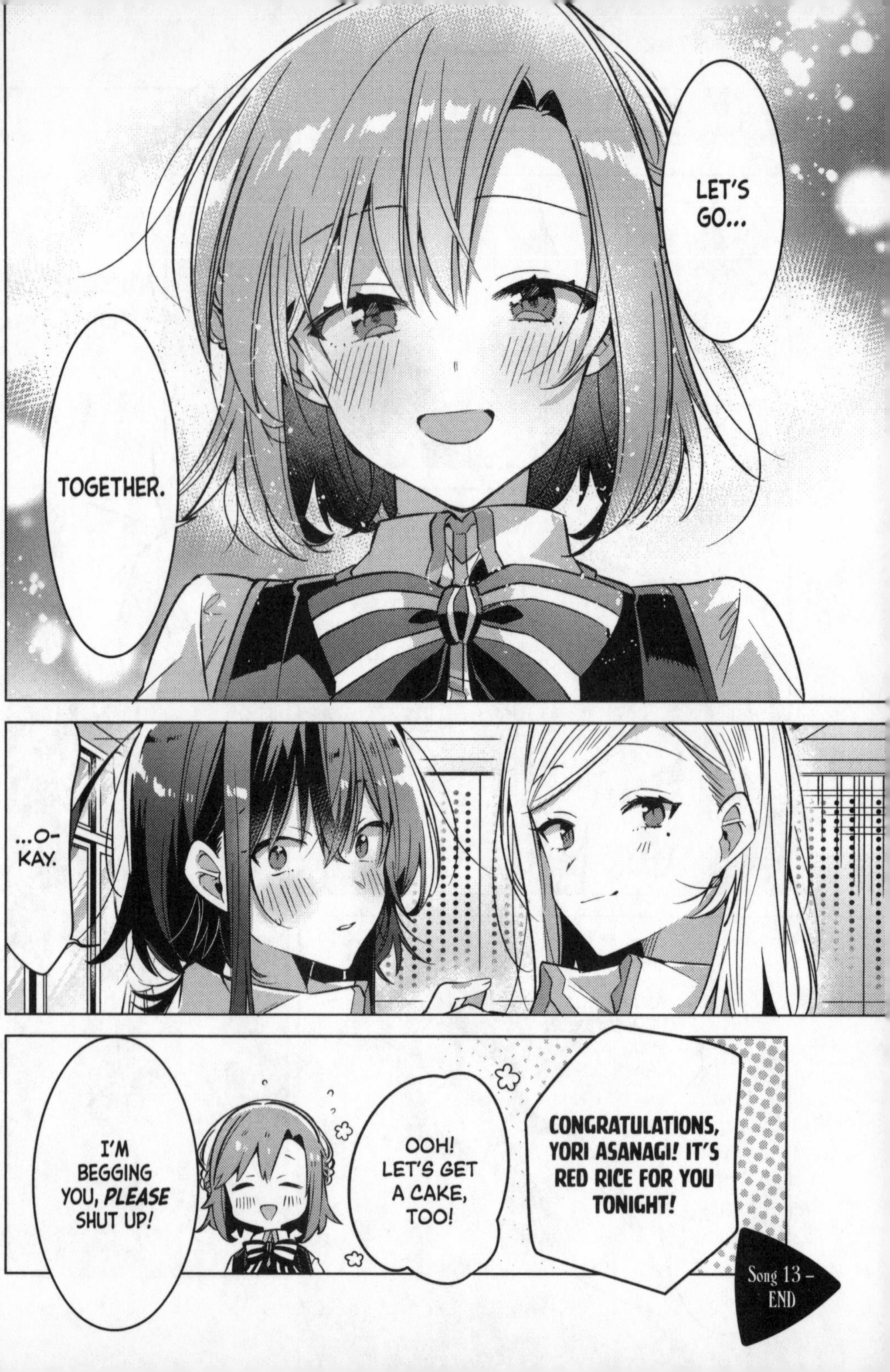
LET'S GO...
TOGETHER.
...O-KAY.
CONGRATULATIONS, YORI ASANAGI! IT'S RED RICE FOR YOU TONIGHT!
OOH! LET'S GET A CAKE, TOO!
I'M BEGGING YOU, *PLEASE* SHUT UP!
Song 13 – END

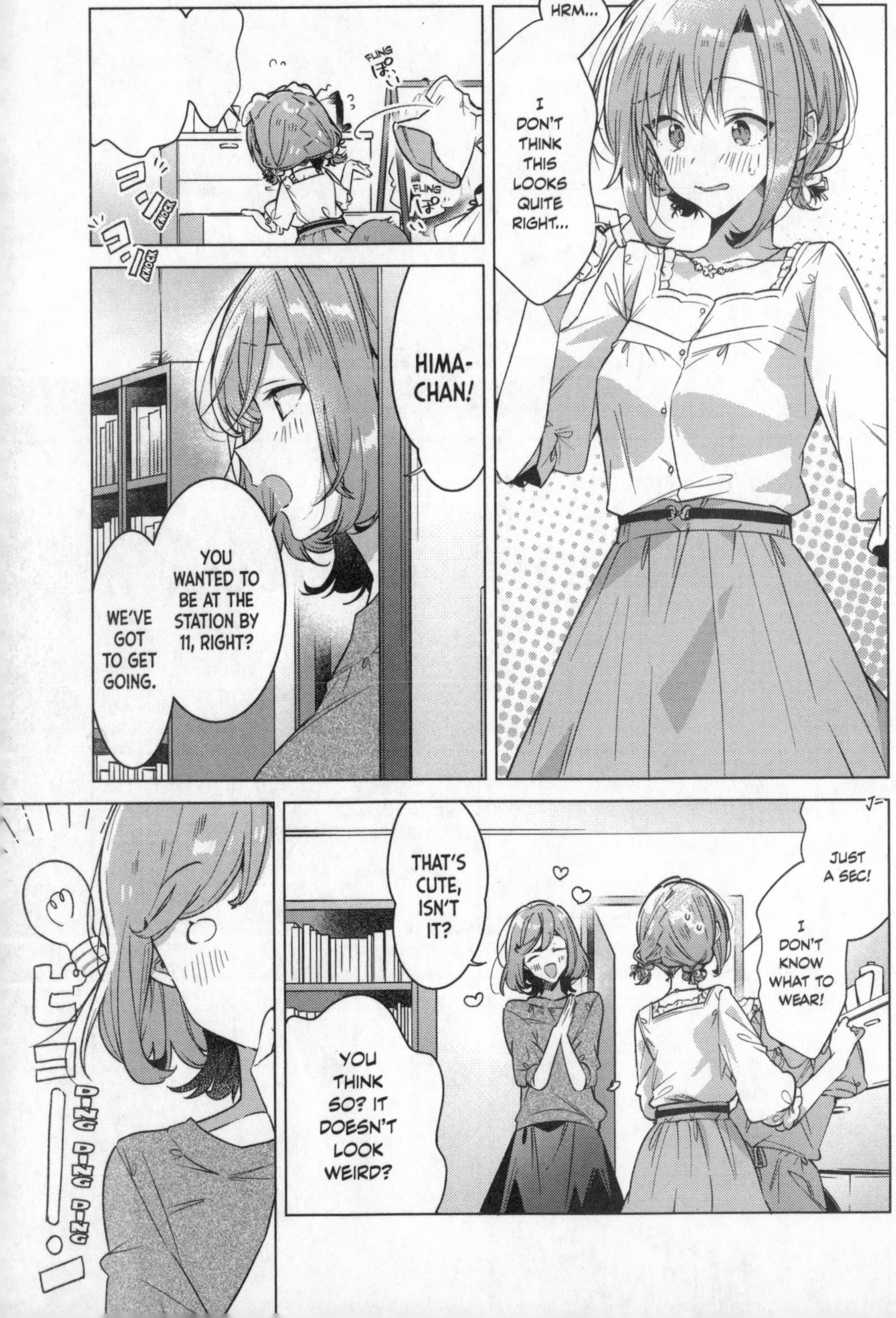
HRM...
I DON'T THINK THIS LOOKS QUITE RIGHT...
FLING ぽい
FLING ぽい
KNOCK
KNOCK
HIMA-CHAN!
YOU WANTED TO BE AT THE STATION BY 11, RIGHT?
WE'VE GOT TO GET GOING.
JUST A SEC!
I DON'T KNOW WHAT TO WEAR!
THAT'S CUTE, ISN'T IT?
YOU THINK SO? IT DOESN'T LOOK WEIRD?
DING DING DING

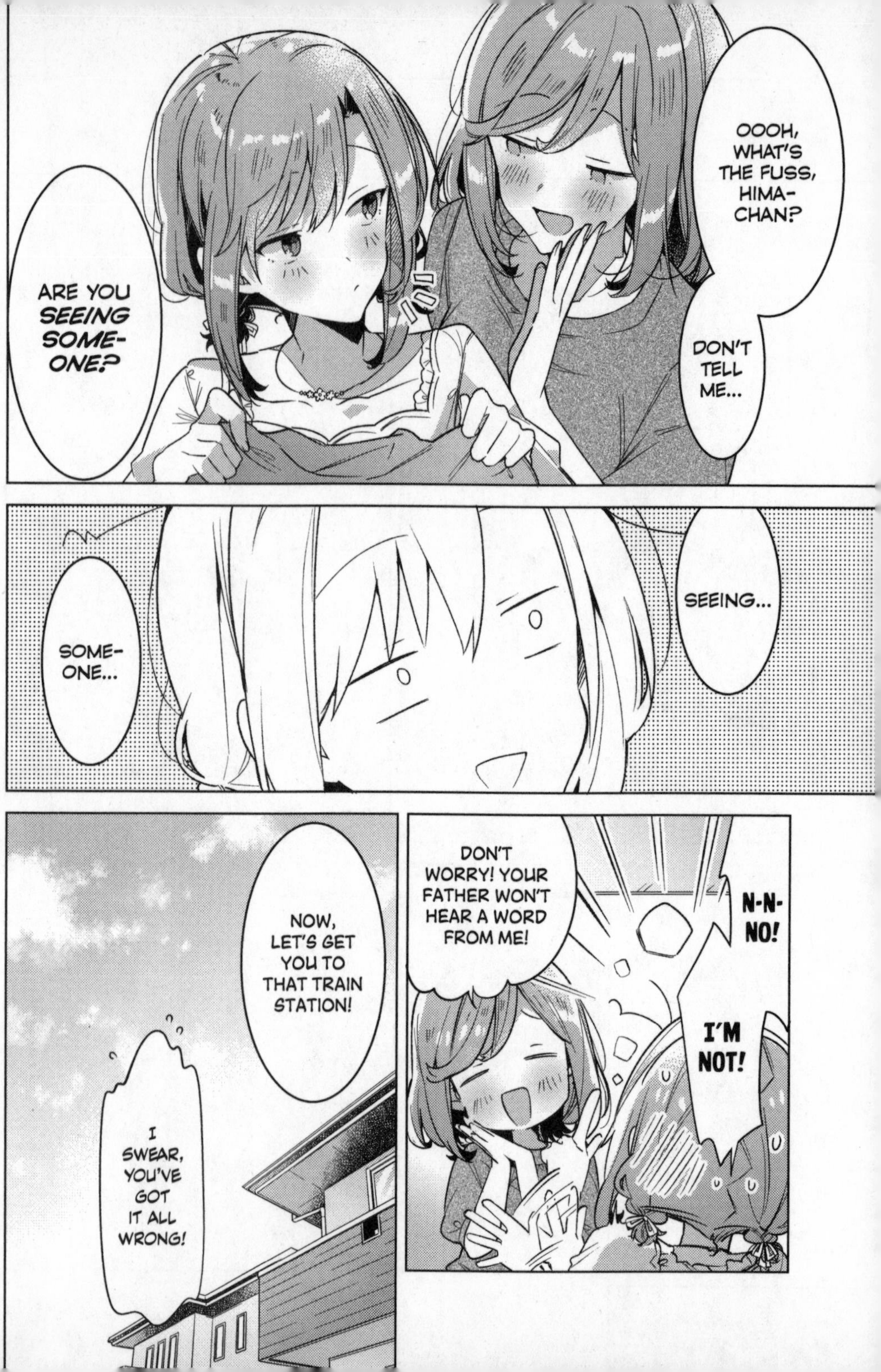
OOOH, WHAT'S THE FUSS, HIMA-CHAN?
DON'T TELL ME...
ARE YOU SEEING SOME-ONE?
SEEING...
SOME-ONE...
N-N-NO!
I'M NOT!
DON'T WORRY! YOUR FATHER WON'T HEAR A WORD FROM ME!
NOW, LET'S GET YOU TO THAT TRAIN STATION!
I SWEAR, YOU'VE GOT IT ALL WRONG!

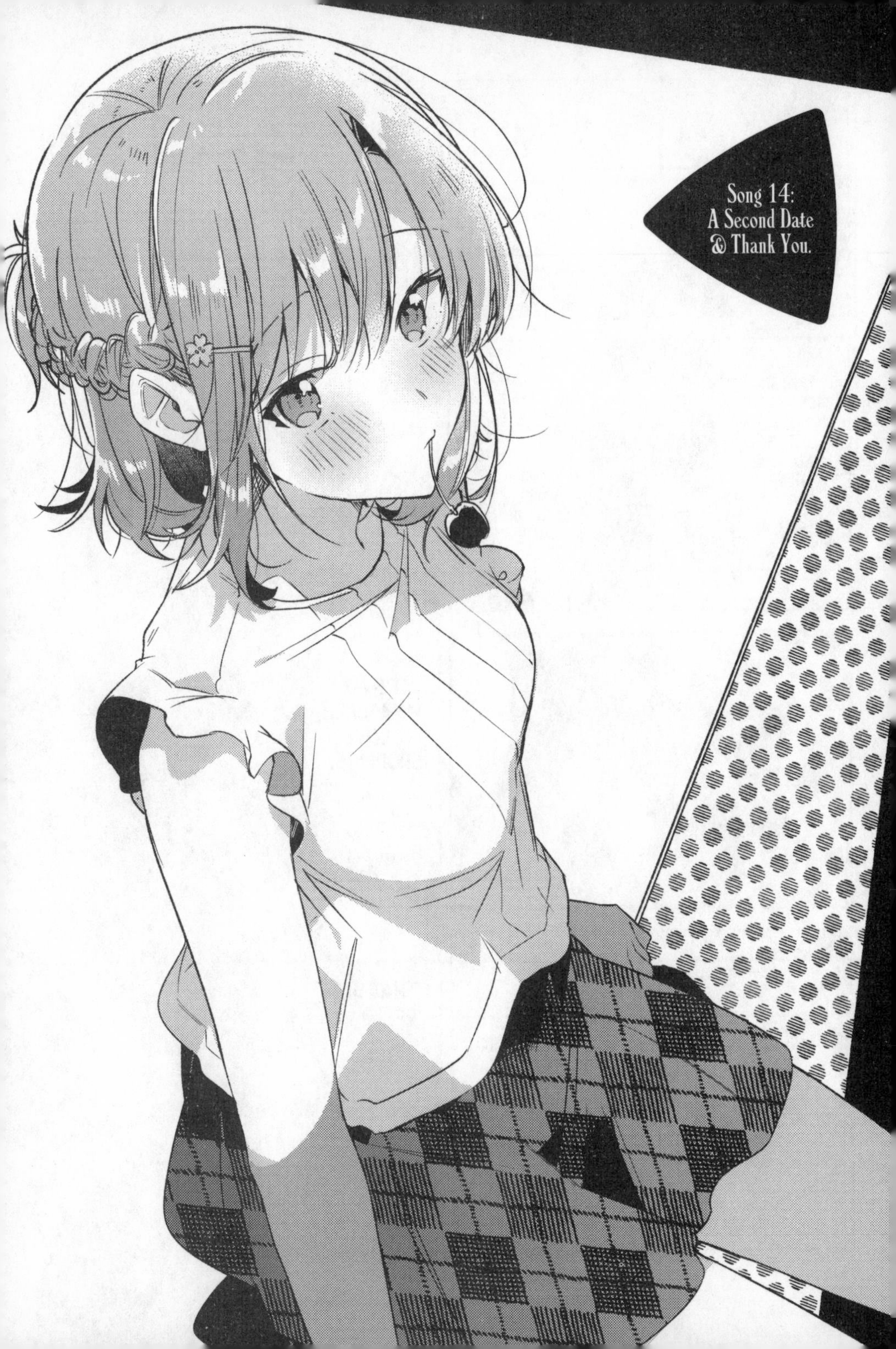
Song 14:
A Second Date
& Thank You.

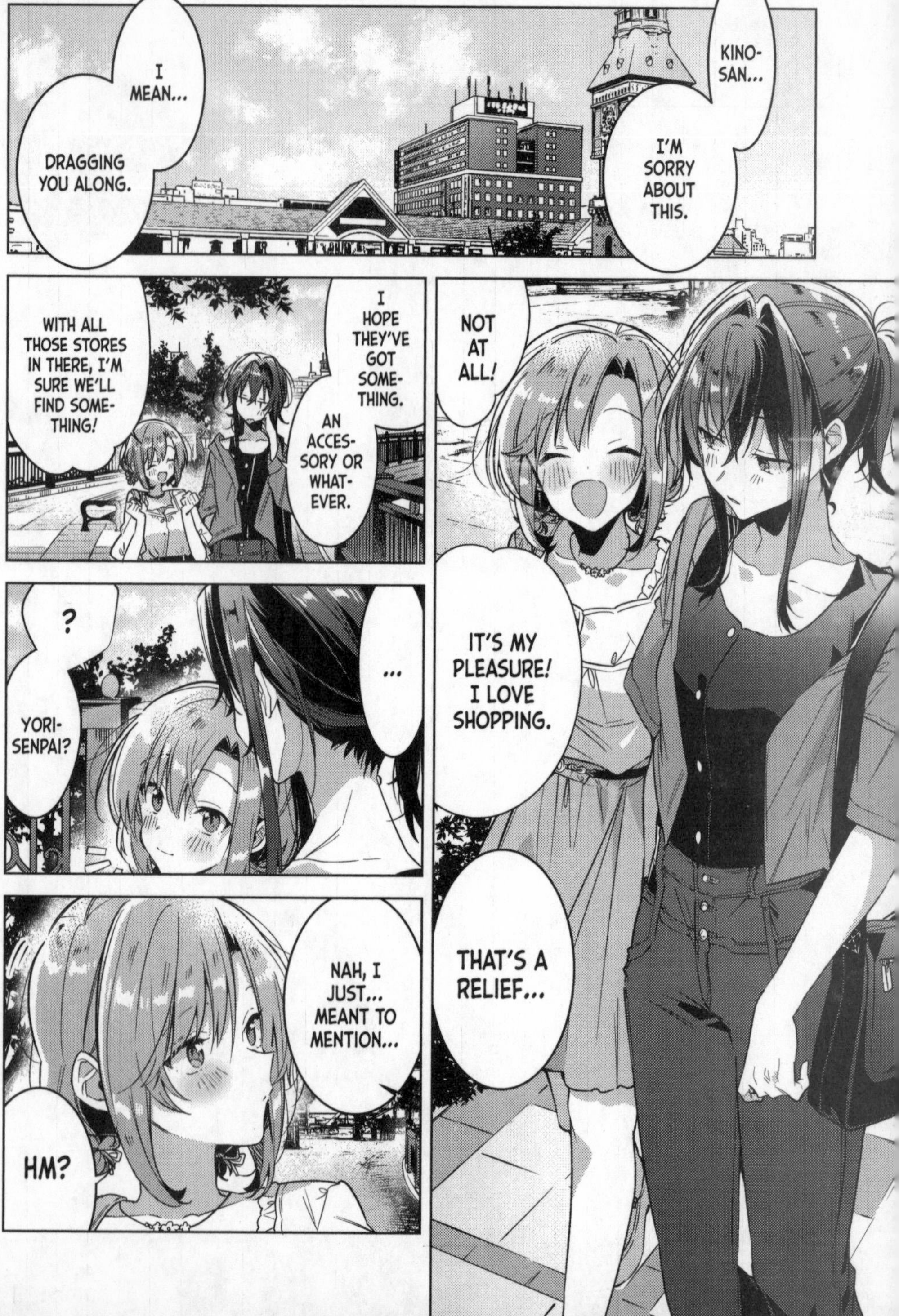
KINO-SAN...
I'M SORRY ABOUT THIS.
I MEAN...
DRAGGING YOU ALONG.
NOT AT ALL!
IT'S MY PLEASURE! I LOVE SHOPPING.
THAT'S A RELIEF...
I HOPE THEY'VE GOT SOME-THING.
AN ACCES-SORY OR WHAT-EVER.
WITH ALL THOSE STORES IN THERE, I'M SURE WE'LL FIND SOME-THING!
...
?
YORI-SENPAI?
NAH, I JUST... MEANT TO MENTION...
HM?

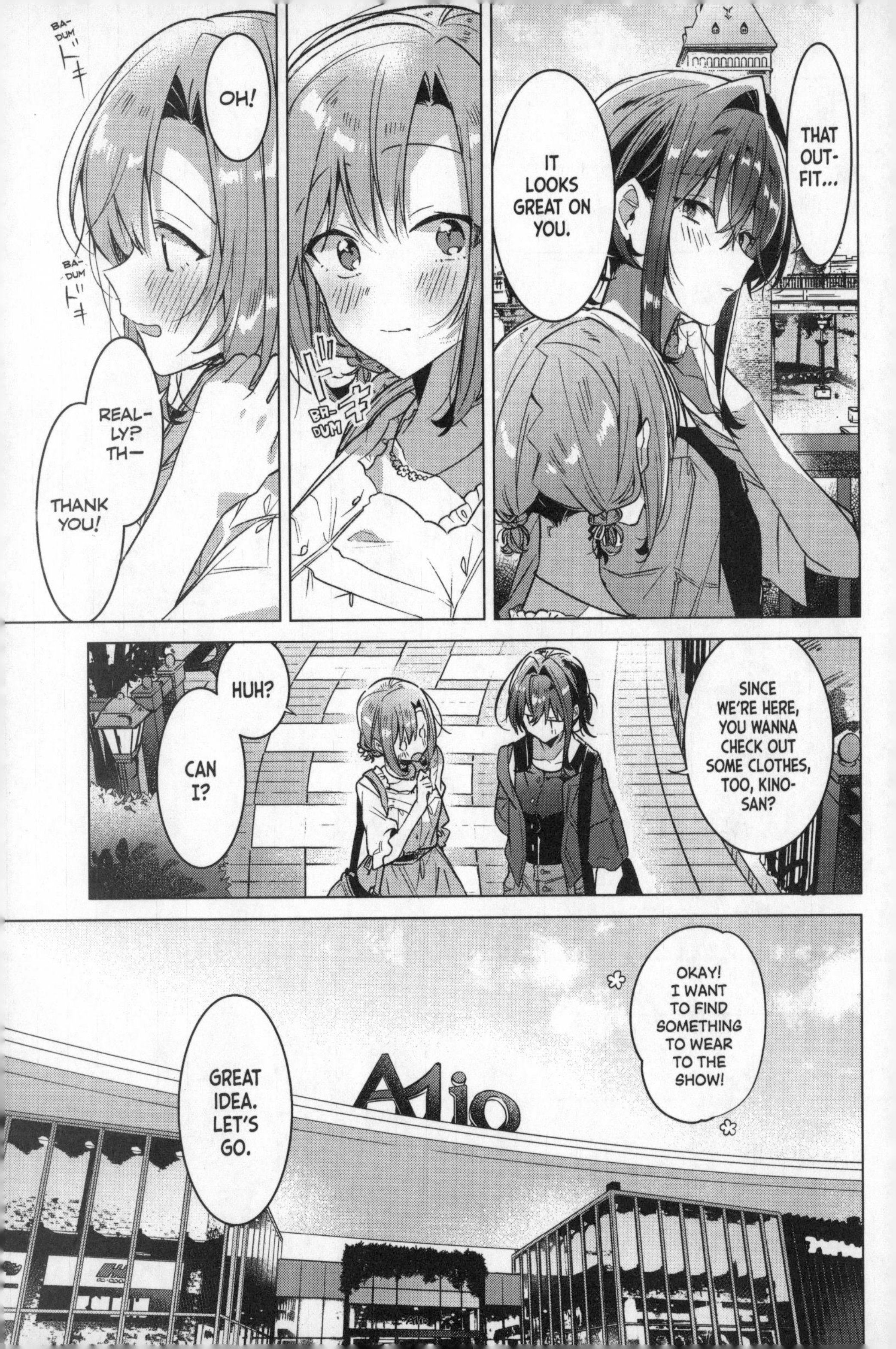
THAT OUT-FIT...
IT LOOKS GREAT ON YOU.
BA-DUM
OH!
BA-DUM
BA-DUM
REAL-LY? TH—
THANK YOU!
SINCE WE'RE HERE, YOU WANNA CHECK OUT SOME CLOTHES, TOO, KINO-SAN?
HUH?
CAN I?
OKAY! I WANT TO FIND SOMETHING TO WEAR TO THE SHOW!
GREAT IDEA. LET'S GO.

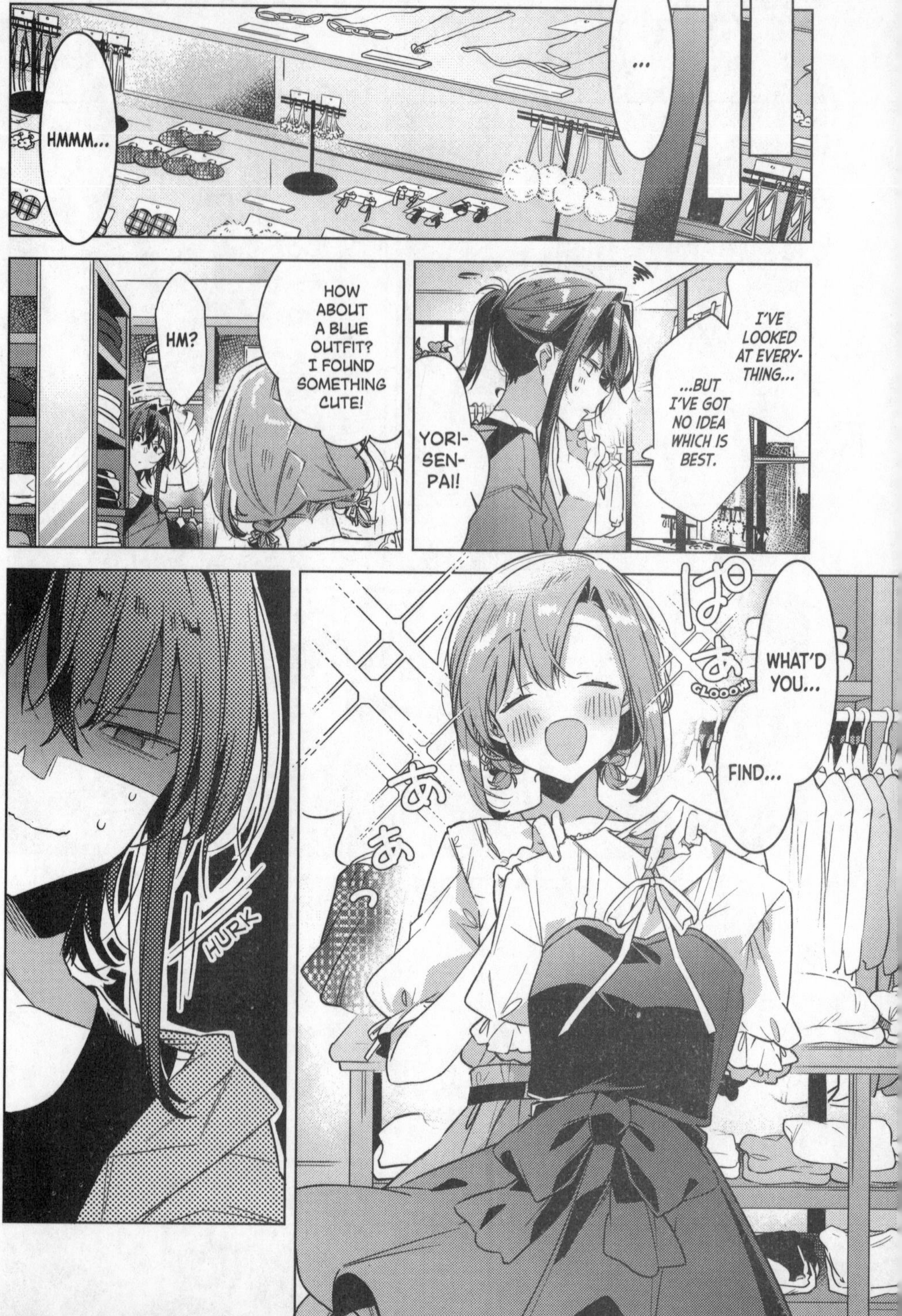
...
HMMM...
I'VE LOOKED AT EVERY-THING...
...BUT I'VE GOT NO IDEA WHICH IS BEST.
YORI-SEN-PAI!
HOW ABOUT A BLUE OUTFIT? I FOUND SOMETHING CUTE!
HM?
ぱぁ
GLOOOW
WHAT'D YOU...
FIND...
あぁっ
HURK

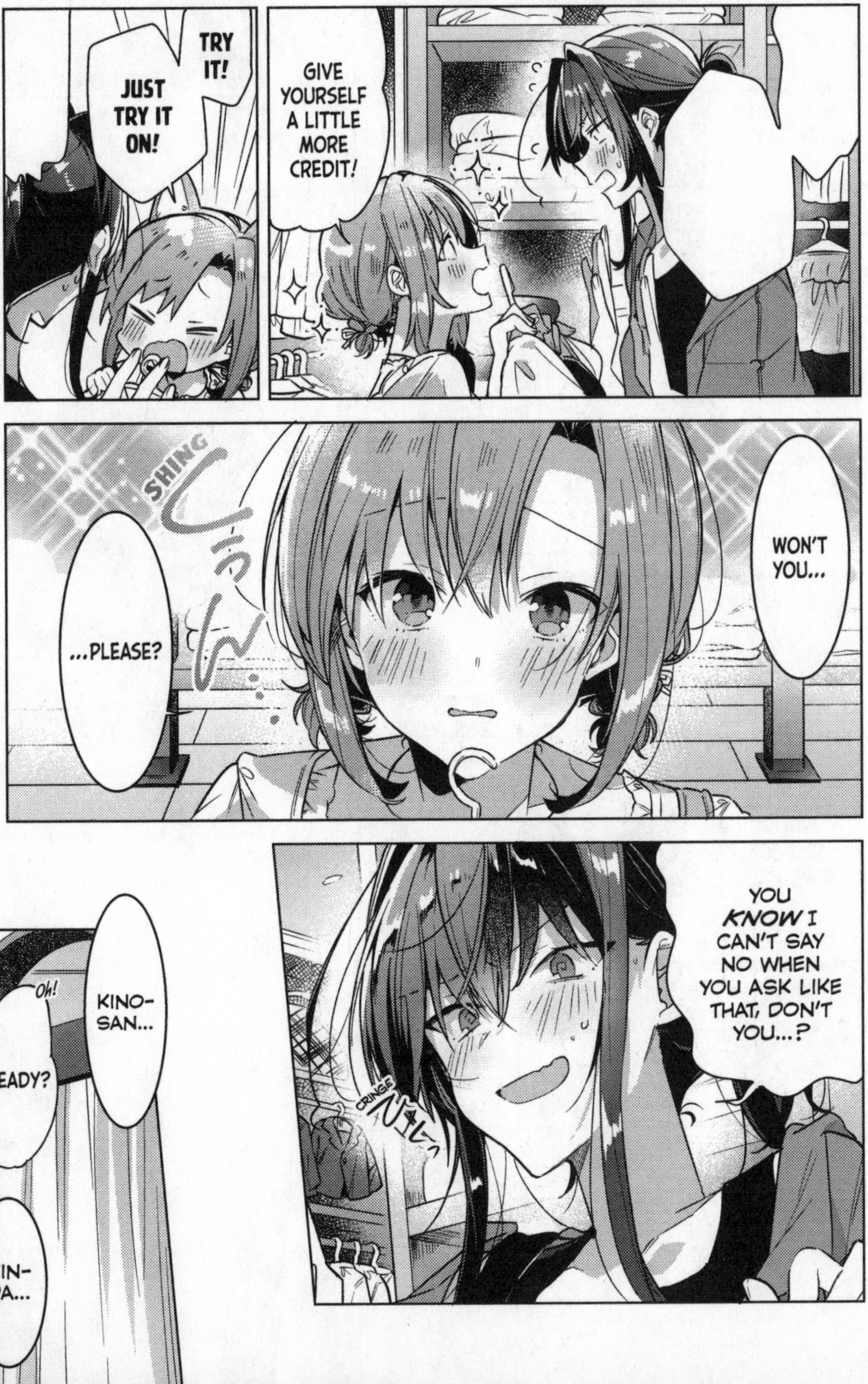
GIVE YOURSELF A LITTLE MORE CREDIT!
TRY IT!
JUST TRY IT ON!
WON'T YOU...
SHING
...PLEASE?
YOU *KNOW* I CAN'T SAY NO WHEN YOU ASK LIKE THAT, DON'T YOU...?
CRINGE
KINO-SAN...
Oh!
READY?
KIN-DA...

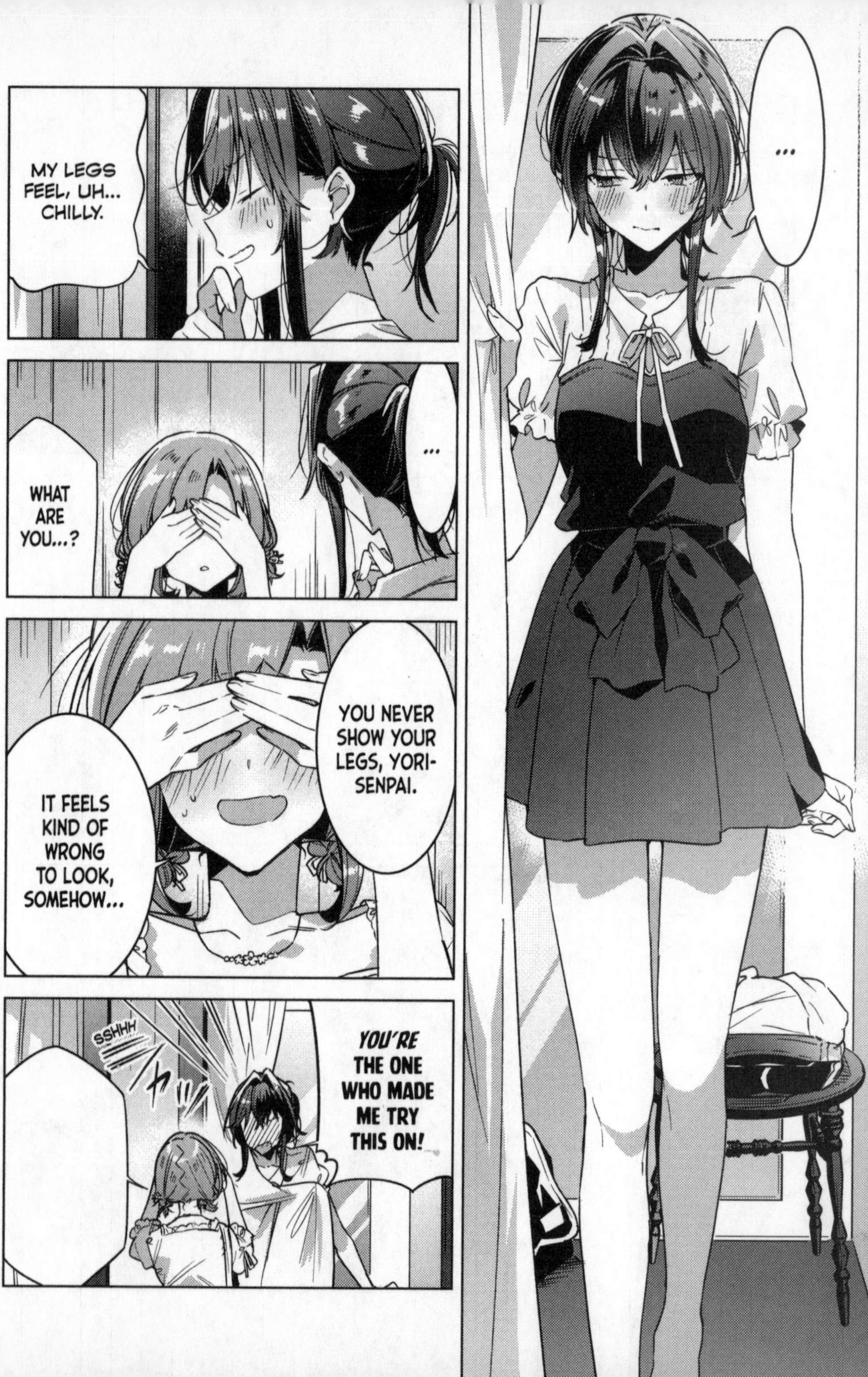
...
MY LEGS FEEL, UH... CHILLY.
...
WHAT ARE YOU...?
YOU NEVER SHOW YOUR LEGS, YORI-SENPAI.
IT FEELS KIND OF WRONG TO LOOK, SOMEHOW...
SSHHH
YOU'RE THE ONE WHO MADE ME TRY THIS ON!

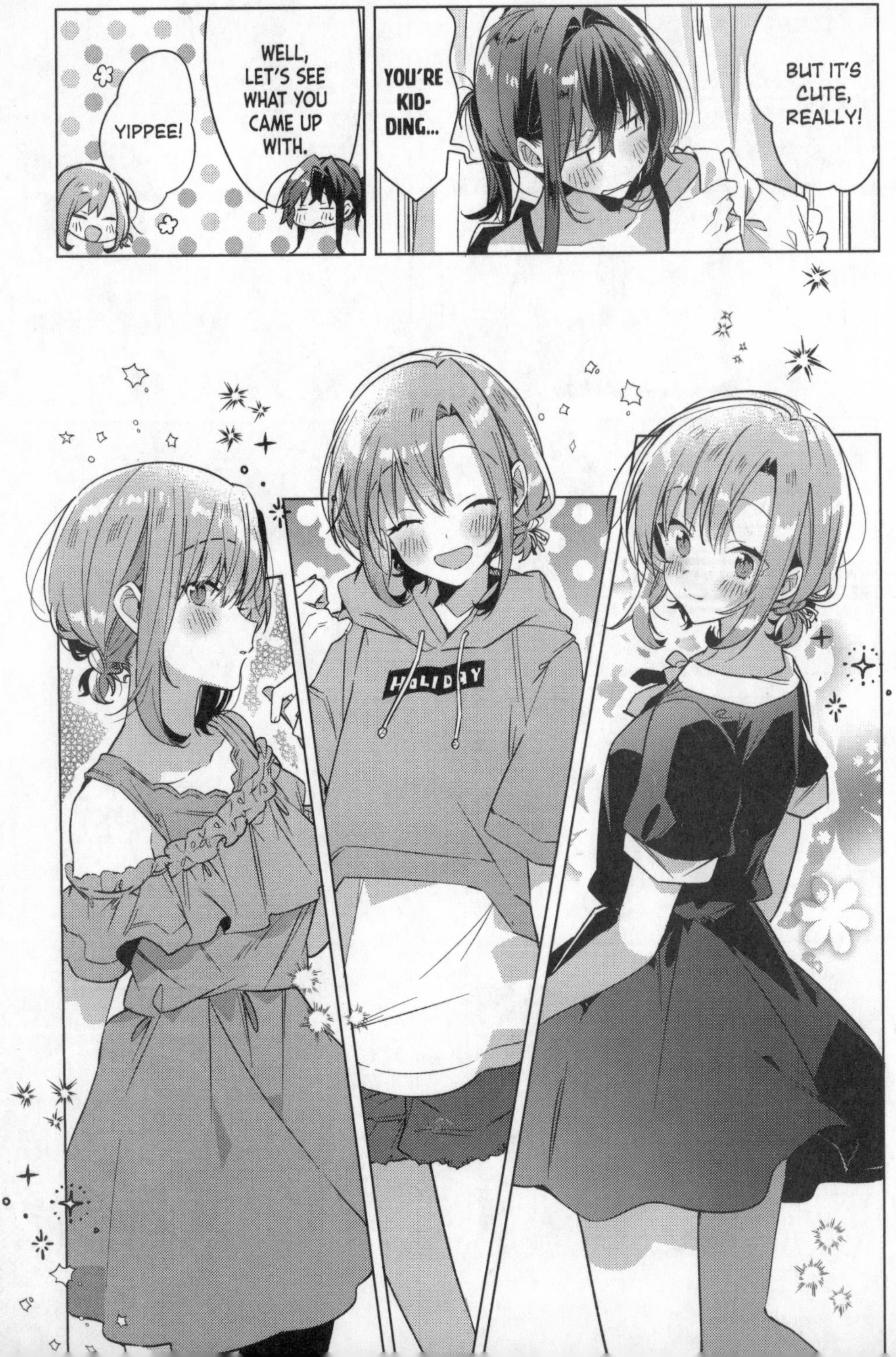

BUT IT'S CUTE, REALLY!
YOU'RE KID-DING...
WELL, LET'S SEE WHAT YOU CAME UP WITH.
YIPPEE!
HOLIDAY

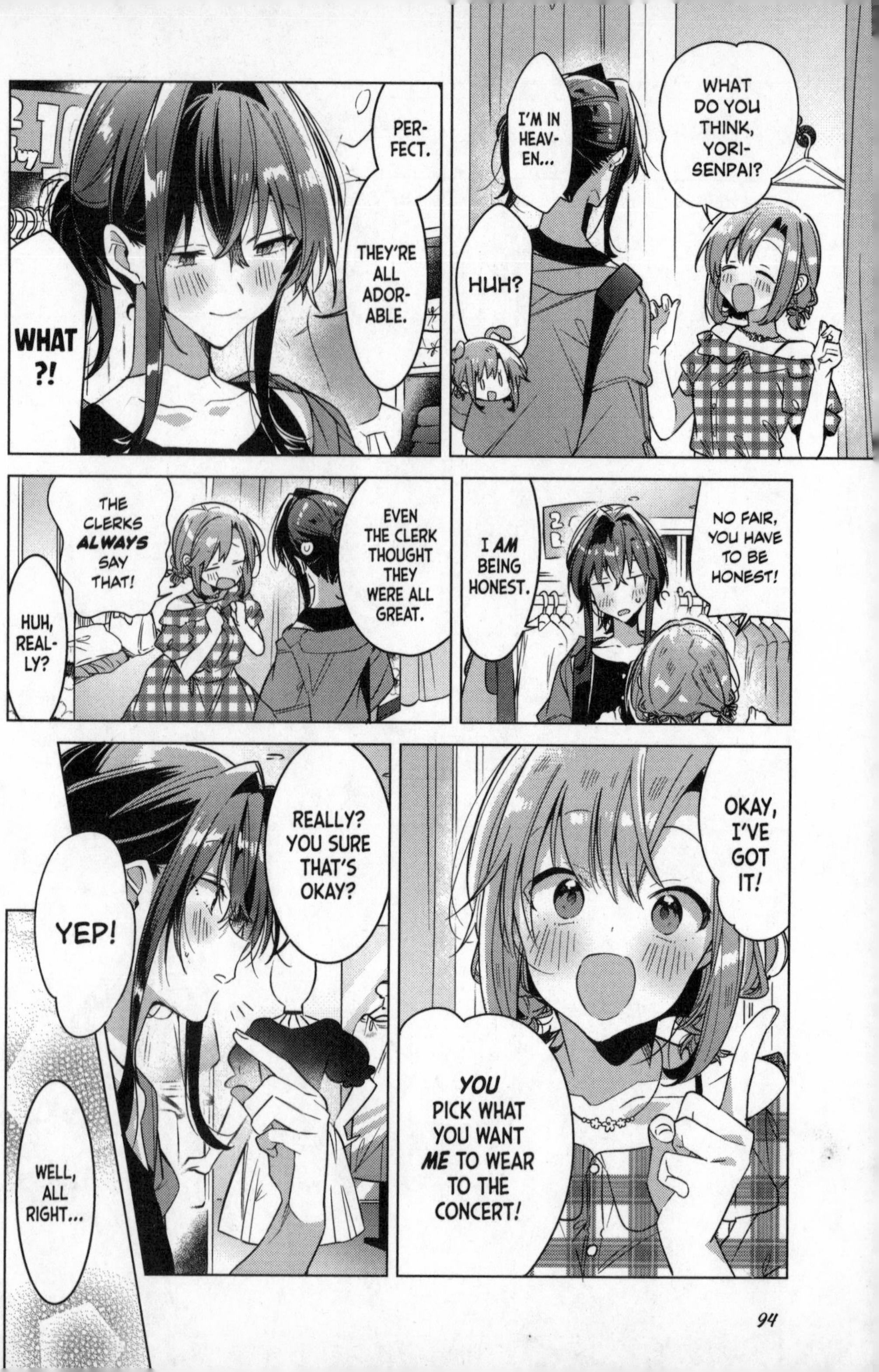
WHAT DO YOU THINK, YORI-SENPAI?
I'M IN HEAVEN...
HUH?
PERFECT.
THEY'RE ALL ADORABLE.
WHAT?!
NO FAIR, YOU HAVE TO BE HONEST!
I *AM* BEING HONEST.
EVEN THE CLERK THOUGHT THEY WERE ALL GREAT.
THE CLERKS *ALWAYS* SAY THAT!
HUH, REALLY?
OKAY, I'VE GOT IT!
YOU PICK WHAT YOU WANT *ME* TO WEAR TO THE CONCERT!
REALLY? YOU SURE THAT'S OKAY?
YEP!
WELL, ALL RIGHT...

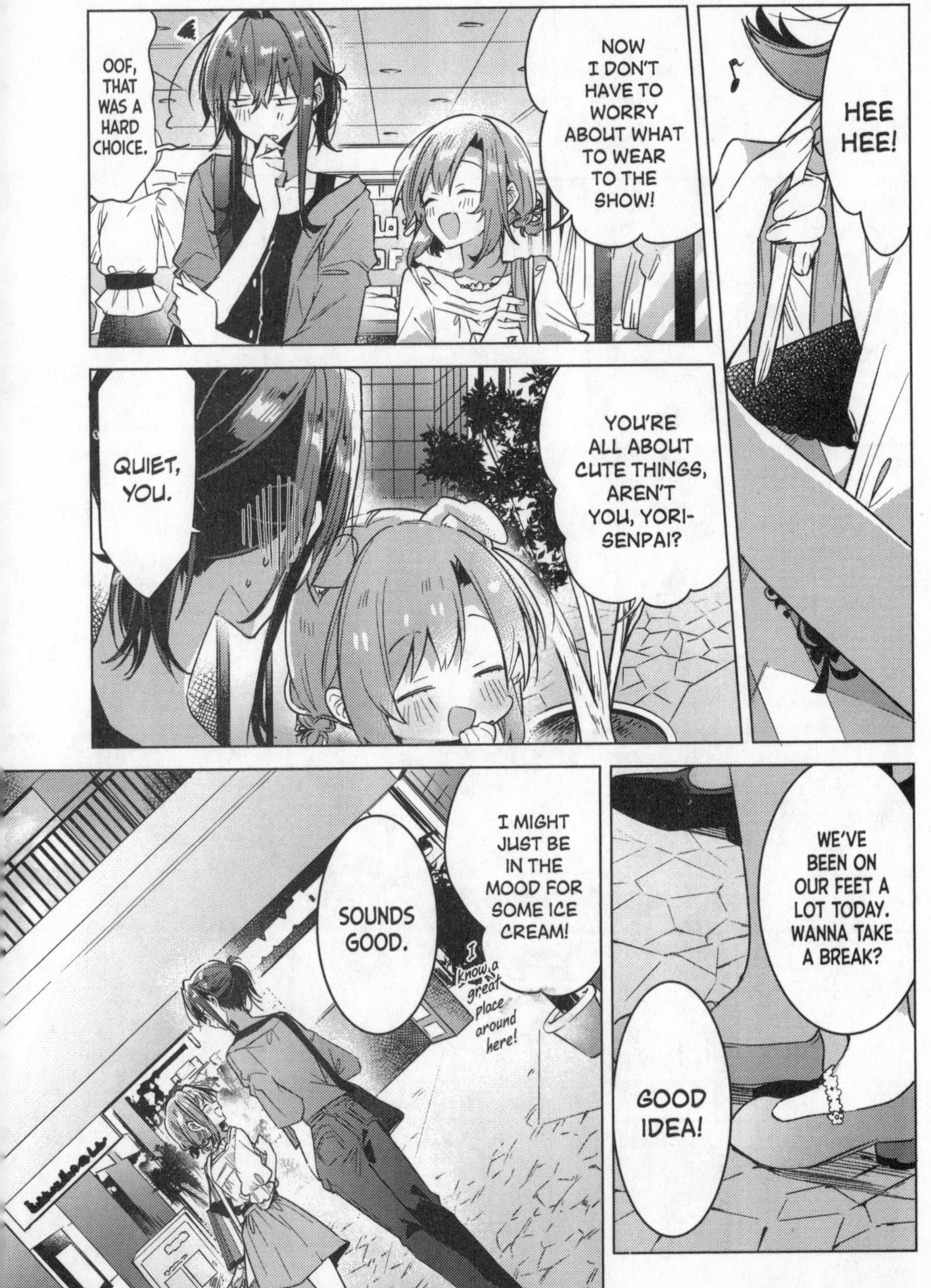
HEE HEE!
NOW I DON'T HAVE TO WORRY ABOUT WHAT TO WEAR TO THE SHOW!
OOF, THAT WAS A HARD CHOICE.
YOU'RE ALL ABOUT CUTE THINGS, AREN'T YOU, YORI-SENPAI?
QUIET, YOU.
WE'VE BEEN ON OUR FEET A LOT TODAY. WANNA TAKE A BREAK?
GOOD IDEA!
I MIGHT JUST BE IN THE MOOD FOR SOME ICE CREAM!
I know a great place around here!
SOUNDS GOOD.

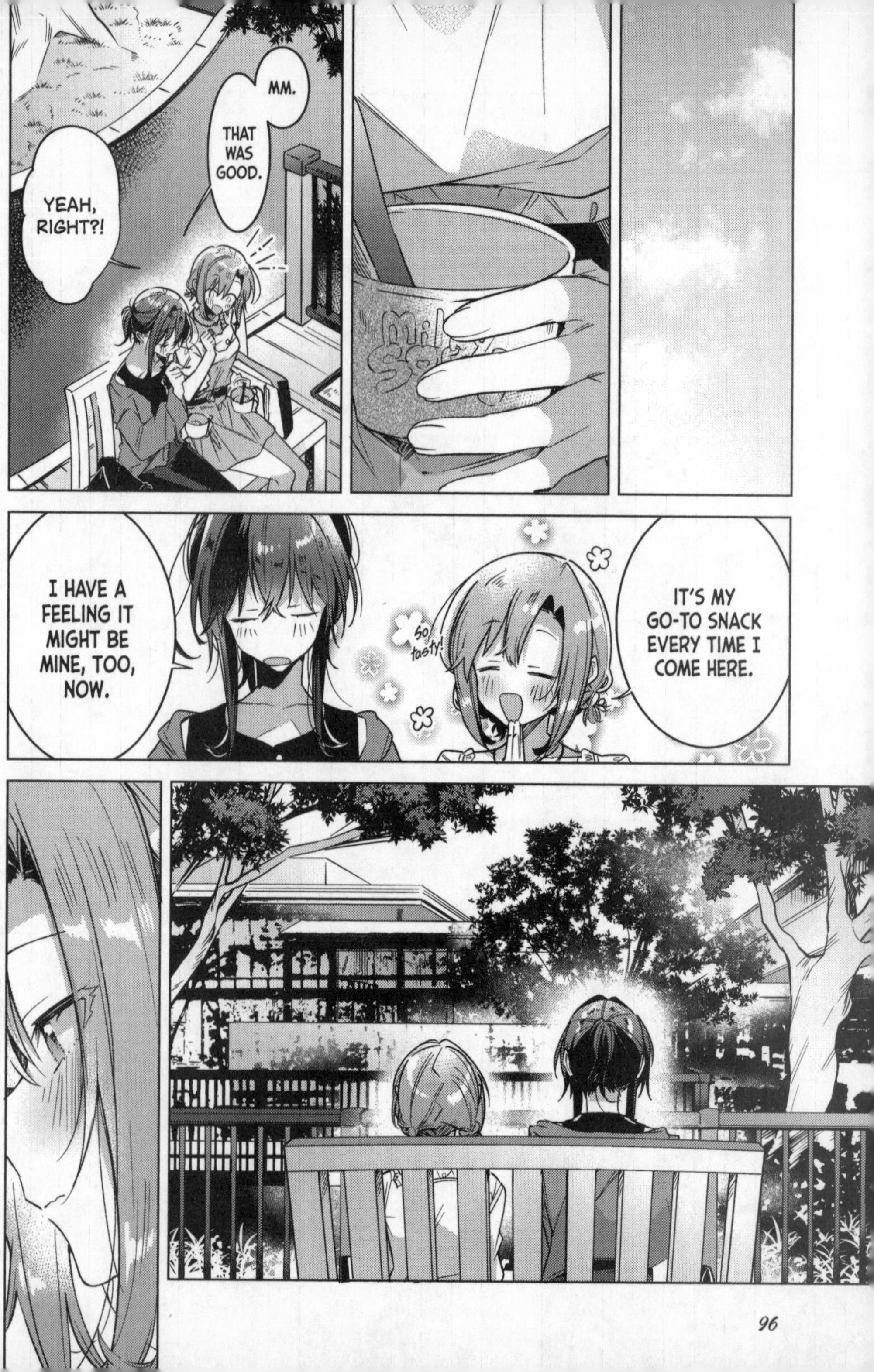
MM.
THAT WAS GOOD.
YEAH, RIGHT?!
IT'S MY GO-TO SNACK EVERY TIME I COME HERE.
So tasty!
I HAVE A FEELING IT MIGHT BE MINE, TOO, NOW.

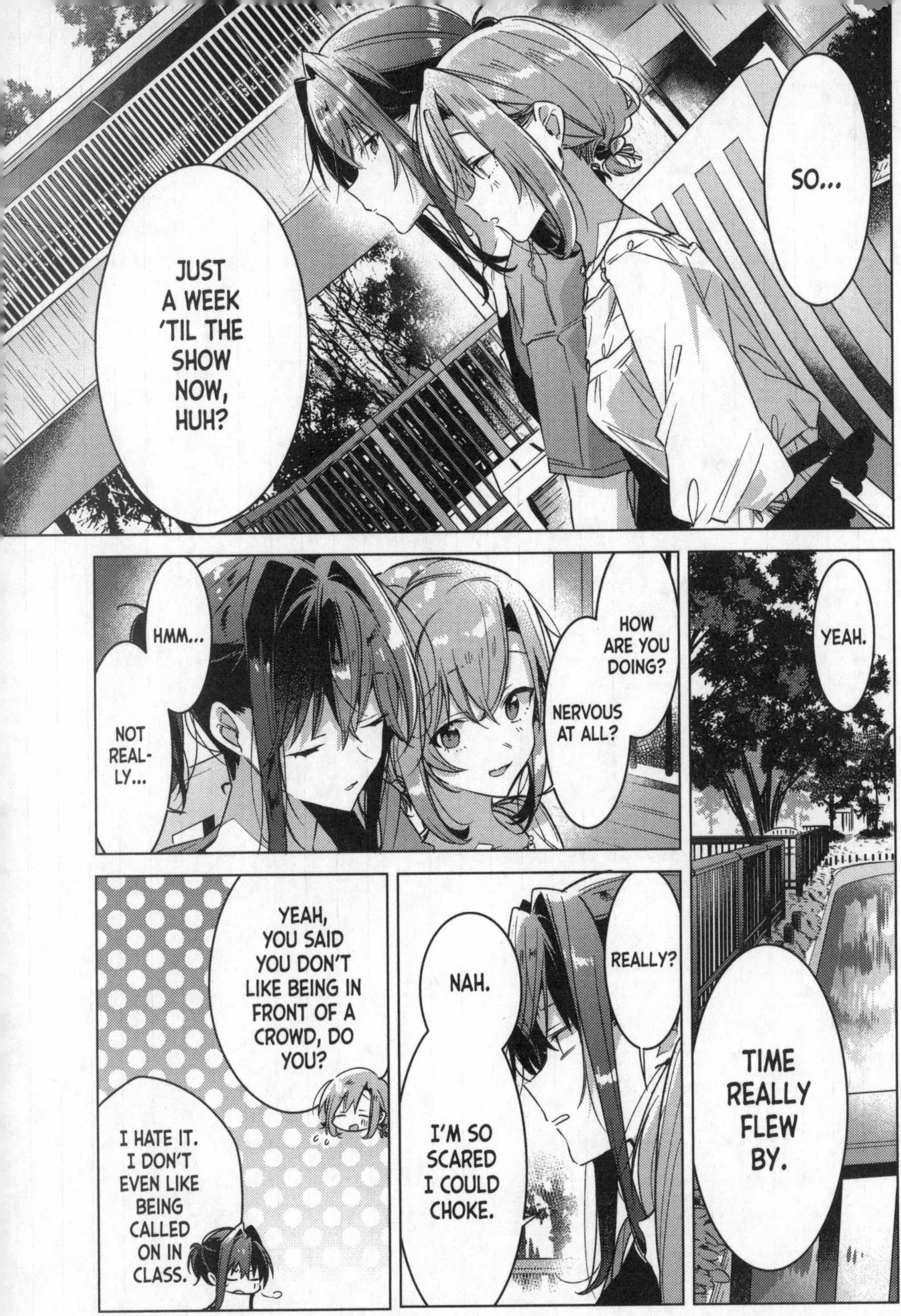
SO...
JUST A WEEK 'TIL THE SHOW NOW, HUH?
YEAH.
TIME REALLY FLEW BY.
HOW ARE YOU DOING?
NERVOUS AT ALL?
HMM...
NOT REALLY...
REALLY?
NAH.
I'M SO SCARED I COULD CHOKE.
YEAH, YOU SAID YOU DON'T LIKE BEING IN FRONT OF A CROWD, DO YOU?
I HATE IT. I DON'T EVEN LIKE BEING CALLED ON IN CLASS.

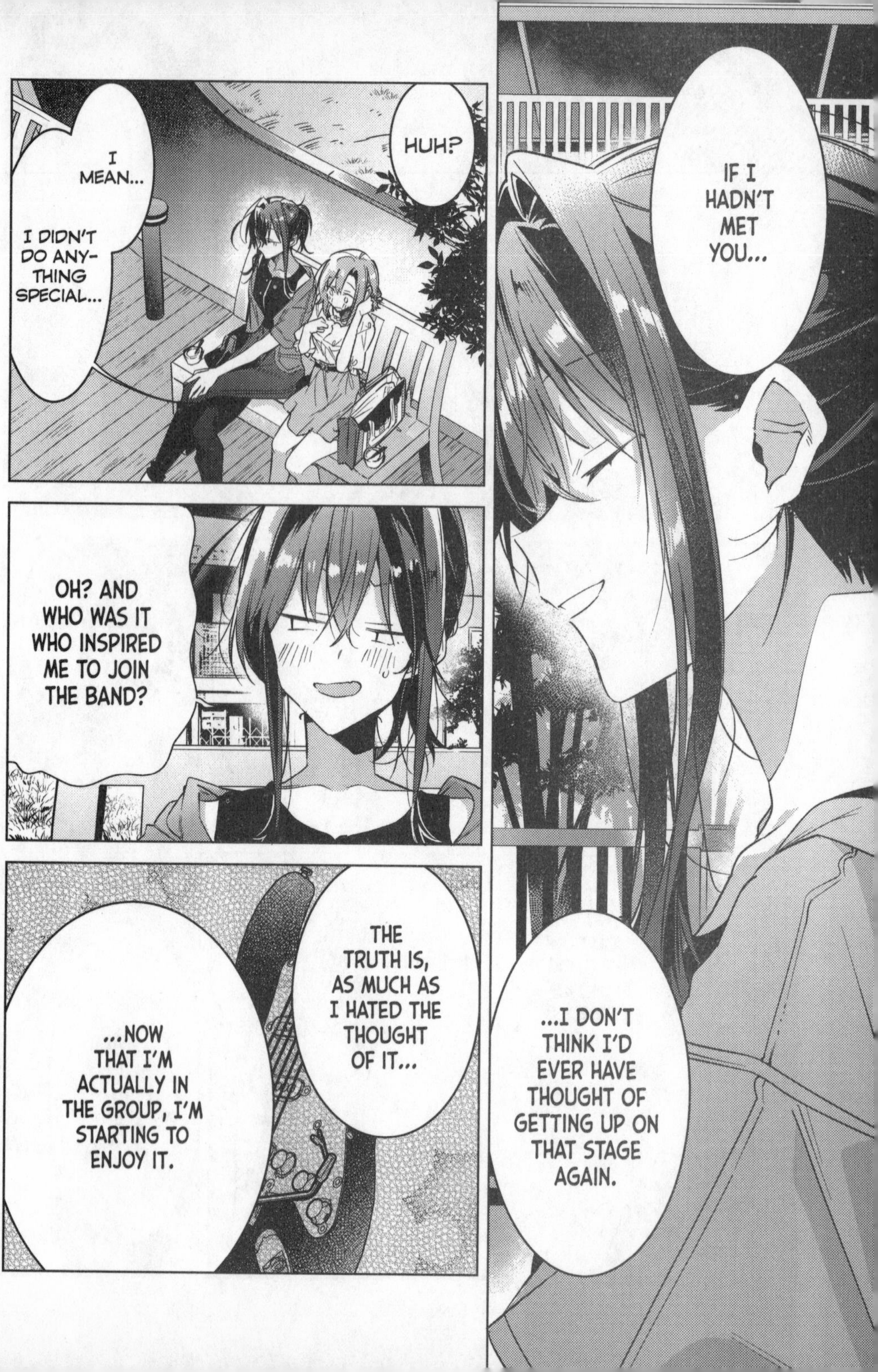
IF I HADN'T MET YOU...
...I DON'T THINK I'D EVER HAVE THOUGHT OF GETTING UP ON THAT STAGE AGAIN.
HUH?
I MEAN...
I DIDN'T DO ANY-THING SPECIAL...
OH? AND WHO WAS IT WHO INSPIRED ME TO JOIN THE BAND?
THE TRUTH IS, AS MUCH AS I HATED THE THOUGHT OF IT...
...NOW THAT I'M ACTUALLY IN THE GROUP, I'M STARTING TO ENJOY IT.

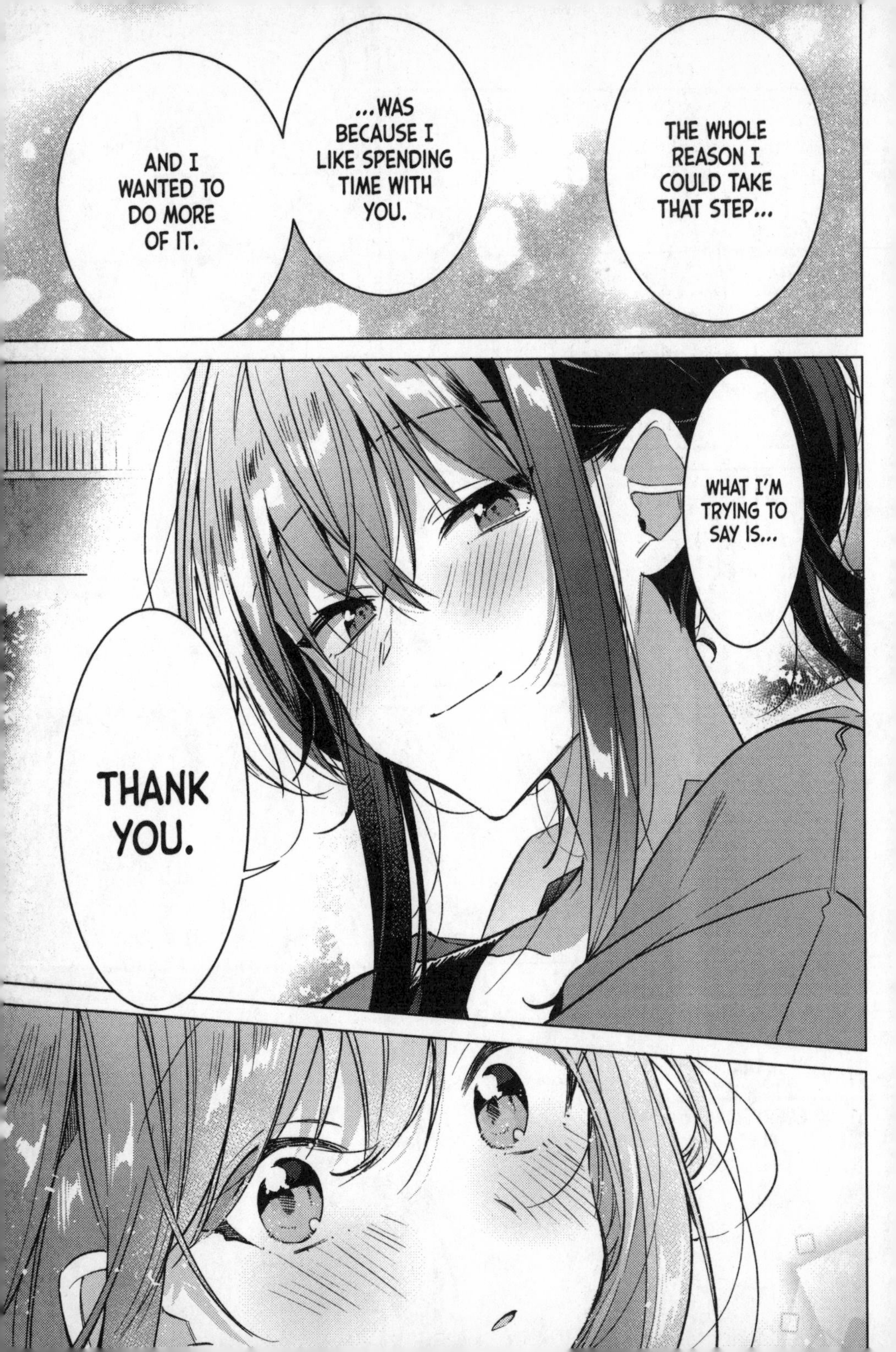
THE WHOLE REASON I COULD TAKE THAT STEP...
...WAS BECAUSE I LIKE SPENDING TIME WITH YOU.
AND I WANTED TO DO MORE OF IT.
WHAT I'M TRYING TO SAY IS...
THANK YOU.

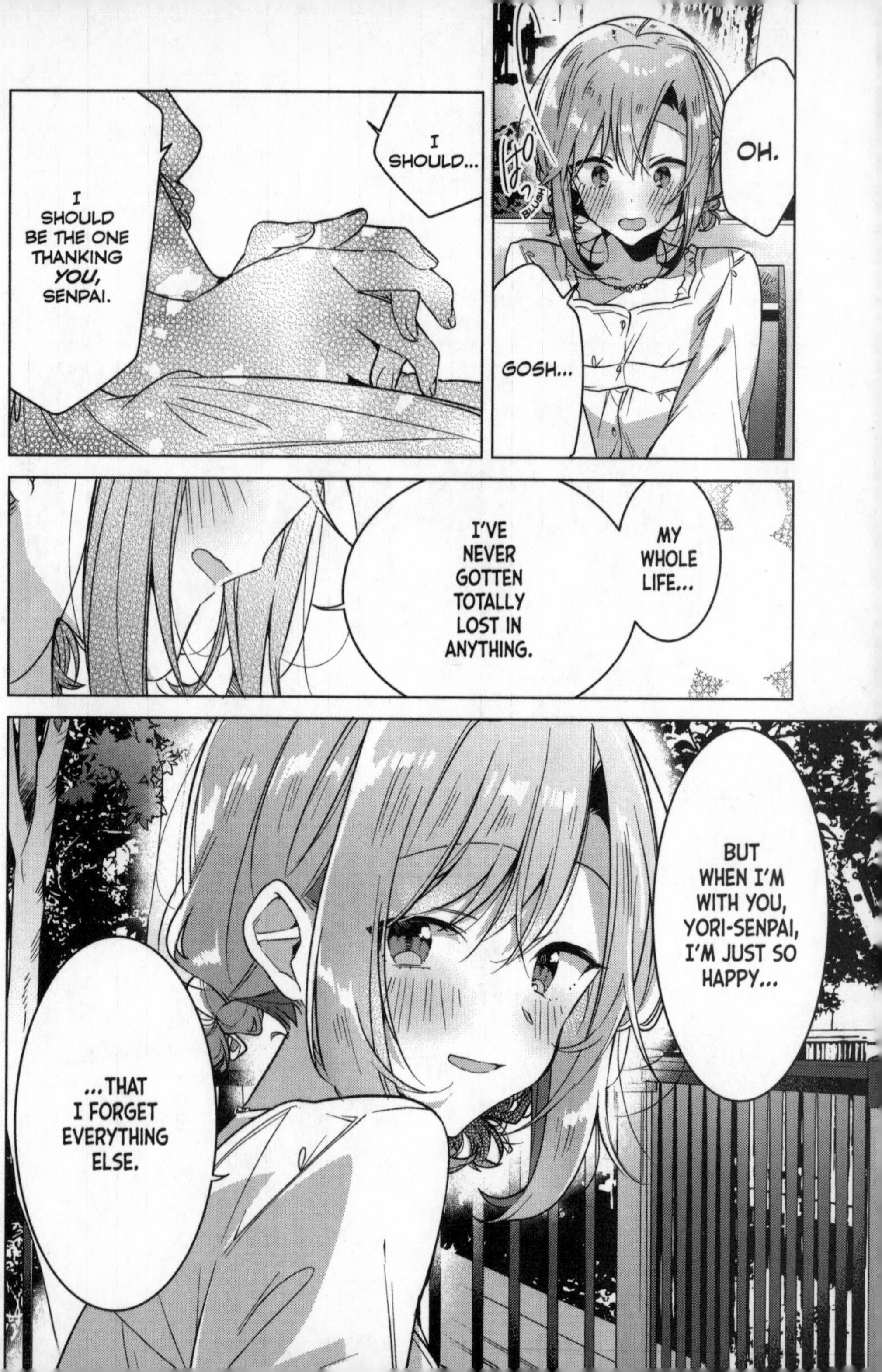
OH.
BLUSH
GOSH...
I SHOULD...
I SHOULD BE THE ONE THANKING *YOU*, SENPAI.
MY WHOLE LIFE...
I'VE NEVER GOTTEN TOTALLY LOST IN ANYTHING.
BUT WHEN I'M WITH YOU, YORI-SENPAI, I'M JUST SO HAPPY...
...THAT I FORGET EVERYTHING ELSE.

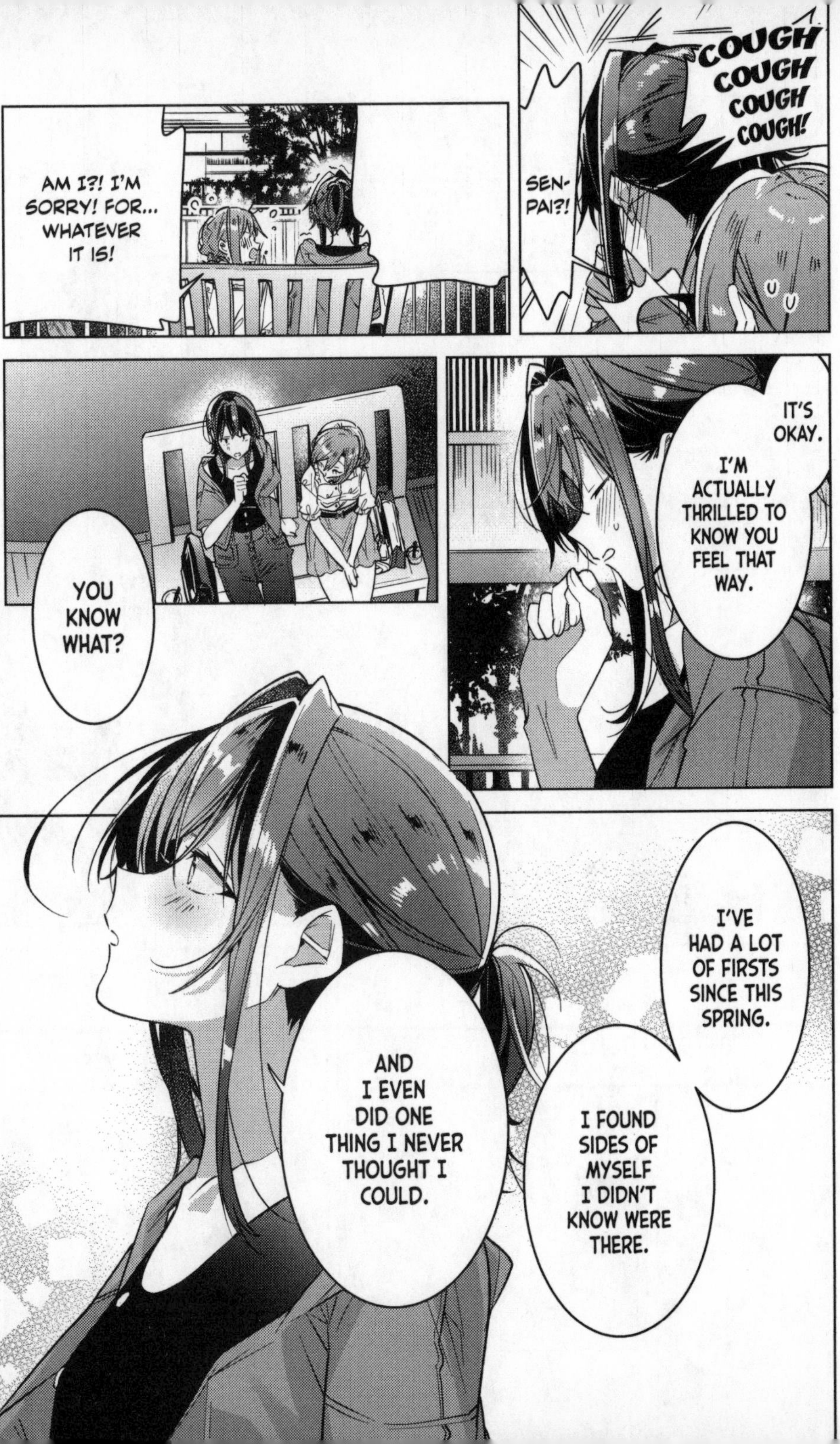
COUGH COUGH COUGH COUGH!
SEN-PAI?!
AM I?! I'M SORRY! FOR... WHATEVER IT IS!
IT'S OKAY.
I'M ACTUALLY THRILLED TO KNOW YOU FEEL THAT WAY.
YOU KNOW WHAT?
I'VE HAD A LOT OF FIRSTS SINCE THIS SPRING.
I FOUND SIDES OF MYSELF I DIDN'T KNOW WERE THERE.
AND I EVEN DID ONE THING I NEVER THOUGHT I COULD.

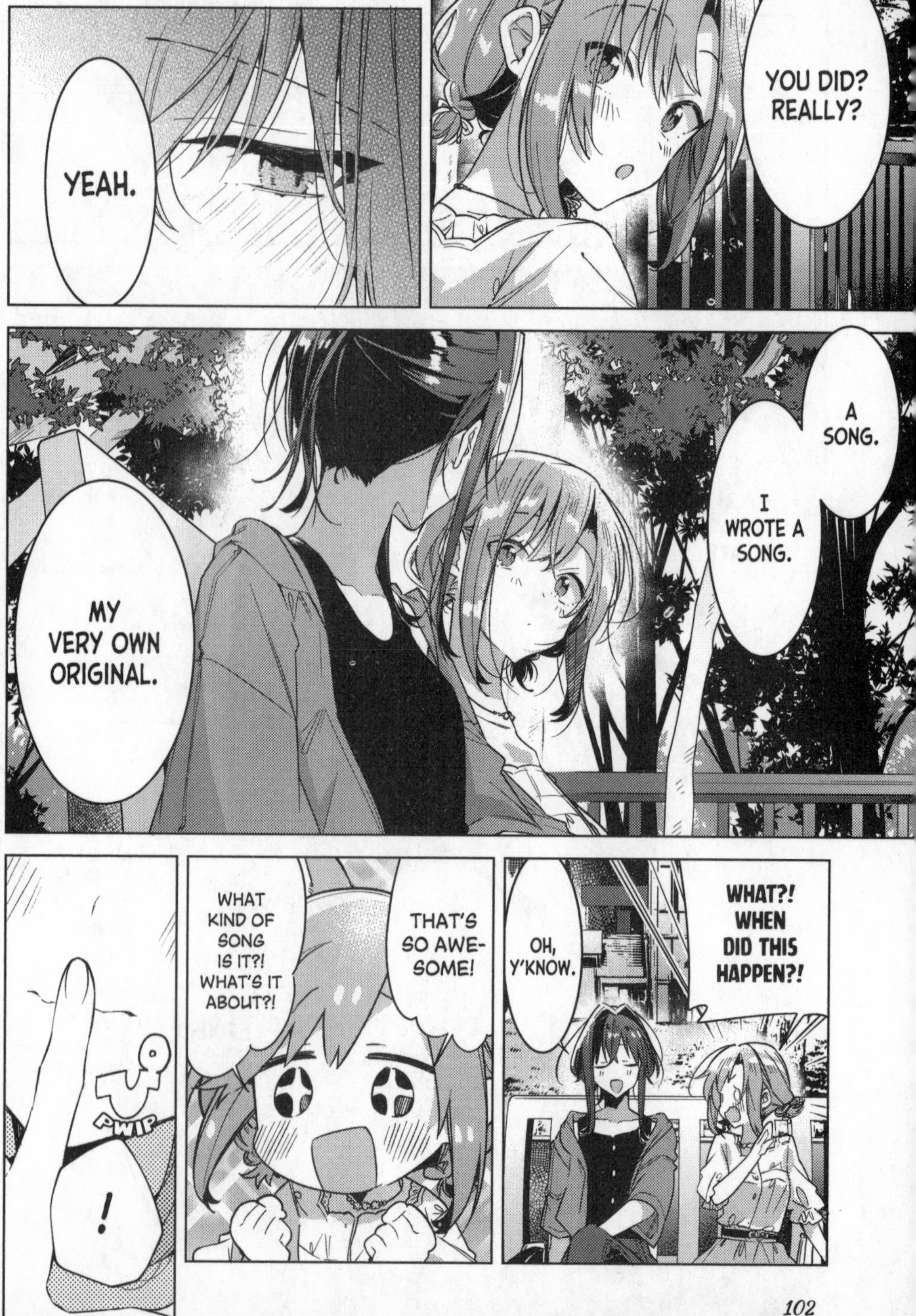
YOU DID? REALLY?
YEAH.
A SONG.
I WROTE A SONG.
MY VERY OWN ORIGINAL.
WHAT?! WHEN DID THIS HAPPEN?!
OH, Y'KNOW.
THAT'S SO AWE-SOME!
WHAT KIND OF SONG IS IT?! WHAT'S IT ABOUT?!
PWIP
!

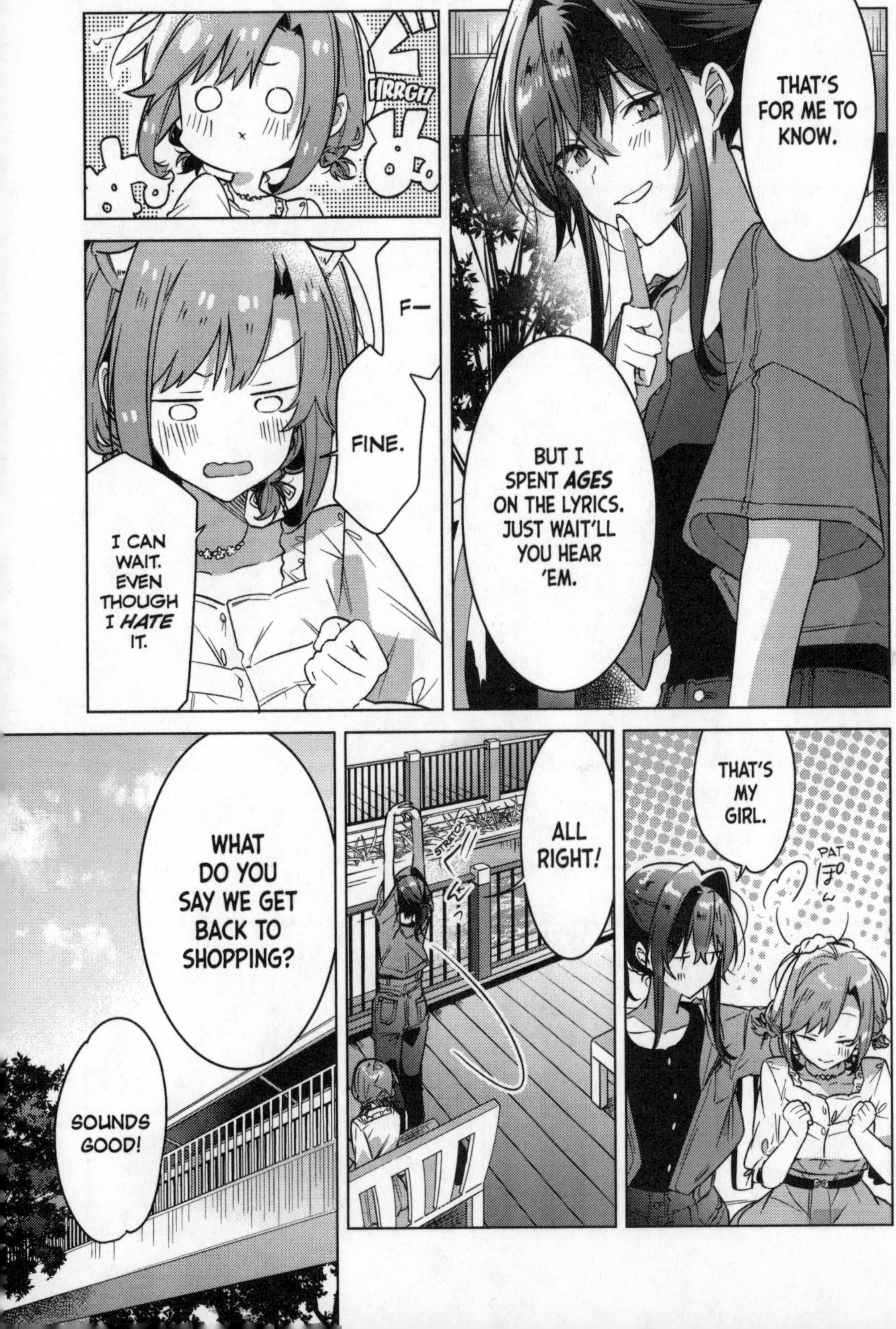
THAT'S FOR ME TO KNOW.
BUT I SPENT *AGES* ON THE LYRICS. JUST WAIT'LL YOU HEAR 'EM.
HRRGH
F—
FINE.
I CAN WAIT. EVEN THOUGH I *HATE* IT.
THAT'S MY GIRL.
PAT
ぽん
ALL RIGHT!
STRETCH
WHAT DO YOU SAY WE GET BACK TO SHOPPING?
SOUNDS GOOD!

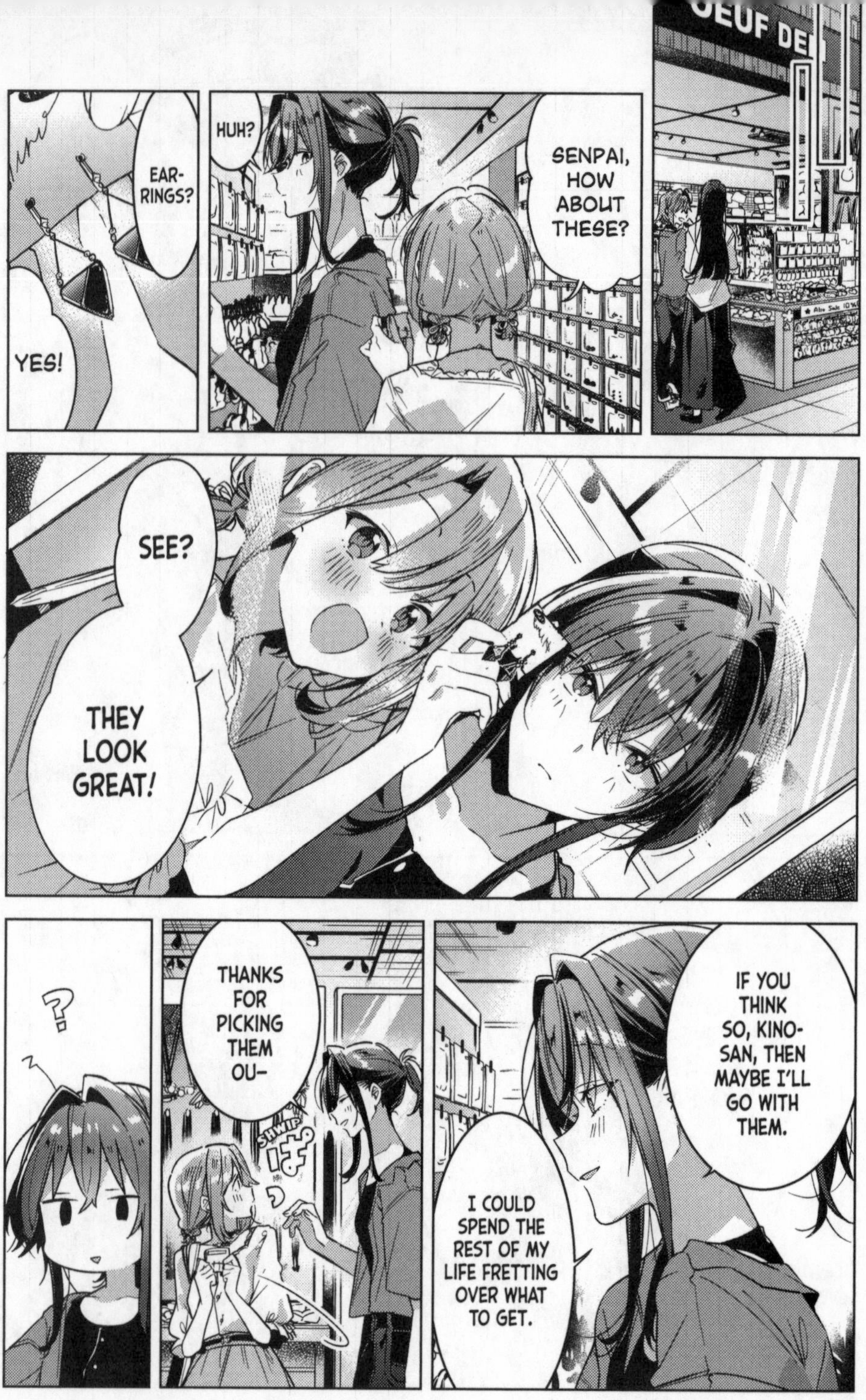
SENPAI, HOW ABOUT THESE?
HUH?
EAR-RINGS?
YES!
SEE?
THEY LOOK GREAT!
IF YOU THINK SO, KINO-SAN, THEN MAYBE I'LL GO WITH THEM.
I COULD SPEND THE REST OF MY LIFE FRETTING OVER WHAT TO GET.
THANKS FOR PICKING THEM OU-
SHWIP
?

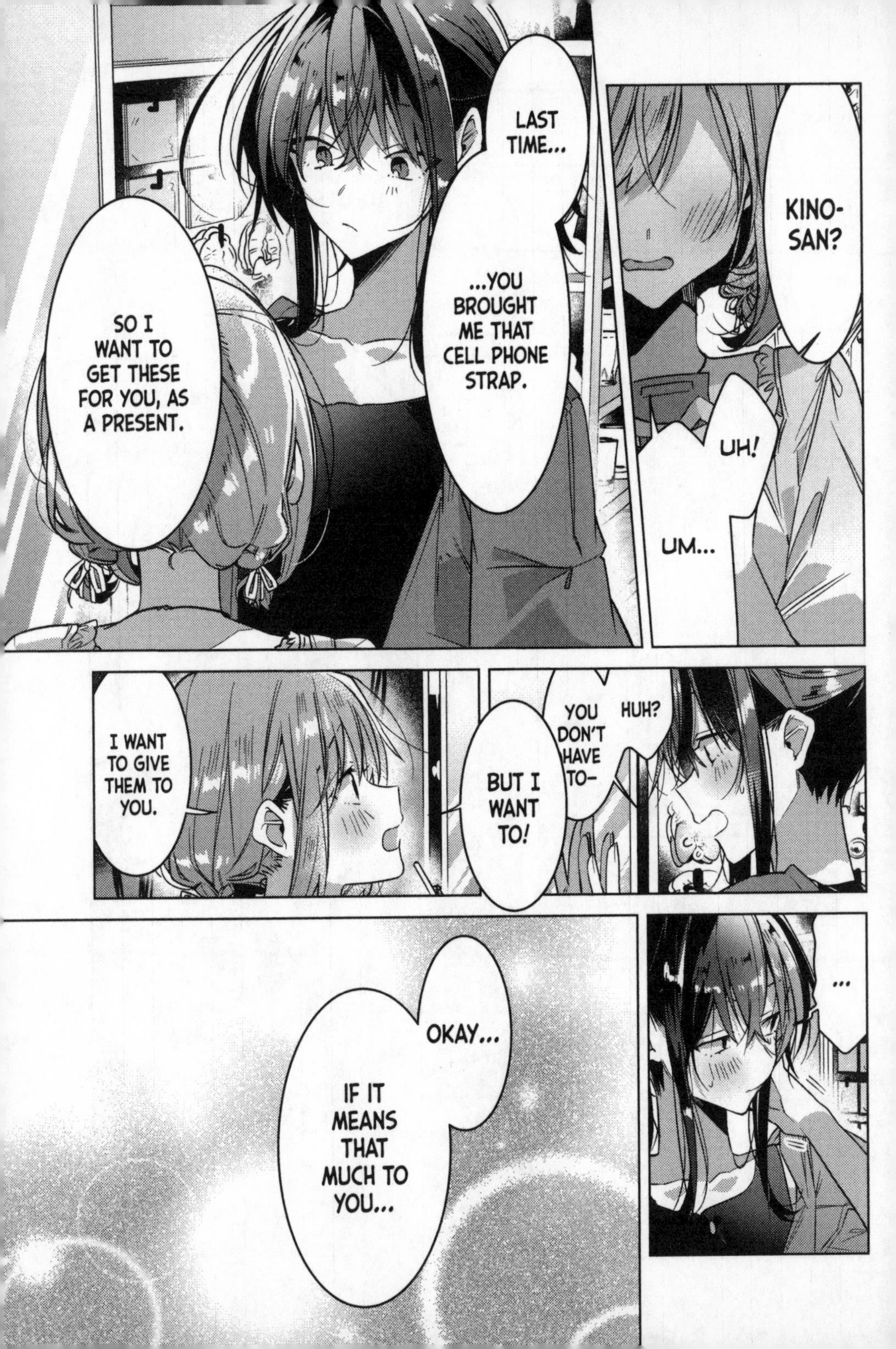

KINO-SAN?
UH!
UM...
LAST TIME...
...YOU BROUGHT ME THAT CELL PHONE STRAP.
SO I WANT TO GET THESE FOR YOU, AS A PRESENT.
HUH?
YOU DON'T HAVE TO—
BUT I WANT TO!
I WANT TO GIVE THEM TO YOU.
...
OKAY...
IF IT MEANS THAT MUCH TO YOU...

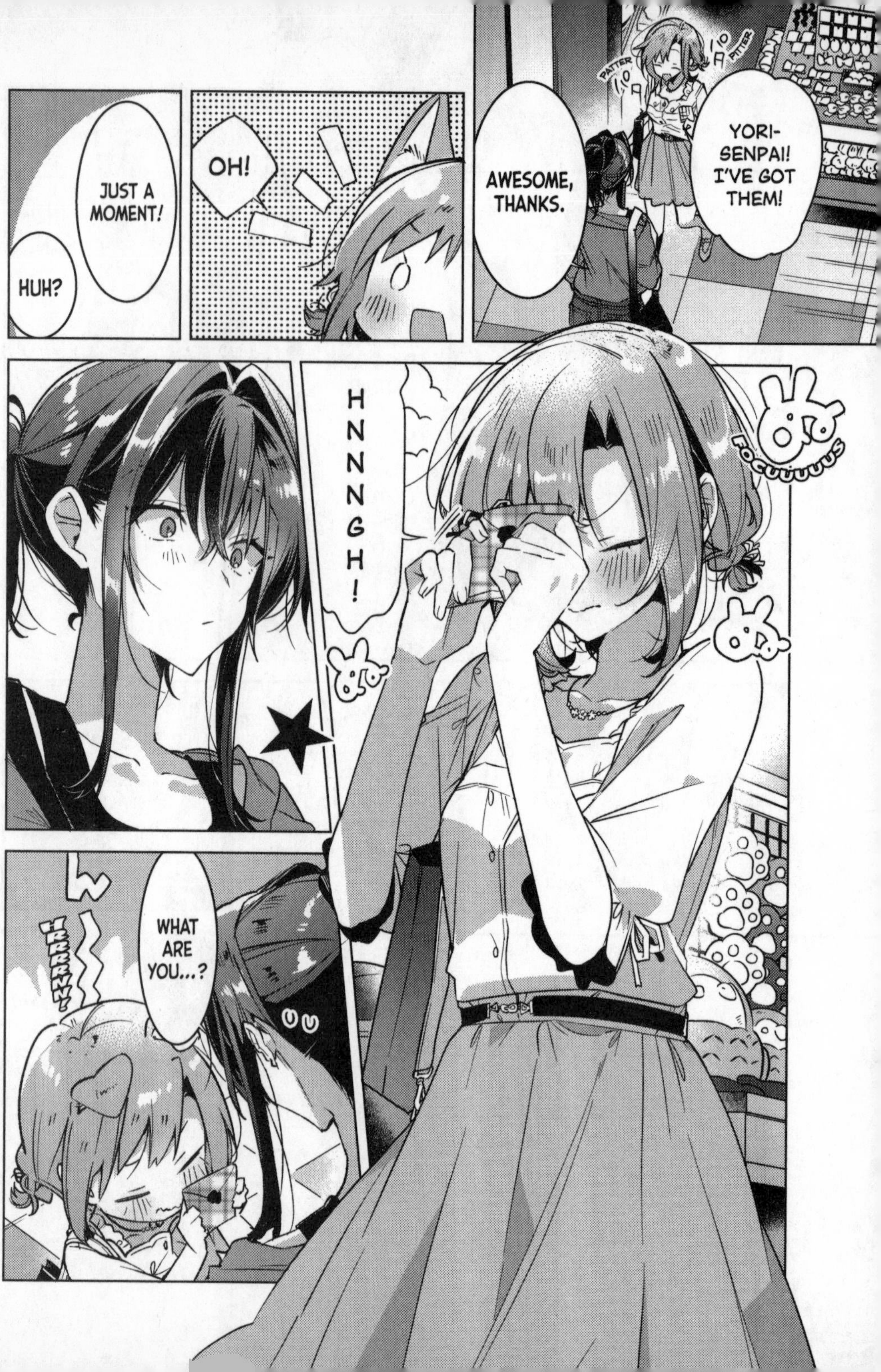
PATTER PATTER
YORI-SENPAI! I'VE GOT THEM!
AWESOME, THANKS.
OH!
JUST A MOMENT!
HUH?
FOCUUUUUS
HNNNGH!
WHAT ARE YOU...?
HRRRNN!

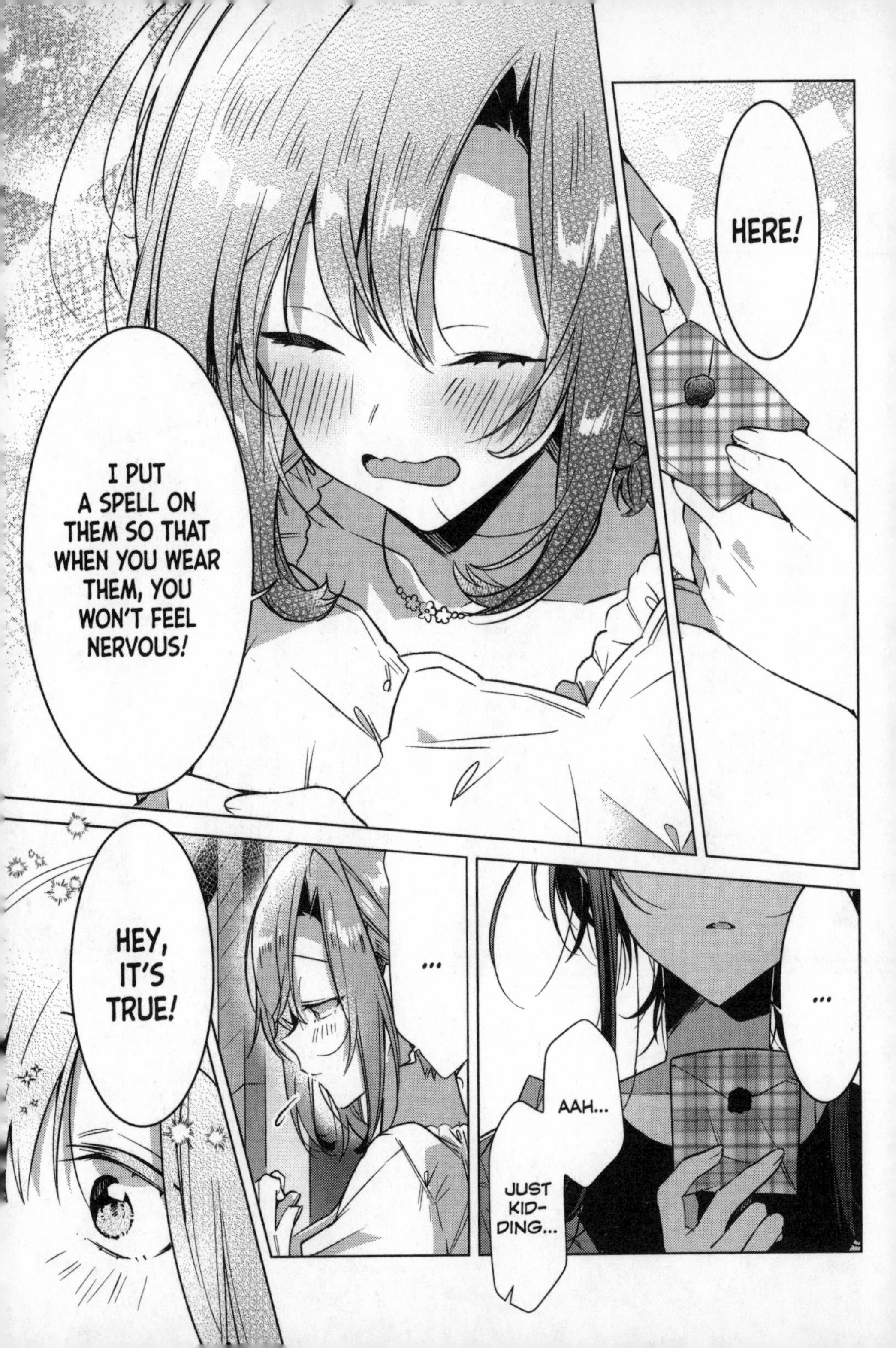
HERE!
I PUT A SPELL ON THEM SO THAT WHEN YOU WEAR THEM, YOU WON'T FEEL NERVOUS!
...
AAH...
JUST KID-DING...
...
HEY, IT'S TRUE!

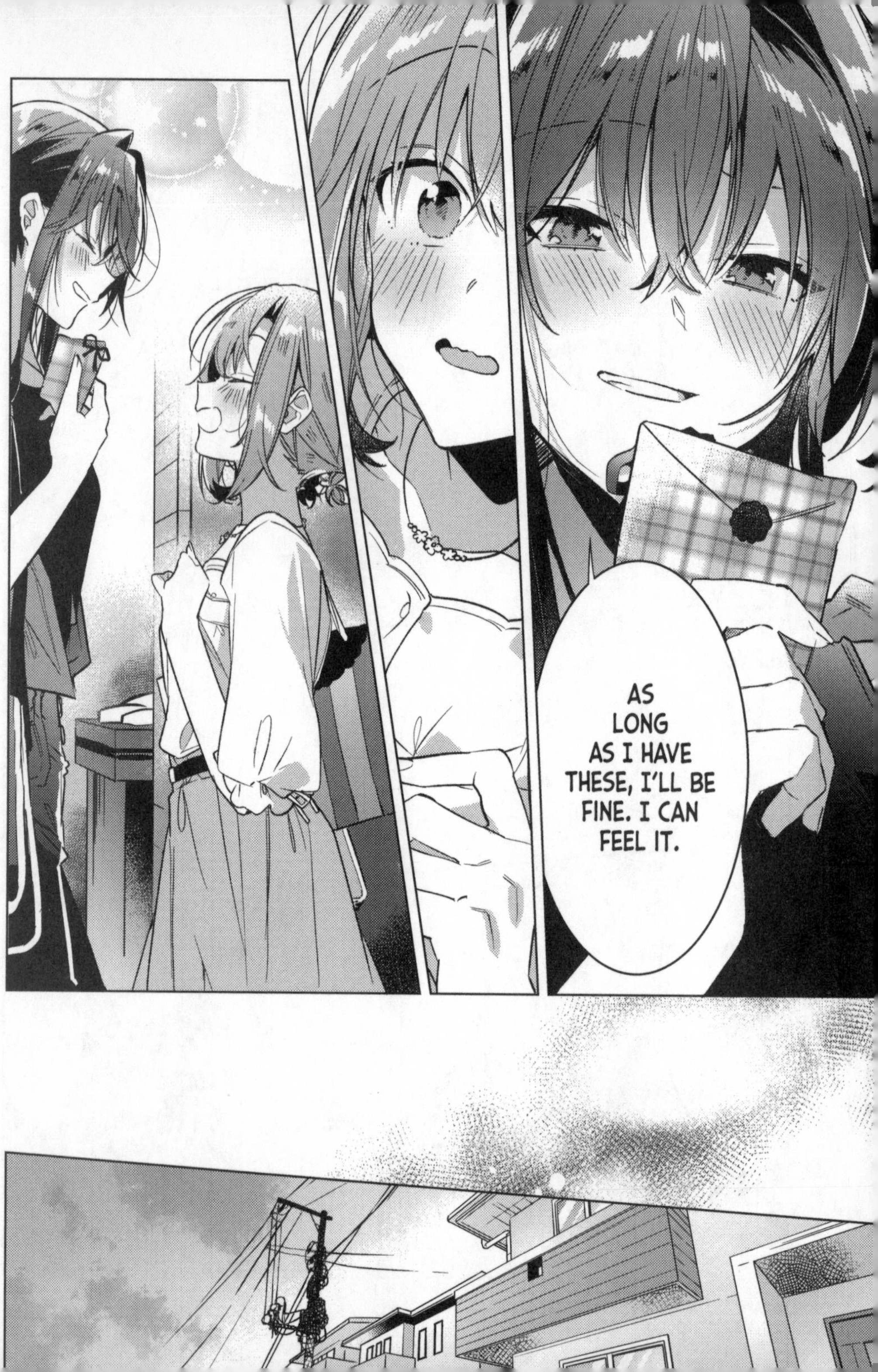
AS LONG AS I HAVE THESE, I'LL BE FINE. I CAN FEEL IT.

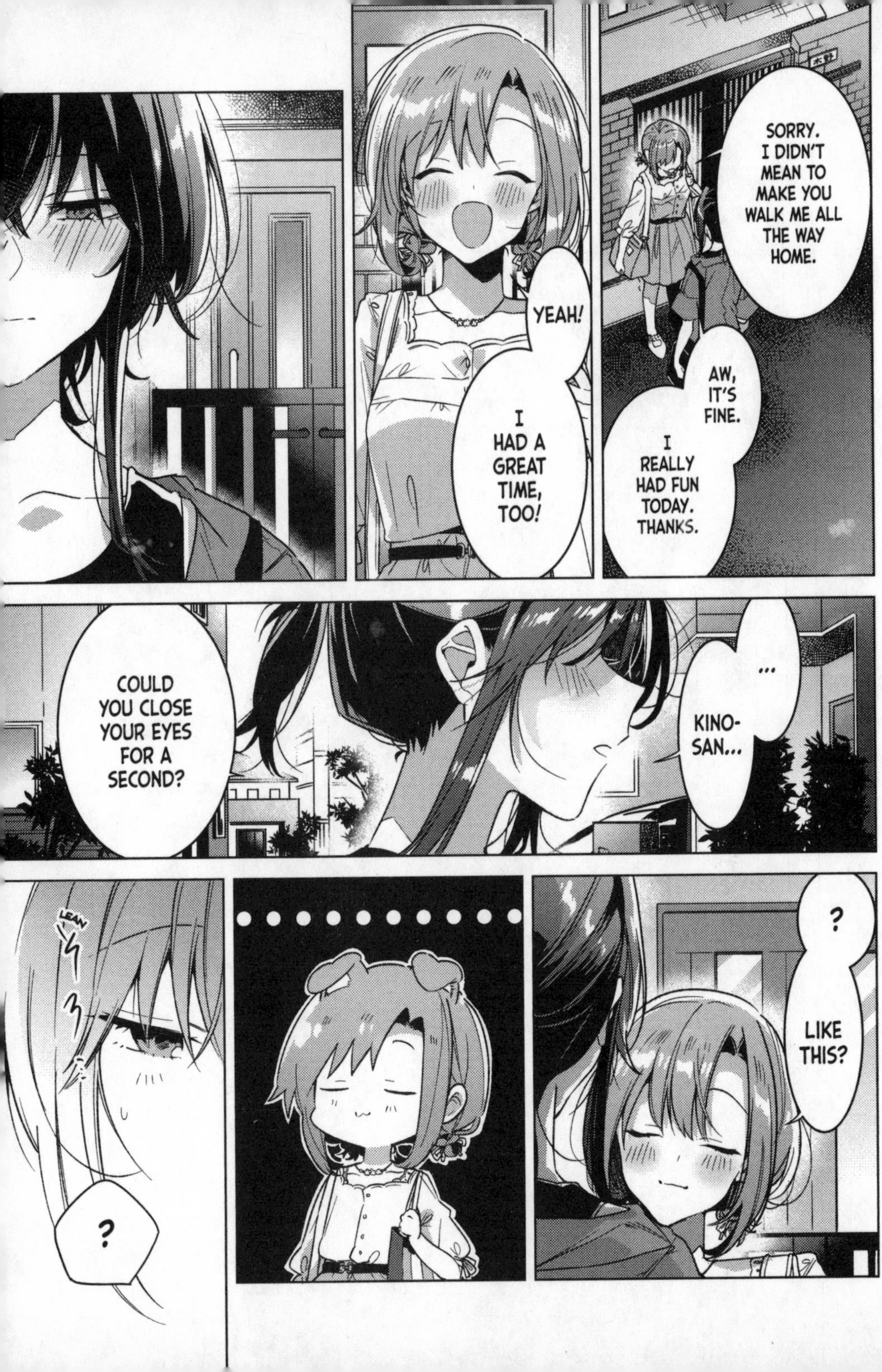
SORRY. I DIDN'T MEAN TO MAKE YOU WALK ME ALL THE WAY HOME.
AW, IT'S FINE.
I REALLY HAD FUN TODAY. THANKS.
YEAH!
I HAD A GREAT TIME, TOO!
...
KINO-SAN...
COULD YOU CLOSE YOUR EYES FOR A SECOND?
?
LIKE THIS?
LEAN
?

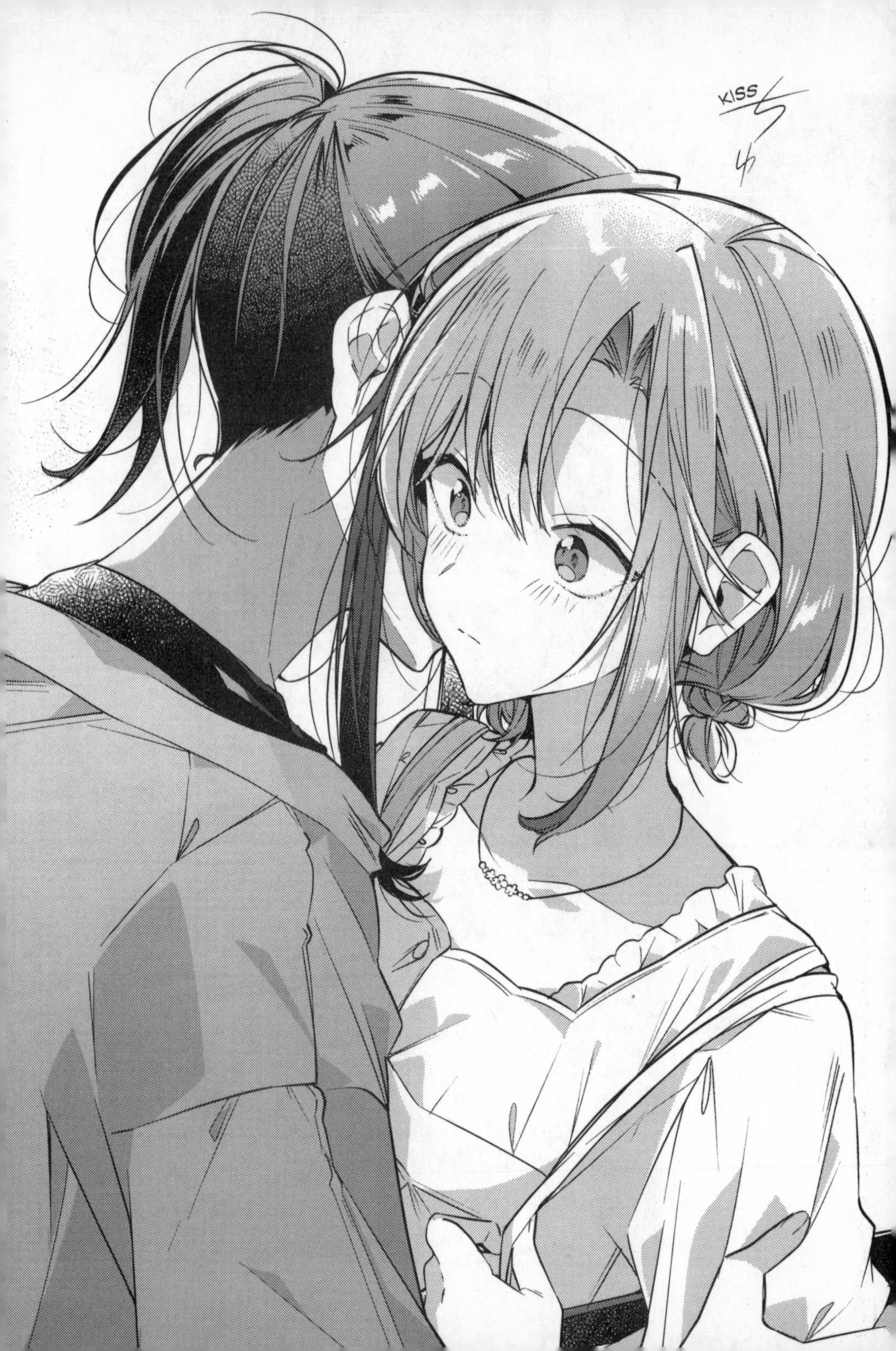
KISS

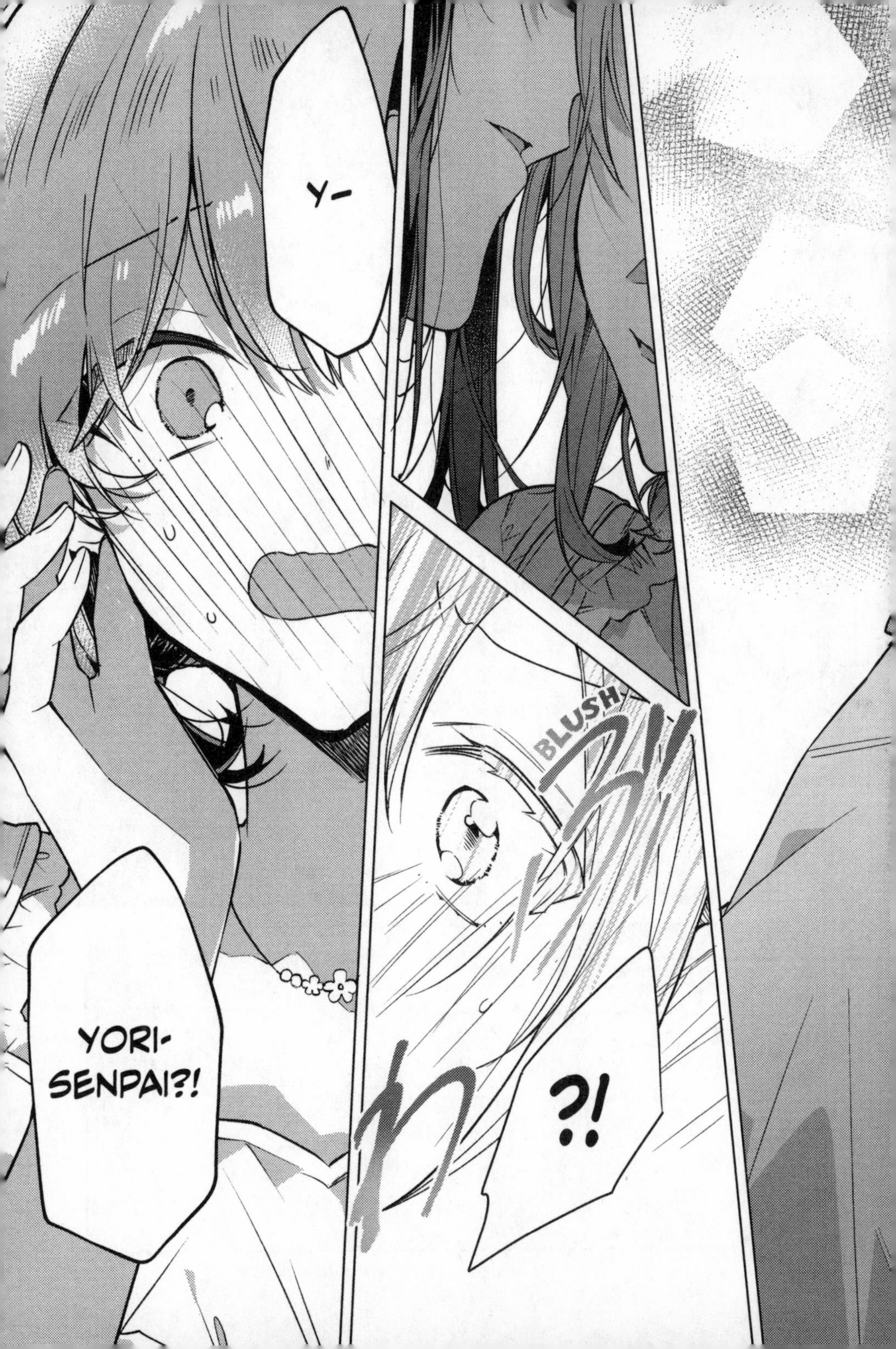
BLUSH
?!
Y–
YORI-SENPAI?!

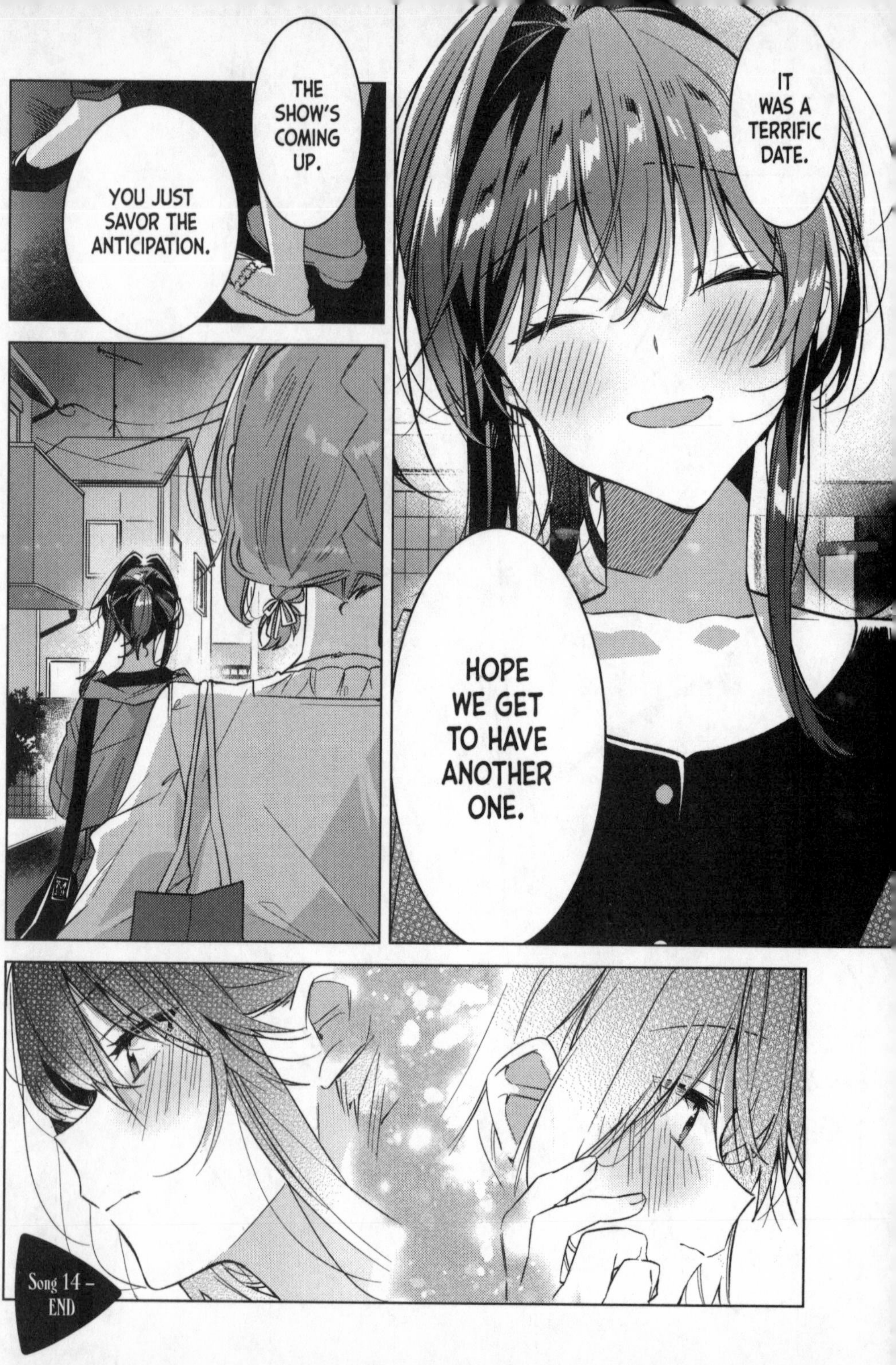
IT WAS A TERRIFIC DATE.
HOPE WE GET TO HAVE ANOTHER ONE.
THE SHOW'S COMING UP.
YOU JUST SAVOR THE ANTICIPATION.
Song 14 – END

Whisper Me A Love Song

Eku
Takeshima

Whisper Me
A Love Song

Eku
Takeshima

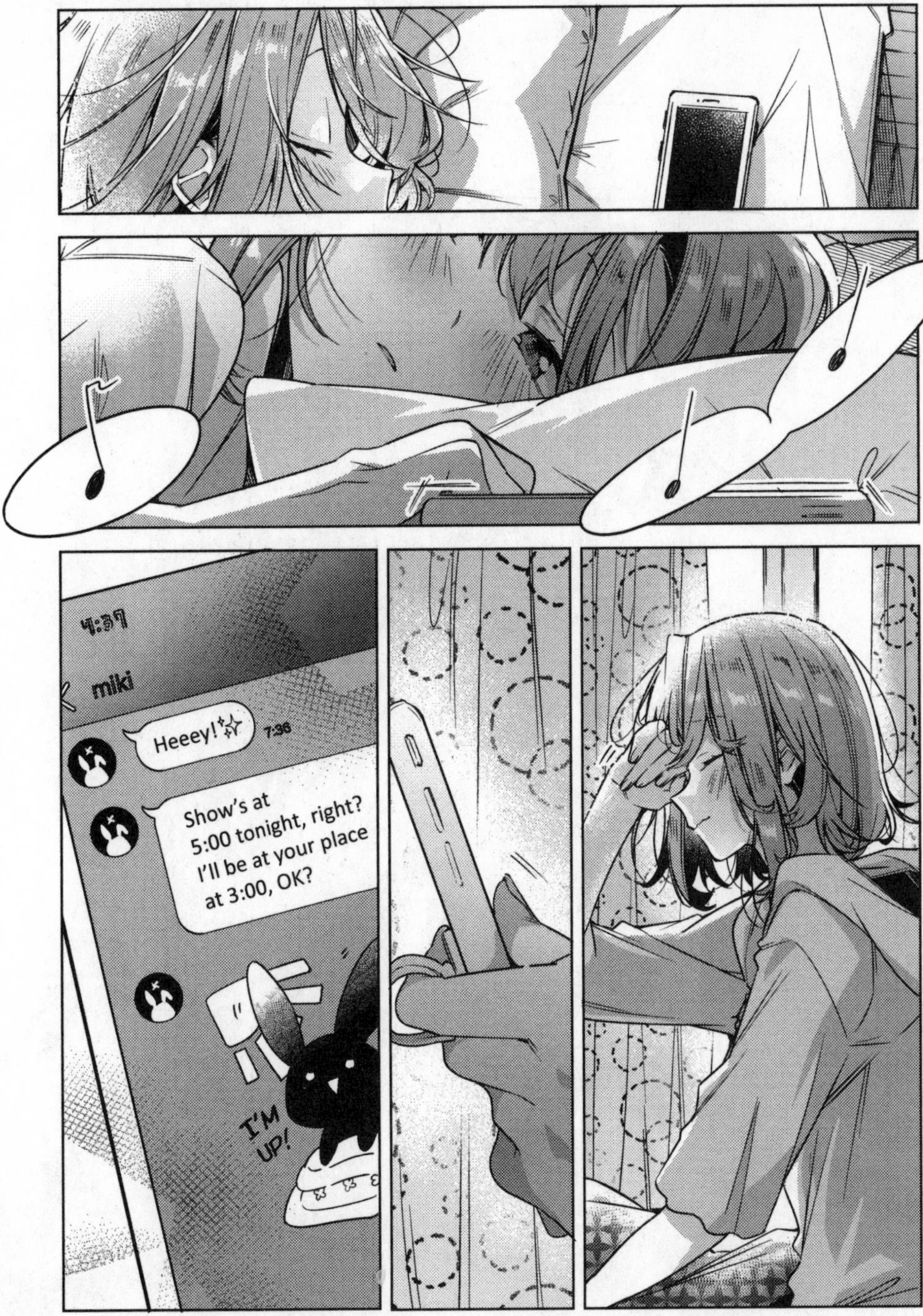
4:37
miki
Heeey!
7:36
Show's at 5:00 tonight, right? I'll be at your place at 3:00, OK?
I'M UP!

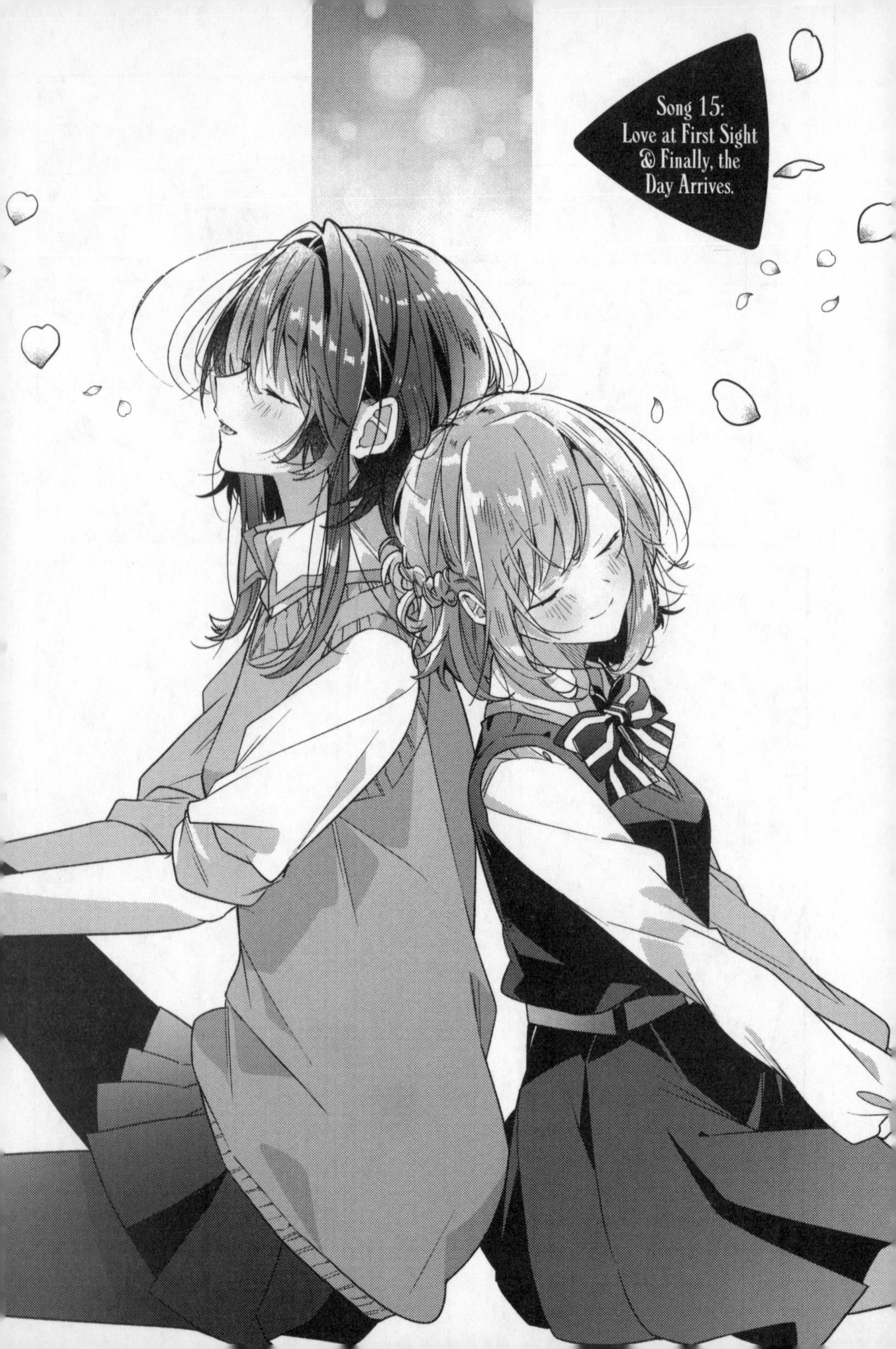
Song 15:
Love at First Sight & Finally, the Day Arrives.

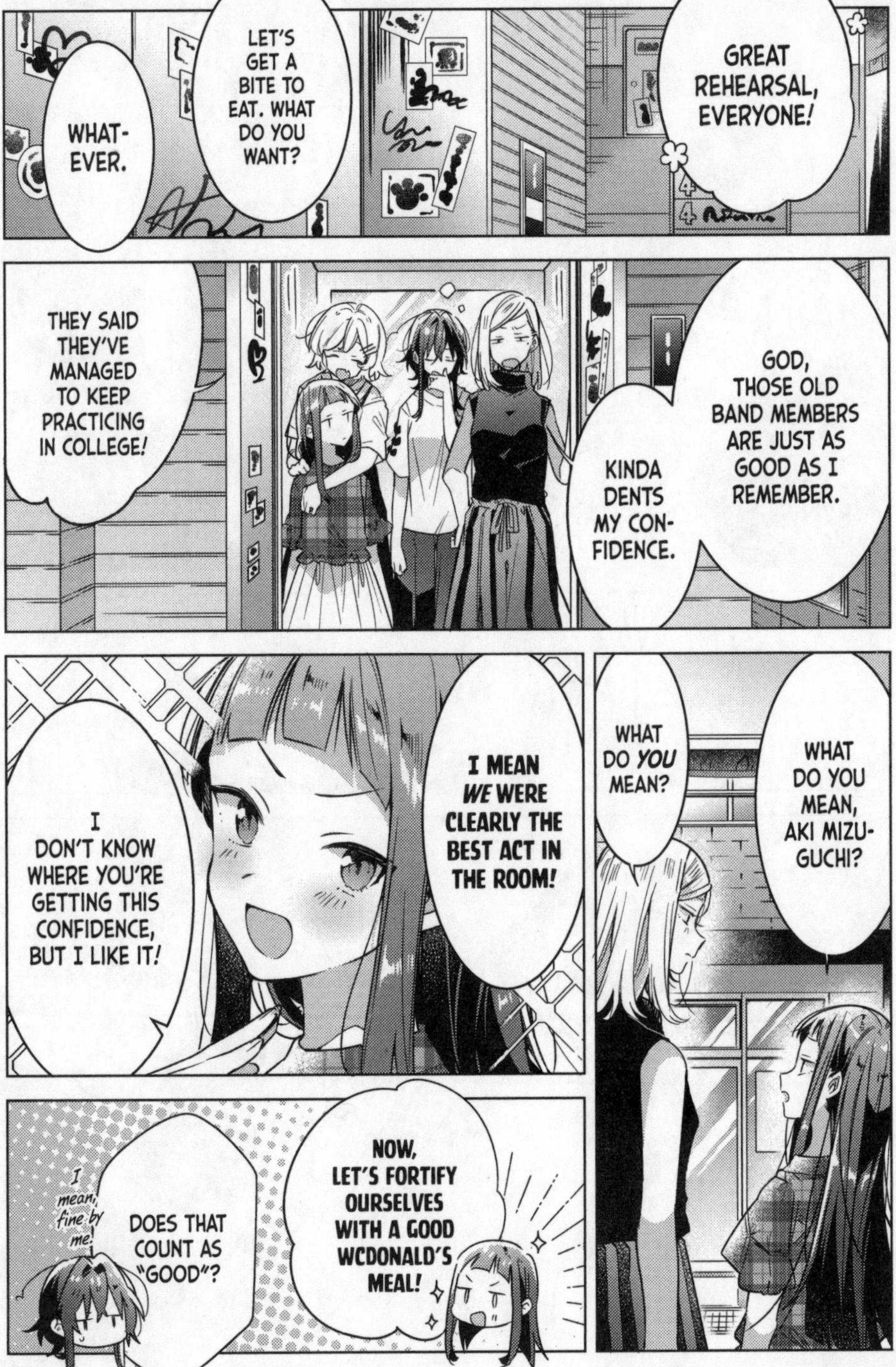
GREAT REHEARSAL, EVERYONE!
LET'S GET A BITE TO EAT. WHAT DO YOU WANT?
WHAT-EVER.
GOD, THOSE OLD BAND MEMBERS ARE JUST AS GOOD AS I REMEMBER.
KINDA DENTS MY CON-FIDENCE.
THEY SAID THEY'VE MANAGED TO KEEP PRACTICING IN COLLEGE!
WHAT DO YOU MEAN, AKI MIZU-GUCHI?
WHAT DO *YOU* MEAN?
I MEAN *WE* WERE CLEARLY THE BEST ACT IN THE ROOM!
I DON'T KNOW WHERE YOU'RE GETTING THIS CONFIDENCE, BUT I LIKE IT!
NOW, LET'S FORTIFY OURSELVES WITH A GOOD WCDONALD'S MEAL!
DOES THAT COUNT AS "GOOD"?
I mean, fine by me.

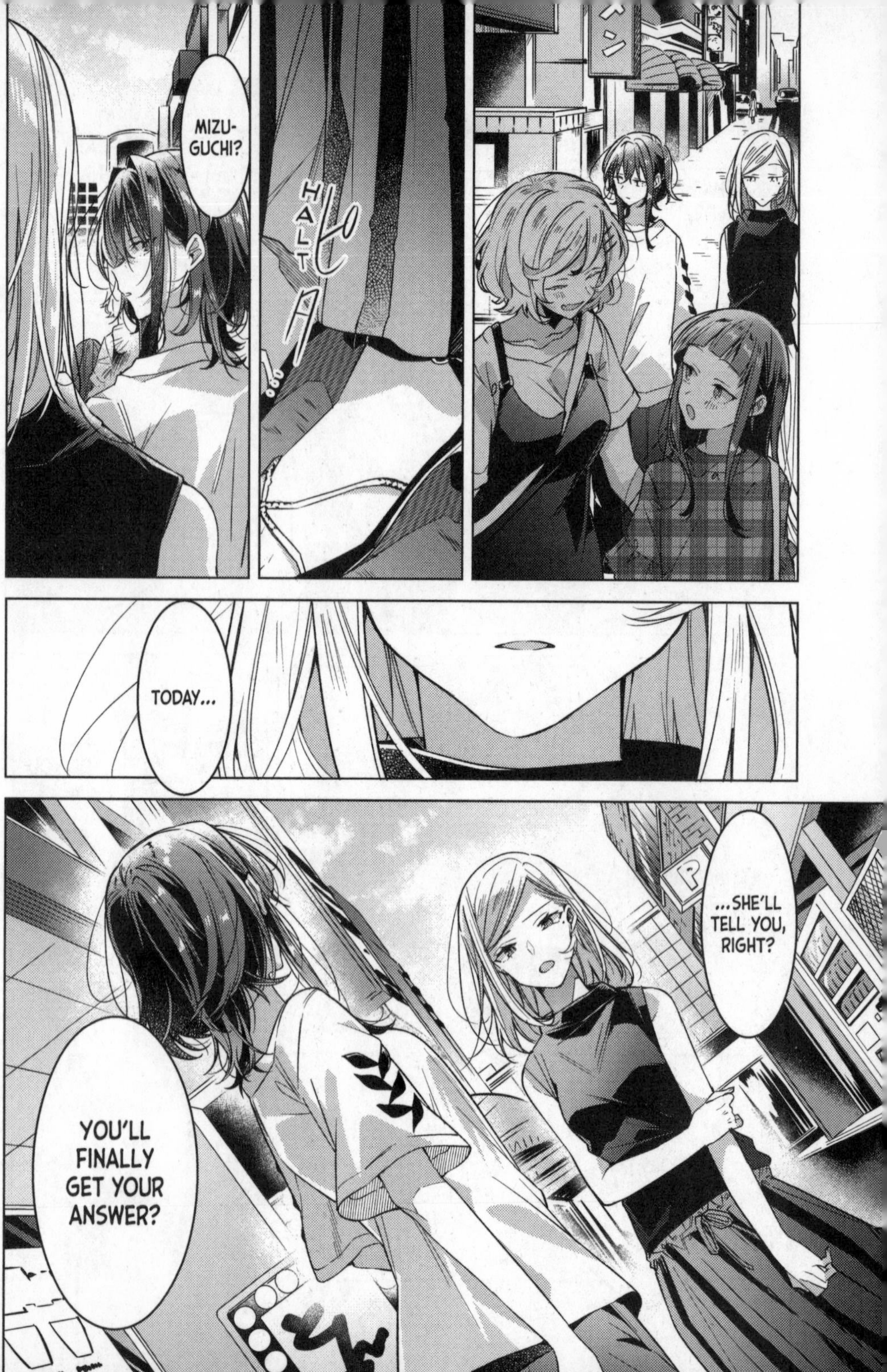

HALT
MIZU-GUCHI?
TODAY...
...SHE'LL TELL YOU, RIGHT?
YOU'LL FINALLY GET YOUR ANSWER?

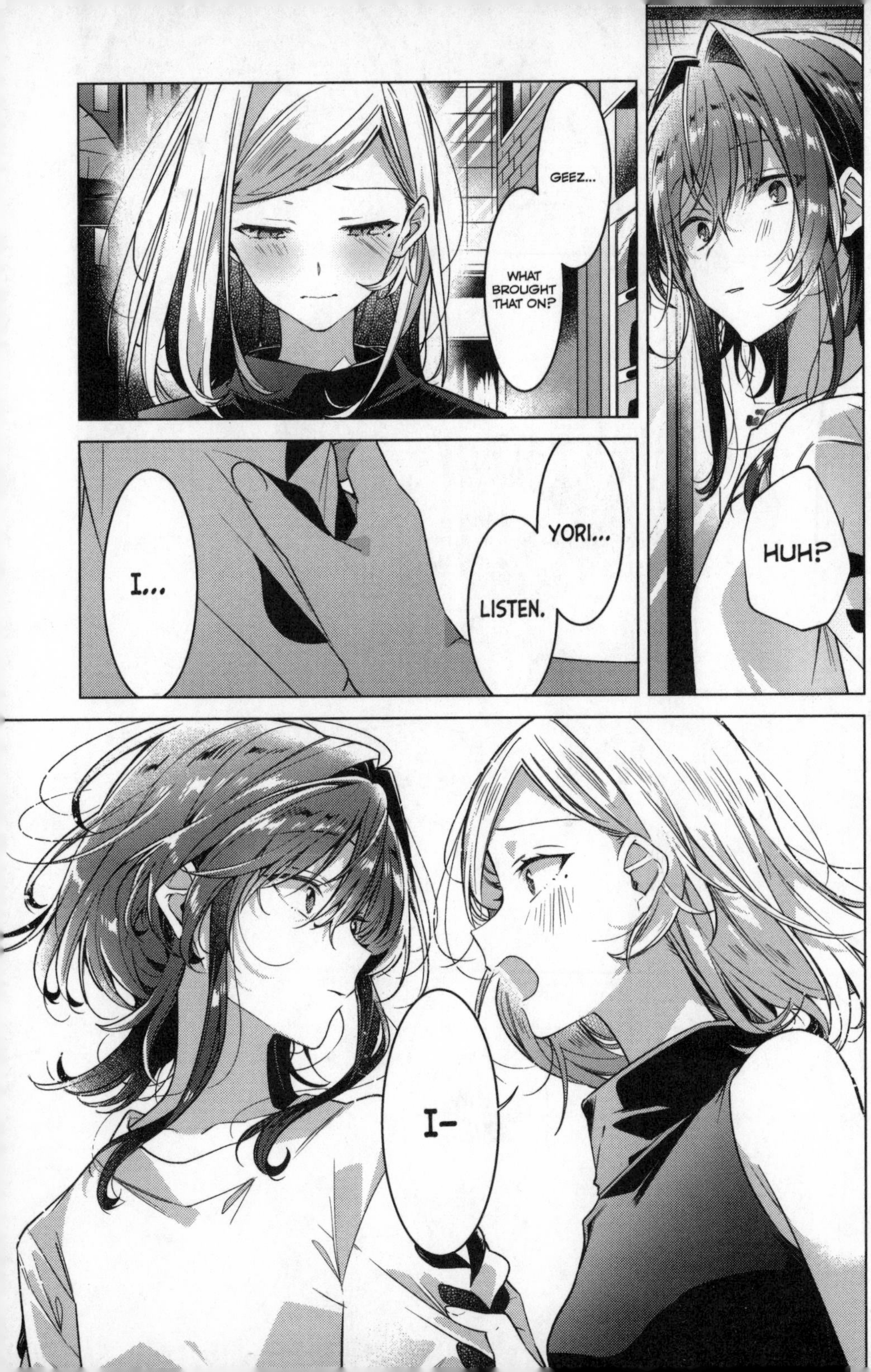
HUH?
GEEZ...
WHAT BROUGHT THAT ON?
YORI...
LISTEN.
I...
I-

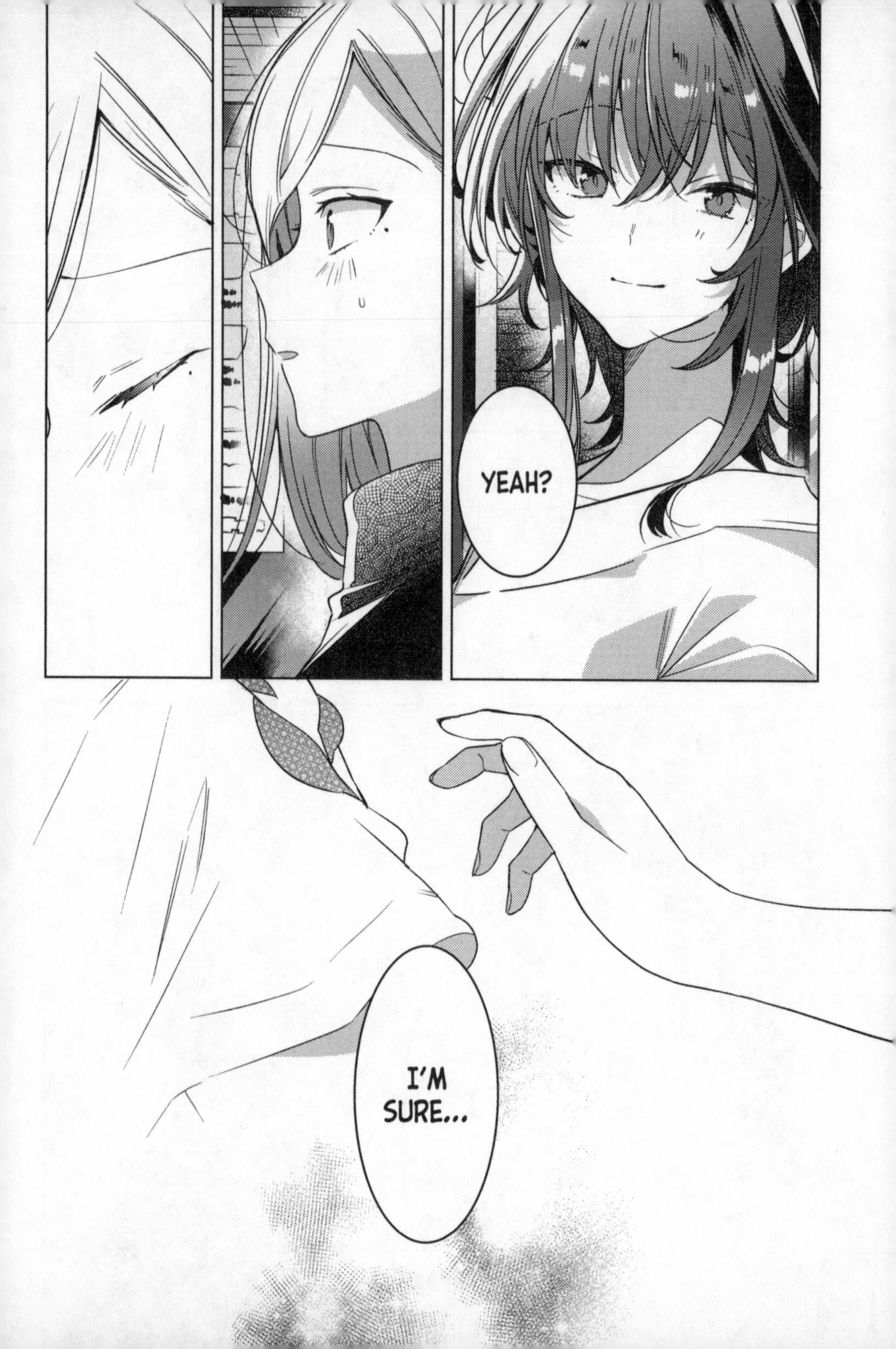
YEAH?
I'M SURE...

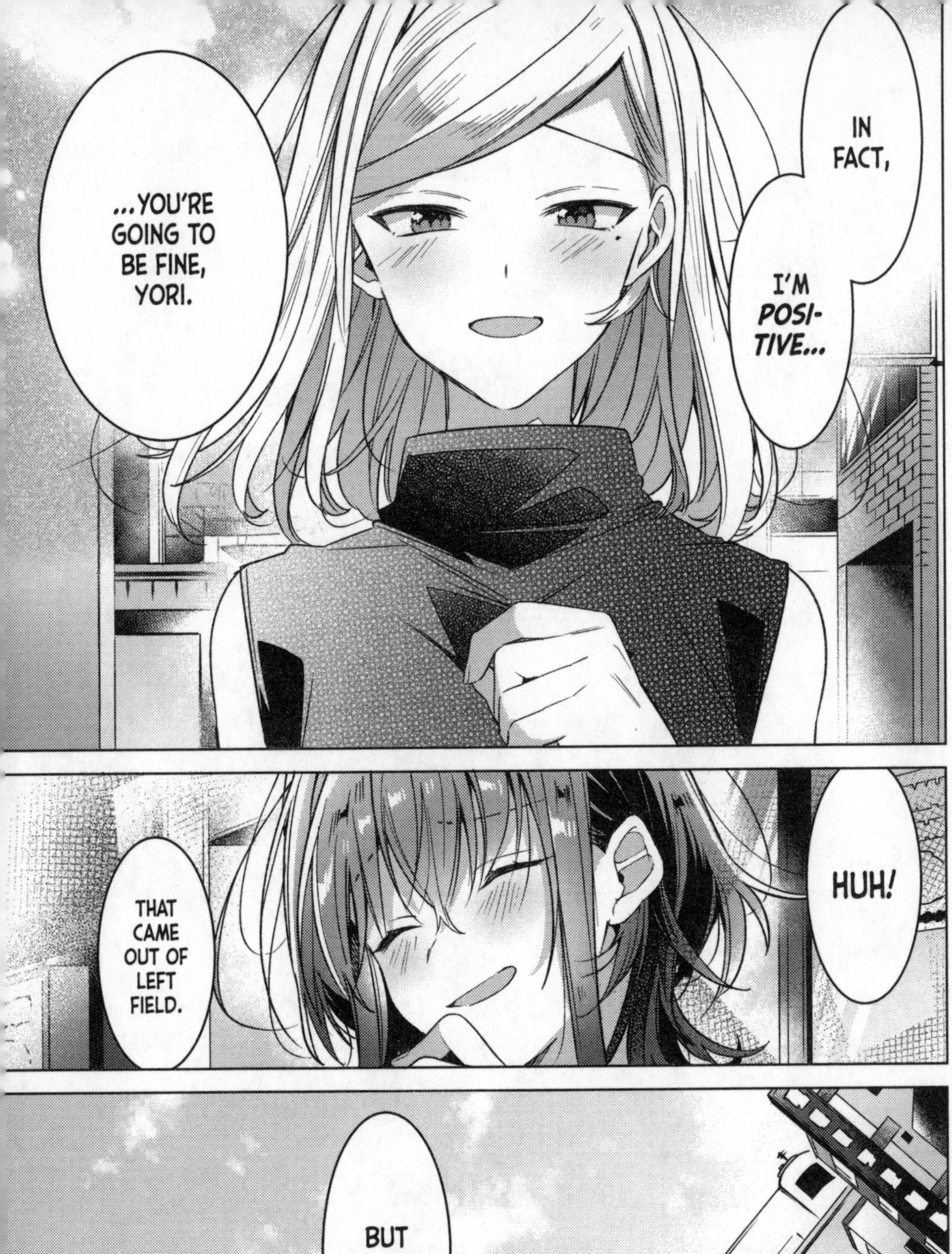
IN FACT,
I'M *POSITIVE*...
...YOU'RE GOING TO BE FINE, YORI.
HUH!
THAT CAME OUT OF LEFT FIELD.
BUT THANKS.

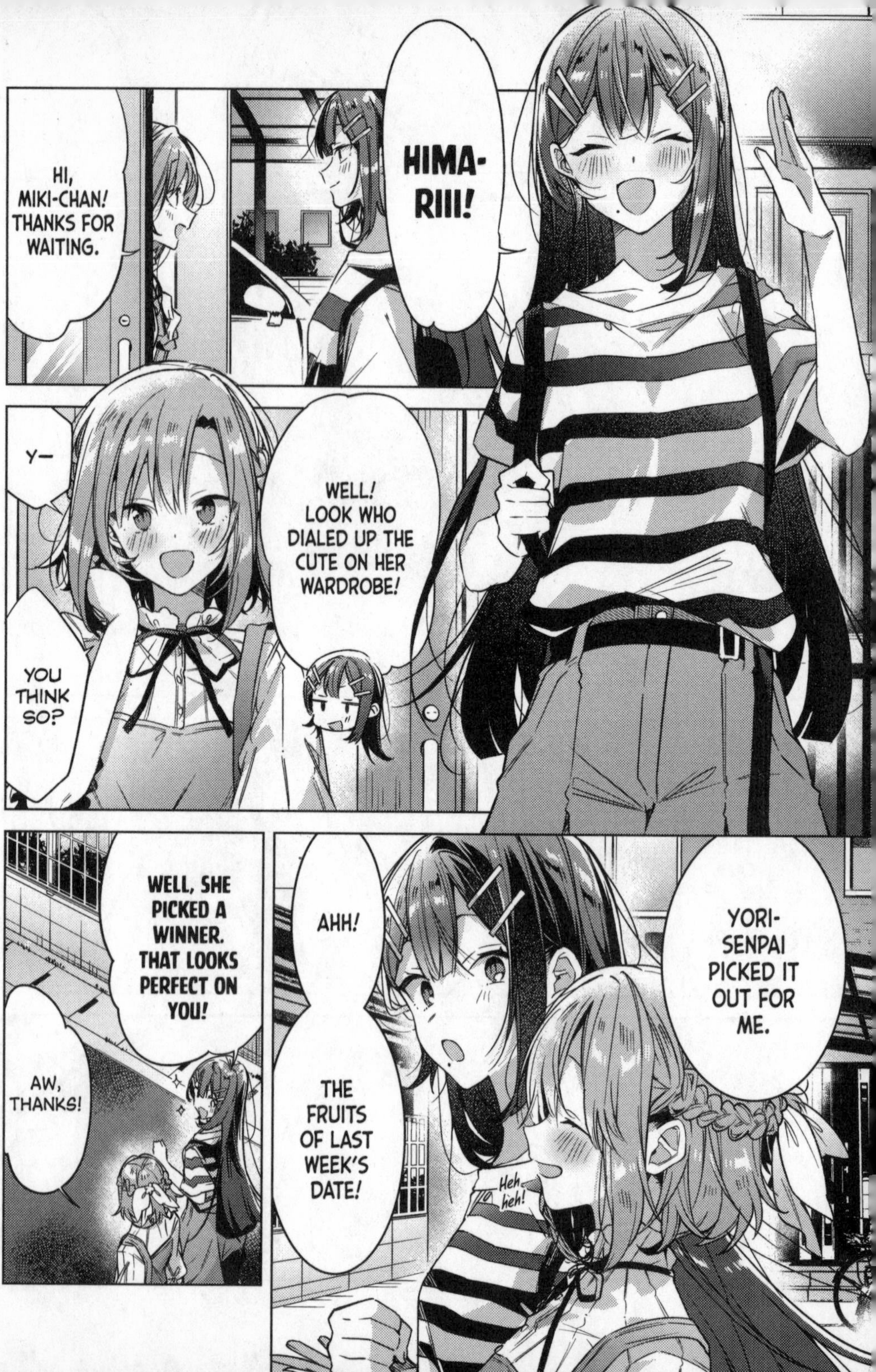
HIMA-RIII!
HI, MIKI-CHAN! THANKS FOR WAITING.
WELL! LOOK WHO DIALED UP THE CUTE ON HER WARDROBE!
Y—
YOU THINK SO?
YORI-SENPAI PICKED IT OUT FOR ME.
AHH!
THE FRUITS OF LAST WEEK'S DATE!
Heh heh!
WELL, SHE PICKED A WINNER. THAT LOOKS PERFECT ON YOU!
AW, THANKS!

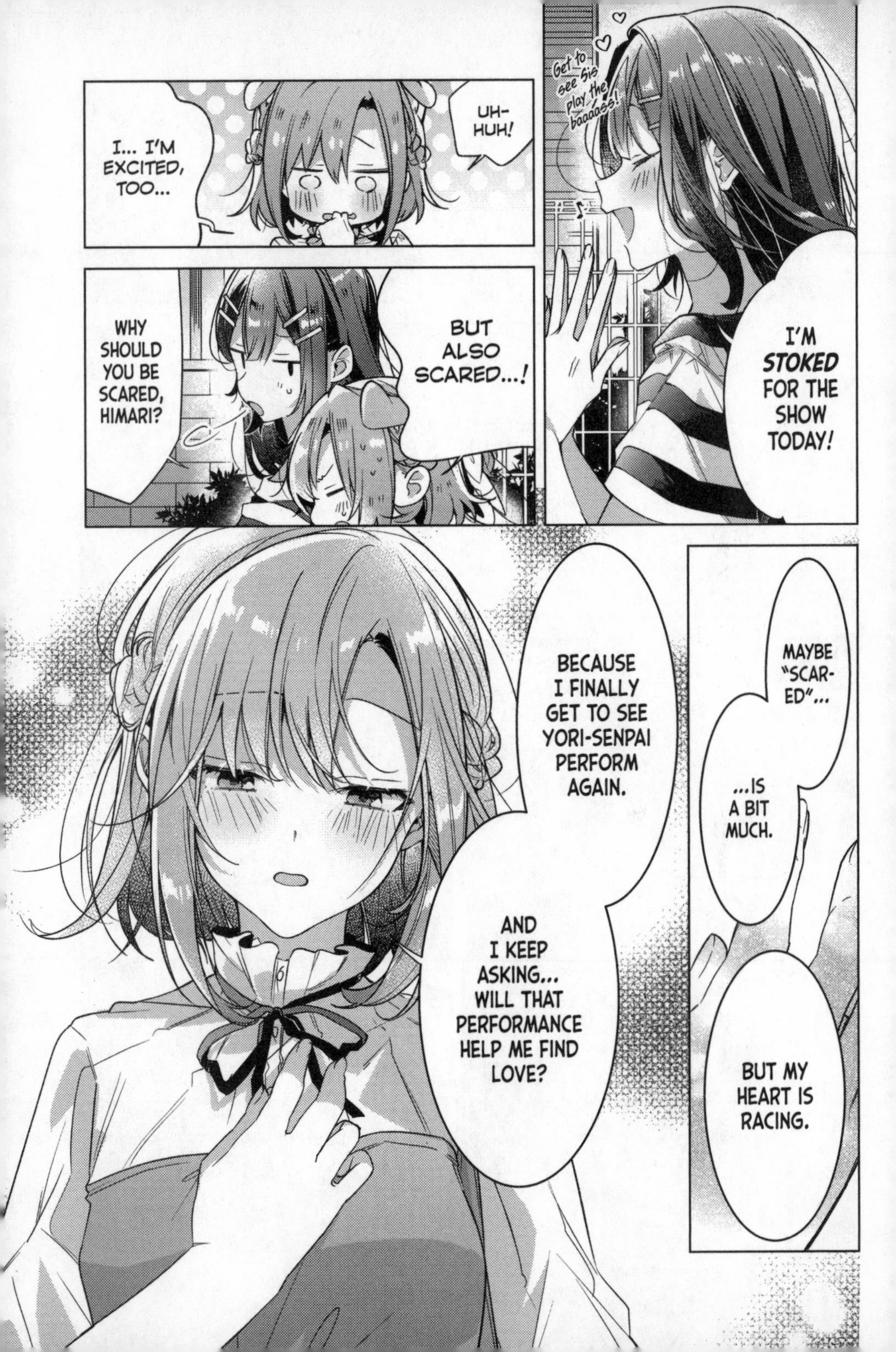
Get to see Sis play the baaaass!
I'M **STOKED** FOR THE SHOW TODAY!
UH-HUH!
I... I'M EXCITED, TOO...
BUT ALSO SCARED...!
WHY SHOULD YOU BE SCARED, HIMARI?
MAYBE "SCAR-ED"...
...IS A BIT MUCH.
BUT MY HEART IS RACING.
BECAUSE I FINALLY GET TO SEE YORI-SENPAI PERFORM AGAIN.
AND I KEEP ASKING... WILL THAT PERFORMANCE HELP ME FIND LOVE?

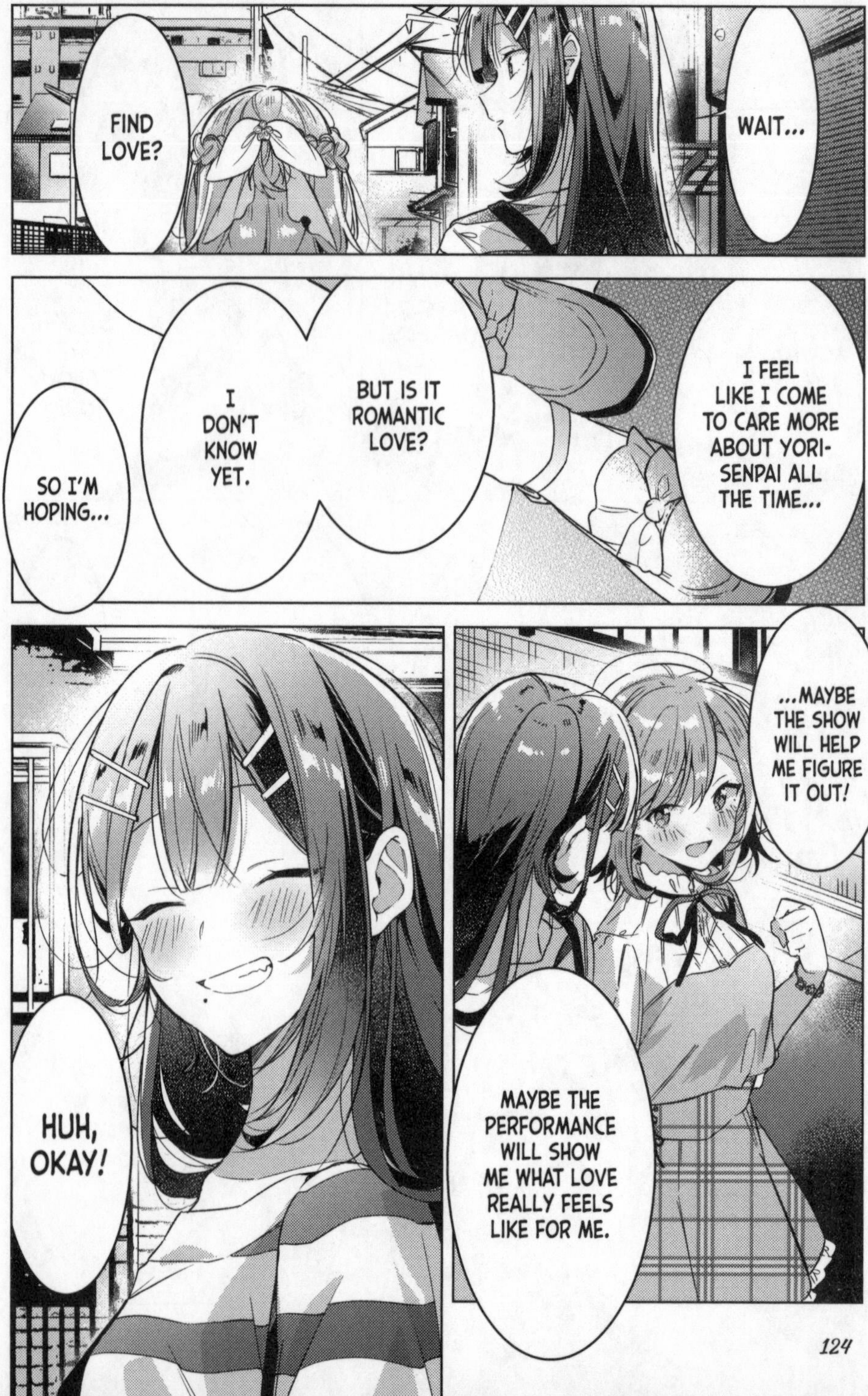
WAIT...
FIND LOVE?
I FEEL LIKE I COME TO CARE MORE ABOUT YORI-SENPAI ALL THE TIME...
BUT IS IT ROMANTIC LOVE?
I DON'T KNOW YET.
SO I'M HOPING...
...MAYBE THE SHOW WILL HELP ME FIGURE IT OUT!
MAYBE THE PERFORMANCE WILL SHOW ME WHAT LOVE REALLY FEELS LIKE FOR ME.
HUH, OKAY!

NOW LISTEN UP!

ASANAGI-SENPAI'S GREAT AND ALL, BUT YOU HAVE TO KEEP ONE EYE ON MY SISTER THIS TIME, ALL RIGHT?

YOU NEVER GIVE UP, MIKI-CHAN!

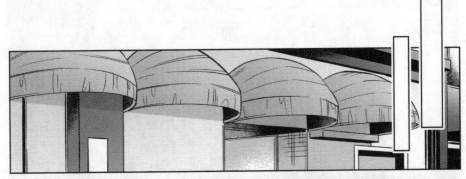

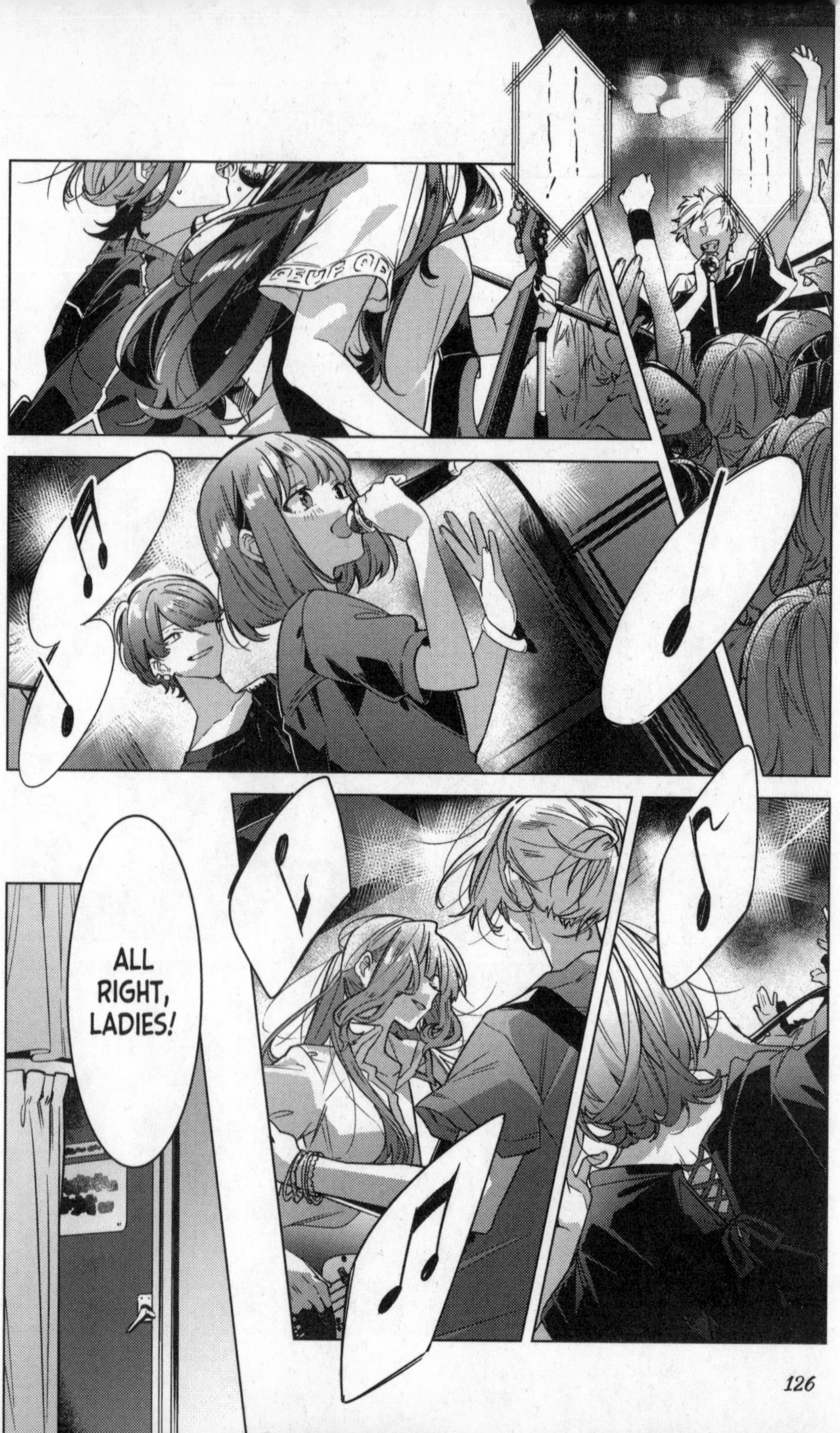
ALL RIGHT, LADIES!

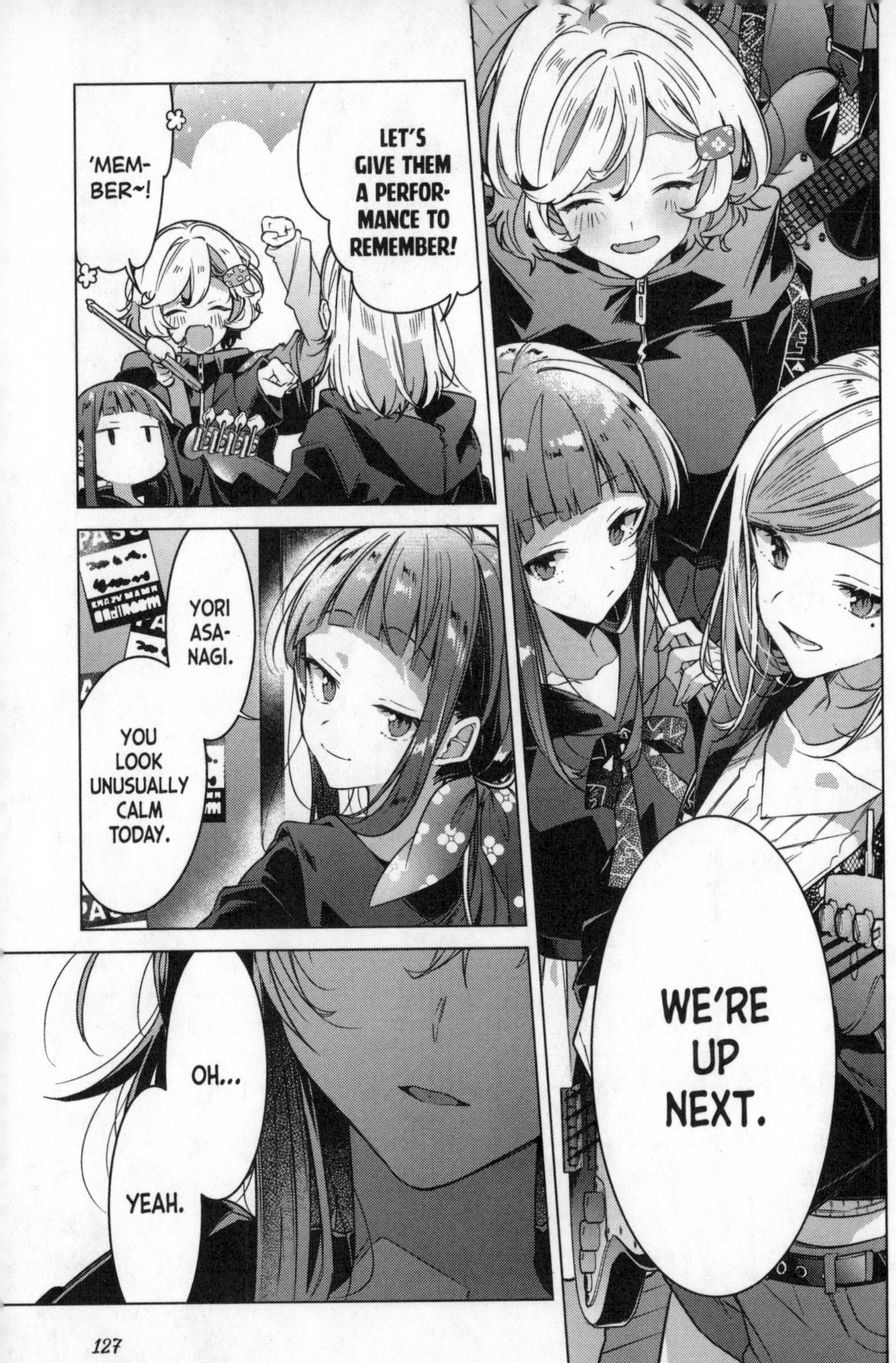
WE'RE UP NEXT.
LET'S GIVE THEM A PERFORMANCE TO REMEMBER!
'MEMBER~!
YORI ASANAGI.
YOU LOOK UNUSUALLY CALM TODAY.
OH...
YEAH.

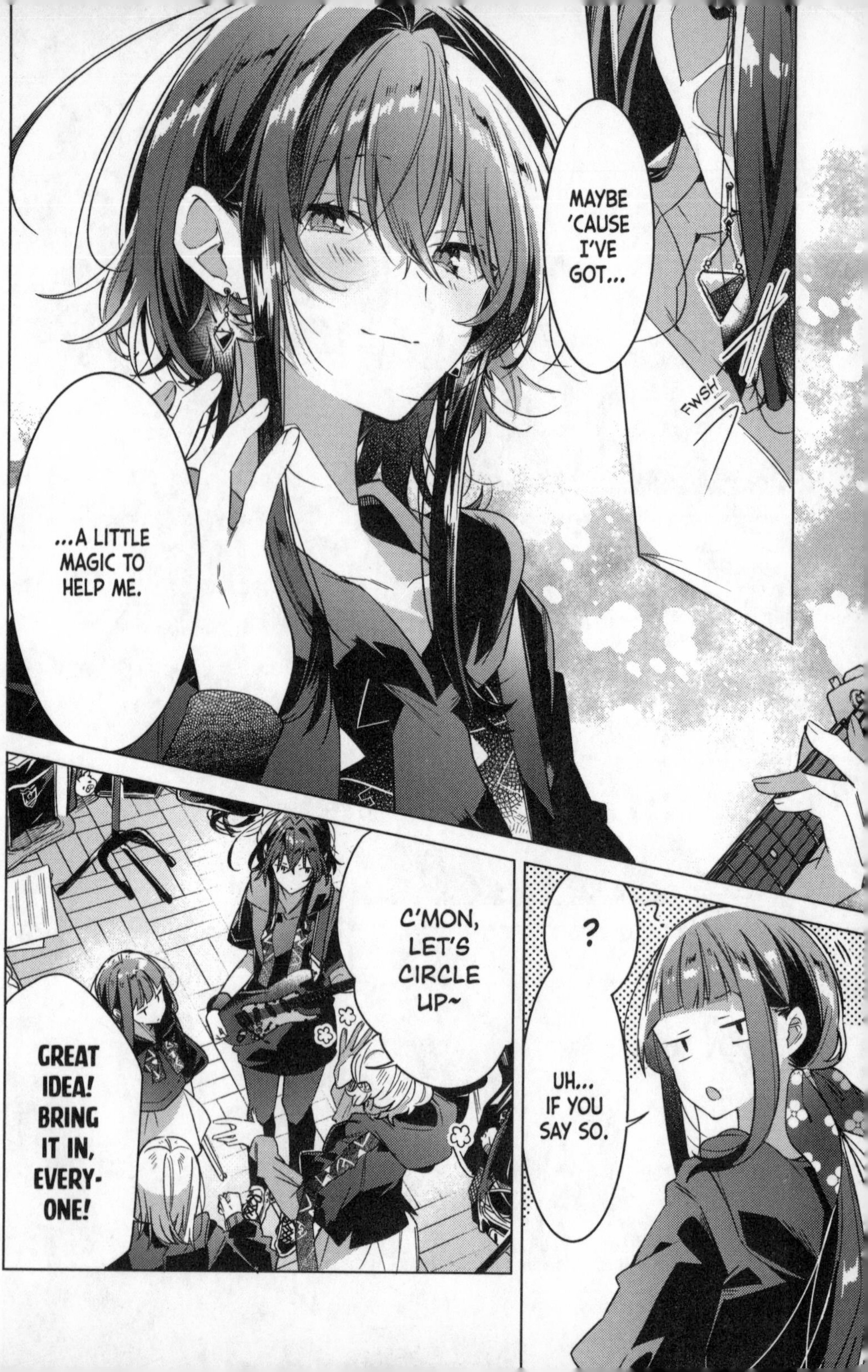
MAYBE 'CAUSE I'VE GOT...
FWSH
...A LITTLE MAGIC TO HELP ME.
?
UH... IF YOU SAY SO.
C'MON, LET'S CIRCLE UP~
GREAT IDEA! BRING IT IN, EVERY-ONE!

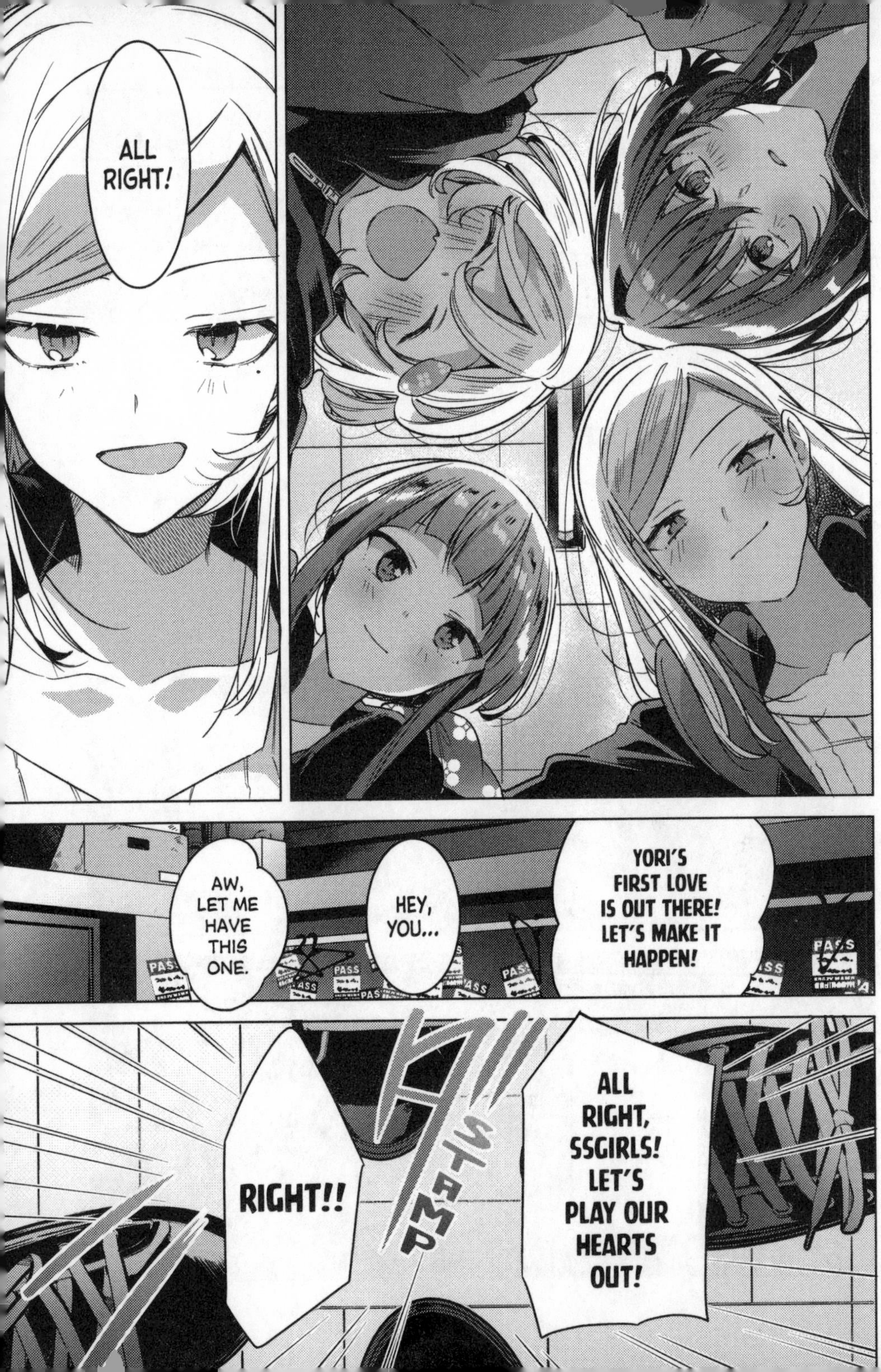
ALL RIGHT!
YORI'S FIRST LOVE IS OUT THERE! LET'S MAKE IT HAPPEN!
HEY, YOU...
AW, LET ME HAVE THIS ONE.
ALL RIGHT, SSGIRLS! LET'S PLAY OUR HEARTS OUT!
STAMP
RIGHT!!

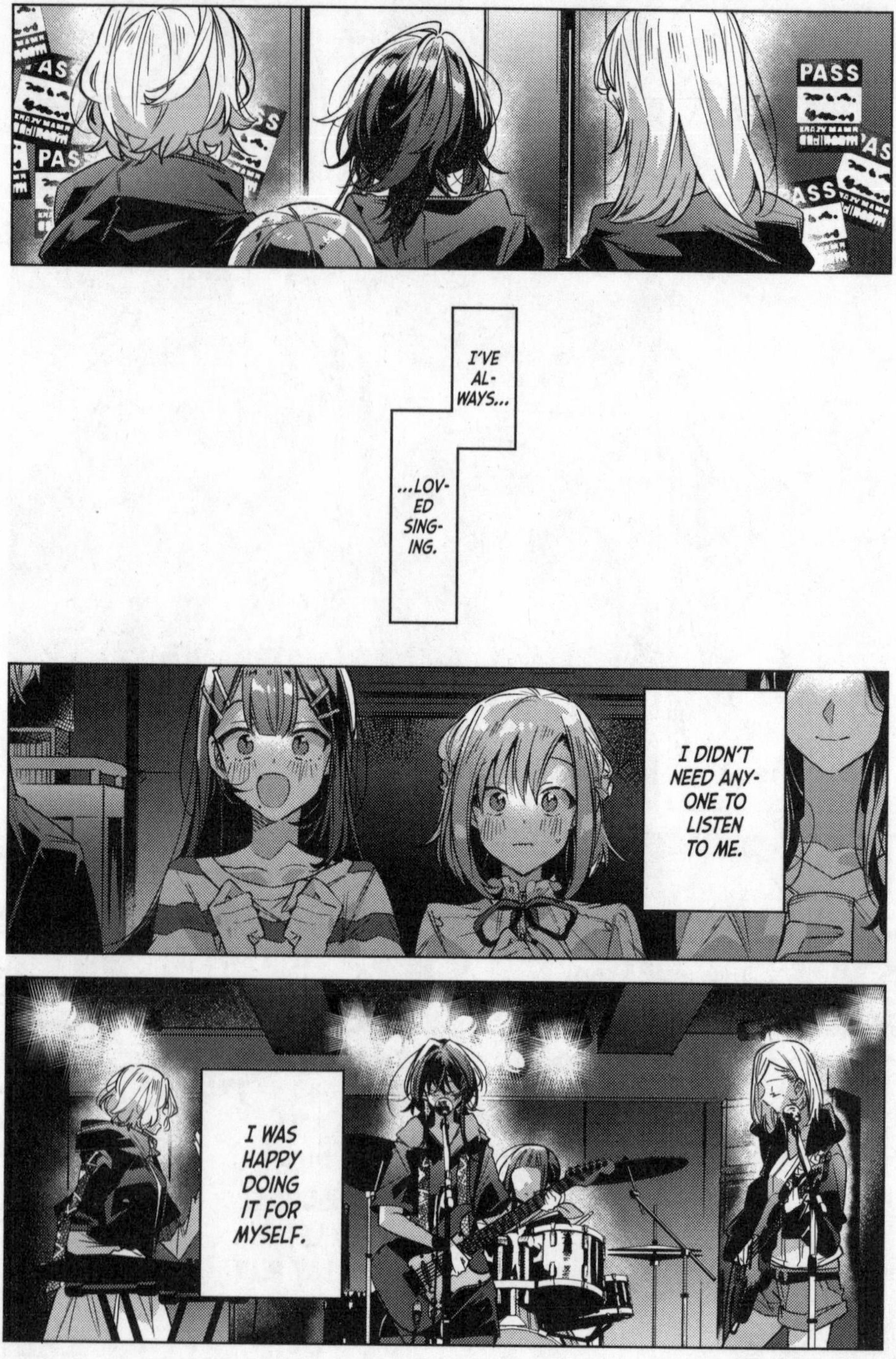
PASS
PASS
I'VE AL-WAYS...
...LOV-ED SING-ING.
I DIDN'T NEED ANYONE TO LISTEN TO ME.
I WAS HAPPY DOING IT FOR MYSELF.

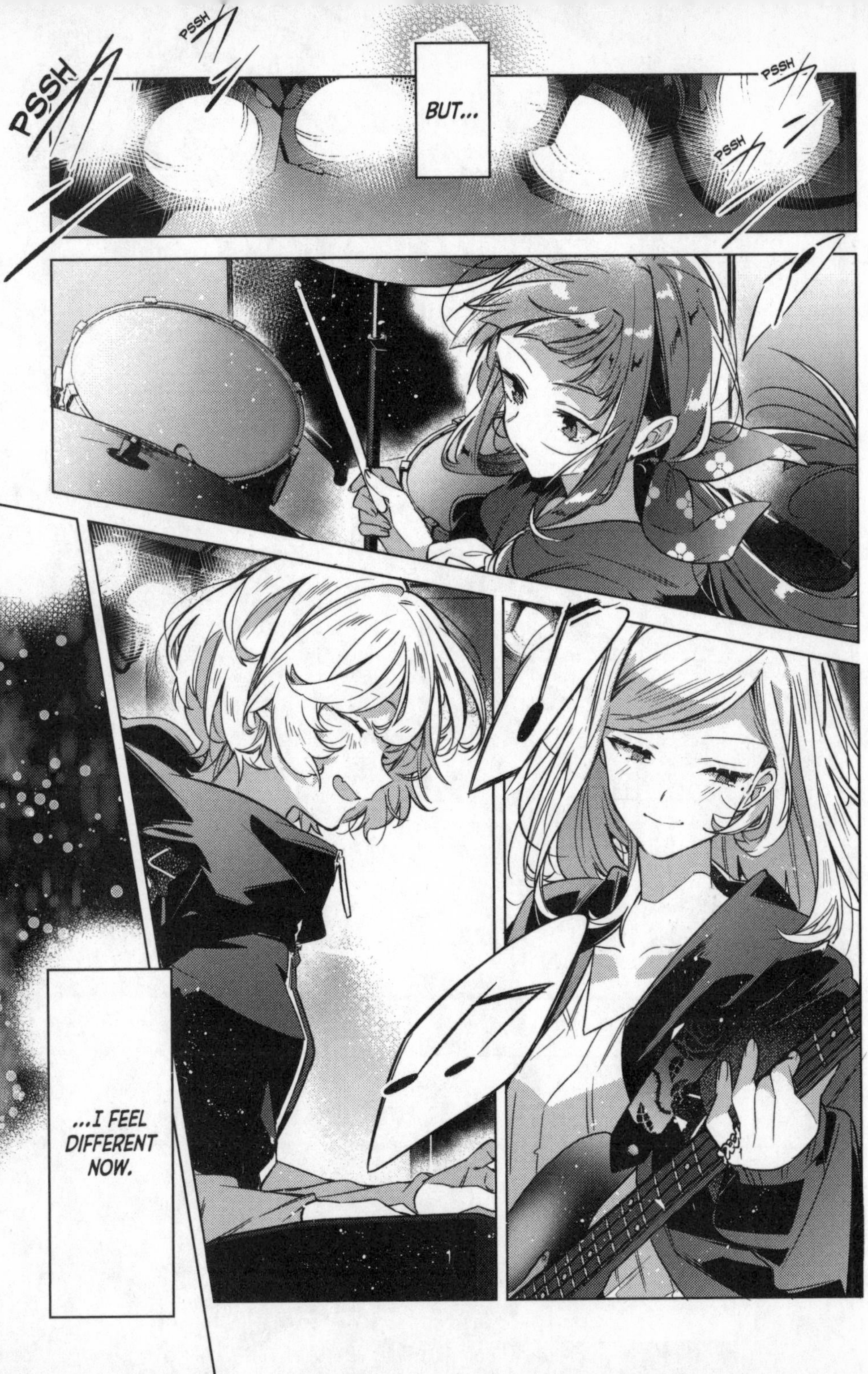
PSSH
PSSH
BUT...
PSSH
PSSH
...I FEEL DIFFERENT NOW.

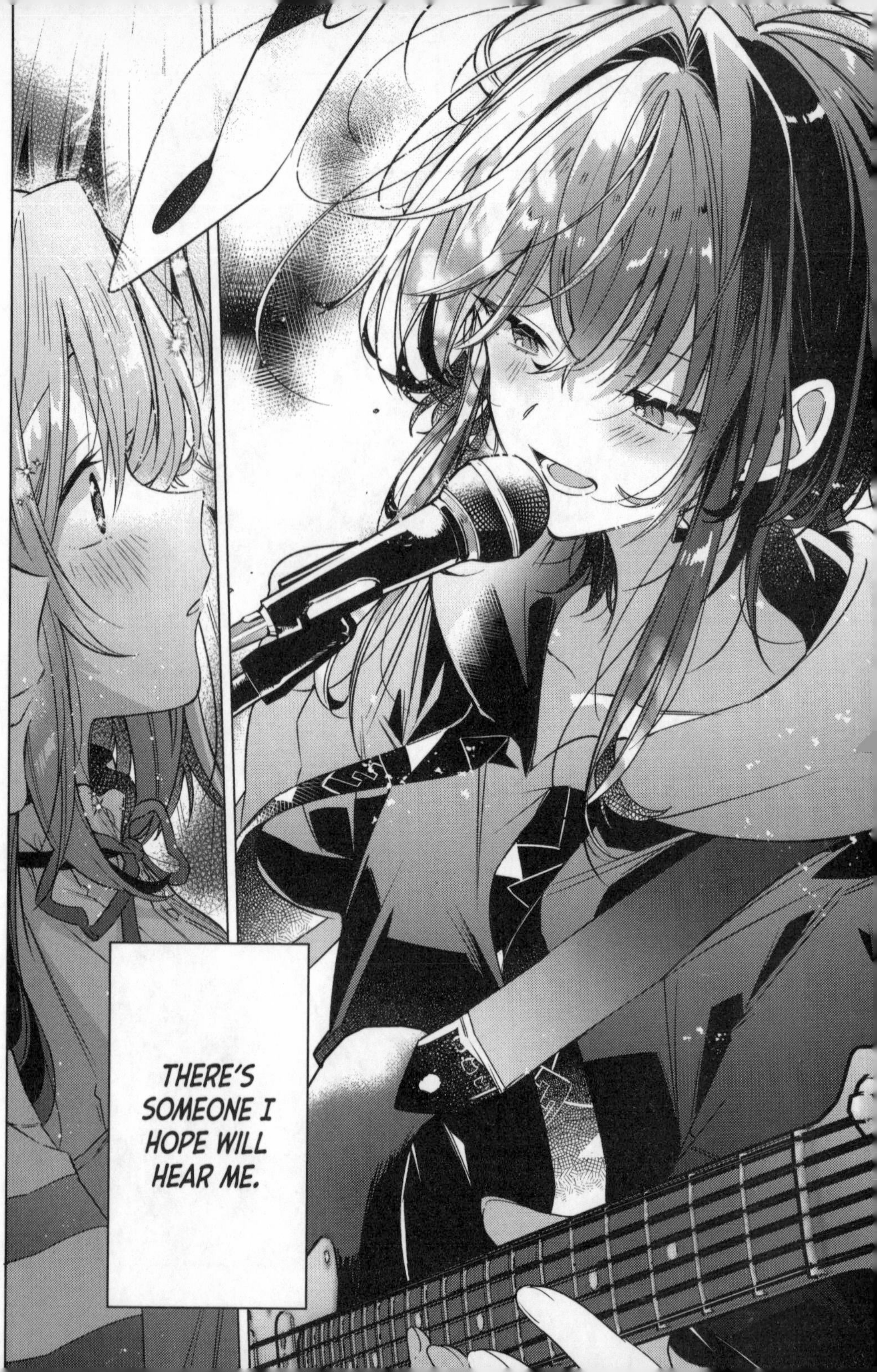
THERE'S SOMEONE I HOPE WILL HEAR ME.

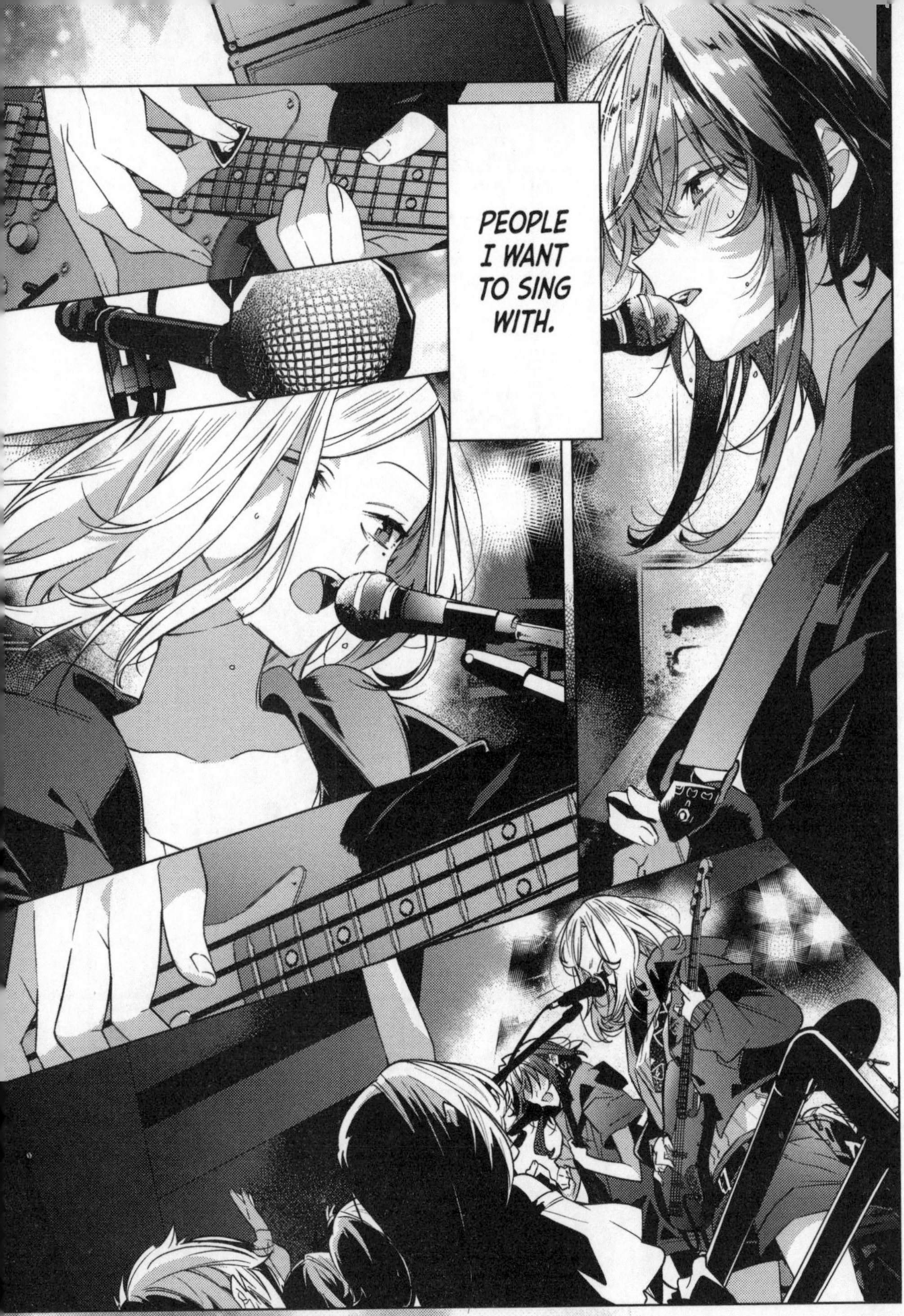
PEOPLE I WANT TO SING WITH.

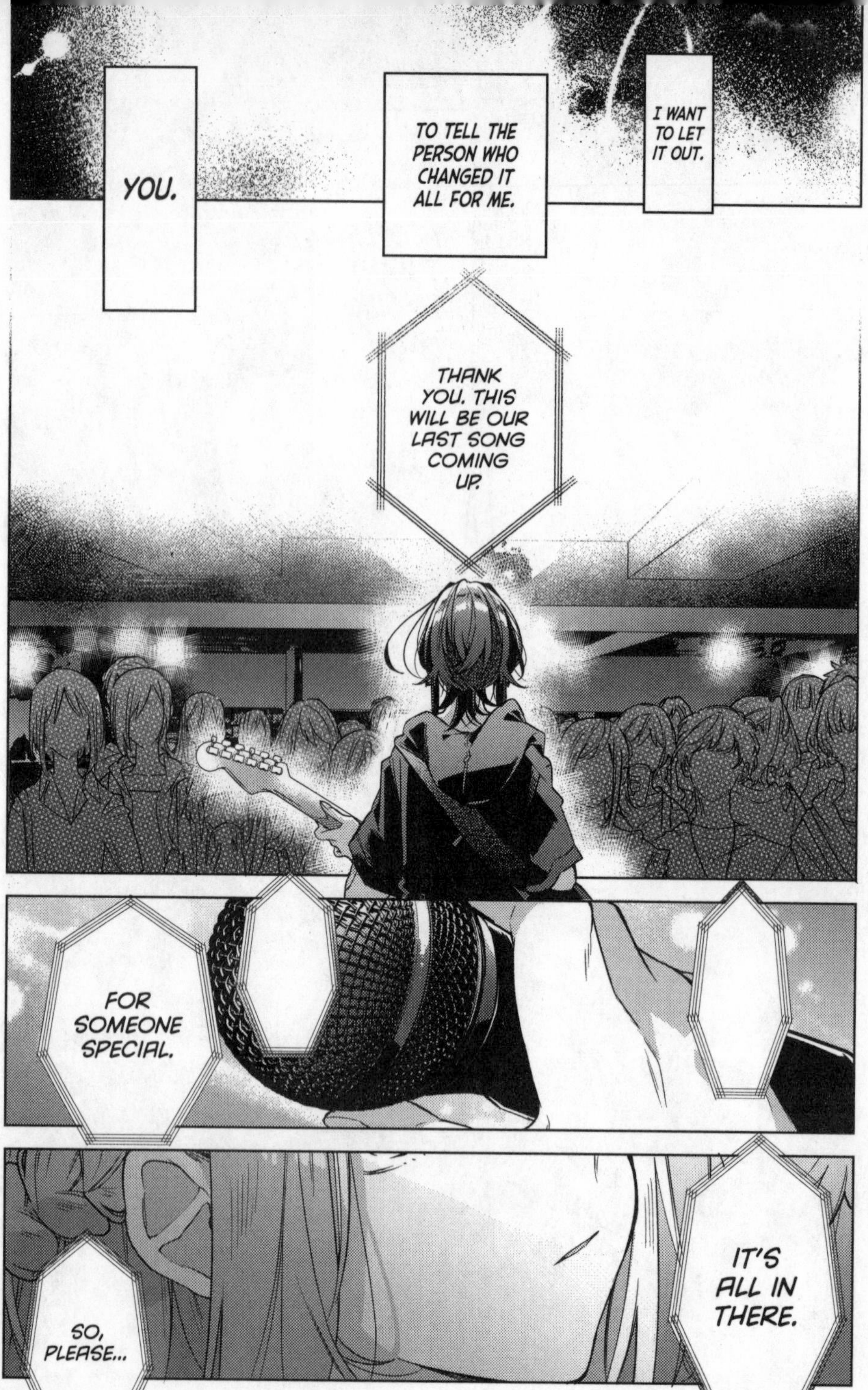
I WANT TO LET IT OUT.
TO TELL THE PERSON WHO CHANGED IT ALL FOR ME.
YOU.
THANK YOU. THIS WILL BE OUR LAST SONG COMING UP.
FOR SOMEONE SPECIAL.
IT'S ALL IN THERE.
SO, PLEASE...

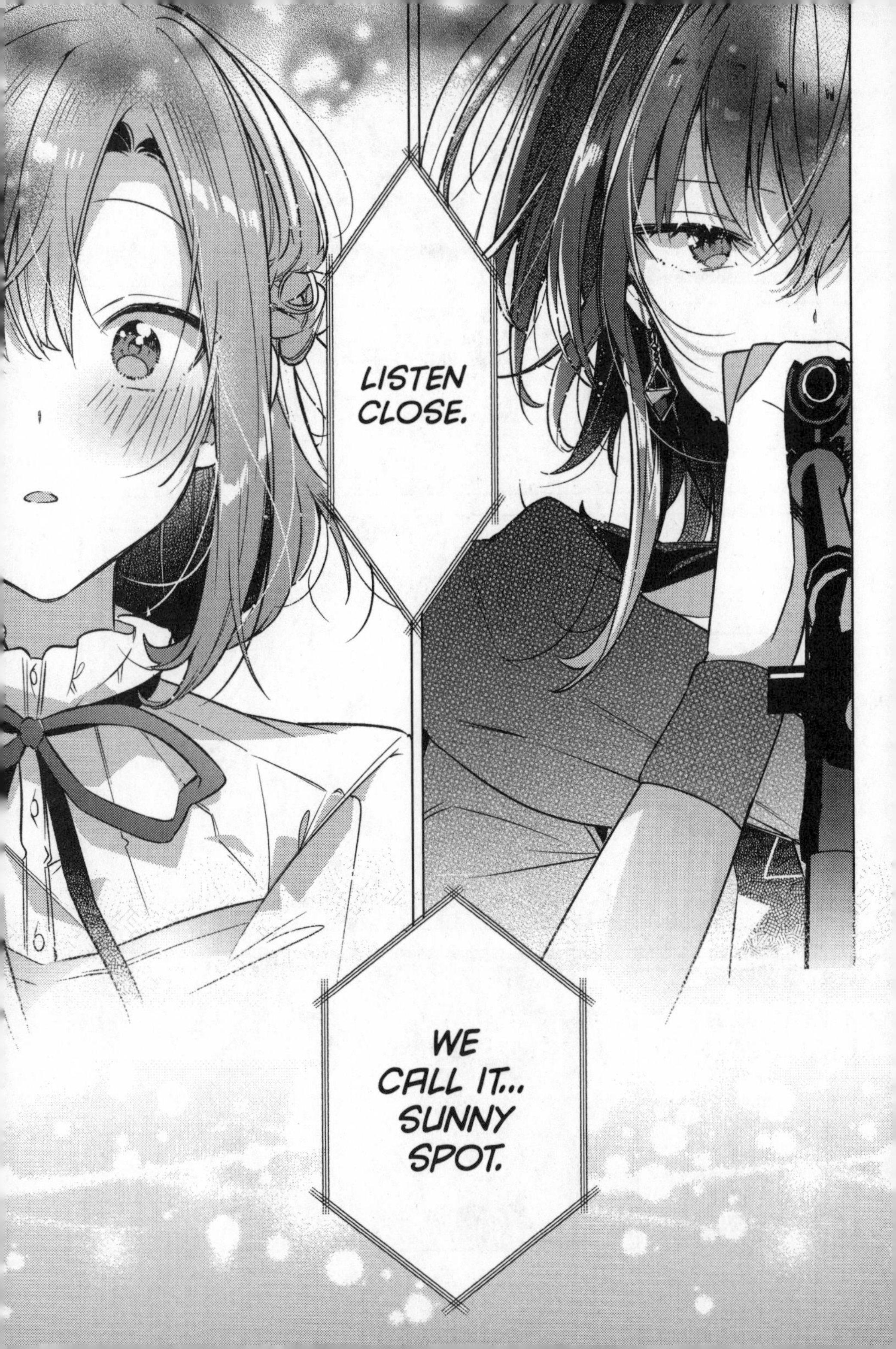
LISTEN CLOSE.
WE CALL IT... SUNNY SPOT.

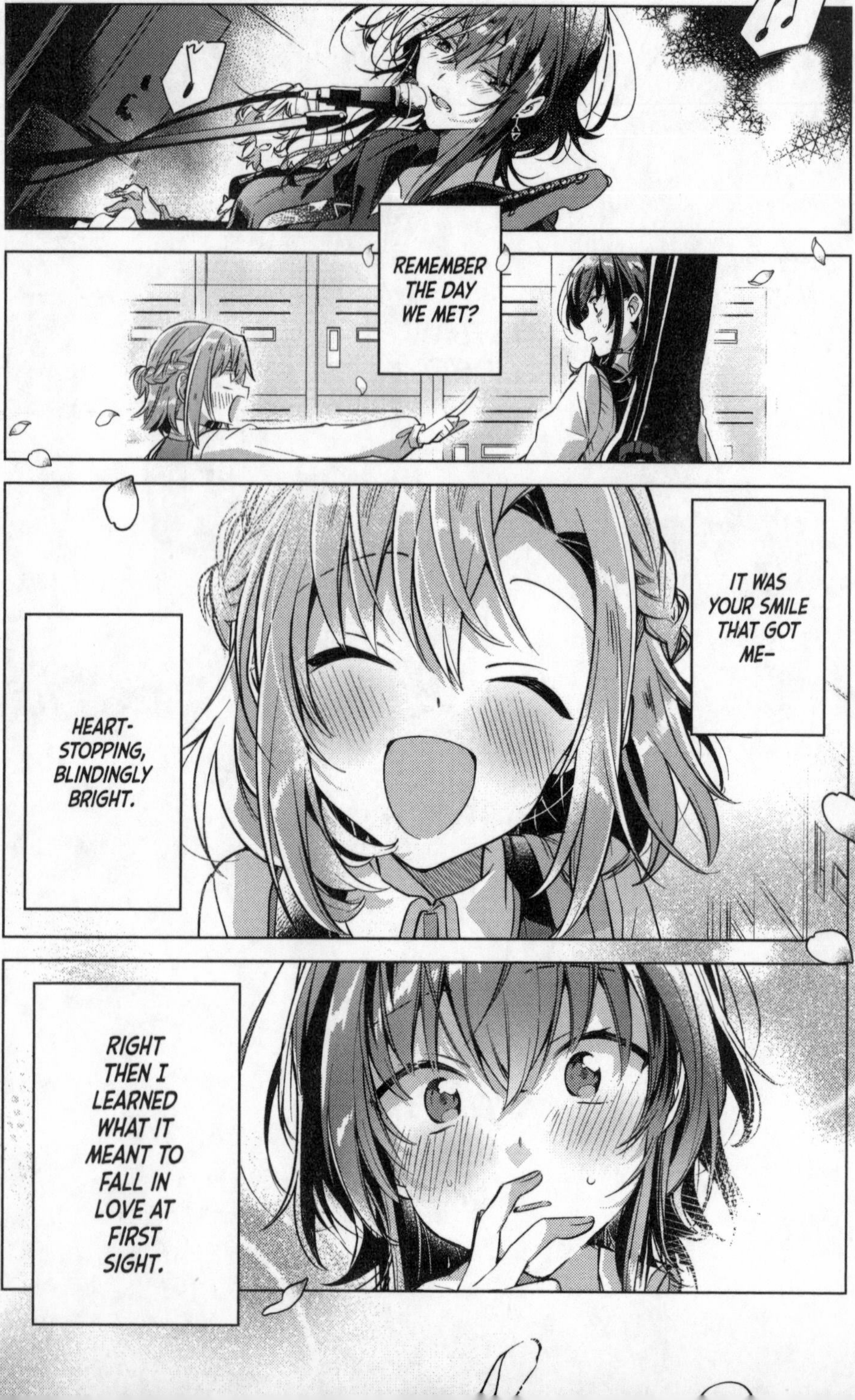
REMEMBER THE DAY WE MET?
IT WAS YOUR SMILE THAT GOT ME–
HEART-STOPPING, BLINDINGLY BRIGHT.
RIGHT THEN I LEARNED WHAT IT MEANT TO FALL IN LOVE AT FIRST SIGHT.

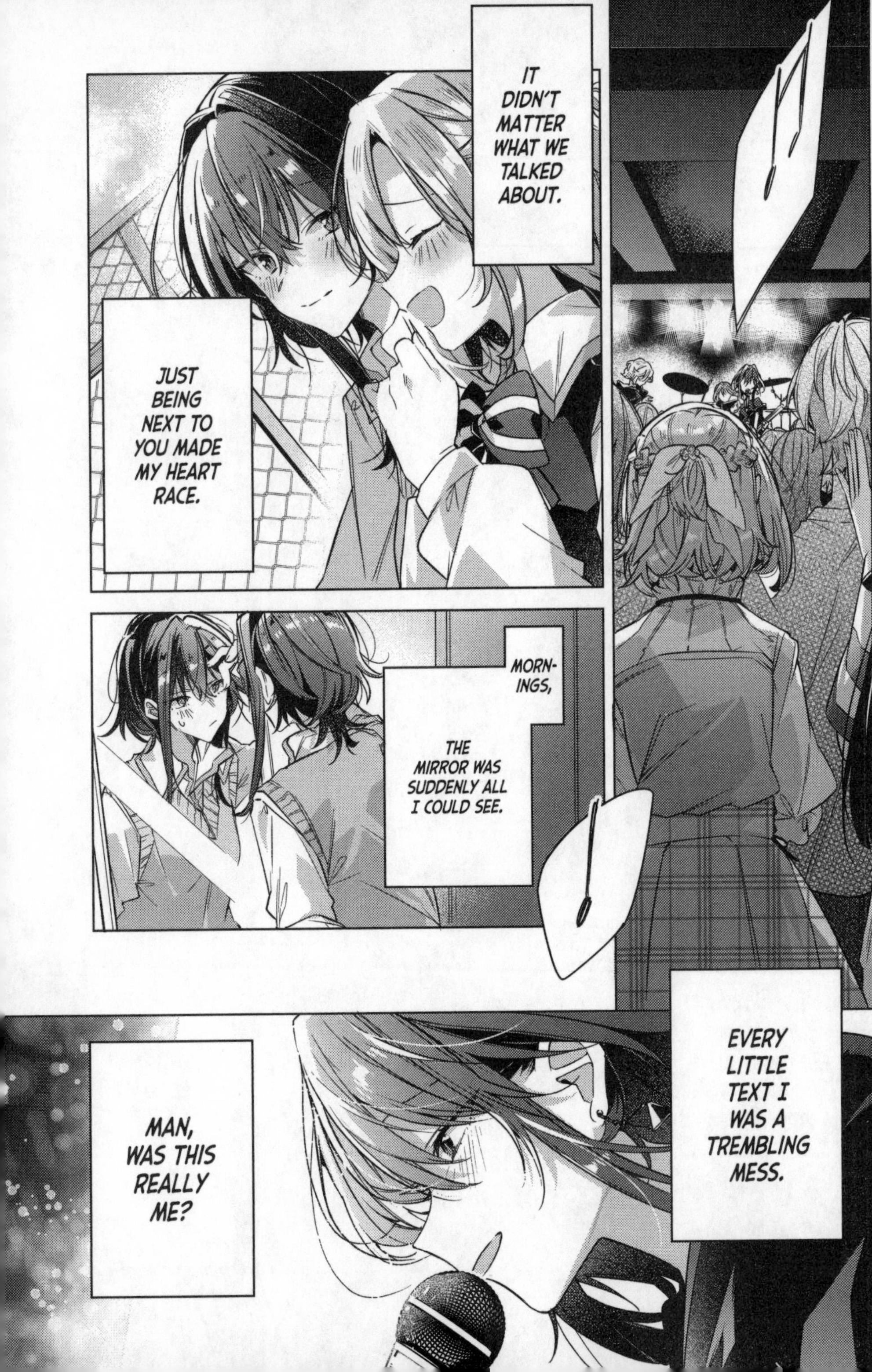
IT DIDN'T MATTER WHAT WE TALKED ABOUT.
JUST BEING NEXT TO YOU MADE MY HEART RACE.
MORNINGS,
THE MIRROR WAS SUDDENLY ALL I COULD SEE.
EVERY LITTLE TEXT I WAS A TREMBLING MESS.
MAN, WAS THIS REALLY ME?

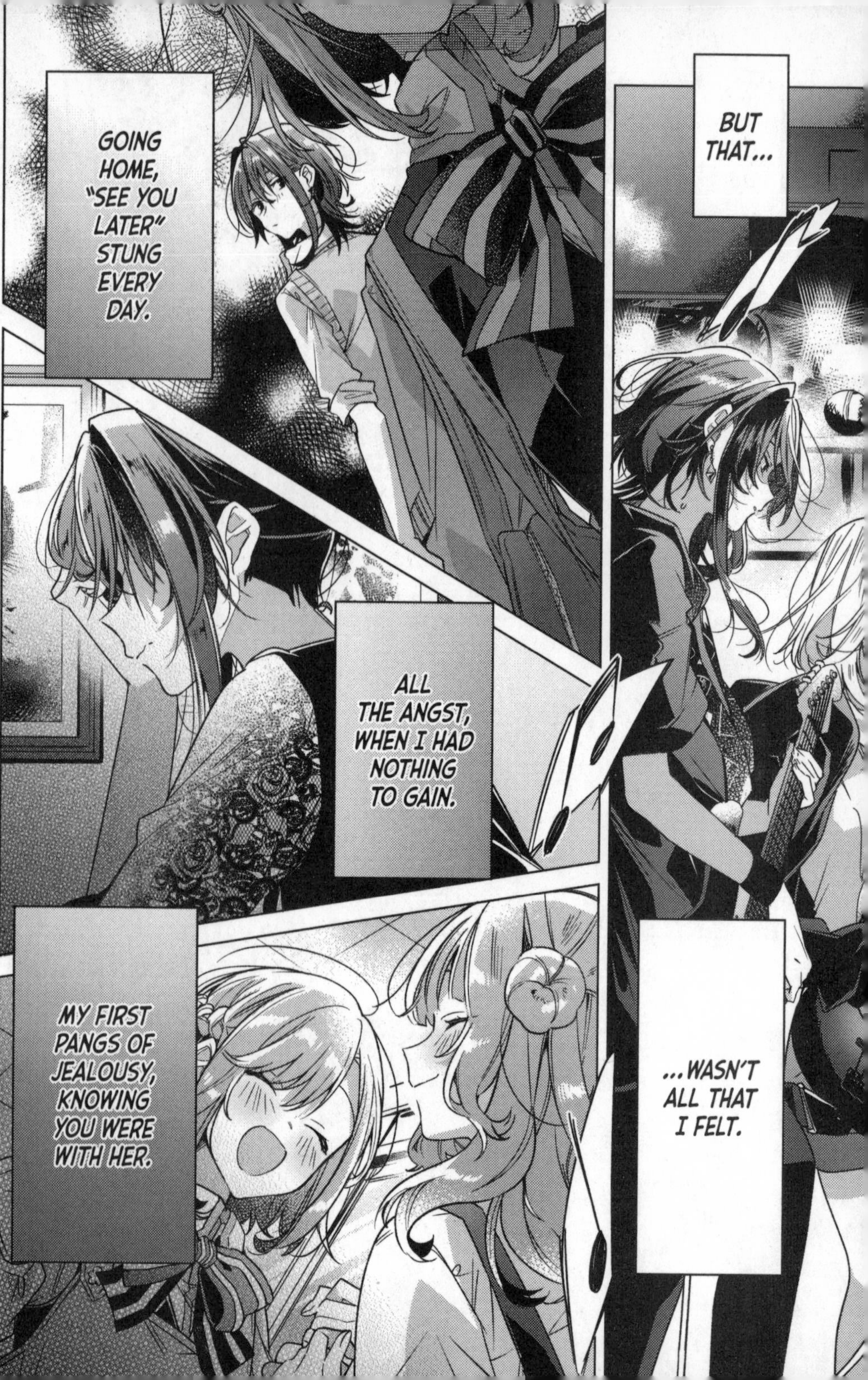
BUT THAT...
...WASN'T ALL THAT I FELT.
GOING HOME, "SEE YOU LATER" STUNG EVERY DAY.
ALL THE ANGST, WHEN I HAD NOTHING TO GAIN.
MY FIRST PANGS OF JEALOUSY, KNOWING YOU WERE WITH HER.

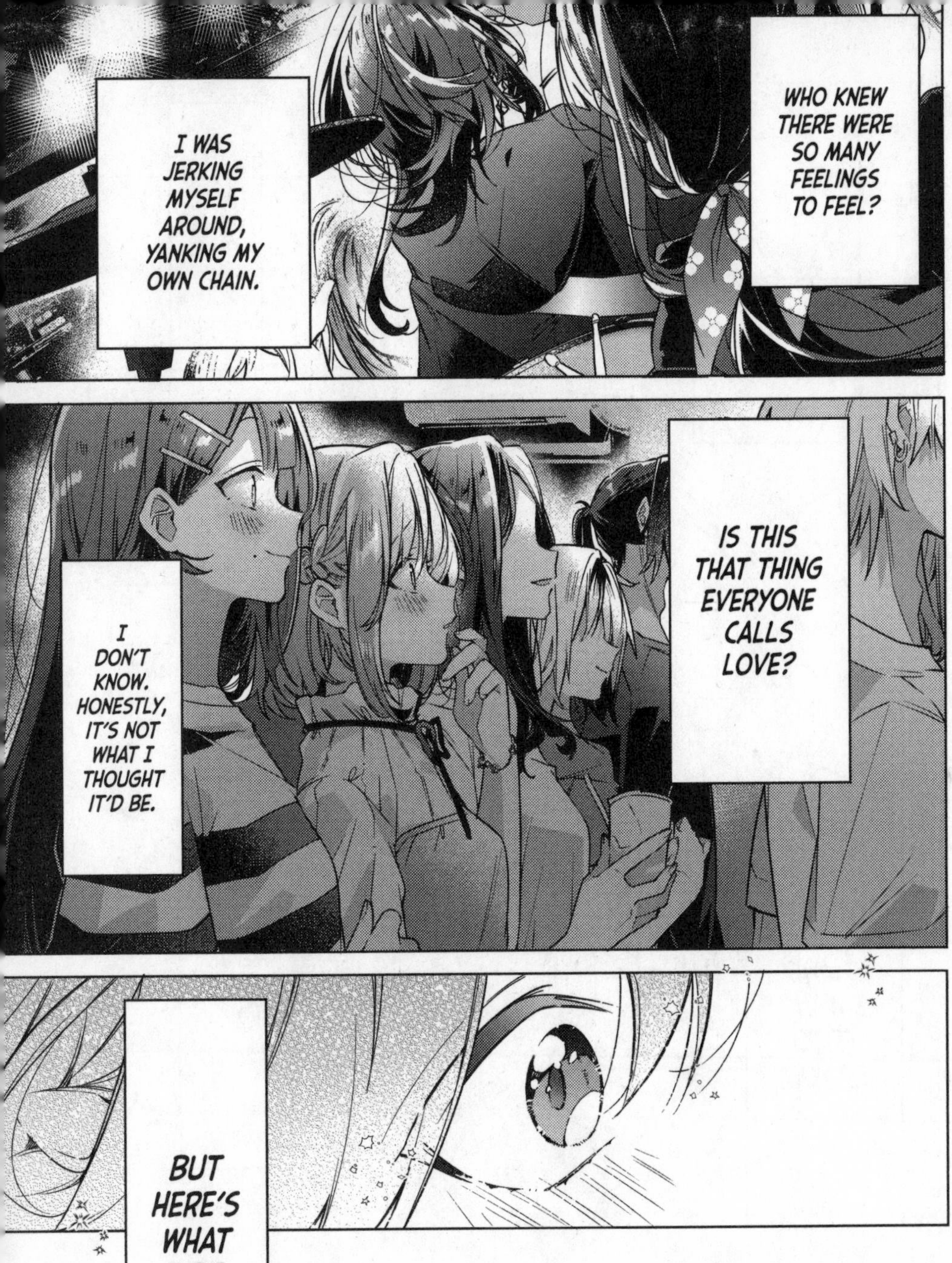
WHO KNEW THERE WERE SO MANY FEELINGS TO FEEL?
I WAS JERKING MYSELF AROUND, YANKING MY OWN CHAIN.
IS THIS THAT THING EVERYONE CALLS LOVE?
I DON'T KNOW. HONESTLY, IT'S NOT WHAT I THOUGHT IT'D BE.
BUT HERE'S WHAT I DO KNOW...

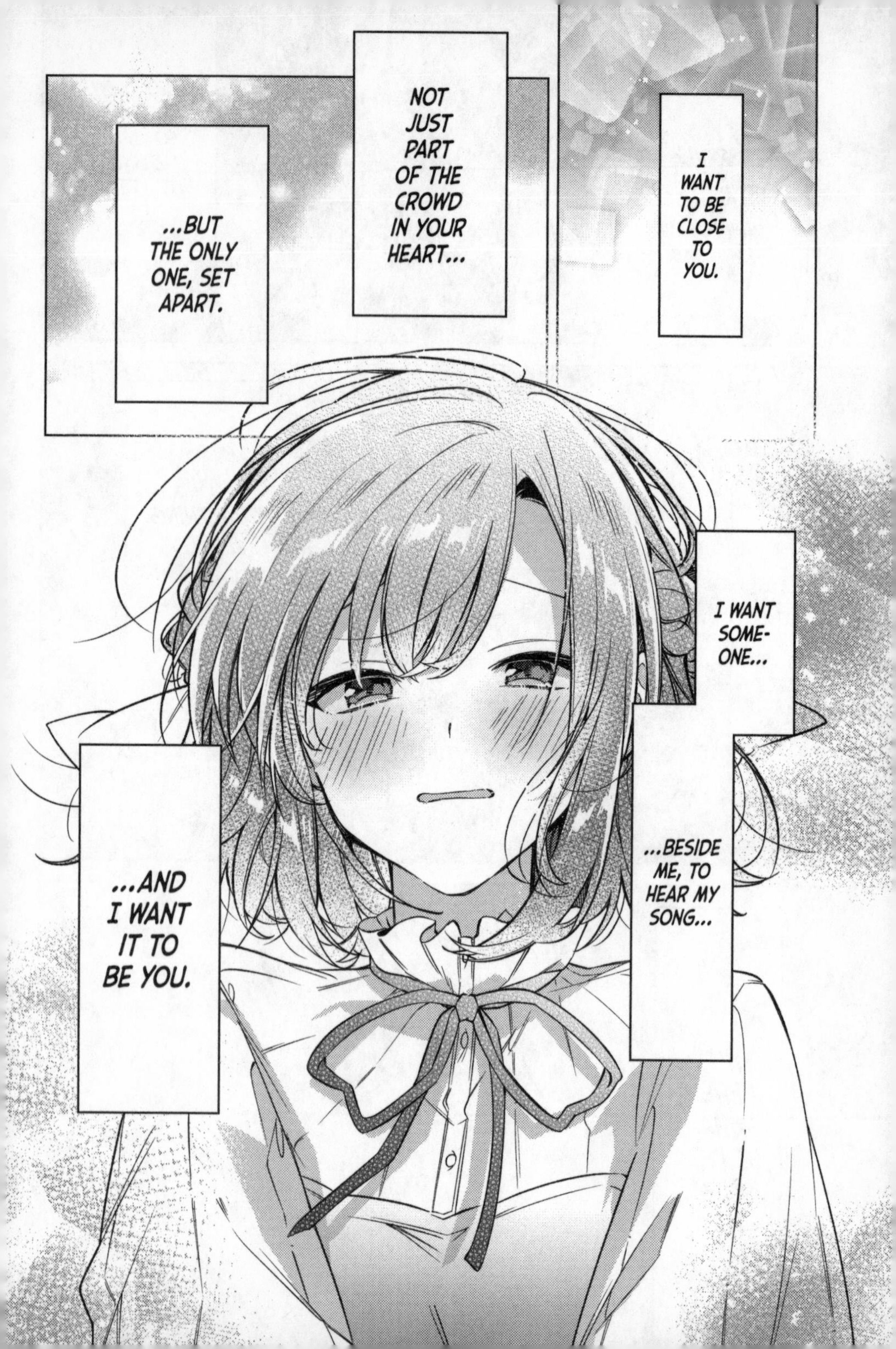
I WANT TO BE CLOSE TO YOU.
NOT JUST PART OF THE CROWD IN YOUR HEART...
...BUT THE ONLY ONE, SET APART.
I WANT SOME-ONE...
...BESIDE ME, TO HEAR MY SONG...
...AND I WANT IT TO BE YOU.

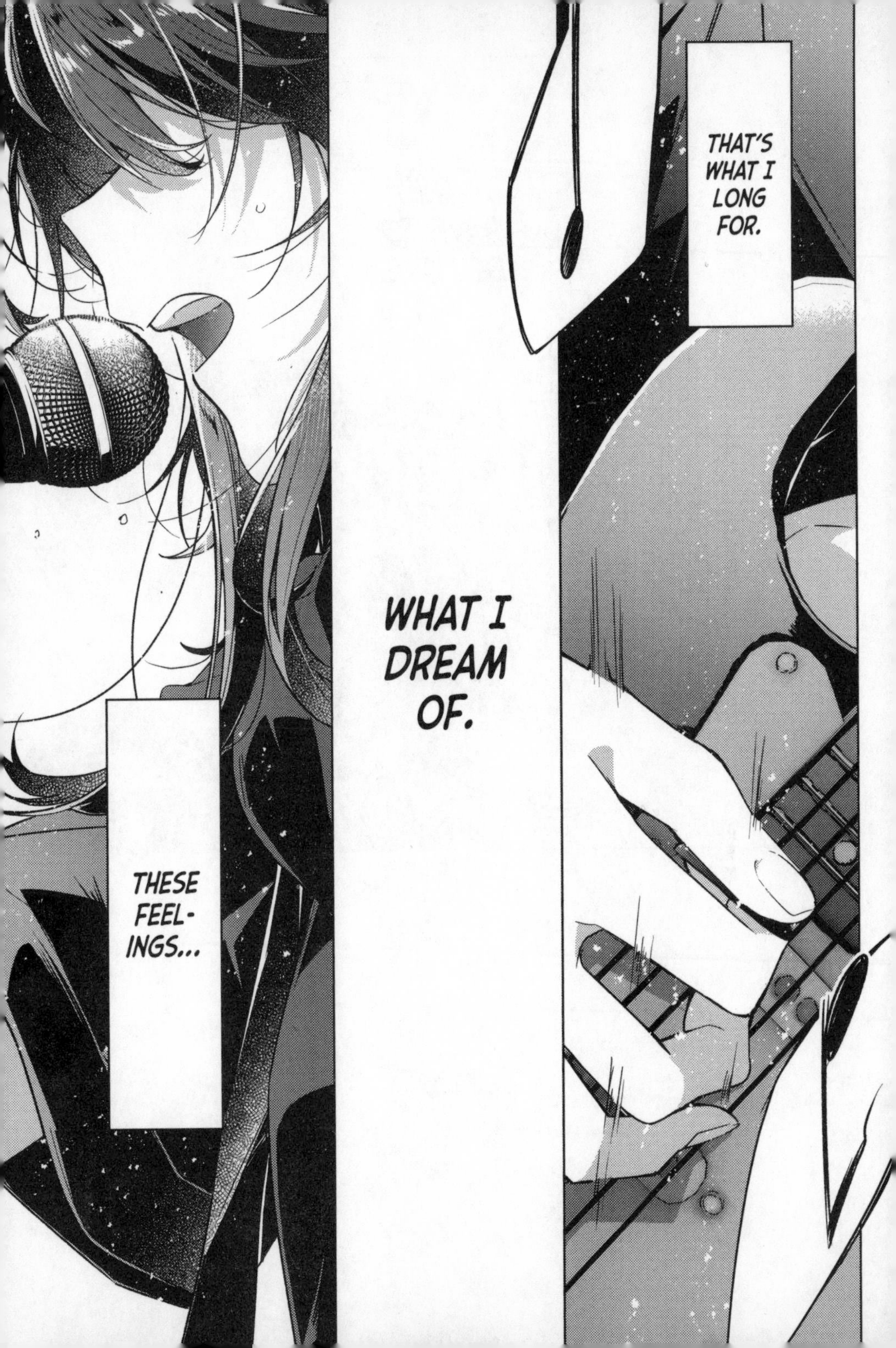
THAT'S WHAT I LONG FOR.
WHAT I DREAM OF.
THESE FEEL-INGS...

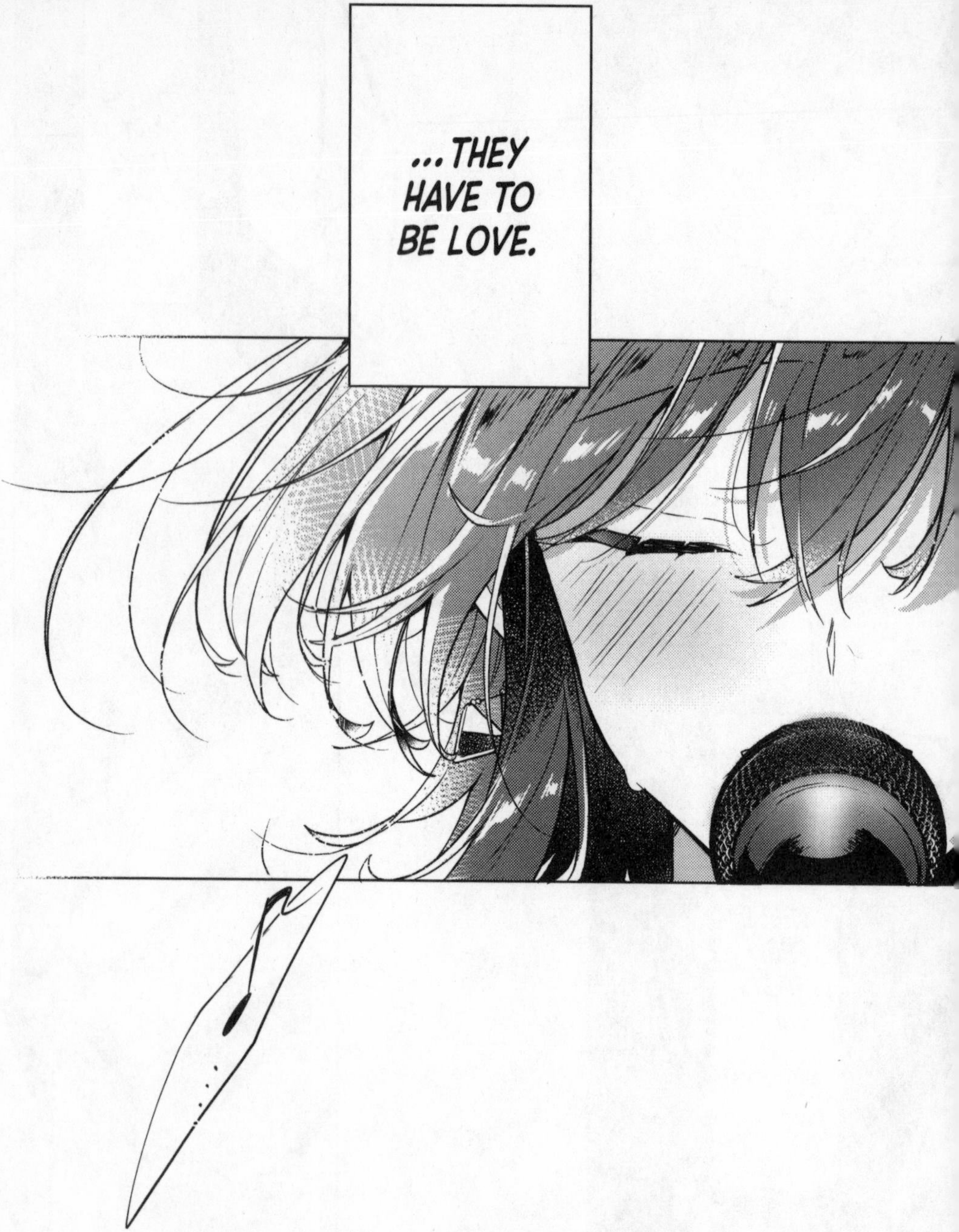
...THEY HAVE TO BE LOVE.

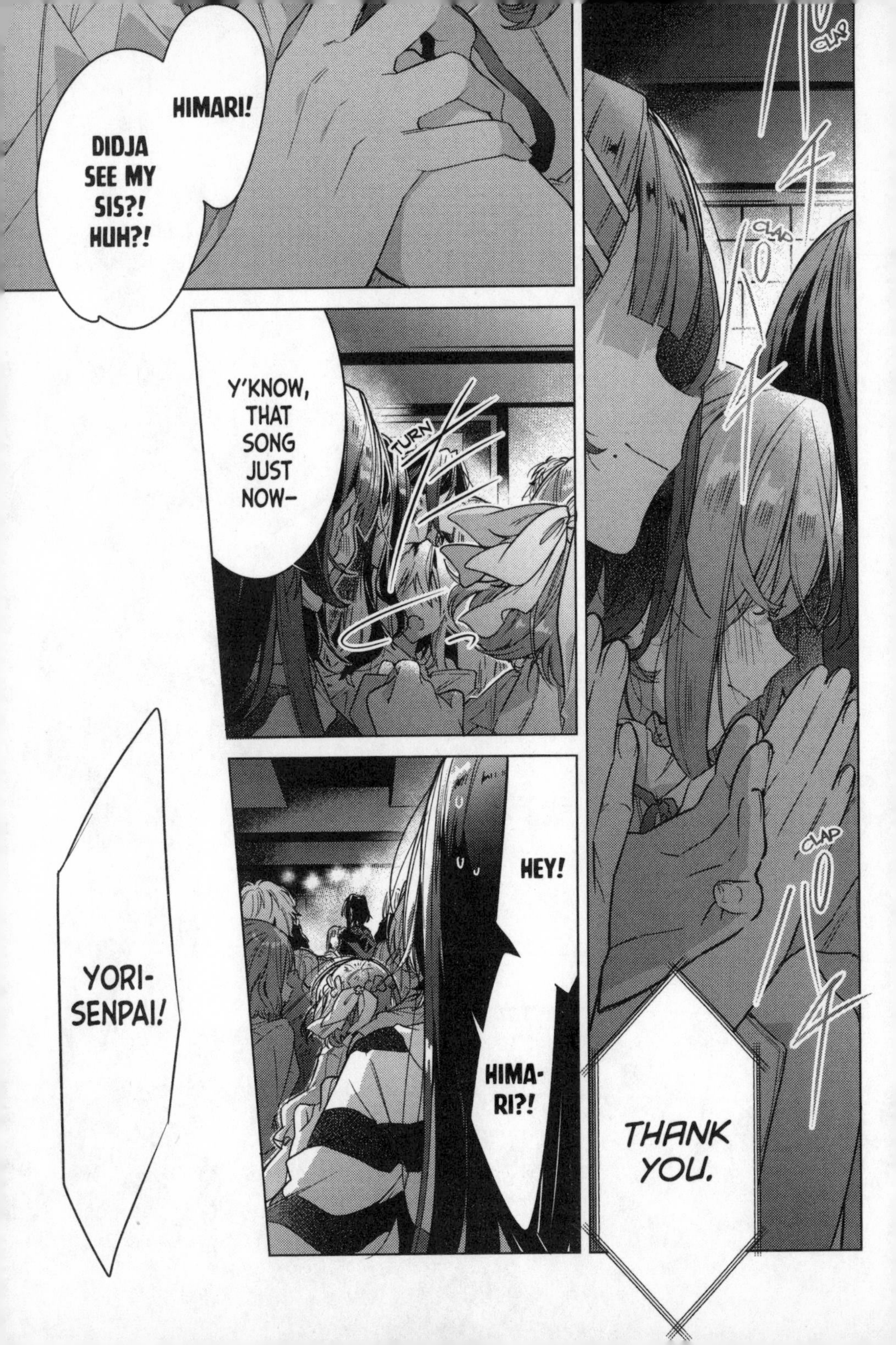
CLAP
CLAP
CLAP
THANK YOU.
HIMARI!
DIDJA SEE MY SIS?! HUH?!
Y'KNOW, THAT SONG JUST NOW–
TURN
HEY!
HIMA-RI?!
YORI-SENPAI!

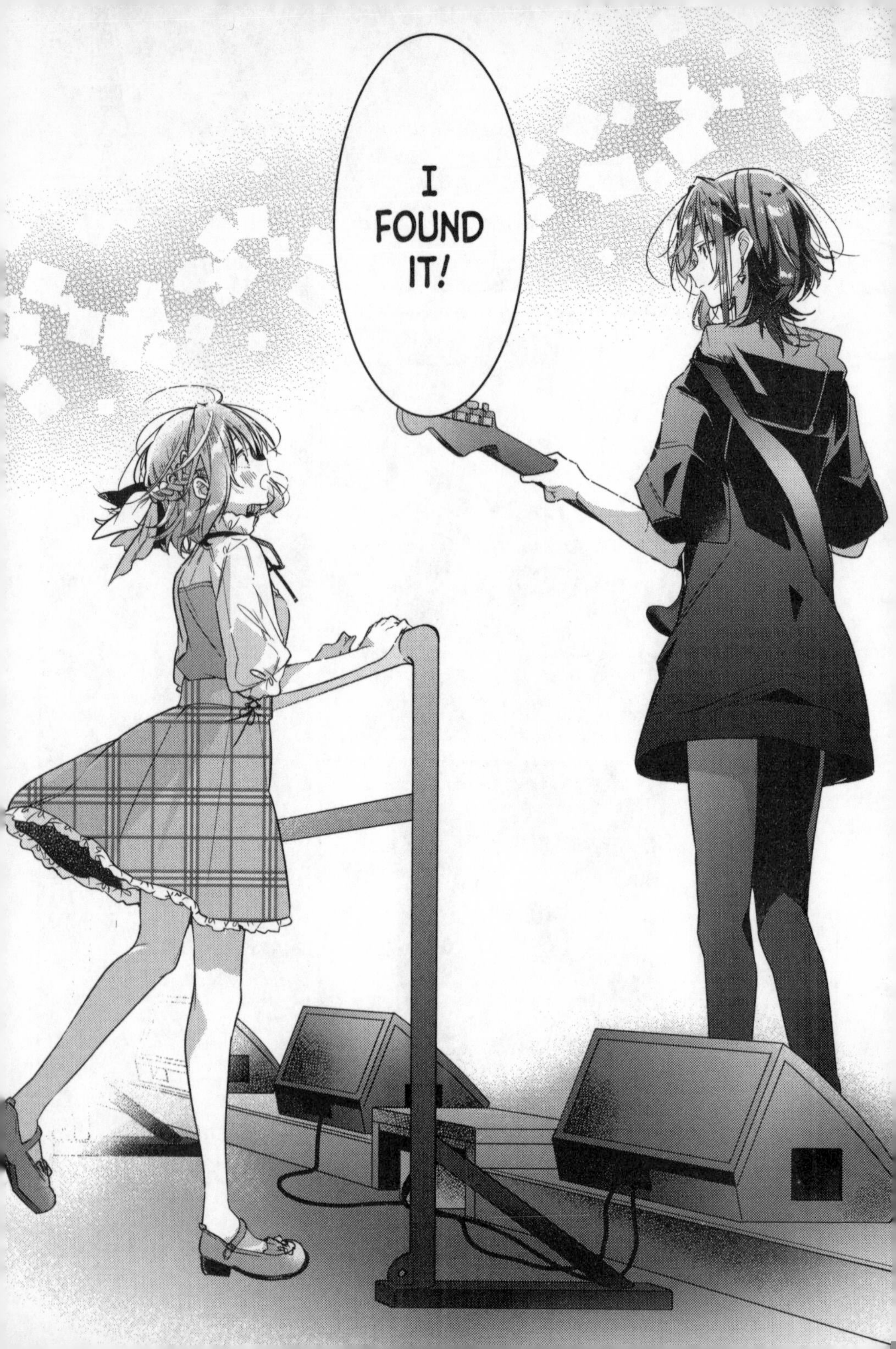
I FOUND IT!

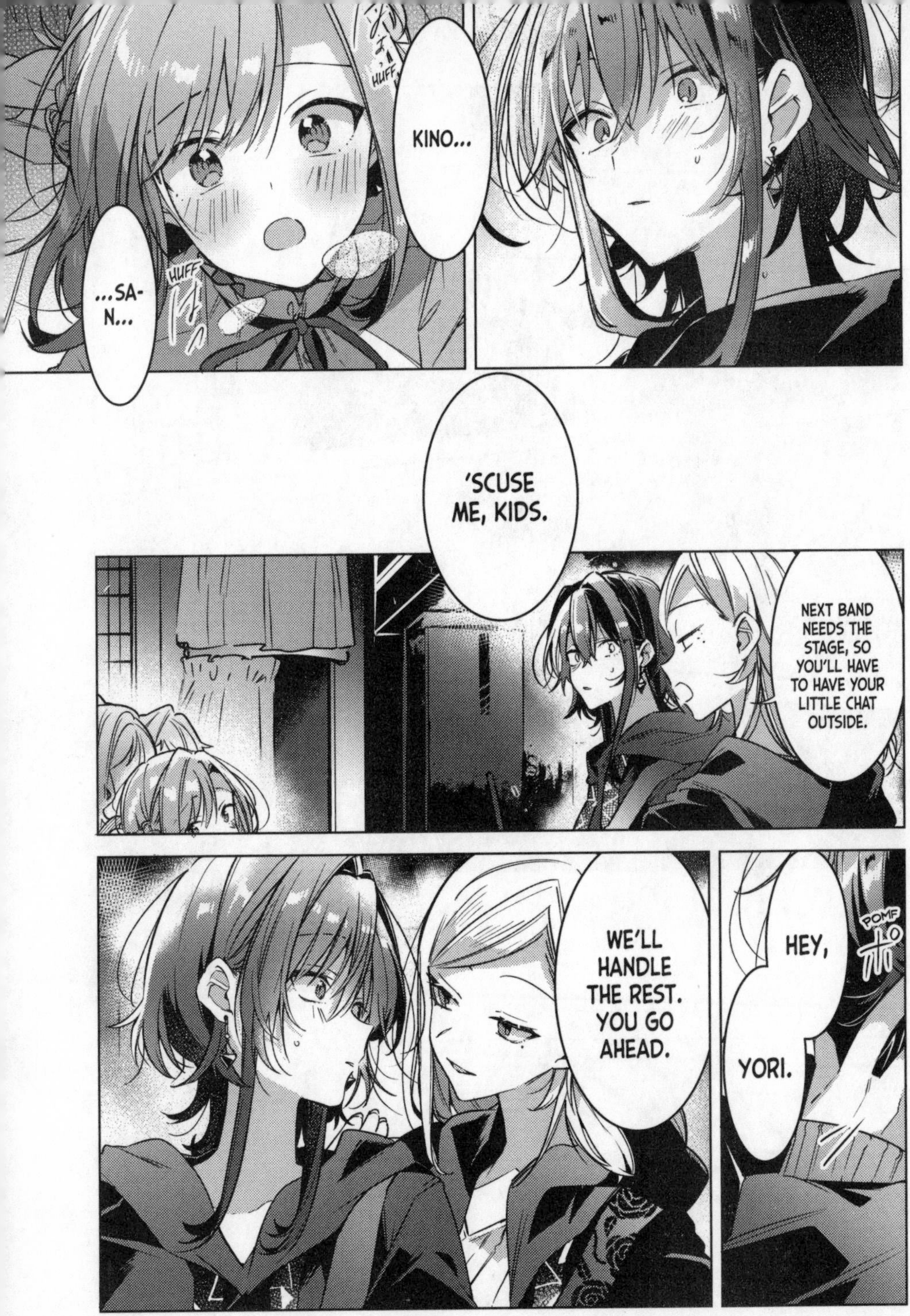
HUFF
KINO...
HUFF
...SA-N...
'SCUSE ME, KIDS.
NEXT BAND NEEDS THE STAGE, SO YOU'LL HAVE TO HAVE YOUR LITTLE CHAT OUTSIDE.
POMF
HEY, YORI.
WE'LL HANDLE THE REST. YOU GO AHEAD.

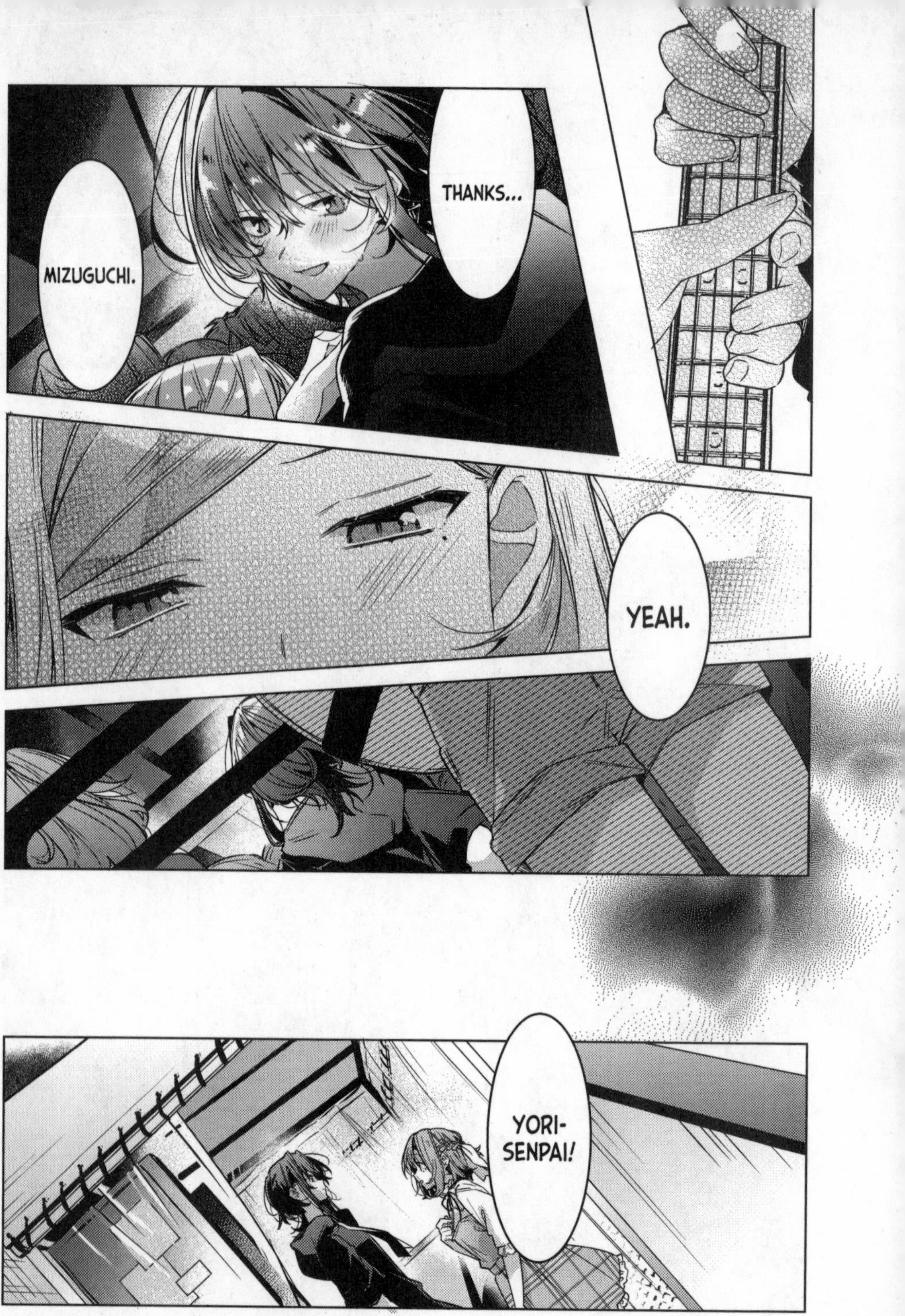
THANKS...
MIZUGUCHI.
YEAH.
YORI-SENPAI!

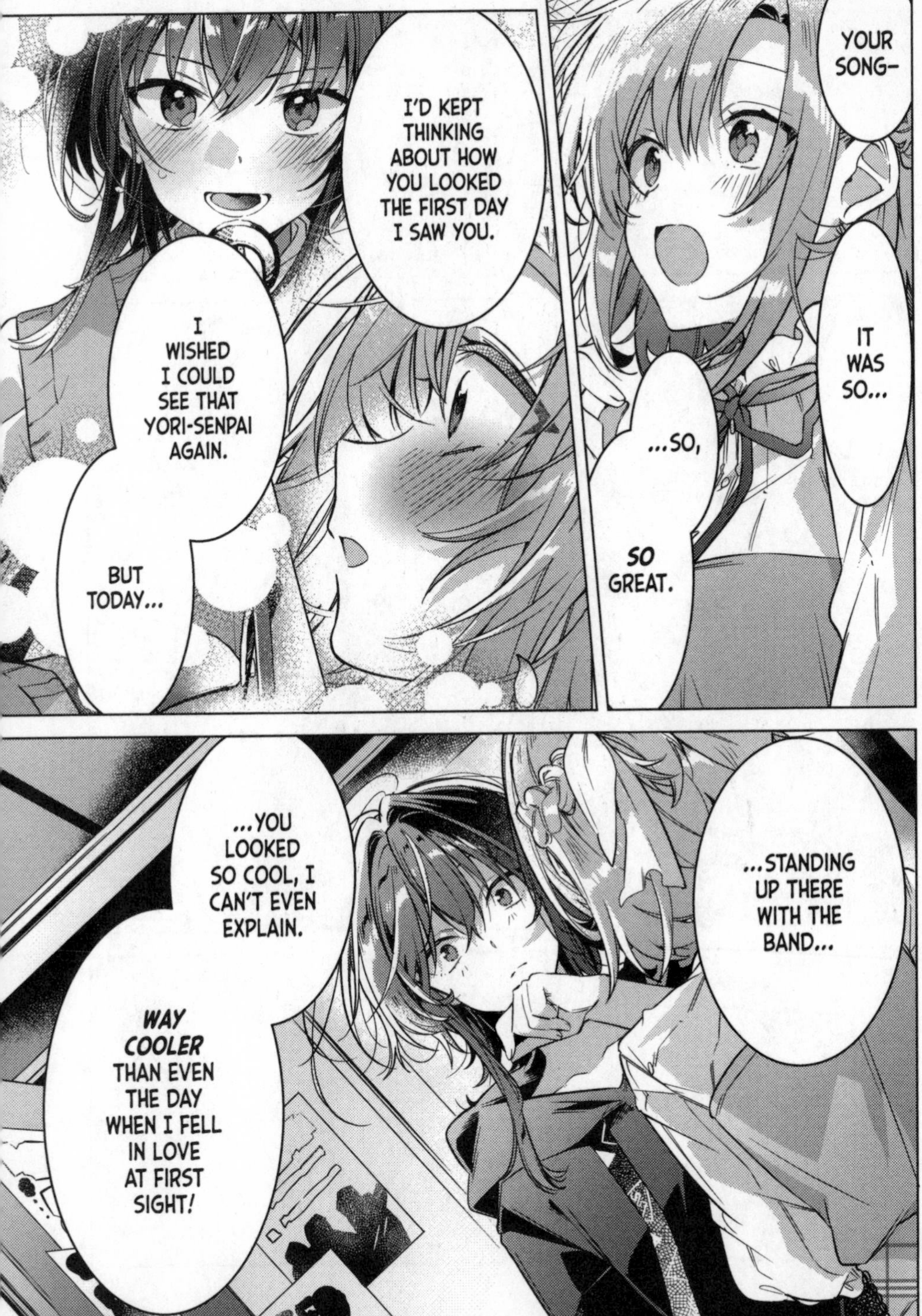
YOUR SONG–
IT WAS SO...
...SO,
SO GREAT.
I'D KEPT THINKING ABOUT HOW YOU LOOKED THE FIRST DAY I SAW YOU.
I WISHED I COULD SEE THAT YORI-SENPAI AGAIN.
BUT TODAY...
...STANDING UP THERE WITH THE BAND...
...YOU LOOKED SO COOL, I CAN'T EVEN EXPLAIN.
WAY COOLER THAN EVEN THE DAY WHEN I FELL IN LOVE AT FIRST SIGHT!

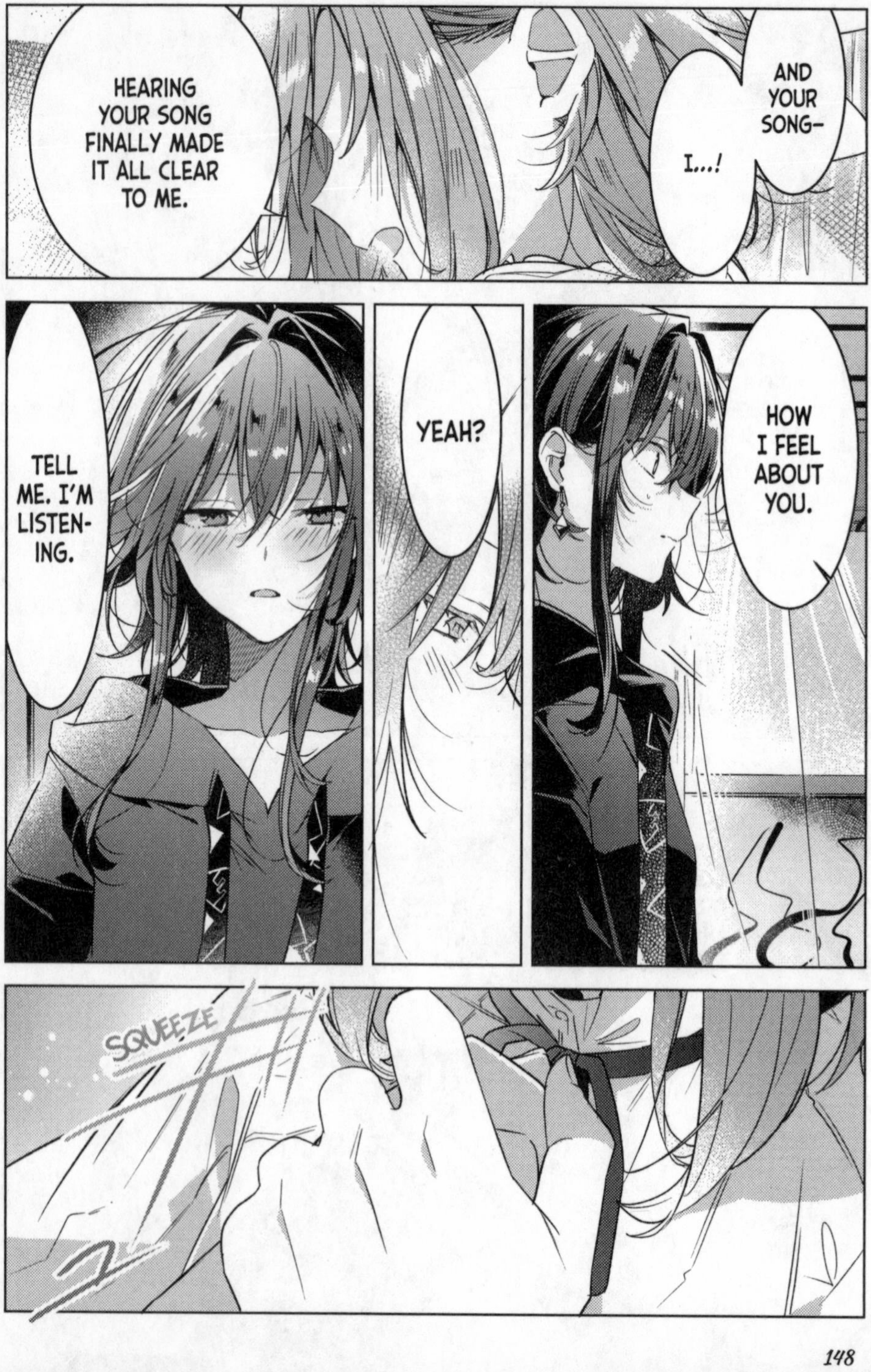
AND YOUR SONG—
I...!
HEARING YOUR SONG FINALLY MADE IT ALL CLEAR TO ME.
HOW I FEEL ABOUT YOU.
YEAH?
TELL ME. I'M LISTENING.
SQUEEZE

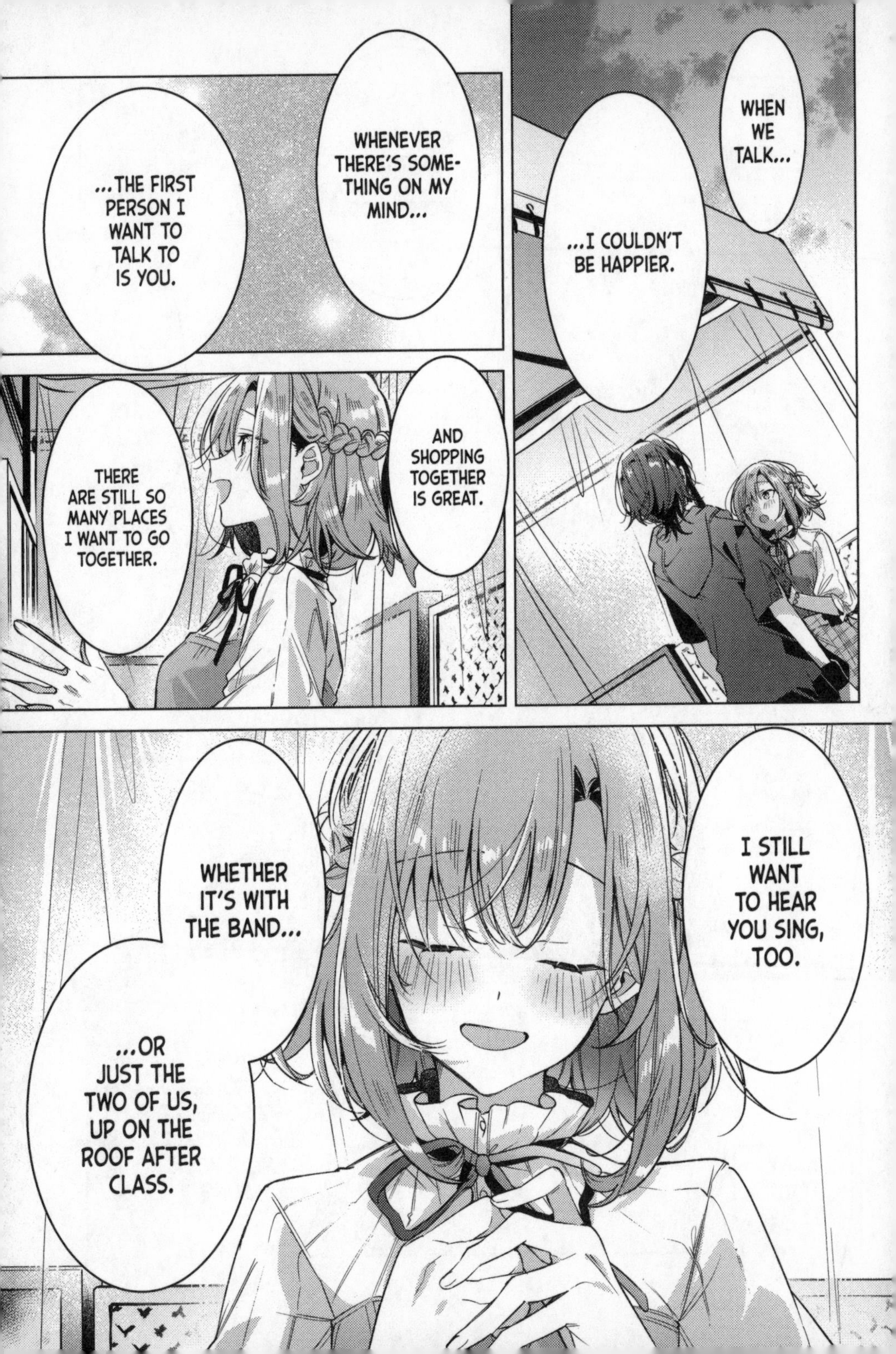
WHEN WE TALK...
...I COULDN'T BE HAPPIER.
WHENEVER THERE'S SOME-THING ON MY MIND...
...THE FIRST PERSON I WANT TO TALK TO IS YOU.
AND SHOPPING TOGETHER IS GREAT.
THERE ARE STILL SO MANY PLACES I WANT TO GO TOGETHER.
I STILL WANT TO HEAR YOU SING, TOO.
WHETHER IT'S WITH THE BAND...
...OR JUST THE TWO OF US, UP ON THE ROOF AFTER CLASS.

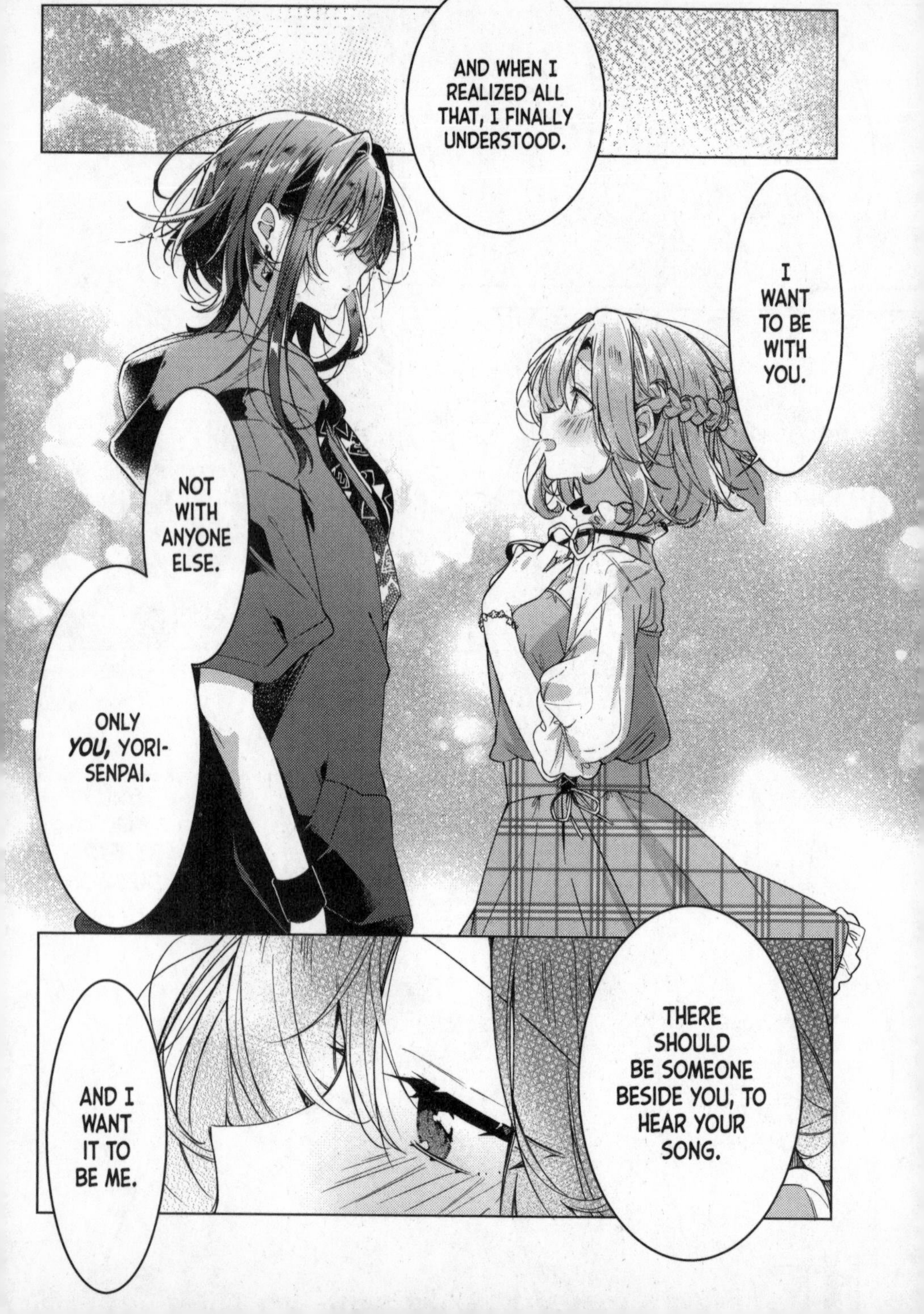
AND WHEN I REALIZED ALL THAT, I FINALLY UNDERSTOOD.
I WANT TO BE WITH YOU.
NOT WITH ANYONE ELSE.
ONLY *YOU,* YORI-SENPAI.
THERE SHOULD BE SOMEONE BESIDE YOU, TO HEAR YOUR SONG.
AND I WANT IT TO BE ME.

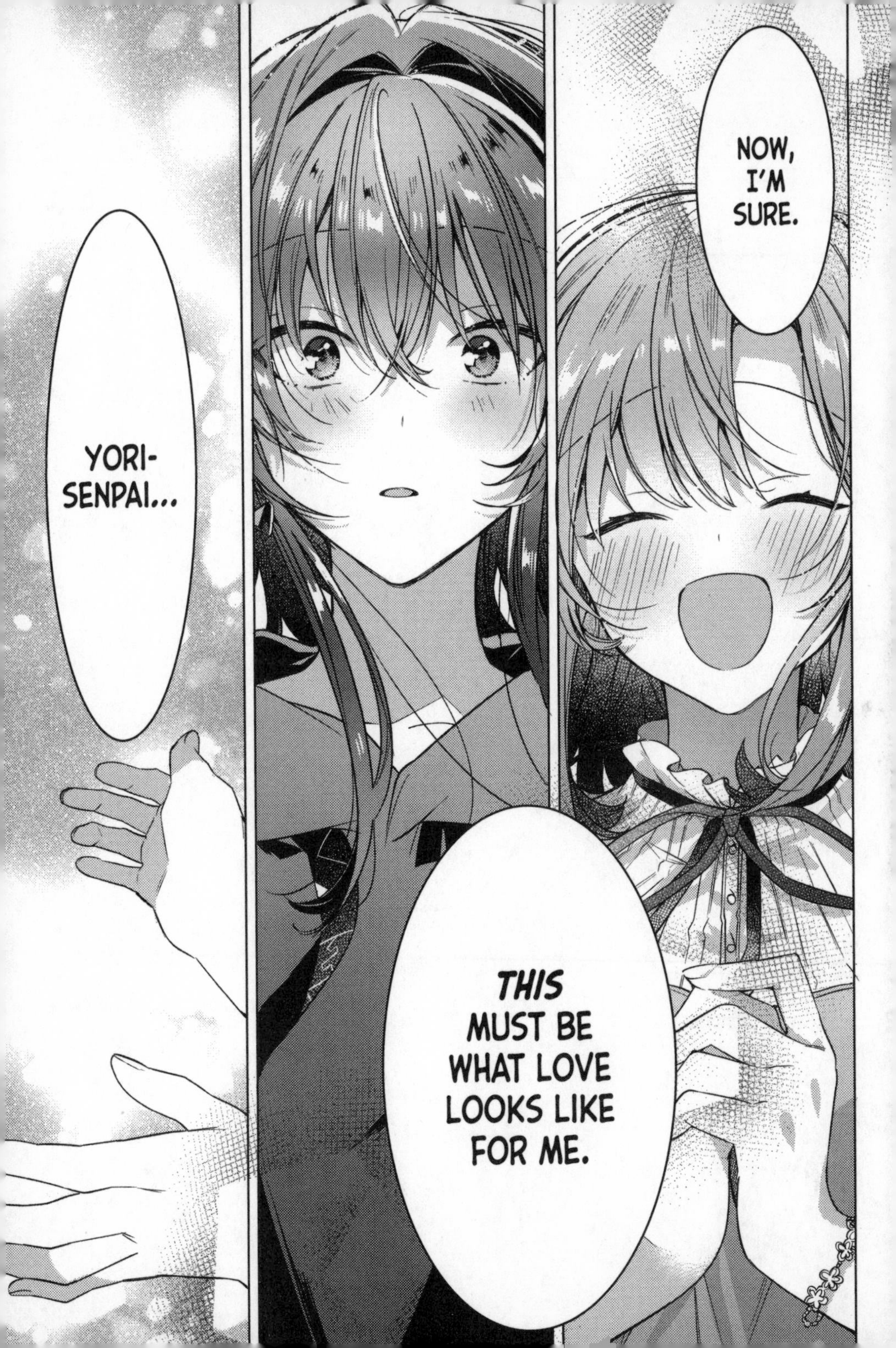
NOW, I'M SURE.
THIS MUST BE WHAT LOVE LOOKS LIKE FOR ME.
YORI-SENPAI...

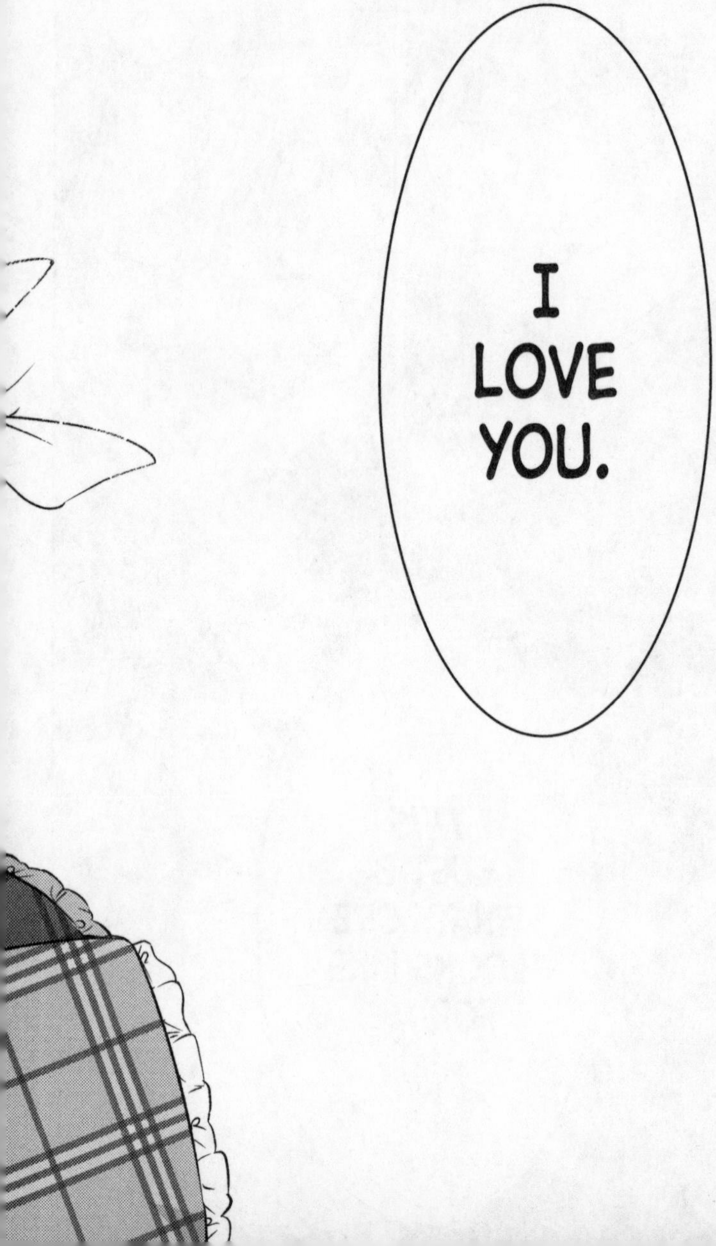
I LOVE YOU.

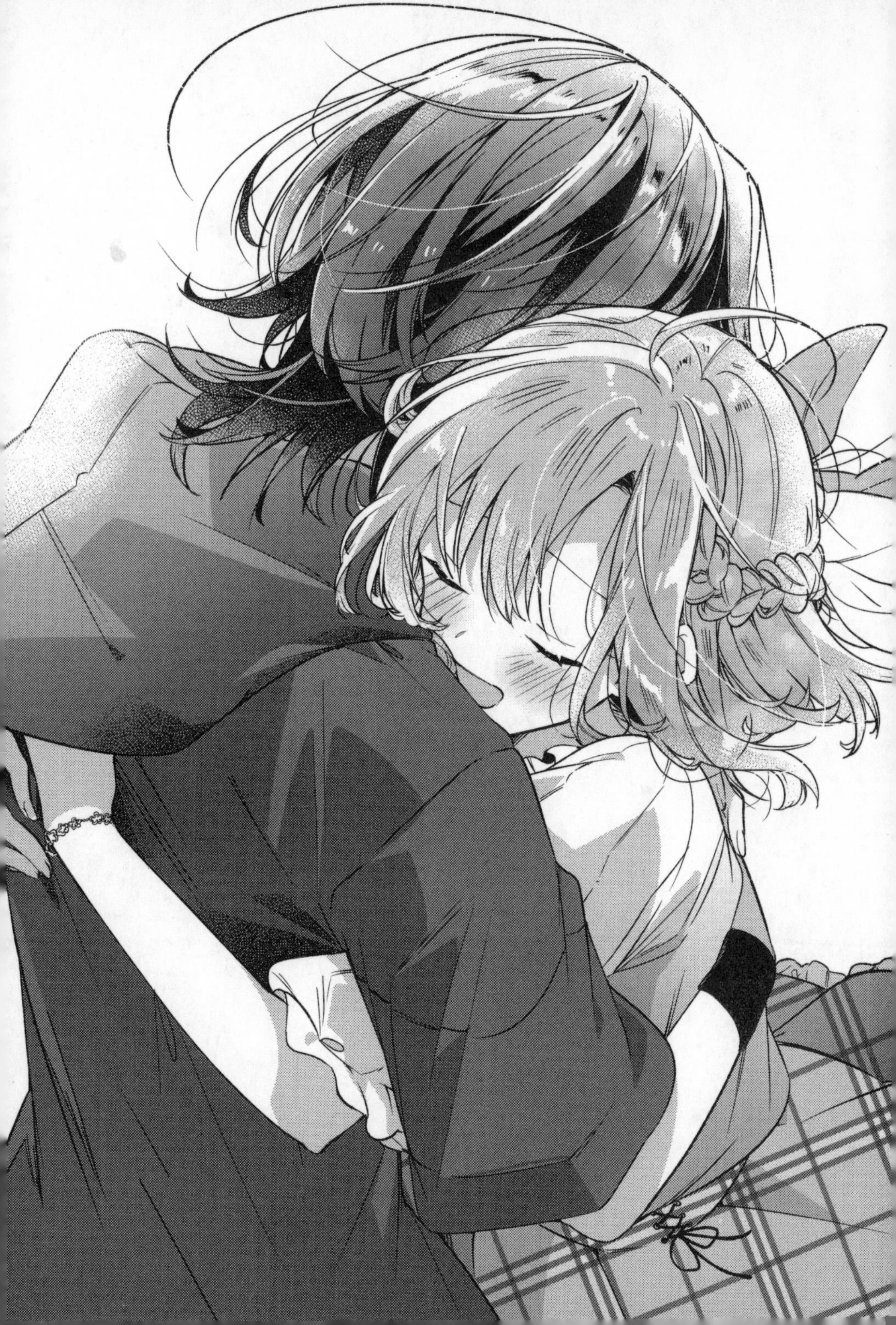

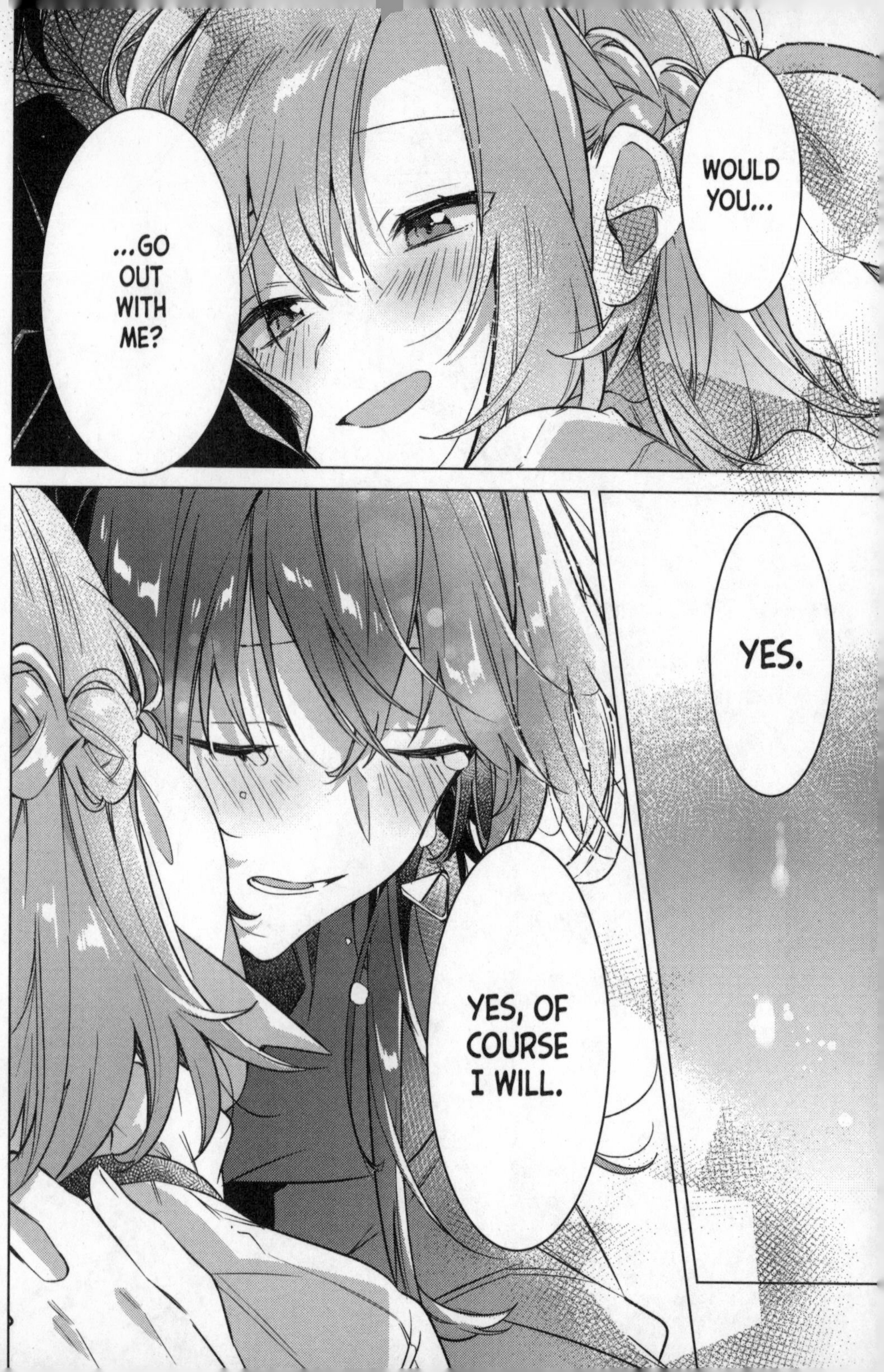
WOULD YOU...
...GO OUT WITH ME?
YES.
YES, OF COURSE I WILL.

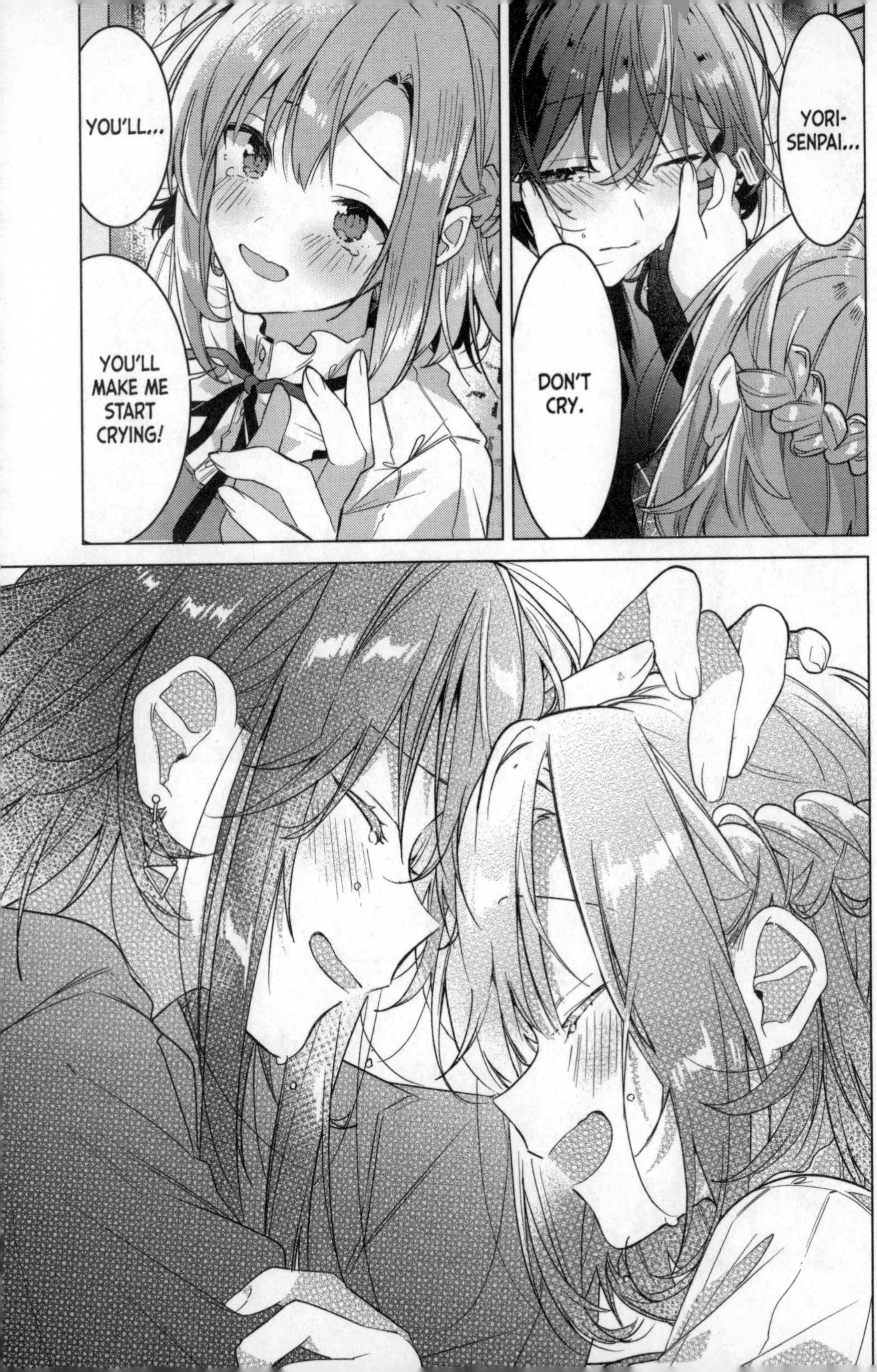
YORI-SENPAI...
DON'T CRY.
YOU'LL...
YOU'LL MAKE ME START CRYING!

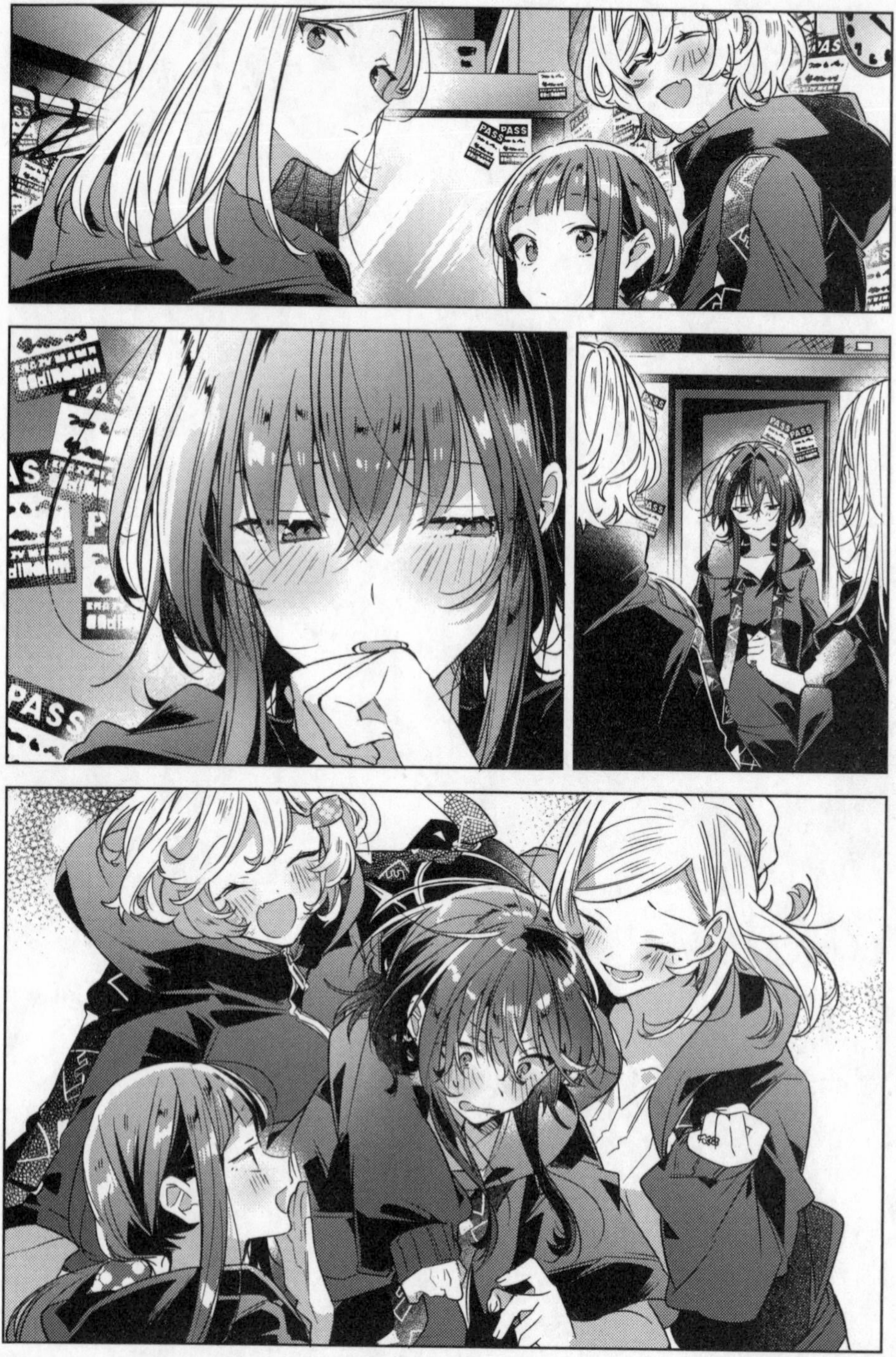

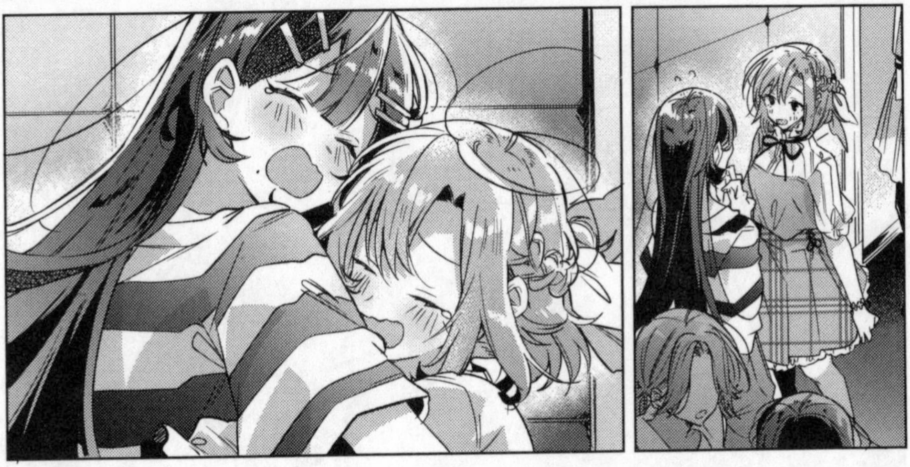

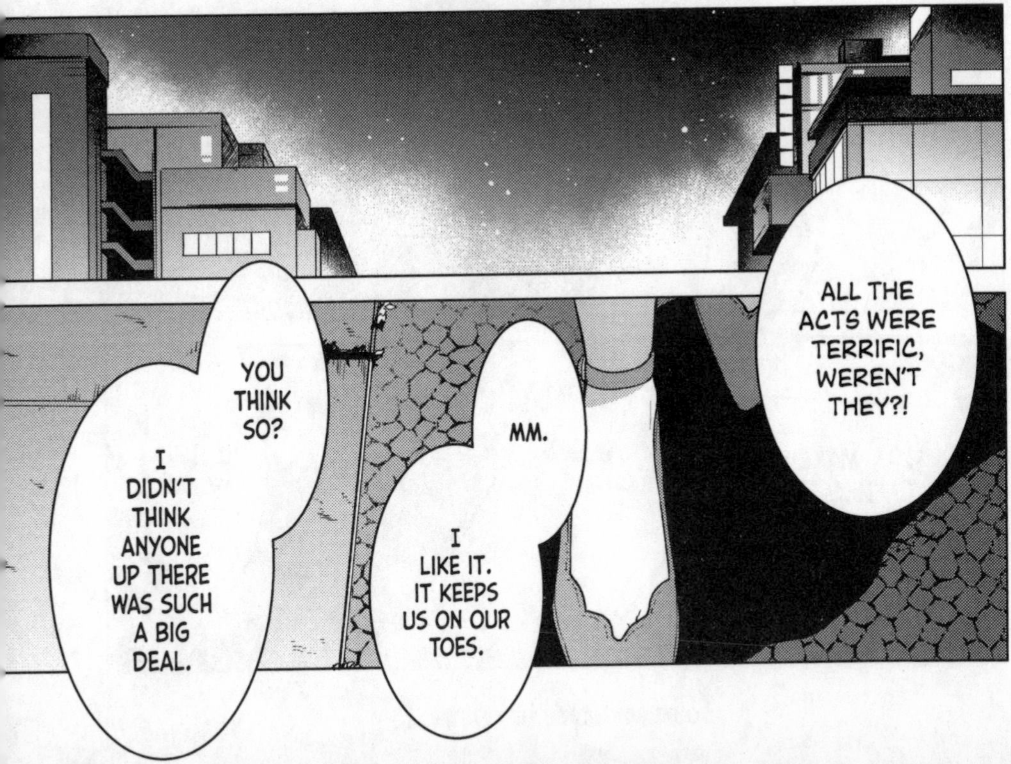

ALL THE ACTS WERE TERRIFIC, WEREN'T THEY?!
MM.
I LIKE IT. IT KEEPS US ON OUR TOES.
YOU THINK SO?
I DIDN'T THINK ANYONE UP THERE WAS SUCH A BIG DEAL.

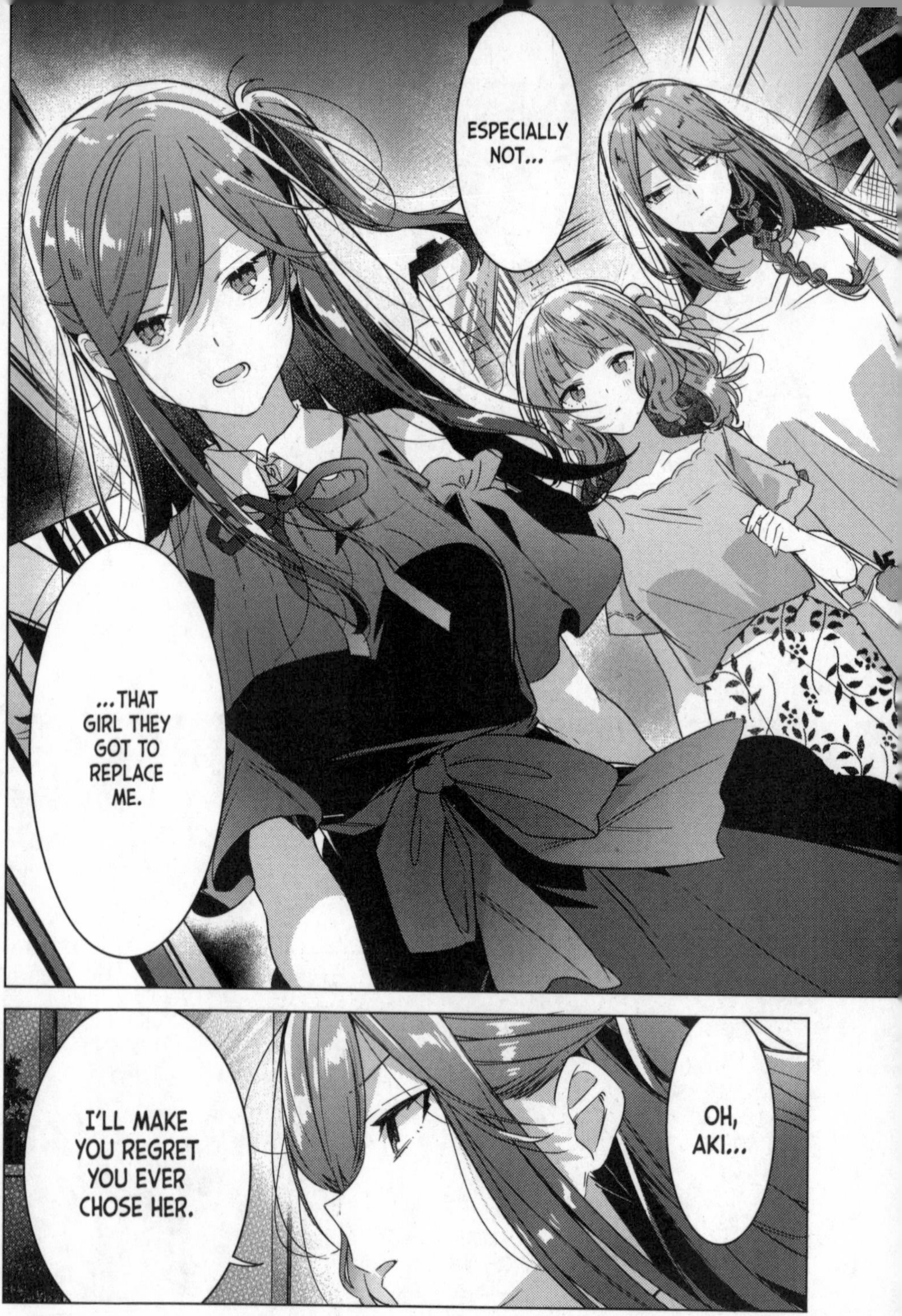
ESPECIALLY NOT...
...THAT GIRL THEY GOT TO REPLACE ME.
OH, AKI...
I'LL MAKE YOU REGRET YOU EVER CHOSE HER.

To be continued in Volume 4

Whisper Me
A Love Song

Eku
Takeshima

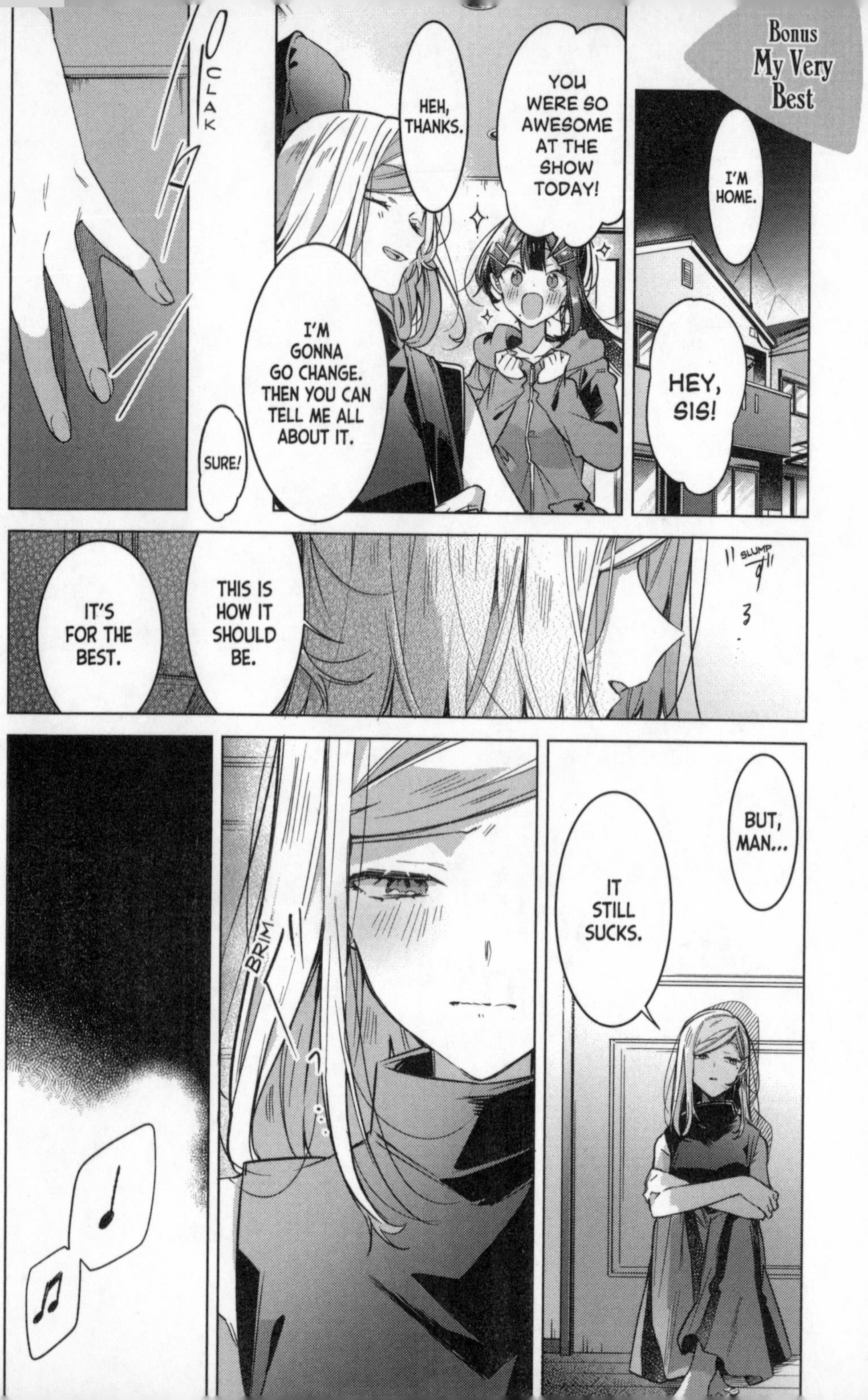
Bonus
My Very Best
I'M HOME.
HEY, SIS!
YOU WERE SO AWESOME AT THE SHOW TODAY!
HEH, THANKS.
I'M GONNA GO CHANGE. THEN YOU CAN TELL ME ALL ABOUT IT.
SURE!
CLAK
SLUMP
THIS IS HOW IT SHOULD BE.
IT'S FOR THE BEST.
BUT, MAN...
IT STILL SUCKS.
BRIM

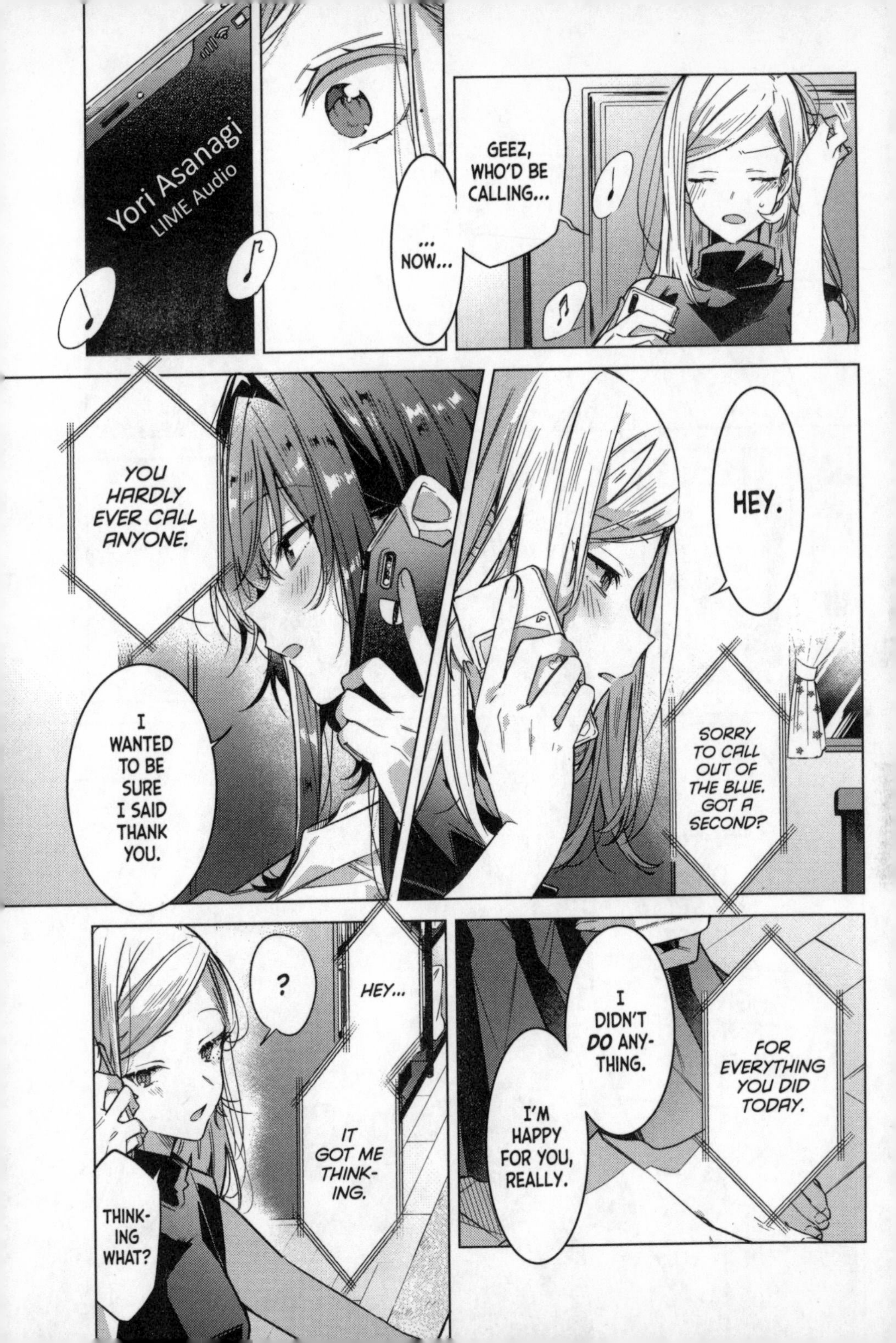
GEEZ, WHO'D BE CALLING...
... NOW...
Yori Asanagi
LIME Audio
HEY.
SORRY TO CALL OUT OF THE BLUE. GOT A SECOND?
YOU HARDLY EVER CALL ANYONE.
I WANTED TO BE SURE I SAID THANK YOU.
FOR EVERYTHING YOU DID TODAY.
I DIDN'T *DO* ANY-THING.
I'M HAPPY FOR YOU, REALLY.
HEY...
?
IT GOT ME THINK-ING.
THINK-ING WHAT?

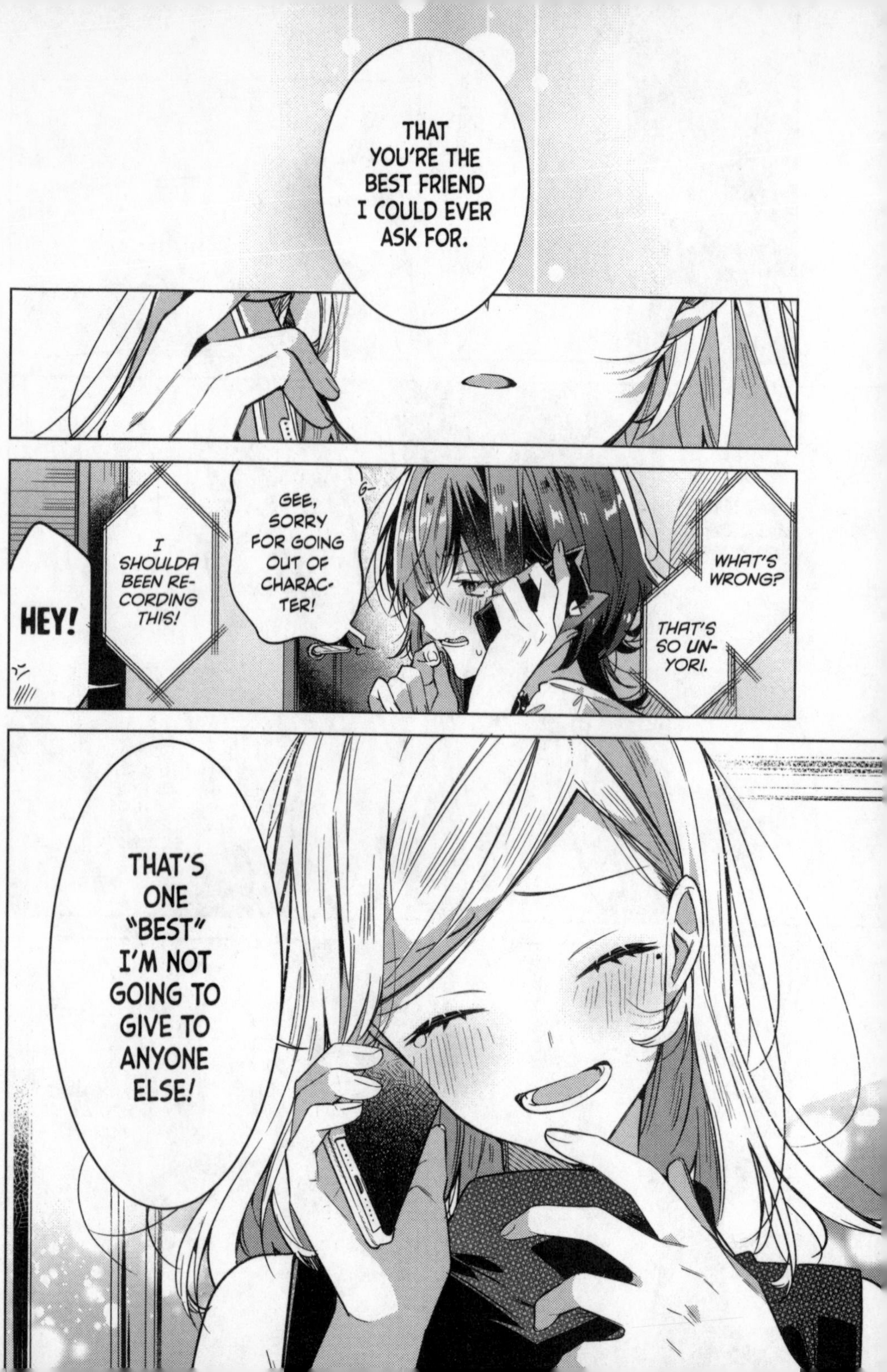
THAT YOU'RE THE BEST FRIEND I COULD EVER ASK FOR.
WHAT'S WRONG?
THAT'S SO UN-YORI.
G-
GEE, SORRY FOR GOING OUT OF CHARAC-TER!
I SHOULDA BEEN RE-CORDING THIS!
HEY!
THAT'S ONE "BEST" I'M NOT GOING TO GIVE TO ANYONE ELSE!

Afterword

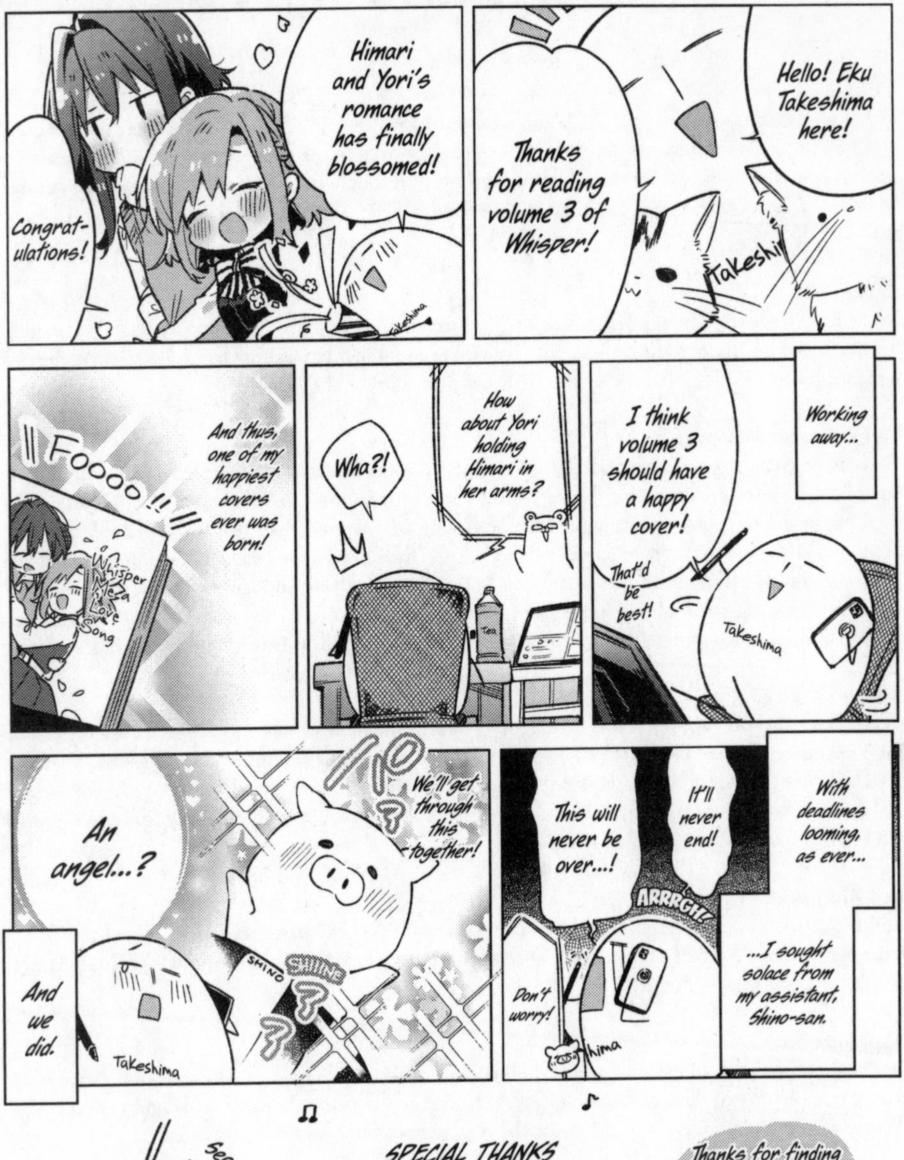

Hello! Eku Takeshima here!
Thanks for reading volume 3 of Whisper!
Takeshi
Himari and Yori's romance has finally blossomed!
Congrat-ulations!
Takeshima
Working away...
I think volume 3 should have a happy cover!
That'd be best!
Takeshima
How about Yori holding Himari in her arms?
Wha?!
Tea
And thus, one of my happiest covers ever was born!
FOOOO!!
Whisper Me a Love Song
With deadlines looming, as ever...
It'll never end!
This will never be over...!
ARRRGH!
...I sought solace from my assistant, Shino-san.
Don't worry!
We'll get through this together!
An angel...?
SHINE
SHINO
And we did.
Takeshima

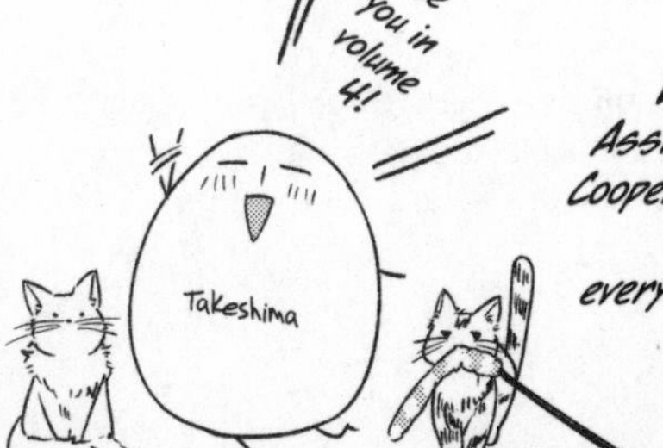

See you in volume 4!
Takeshima

SPECIAL THANKS
Editor - Ten-san
Design - SALIDAS-sama
Assistant - Hirofumi Shino-san
Cooperation - CRAZY MAMA-sama
And–
everyone who picked up this book!
Thank you all so much!

Thanks for finding time to let me visit your studio to help with chapter 15!

TRANSLATION NOTES

6 PM, page 24
Although there's no national standard, different municipalities and different schools may set specific times by which students must leave school grounds. As this is often in the name of making sure students don't have to go home in the dark, the exact time might vary throughout the year. For example, the cutoff might be 5:00 PM in the winter, but 6:00 PM in the summer. (The Japanese school day proper usually ends around 3:00 PM.)

X, page 42
In the first panel on page 42, Yori makes an "X" shape with her hands. Called the *batsu* in Japanese, it represents negation, falseness, or denial. (*Batsu* can be encountered in written texts as well, where they have the same meaning.) As a gesture, it may mean "Uh-uh" or "No way."

Bathroom Sandals, page 69
We've noted before that it's considered inappropriate to wear outdoor footwear into many buildings in Japan, but it's also considered inappropriate to wear your indoor sandals into parts of a building where the floor might not be clean, especially the bathroom. Instead, there will be a pair (or, in school, several pairs) of sandals at the bathroom door specifically to be used there. You leave your indoor slippers at the door and put on a pair of bathroom slippers, then trade back when you come out. (In the fourth panel on page 69, we see Aki tapping one foot as she puts her indoor slippers back on.) Leaving the bathroom with the toilet slippers still on is just as much a faux pas as entering the bathroom wearing your regular indoor footwear.

Akanbe, page 83
In the first panel on page 83, Aki is making the gesture known in Japanese as *akanbe* (a slightly corrupted form of the words *akai me,* "red eye"). The person pulls down the skin under one eye with their finger, revealing the red flesh underneath, hence the name. It's often accompanied by sticking out the tongue and exclaiming *"Beh!"* In terms of both its meaning and its level of maturity, it's roughly equivalent to sticking out one's tongue and saying "nyah nyah!"

Red Rice, page 84
Called *o-sekihan* in Japanese, this is rice made with *azuki* (red bean paste) and other ingredients to give it a red color. It may be served on a number of celebratory occasions, such as a wedding or engagement, as well as other occasions...

Alio, page 89
The name of the shopping center Yori and Himari go to appears to be Alio. The style of the logo bears a strong resemblance to the real shopping center chain Ario. (Because the Japanese language doesn't really distinguish between the phonemes *l* and *r*, the two names would sound almost identical.)

"We ended up on the inside cover... again," page 168
In the Japanese edition of *Whisper Me a Love Song,* the bonus comics on pages 167 and 168 originally appeared on the inside cover of the paperback, hidden beneath the book's dust jacket.

Whisper Me
A Love Song
Eku
Takeshima

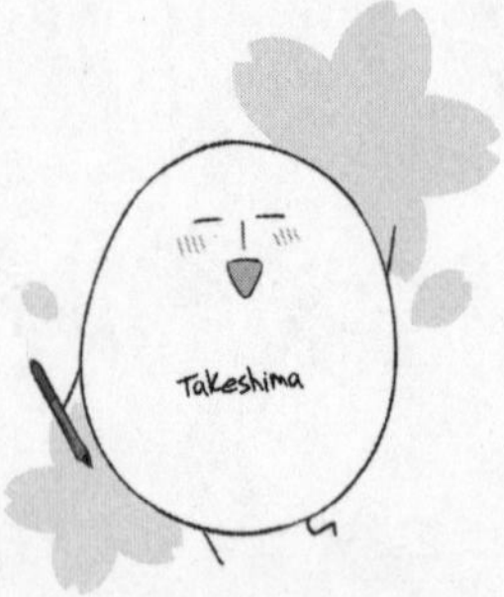
Takeshima

It's been 18 months since I started doing *Whisper.* I can't tell if the time flew by or dragged on. It's your encouragement and support that enables me to keep drawing, so thank you so much! I hope you enjoy volume 3.

–Eku Takeshima

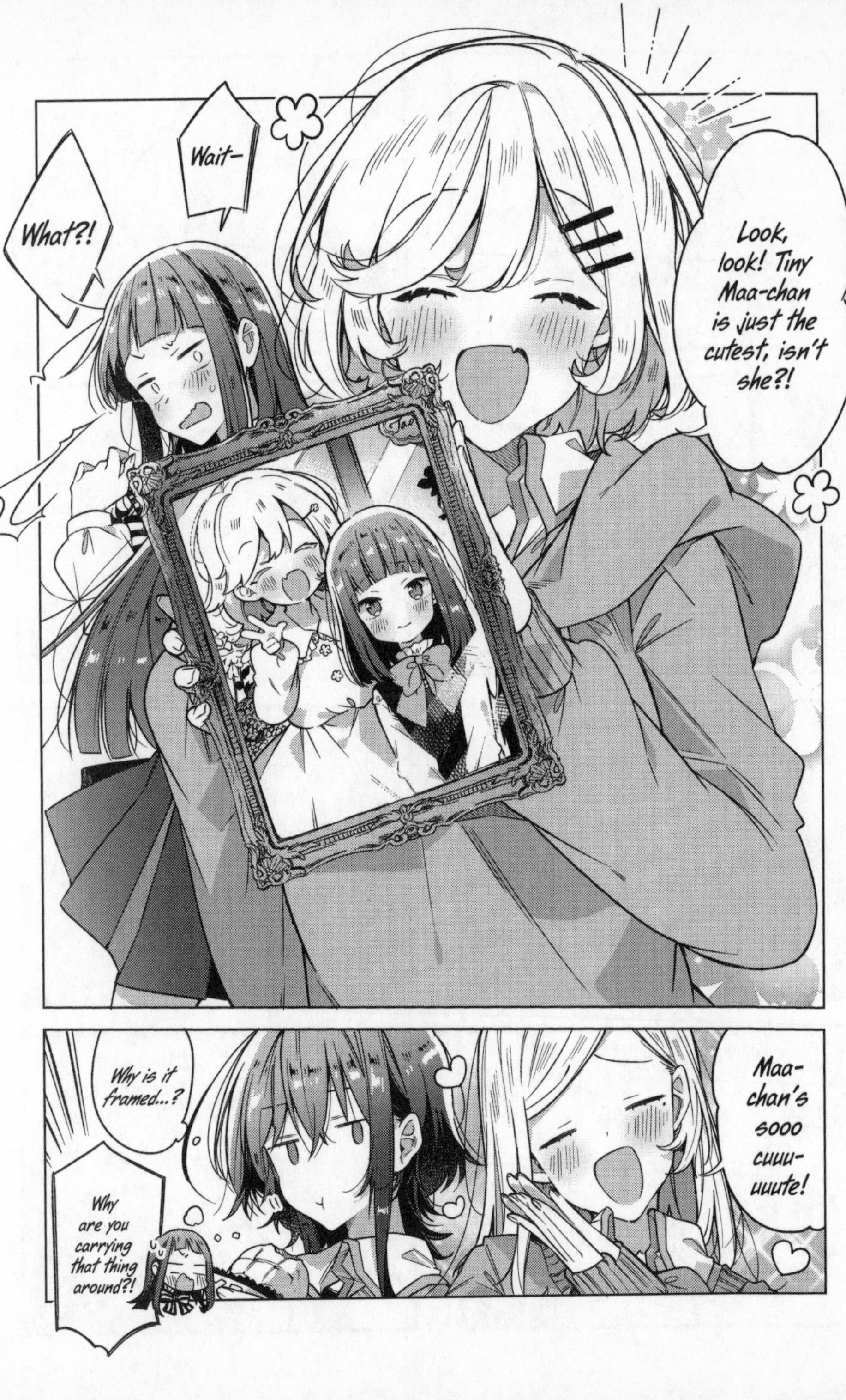
Look, look! Tiny Maa-chan is just the cutest, isn't she?!
Wait-
What?!
Maa-chan's sooo cuuu-uuute!
Why is it framed...?
Why are you carrying that thing around?!

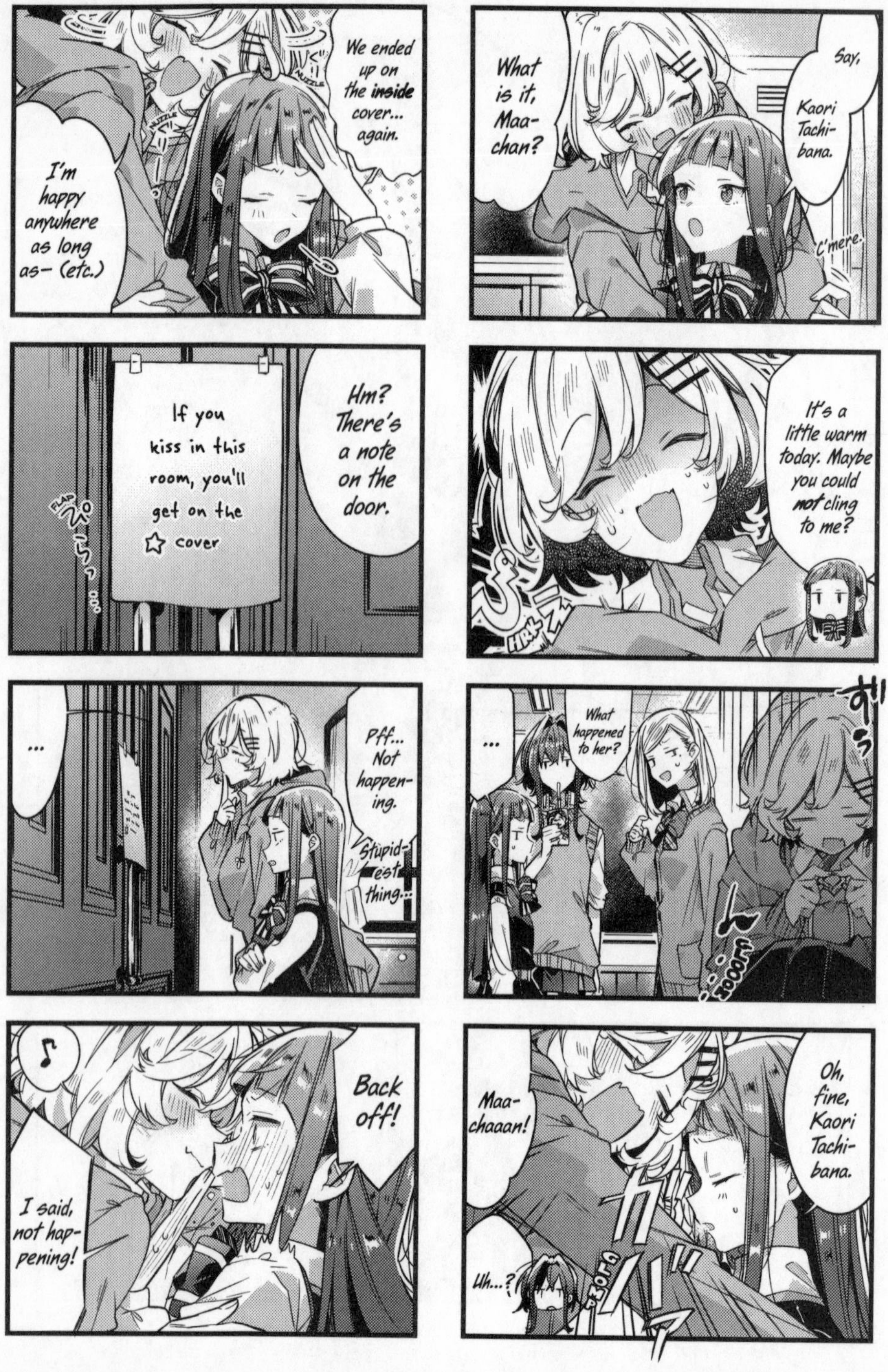
Say, Kaori Tachibana.
What is it, Maa-chan?
C'mere.
We ended up on the **inside** cover... again.
NUZZLE
I'm happy anywhere as long as– (etc.)
It's a little warm today. Maybe you could **not** cling to me?
HRK
Hm? There's a note on the door.
If you kiss in this room, you'll get on the ☆ cover
FLAP
What happened to her?
...
ZOOOOM...
Pff... Not happening.
Stupid-est thing...
...
Oh, fine, Kaori Tachibana.
Maa-chaaan!
Uh...?
Back off!
♪
I said, not hap-pening!

Yuri Is My Job!

miman

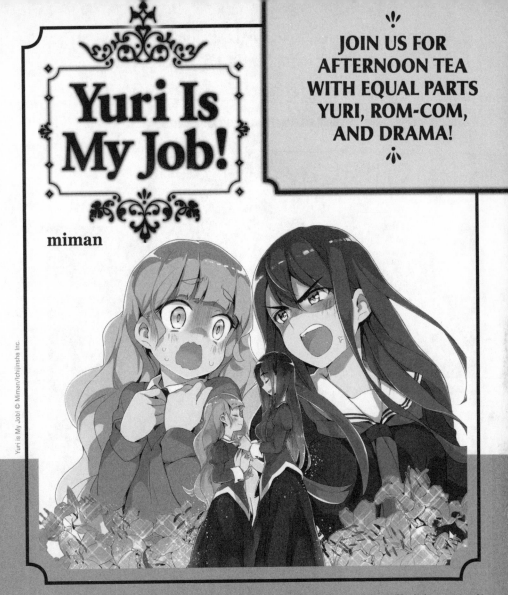

Hime is a picture-perfect high school princess, so when she accidentally injures a café manager named Mai, she's willing to cover some shifts to keep her façade intact. To Hime's surprise, the café is themed after a private school where the all-female staff always puts on their best act for their loyal customers. However, under the guidance of the most graceful girl there, Hime can't help but blush and blunder! Beneath all the frills and laughter, Hime feels tension brewing as she finds out more about her new job and her budding feelings...

KC
KODANSHA COMICS

"A quirky, fun comedy series... If you're a yuri fan, or perhaps interested in getting into it but not sure where to start, this book is worth picking up."
— Anime UK News

A SMART, NEW ROMANTIC COMEDY FOR FANS OF *SHORTCAKE CAKE* AND *TERRACE HOUSE*!

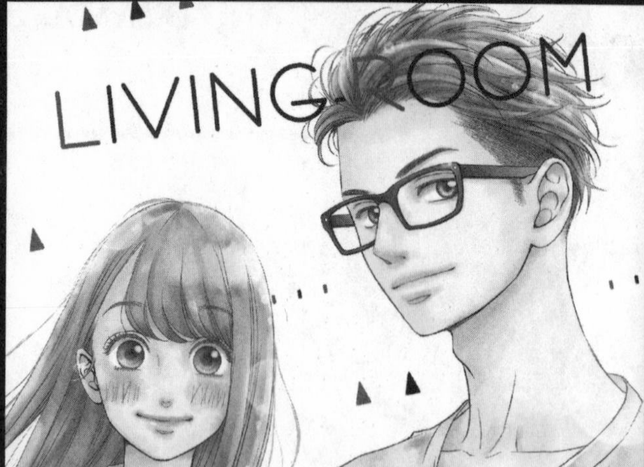
LIVING-ROOM
MATSUNAGA-SAN
1
Keiko Iwashita

A romance manga starring high school girl Meeko, who learns to live on her own in a boarding house whose living room is home to the odd (but handsome) Matsunaga-san. She begins to adjust to her new life away from her parents, but Meeko soon learns that no matter how far away from home she is, she's still a young girl at heart — especially when she finds herself falling for Matsunaga-san.

KC KODANSHA COMICS

PERFECT WORLD

Rie Aruga

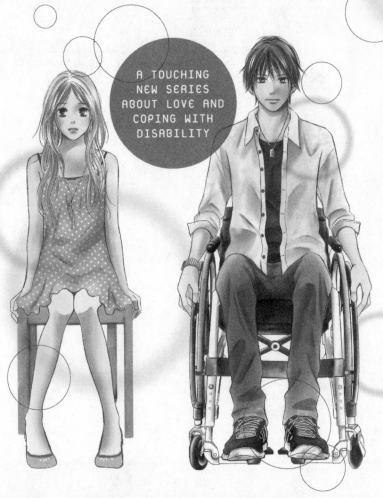

A TOUCHING
NEW SERIES
ABOUT LOVE AND
COPING WITH
DISABILITY

An office party reunites Tsugumi with her high school crush Itsuki. He's realized his dream of becoming an architect, but along the way, he experienced a spinal injury that put him in a wheelchair. Now Tsugumi's rekindled feelings will butt up against prejudices she never considered — and Itsuki will have to decide if he's ready to let someone into his heart...

"Depicts with great delicacy and courage the difficulties some with disabilities experience getting involved in romantic relationships... Rie Aruga refuses to romanticize, pushing her heroine to face the reality of disability. She invites her readers to the same tasks of empathy, knowledge and recognition."
—Slate.fr

"An important entry [in manga romance]... The emotional core of both plot and characters indicates thoughtfulness... [Aruga's] research is readily apparent in the text and artwork, making this feel like a real story."
—Anime News Network

KC
KODANSHA
COMICS

Knight of the Ice ©Yayoi Ogawa/Kodansha Ltd.

Yayoi Ogawa

SKATING THRILLS AND ICY CHILLS WITH THIS NEW TINGLY ROMANCE SERIES!

A rom-com on ice, perfect for fans of *Princess Jellyfish* and *Wotakoi*. Kokoro is the talk of the figure-skating world, winning trophies and hearts. But little do they know... he's actually a huge nerd! From the beloved creator of *You're My Pet* (*Tramps Like Us*).

Chitose is a serious young woman, working for the health magazine *SASSO*. Or at least, she would be, if she wasn't constantly getting distracted by her childhood friend, international figure skating star Kokoro Kijinami! In the public eye and on the ice, Kokoro is a gallant, flawless knight, but behind his glittery costumes and breathtaking spins lies a secret: He's actually a hopelessly romantic otaku, who can only land his quad jumps when Chitose is on hand to recite a spell from his favorite magical girl anime!

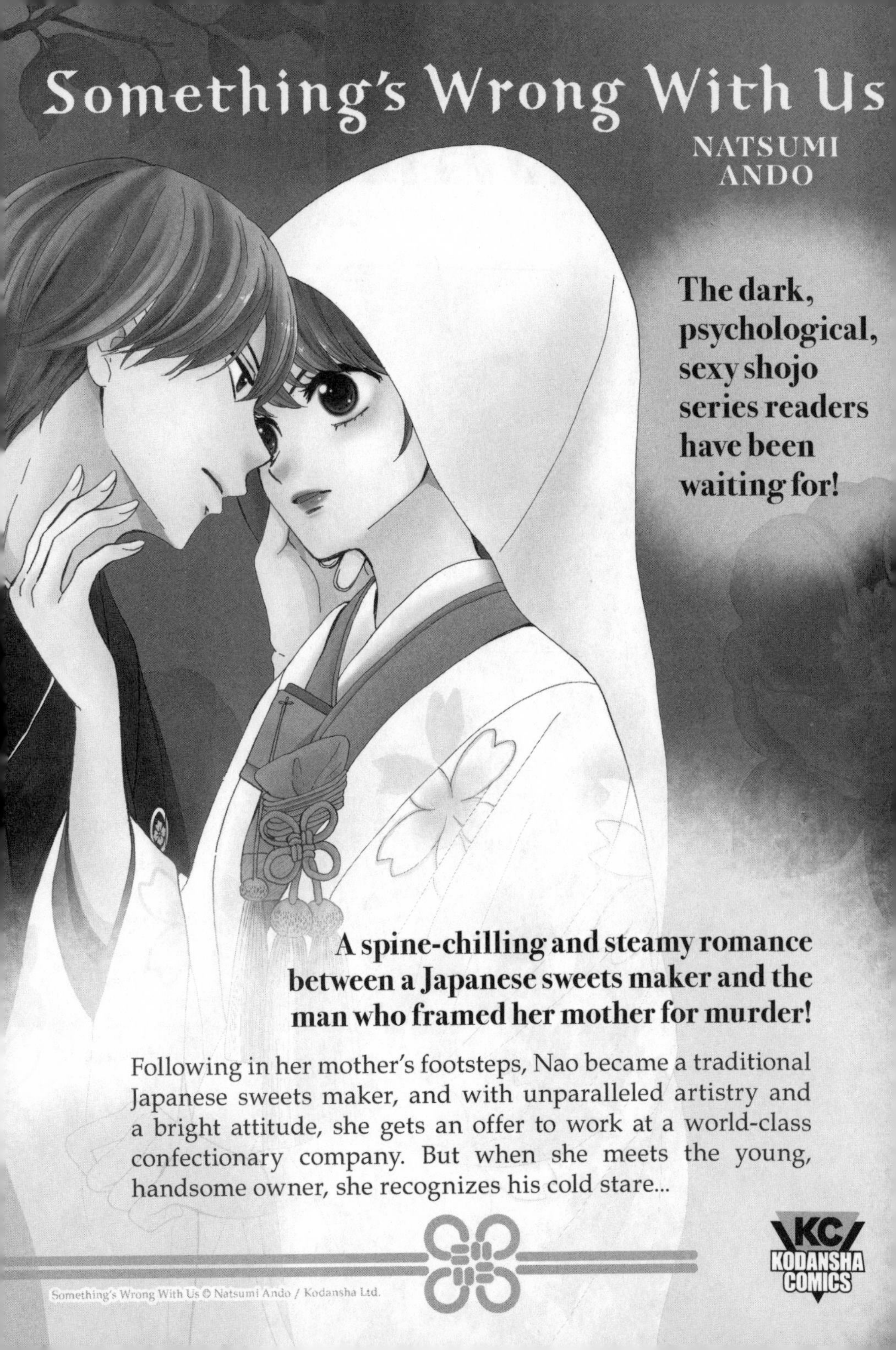
Something's Wrong With Us
NATSUMI ANDO
The dark, psychological, sexy shojo series readers have been waiting for!
A spine-chilling and steamy romance between a Japanese sweets maker and the man who framed her mother for murder!
Following in her mother's footsteps, Nao became a traditional Japanese sweets maker, and with unparalleled artistry and a bright attitude, she gets an offer to work at a world-class confectionary company. But when she meets the young, handsome owner, she recognizes his cold stare...
KC KODANSHA COMICS
Something's Wrong With Us © Natsumi Ando / Kodansha Ltd.

The slow-burn queer romance that'll sweep you off your feet!

10 DANCE

Inouesatoh presents

"A FANTASTIC DEBUT VOLUME... ONE OF MY FAVORITE BOOKS OF THE YEAR..."
— AiPT!

"10 DANCE IS A MUST-READ FOR ANYONE WHO'S ENJOYED MANGA AND ANIME ABOUT COMPETITIVE DANCE (ON OR OFF THE ICE!)."
—Anime UK News

Shinya Sugiki, the dashing lord of Standard Ballroom, and Shinya Suzuki, passionate king of Latin Dance: The two share more than just a first name and a love of the sport. They each want to become champion of the 10-Dance Competition, which means they'll need to learn the other's specialty dances, and who better to learn from than the best? But old rivalries die hard, and things get further complicated when they realize there might be more between them than an uneasy partnership...

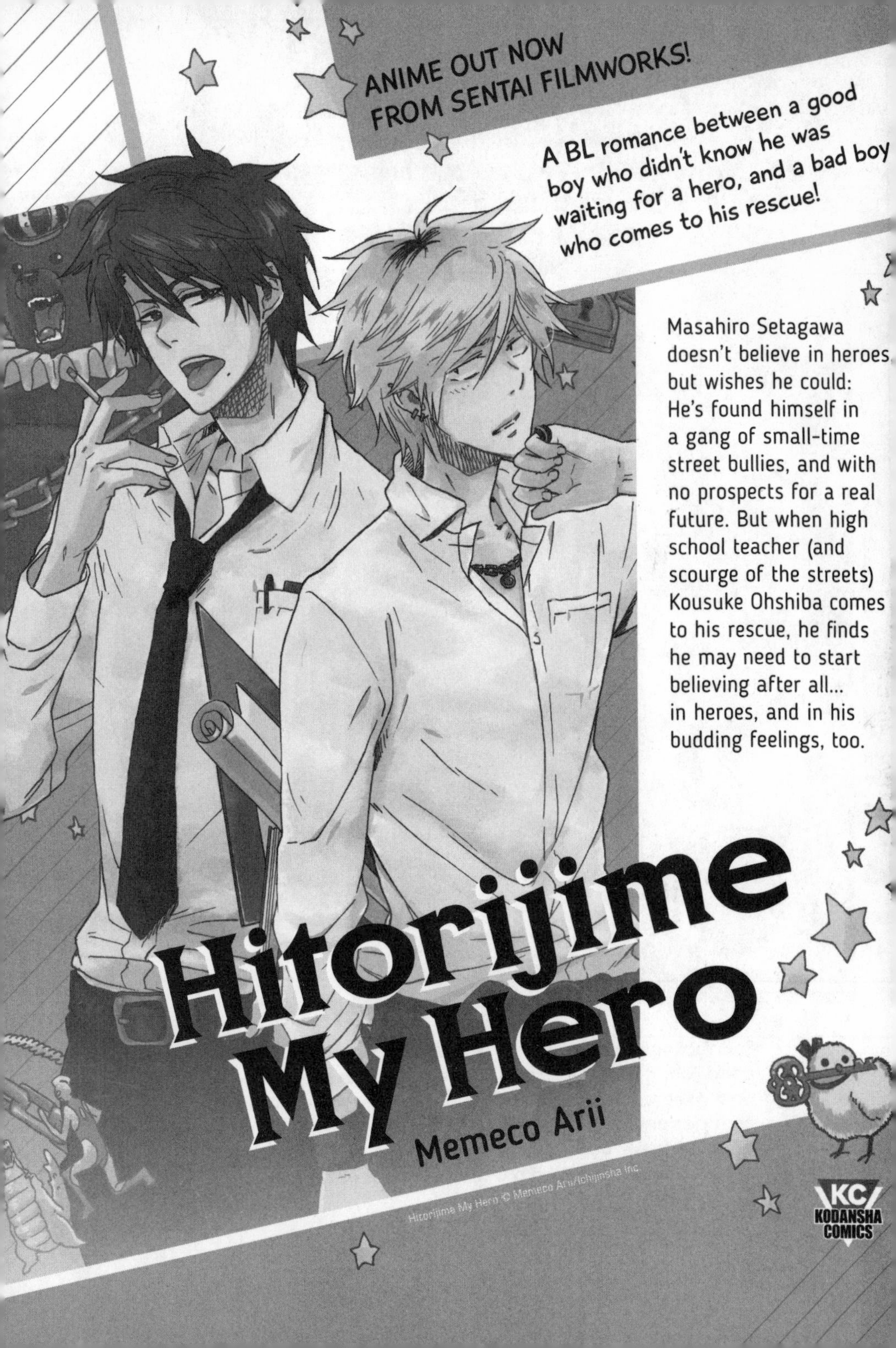
ANIME OUT NOW FROM SENTAI FILMWORKS!
A BL romance between a good boy who didn't know he was waiting for a hero, and a bad boy who comes to his rescue!
Masahiro Setagawa doesn't believe in heroes but wishes he could: He's found himself in a gang of small-time street bullies, and with no prospects for a real future. But when high school teacher (and scourge of the streets) Kousuke Ohshiba comes to his rescue, he finds he may need to start believing after all… in heroes, and in his budding feelings, too.
Hitorijime My Hero
Memeco Arii
Hitorijime My Hero © Memeco Arii/Ichijinsha Inc.
KC KODANSHA COMICS

CLAMP

Chobits
20TH ANNIVERSARY EDITION

Chobits © CLAMP·ShigatsuTsuitachi CO.,LTD./Kodansha Ltd.

Poor college student Hideki is down on his luck. All he wants is a good job, a girlfriend, and his very own "persocom"—the latest and greatest in humanoid computer technology. Hideki's luck changes one night when he finds Chi—a persocom thrown out in a pile of trash. But Hideki soon discovers that there's much more to his cute new persocom than meets the eye.

KC
KODANSHA
COMICS

THE SWEET SCENT OF LOVE IS IN THE AIR! FOR FANS OF OFFBEAT ROMANCES LIKE *WOTAKOI*

Sweat and Soap © Kintetsu Yamada / Kodansha Ltd.

In an office romance, there's a fine line between sexy and awkward... and that line is where Asako — a woman who sweats copiously — meets Koutarou — a perfume developer who can't get enough of Asako's, er, scent. Don't miss a romcom manga like no other!

KC KODANSHA COMICS

In love, there are no save points.

NOW AN ANIME!

ヲタクに恋は難しい

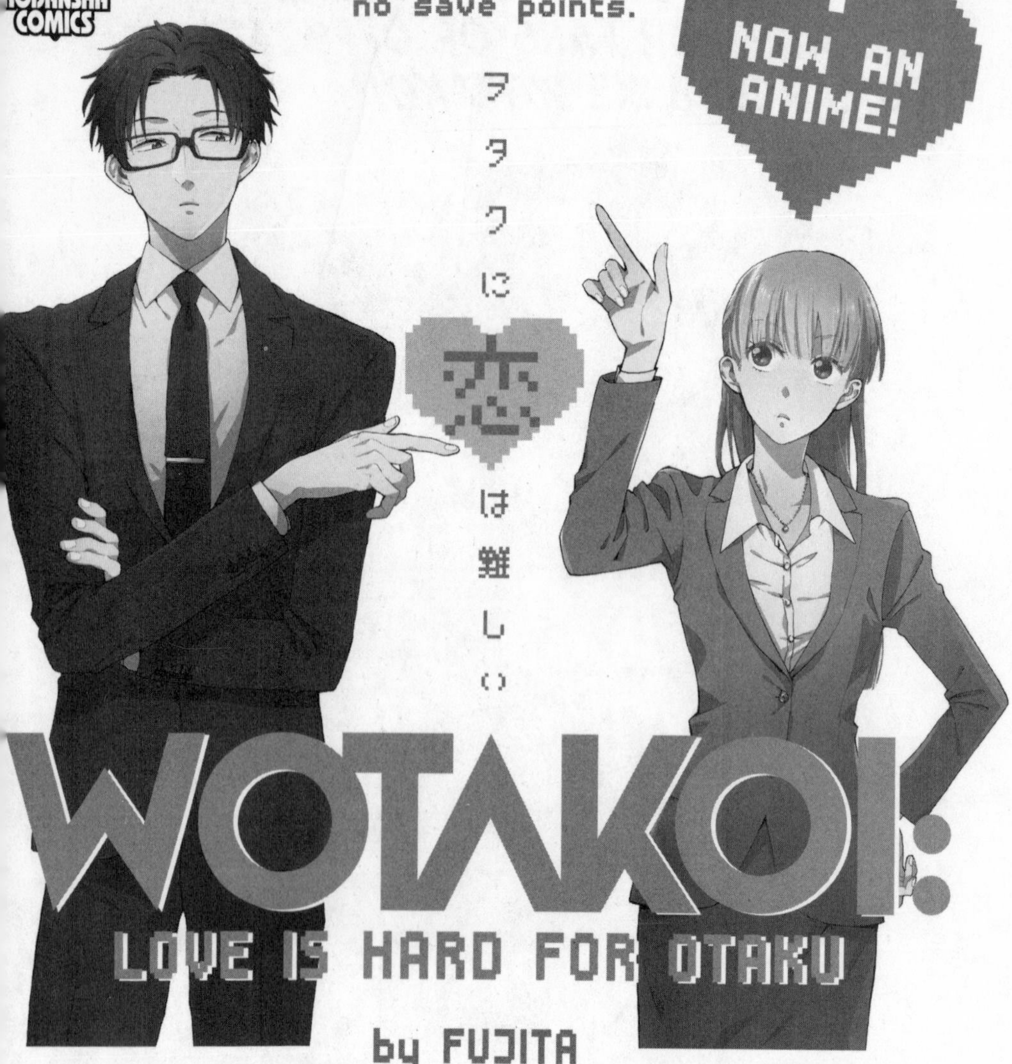

WOTAKOI: LOVE IS HARD FOR OTAKU

by FUJITA

Narumi has had it rough: Every boyfriend she's had dumped her once they found out she was an otaku, so she's gone to great lengths to hide it. At her new job, she bumps into Hirotaka, her childhood friend and fellow otaku. When Hirotaka almost gets her secret outed at work, she comes up with a plan to keep him quiet. But he comes up with a counter-proposal: Why doesn't she just date him instead?

A Kodansha Comics Trade Paperback Original
Whisper Me a Love Song 3 copyright © 2020 Eku Takeshima
English translation copyright © 2021 Eku Takeshima

All rights reserved.

Published in the United States by Kodansha Comics, an imprint of Kodansha USA Publishing, LLC, New York.

Publication rights for this English edition arranged through Kodansha Ltd., Tokyo.

First published in Japan in 2020 by Ichijinsha Inc., Tokyo as *Sasayaku you ni koi wo utau*, volume 3.

ISBN 978-1-64651-147-1

Original cover design by SALIDAS

Printed in the United States of America.

www.kodansha.us

2nd Printing
Translation: Kevin Steinbach
Lettering: Jennifer Skarupa
Editing: Tiff Joshua TJ Ferentini
Kodansha Comics edition cover design: Matt Akuginow

Publisher: Kiichiro Sugawara

Director of publishing services: Ben Applegate
Associate director of operations: Stephen Pakula
Publishing services managing editors: Alanna Ruse, Madison Salters
Assistant production managers: Emi Lotto, Angela Zurlo
Logo and character art ©Kodansha USA Publishing, LLC